YALE HISTORICAL PUBLICATIONS

Leonard Woods Labaree · Editor

MISCELLANY

XXXIV

PUBLISHED UNDER THE DIRECTION OF
THE DEPARTMENT OF HISTORY
FROM THE INCOME OF
THE FREDERICK JOHN KINGSBURY
MEMORIAL FUND

FIRST LEVEL CANAL FROM GATE-HOUSE
ABOUT 1875

SECOND LEVEL CANAL FROM CONNECTICUT
RIVER R.R. BRIDGE, ABOUT 1875

HOLYOKE
MASSACHUSETTS

A CASE HISTORY
OF THE INDUSTRIAL REVOLUTION
IN AMERICA

BY

CONSTANCE McLAUGHLIN GREEN
INSTRUCTOR IN HISTORY AT SMITH COLLEGE

NEW HAVEN · YALE UNIVERSITY PRESS
LONDON · HUMPHREY MILFORD · OXFORD UNIVERSITY PRESS

1939

Copyright, 1939, by Yale University Press

Printed in the United States of America

TO

MY HUSBAND

A GENTLEMAN AND

A MANUFACTURER

PREFACE

WHEN Jefferson in 1801 spoke of the United States as "a chosen country, with room enough for our descendants to the thousandth and thousandth generation," a map of North America would have revealed so few towns and cities that the President's estimate would seem conservative. Today, five generations later, the country from Atlantic to Pacific is dotted with cities. How has this almost fabulous growth come about? What has determined its urban character? What factors have been instrumental in locating these cities? Geographical influences have indicated the sites. Immigration and natural increase of the native population; a revolution in means of communication and transportation; the mechanization of life until the farm itself has been brought within the realm of the machine world; these are general answers to the question, why cities have arisen.

At the fall line of the rivers mill towns had begun to arise in Jefferson's day. But still in 1850, indeed in 1860, the United States was rural. The phenomenon of widespread urbanization was a development of the last quarter of the nineteenth century. Only within the last decades has the transmission of electric power induced the de-centralization of industry and thus a relaxing, even a reversal, of the process of urbanization. The crowding of people into limited areas in order to be near their work, the diversification of racial stock and hence the variations of social background which the floods of old-world immigrants have brought into American cities, the growing impersonality of industry and the widening of the gulf between poor and rich, all these factors of the modern city have created problems in American life before which "the apostle of Americanism" would doubtless stand appalled. The fact of the twentieth century American city is familiar to everyone. Just how it came into being can only be fully understood by studying the rise of individual cities. The problem in the large is only to be comprehended by examining it as produced *in parvo*.

The particular city under scrutiny in this study has probably no more unique characteristics than many another. The dramatic quality of its history can perhaps be often paralleled. In 1917 at its peak Holyoke boasted about 63,000 inhabitants; till 1850 it had no separate corporate existence at all. The city is situated in the heart of New England, yet has no old New England traditions, no prominent original families, little stock of inherited wealth. A farming district transformed into a mill town by the exploitation of its water power, the history of the town is the chronicle of the rise of a water-power city. Unlike most New England towns it was the outgrowth of deliberately planned and consistently promoted financial investment. It was the design of the promoters, Boston capitalists, who between 1821 and 1843 had netted fortunes in the power development of the Merrimack River and the building of Lowell and Lawrence, to repeat those profitable ventures on a still larger scale by the creation of a mightier water power on the Connecticut River and the building of an even greater cotton textile city. Actually with the partial miscarriage of the original plan, there grew up a town of diversified industry—paper, papeteries, machinery, silk, and wool, as well as cotton textiles. In the eighty-odd years of its civic career this community offers an example of the changing modes of life and readjustments of thought forced upon America by the coming of the machine age. The story has been carried through the depression immediately following the war. By that time the main lines of the city's development had been established, the peak of population had been passed, and the era of expansion was at an end.

The location of the city was determined by the geographical advantages of the site; the development of the community has been conditioned by the character of the men and women who have made it their home. The story should be typical of the American scene; unquestionably it is distinctive. The history of Holyoke is the history of Massachusetts industrialism and all its social consequences.

Much of the data for this study has had to be obtained from living persons. The number of Holyoke citizens who have contributed information and given me access to records is too large to mention all by name, but to each I wish to give my thanks. The files of the Holyoke *Transcript*, the only newspaper in the city with a continuous existence since the founding of the town, have been most courteously put at my disposal and to the owners of the *Transcript* I am also much indebted. To Professor Ralph Gabriel of Yale University, where in an earlier form this study was first submitted as a doctoral dissertation, I make my acknowledgement with utmost gratitude. And finally to my husband, whose technical knowledge and human wisdom have contributed greatly to the content of this book, and whose patience and humor have eased its preparation, I wish to make acknowledgement.

C.McL.G.

Holyoke, Massachusetts,
  December, 1938.

CONTENTS

ILLUSTRATIONS

HOLYOKE MASSACHUSETTS

I

THE AGRARIAN BACKGROUND

IN the early forties of the last century a traveler northward bound from West Springfield, Massachusetts,
would have journeyed by stagecoach over the county
road along the right bank of the great Connecticut River.
Rising a few miles ahead of him he would have seen on
right bank and left the Mt. Tom and Mt. Holyoke ranges
between which the river cut. Stretching down to the river
lay fertile farm lands. As he drove through the northern
parish of West Springfield he would have seen at the bend
of the Connecticut the beautiful Hadley falls where the
river, swinging eastward in a great arc, dropped nearly
sixty feet. There on the left bank he must have seen the
thriving hamlet of Canal Village with its transportation
canal and locks for river boats carrying freight north or
south. There too below the mouth of the canal he could
have seen a wing dam at the village factories, the gristmill, the flaxseed oil mill, and the two busy paper mills. On
the right bank opposite, a cluster of buildings would have
met his eye and another small wing dam feeding water to a
wheel for a tiny cotton mill. But the imaginative Yankee
must have watched with speculative interest the vast power
of the river pouring unused over the falls.

Over two hundred years had passed since the first traders from the Bay colony had built their trading post on
the Connecticut at the confluence of the Agawam or Westfield River. Furs had been the objective of those firstcomers, but the colonists who had followed to make a permanent settlement on the east bank of the Connecticut had

been planters.[1] Nearly a hundred miles of wilderness had lain between Springfield and the nearest English settlement on the coast. The rich bottom lands of the Connecticut had yielded abundant crops of corn which together with lumber early formed the chief exports from the valley, and Springfield had thrived.[2] In 1653 Northampton, eighteen miles upstream on the west bank, and in 1659 Hadley on the east bank had been settled.

The section of Springfield by the great falls of the Connecticut had developed slowly. After the more accessible lots near the main settlement had been assigned, the proprietors of Springfield in 1660 had granted out a first lot on the west side of the Connecticut, twenty-four acres "about halfe a mile below the higher falls in the Great River."[3] And three years later they had assigned land in this part of the town to a Protestant Irishman named Riley.[4] From Riley's nationality the place took its name, Ireland, for nearly two centuries, and in 1850, after the stagecoach had given way to the railroad, Ireland or Ireland Parish was to be set off as the town of Holyoke.

In the seventeenth century development of this part of

1. Harry A. Wright, ed., *Indian Deeds of Hampden County*, pp. 11–13; William B. Sprague, "Historical Discourse . . . 1824," Appendix A, in *Sermons*, II, 45. The advantages of the site of the original trading post were obvious for purposes of barter with the Indians, since native fur traders had easy access thither not only from the upper Connecticut, but also from the back country to the west drained by the Westfield River. But the location of the trading house on the west bank was unfortunate because it was on low land subject to inundation in the spring. Hence, presumably, the move to the east bank.

2. In the seventeenth century the fur trade and commerce with the Indians in general was a privilege confined to a specified few. Nathaniel Shurtleff, ed., *Records of the Governor and Company of the Massachusetts Bay in New England*, I, 179, 322–323; III, 424. But as settlement advanced along the valley, the fur trade shrank and other exports became more important. See William B. Weeden, *Economic and Social History of New England, 1620–1789*, I, 160–164.

3. Springfield Town Records, I, 207.

4. *Ibid.*, I, 207, 232, 257, 261, 265; II, 16, 75, 76, 77, 103; III, 170, 173, 344, 366. The first land granted to Riley was apparently south of Riley's Brook, and it was the later allotments or purchases which are truly Ireland. For the location of Chicopee Plain see Charles H. Barrows, *An Historical Address . . . with Five Appendices*, p. 33.

the valley was hampered somewhat by fear of Indian hostility after the terrifying experiences of King Philip's War. In earlier years relations between white men and red men in this locality had been unstrained and the planters had dealt with the river Indians with a certain matter-of-factness. The treachery of the Agawams which resulted in the burning of Springfield in 1675 had been utterly unexpected.[5] At the end of King Philip's War they fled to the West, and after 1676 there is rarely mention of any but an occasional Indian squatter. Nevertheless the effect of the Indian war was to retard local settlement. The houses on the west side of the river had not been destroyed; but to attacks from the north and west the settlers on the right bank were more exposed than the planters who lived in the main settlement.[6] For seventy-five years Ireland, like other outlying districts, lay open to raids from Indian allies of New France. Though the settlers suffered little from attacks the fear remained, and as late as 1745 the six resident families were said to have "forted together nights for fear of the Indians."[7] Not until the close of the French and Indian War in 1763 could the Ireland farmer plough his fields without danger from an occasional marauder.

Still, life went on here down to the Revolution much as

5. Henry Morris, *Early History of Springfield, passim;* Oliver B. Morris, *An Historical Address, Delivered on the 200th Anniversary of the Settlement of Springfield, May 25, 1836,* pp. 22–33. Hampshire County Court Records abound with instances of Indians being hailed into court to answer for misdemeanors, and include occasional cases of natives, like white men, seeking redress there. Hampshire County Records, I, 98 and *passim* (Registry of Probate, Northampton). Thus Springfield settlers trusted their Indian neighbors. This confidence of the planters in their security may long have been based on delusion. The threats of Indian attacks against all the New England settlements from the time of the great Narragansett conspiracy of 1643 down to the summer of 1675 had become so familiar to Massachusetts colonists that probably even the more uneasy had come to regard the occasional rumors of trouble as mere cries of "Wolf! Wolf!" See *Acts of the Commissioners of the United Colonies of New England,* in David Pulsifer, ed., *Records of the Colonies of New Plymouth in New England,* IX and X.

6. Henry Morris, *Early History of Springfield,* p. 80 and *passim.*

7. Letter of Colonel Benjamin Ball, cited by George H. Allyn, "Sketch of Holyoke," *Thirtieth Anniversary Holyoke Daily Transcript.*

in other remote New England localities. In 1685 with the establishment of the Dominion of New England, in order to avoid *quo warranto* proceedings against the town and forfeiture of the common lands, Springfield voted to lay the commons out into proprieties and to allot individual holdings. But final division of the outer commons did not take place until well into the eighteenth century. Meanwhile the business of living went on: clearing, planting, harvesting, building houses and barns, tending cattle and swine, netting shad and salmon at the falls of the river, or occasionally carting by ox team a few hogsheads of rum or other cargo around the falls. In 1696 the settlers on the west side of the river were allowed to set up a ministry for themselves so that they need not cross the great river to attend meeting every Sabbath.[8] Much of the time the river might be a satisfactory highway, but there were many weeks of the year even after a ferry was established in 1683 when the mighty stream was an obstacle.

Thenceforward the contacts between Ireland and the parent settlement were fewer. No school fund was assigned to the place until 1731 although, in keeping with Massachusetts laws of an early date, the west side of the river as a whole was rather generously provided for. A good deal of land in this northwestern section was allotted to persons who dwelt in other parts of the town, so that attention to the needs of the actual residents was given tardily.[9]

Between 1720 and 1730 settlers from the town of Hadley had moved down to the land south of Mt. Holyoke on the east side of the river above the falls. In 1753 this territory below the Mt. Holyoke range south to the Springfield boundary was made a separate district, South Hadley, but was not recognized as a legally distinct town until

8. Springfield Town Records, III, 122, 136, 210, 221, 222; IV, 32, 67, 114, 180; George Bliss, *An Address delivered at the Opening of the Town Hall in Springfield, March 24, 1828,* pp. 26, 27; W. B. Sprague, "Historical Discourse . . . 1824," Appendix D, in *Sermons,* II, 50.

9. Springfield Town Records, III, 31, 296, 326, 356, 366, 380, 404, 424. See the remonstrance of the Second Parish to the General Court, Records of the Second Parish of Springfield (office of town clerk of West Springfield).

after the Revolution.[10] South Hadley, like West Springfield, was a quiet agricultural community.

In 1750 the inhabitants of Ireland joined with the people in Chicopee, the northernmost section of Springfield on the east side of the river, to petition the General Court of the province to set them off as a new parish, and the next year the fifth parish of Springfield was created, comprising some six square miles on the east side of the river and four square miles on the west side. A meetinghouse was built in Chicopee at once and a pastor secured. Although Irelanders were obliged now to cross the river to attend meeting, they obviously preferred the arrangement and the local autonomy thus attained. In fact the fifth parish soon formally petitioned the town to set it off into a distinct district, and, although refused, the request is significant as marking a growing self-consciousness. Nevertheless, whether because of remoteness or because of sparsity of settlement, Ireland continued through the remaining years of her connection with the mother town to play a minor role in the town life of Springfield.[11]

The act of 1773 which cut off from Springfield all the township lying west of the Connecticut River, making a separate town of West Springfield, made Ireland part of West Springfield. The years 1775 and 1776 saw West Springfield and Ireland entering into the struggle against the British king with vigor and sending off their soldiers to join the Continental Army. During the excitements of the ensuing decade Ireland apparently bore its share of the burdens, filled its quota of town offices, and took its part in discussions of public policies. In the troubled years which immediately preceded and followed peace all the township shared in the discontent general in western Mas-

10. R. O. Dwight, "Historical Address," in *A History of the Sesqui-Centennial Anniversary Celebration of the Town of South Hadley, Mass.*, pp. 47–49 (hereafter cited as *A History . . . of South Hadley*).

11. Springfield Town Records, IV, 170, 186–187. A list of polls of the fifth parish before 1760 shows just under forty for the west side of the river, and scarcely more than forty after 1760. This did not include children. Connecticut Valley Historical Society Library, MSS., Chicopee.

sachusetts. But with the outbreak of actual violence under
Daniel Shays, they who had stakes in the soil had more to
lose than gain from the harum-scarum army of "rebels,"
and at the approach of his motley contingent, tradition
has it, most of the householders of Ireland bolted their
doors.[12]

In 1786 Ireland was officially made a separate parish of
West Springfield, properly called the Third or North
Parish, but generally still called Ireland Parish. Since
1774 it had been in the curious position of being part of
the town of West Springfield, but still an ecclesiastical
unit with a parish of Springfield. Now Ireland was to be a
unit to itself. Legal recognition as a parish entailed, according to Massachusetts law, responsibility for the support of a minister. Hitherto Ireland had been able to share
or evade much of that burden, but by 1792 Ireland Parish
had no legal excuse for not setting up its own ministry.[13]
Although population had increased, the new settlers were
mostly Baptists and as such were loath to contribute to the
maintenance of an orthodox Congregational minister. The
new colony took up farms on "Back Street" some two miles
from the river south of Mt. Tom and formed there the
nucleus of "Baptist Village." In 1787 they undertook to
build a Baptist meetinghouse, the "Lord's Barn," but,

12. Springfield Town Records, IV, 203, 388, 390–391, 396–397, 408–410;
West Springfield Town Records, I, 19, 21, 36, 57, 60; Records of the Second Parish of Springfield; Alfred Copeland, ed., *A History of Hampden
County* (hereafter cited as *Hampden County History*), III, 2, 8. A few
days before Shays' march upon the United States arsenal at Springfield,
his second-in-command is said to have addressed his men as follows: "My
boys, you are going to fight for liberty. If you wish to know what liberty
is, I will tell you. It is for every man to do what he pleases, to make
other folks do as you please to have them, and to keep folks from serving
the devil." Quoted in *History of the Connecticut Valley in Massachusetts*
(Philadelphia, 1879; hereafter cited as *History of Conn. Valley*), I, 77.

13. Records of the Second Parish of Springfield; Connecticut Valley
Historical Society Library, MSS., Chicopee. The financial difficulties in
which the old fifth parish of Springfield (after 1783 the second parish)
found itself after the Revolution in its dealings with its minister led to
six years of parley between the two divisions, Ireland and Chicopee.
W. B. Sprague, "Historical Discourse . . . 1824," Appendix K, in *Sermons*, II, 58.

funds giving out, the project came to a standstill. At this juncture a Congregational Society was formed, purchased the unfinished Baptist structure, moved it north one-half mile and attempted to organize the parish. But without the Baptists' financial aid the Congregationalists were helpless.[14] In 1802 the inhabitants of the third parish were summoned by the sheriff to answer in County Court for their neglect of duty in not "Settling a Minister of Piety Religion & Morality."[15] Then the Congregationalists yielded and effected a working compromise with the Baptists whereby a Baptist minister was secured and maintained by both denominations. This arrangement endured until 1826 when the Baptists built a meetinghouse of their own.[16]

Although only eleven persons including the minister made up the Baptist church when it was constituted in 1803, it grew rapidly. Twice in the first quarter century it was quickened by a revival. In 1816 seventy-seven members were added by baptism and ten years later sixty-six

14. A. Judson Rand, "Early Life in this Locality," Holyoke *Daily Transcript*, Aug. 27, 1923 (hereafter cited as Holyoke *Transcript*); "Early Life in Our Valley," Holyoke *Telegram*, Sept. 1, 1923; Records of the First Orthodox Congregational Church in Holyoke, I. Since 1740 West Springfield had contained a small community of Baptists who as a religious society had supported their own pastor. By incorporating as a separate religious society Baptists could avoid paying the tithe in support of the Congregational minister. W. B. Sprague, "Historical Discourse . . . 1824," Appendices L and M, in *Sermons*, II, 60–61; Josiah G. Holland, *History of Western Massachusetts*, II, 151.

15. Writ in possession of Mrs. William F. Whiting of Holyoke.

16. Records of the First Orthodox Congregational Church in Holyoke, I. Only once in every two months the Congregationalists had a neighboring Congregational pastor administer communion to them. Three Sundays in four the Baptists had the use of the church building and the fourth Sunday the Congregationalists met there.

The fundamental importance to the Baptists of the doctrine of baptism by immersion is revealed in the wording of the deeds for pews in the new meetinghouse: "The Minister who shall occupy said house shall profess & preach the doctrine of free Salvation by Grace through faith in God our Divine Redeemer he shall practice baptism by immersion only on profession of faith & in order that any person shall take a part in the Government of the worship in said house, he shall profess & practice the same as is herein required of the Minister." (Deed in possession of Mrs. E. T. Hastings of Holyoke.)

were baptized in the course of a few months.[17] On several
occasions the Connecticut of a Sunday morning must have
resembled the Jordan. Small wonder that the neighborhood of the meetinghouse came to be called Baptist Village. In fact the strength of the Baptist church was to be
a characterizing feature of the community for three generations.

As the parish took on more semblance of a distinct community schools increased in number. By 1802 there were
three district schools and twenty-five years later there were
seven. Readers, "rhetorics," and the Bible served as school
books. Women began to be employed as teachers, first for
a summer term and then more regularly. But the education offered was limited in scope. Most of the pupils were
farmer children who could attend only part of the year,
and these came winter after winter until they were adult.
In 1805 the Baptist minister opened a school in which for
twenty-five cents a week a boy might be made ready for
college and the ministry. Girls also were admitted. Here
Greek, Latin, and geometry were taught. This academy
was supplemented after 1818 by a town grammar school.[18]

Education was of course the handmaid of religion. Here
prevailed a kind of simple Puritanism. The local justice of
the peace fined culprits more severely for travelling on the
Sabbath or for uttering profane oaths than for assault;
and for shad-fishing on Sunday the fine was as much as
four dollars.[19] But rum-drinking was not a sin and the

17. Records of the Second Baptist Church in West Springfield, Mass.
(in possession of clerk of First Baptist Church of Holyoke). It is true
that a large proportion of these converts later moved to other localities.
Of the seventy-seven baptized in 1816, twenty-four were dismissed to other
churches, and of the sixty-six immersed in 1826, thirty-seven were dismissed in the course of years. This is probably numerical testimony to
the fluid character of even the farming population of this section at the
time.

18. Plan of Ireland Parish, West Springfield, 1827, reproduced in *Early
Maps of the Connecticut Valley in Massachusetts* (published by Wright
& DeForest, Springfield, 1911); Gertrude Dunn, History of the Schools
of Ireland Parish, West Springfield, Massachusetts, 1720–1850 (Master's
Thesis in Library of Smith College).

19. Records of Lucas Morgan, Justice of the Peace in Ireland Parish,
1796–1797 (in possession of Mrs. W. F. Whiting of Holyoke).

Ireland farmer or riverman enjoyed an occasional mug of flip with an easy conscience.

The years immediately following the Revolution saw not only schools but some new business ventures arise. An inn was built in 1785 on the main road "to Hanover and Dartmouth College," as old maps label it, and Abner Miller's tavern became the popular stopping place for stagecoach travelers north- or south-bound. About this time also the town laid out a road connecting the great falls with the main road north. Thus not only was carting of goods around the falls made easier but the gristmill and the sawmill at the falls were made more accessible. The latter was built in 1783 and the corn mill just above it soon after.[20] Another corn mill was located in the southwestern corner of the parish upon Tannery Brook and "iron works," so called, just above it. Bog iron was dug not far away but the quantity was apparently not sufficient to supply the iron works indefinitely. By the time of the second town survey in 1827 the iron works had given way to an "hydraulic cement manufacture," limestone for which was quarried in the nearby hills. Some of this cement is said to have been used in building the stonework of the New Haven–Northampton Canal in the late 1820's, but later the quality proved inferior and the cement works were transformed into a straw paper mill.[21] As such it operated until long after Ireland Parish ceased to exist.

Besides these enterprises, a tannery was established in 1786 where the proprietor eked out from his farm the returns from the shoe- and harness-making business. This

20. West Springfield Town Records, I, 219–220, 315–316; Plan of the Town of West Springfield, 1795, reproduced in *Early Maps of the Connecticut Valley in Massachusetts.*

21. A. J. Rand, "Early Life in Our Valley," Holyoke *Telegram,* Sept. 1, 1923. This variety of manufacture to which one building could be successively devoted is typical of the neighborhood. It was strikingly true in South Hadley and in Northampton, too. *A History . . . of South Hadley, passim.* Although these little mills lay within Ireland Parish, when Holyoke was marked off in 1850 the parish line was not followed exactly, and these properties were included in West Springfield. Caleb J. Humeston, "Early Education and Business Enterprises," Holyoke *Telegram,* Aug. 31, 1923.

tannery was maintained more than a generation, super-
seded at length partly by one built near the mouth of Riley's Brook and by the flourishing Bardwell tan works in
South Hadley. The earlier business was conducted mostly
on a barter basis, boot-making or cobbling being done in
return for hides, lumber, corn, or "boarding" of cows or
sheep. Two blacksmithies, a cider mill, a wheelwright establishment and a wagon shop, a winter clock-making business
which was in summer abandoned for farming, and a mill
for sawing shingles and grinding paint were scattered
through the parish before many years. In the twenties a
fulling mill was located at the great falls for a time where
homespun was brought for finishing.[22] But such minor
ventures gave no permanent industrial character to the
community. They were merely the necessary concomitants
of the economic self-sufficiency common to rural New England of the time.

Here was a farming region distinctly, producing grain
for foodstuffs, raising livestock, breeding sheep. Sheep-
raising declined markedly after the thirties and by the
middle of the nineteenth century had virtually disap-
peared. The chief crops were hay, corn, rye, potatoes, and
oats, but there were occasional fields of turnips, beans, and
esculent vegetables, and even some tobacco. It was a bal-
anced, not a staple, economy.[23]

Only the spring salmon and shad fisheries at the river
varied the agricultural scheme of life in Ireland Parish
until well into the nineteenth century. In the latter part of
the eighteenth century people came from many miles in
April and May to fish at the falls where the most abundant
supply could be netted. As many as 1,500 horses at one
time were said to have been drawn up on the river banks

22. Account Book of Caleb Humeston, 1787–1813 (in possession of
Thomas Humeston of Holyoke); A. J. Rand, "Early Life in this Locality," Holyoke *Transcript*, Aug. 27, 1923.

23. *Statistical Tables . . . of Industry in Massachusetts, 1837* (hereafter cited as *Statistical Tables of Industry in Mass., 1837*), p. 93; *Statistics . . . of Industry in Massachusetts, 1845* (hereafter cited as *Statistics of Industry in Mass., 1845*), p. 187.

a day or two after the fish had begun to run. The inn on the South Hadley side of the river was filled with fishermen; and farm houses on east and west shore alike accommodated the thrifty householders who came to secure their supply of salmon or shad to salt down. As time went on ne'er-do-wells too came to drink rum and gamble with others of their kind for a few days. But the season was short and after it was by Ireland Parish settled down again to the quiet of agrarian existence.[24]

While the farming life of Baptist Village thus went on, commercial developments were taking place at the river. As the stream of migration had steadily pushed up the Connecticut, the importance of the river as a highway of commerce had increased. River settlements in New Hampshire and what was later Vermont had grown up during the eighteenth century and the river naturally served these as the easiest means of communication with the seaboard. Household goods were poled upstream and sawn lumber and farm produce shipped down. Every sizeable fall or rapids necessitated a carting around the white water and interfered by so much with the ease and cheapness of transport. Ireland farmers had long done some teaming of cargoes around the Hadley falls but the enterprising landowners on the South Hadley side had largely anticipated them in the business. Since 1755 South Hadley farmers had regularly carted boards and sawn lumber south across "Falls Field" and had had a good road around the falls since 1765. After the Revolution when interest in the improvement of roads and waterways was general, great enthusiasm was aroused in the project of constructing a canal around these falls at South Hadley, and in 1792 a company was chartered, "The Proprietors of the Locks and Canals on Connecticut River," to make the river navigable from the mouth of the Chicopee River northward to the state line. Capital was with some difficulty secured, mostly in the valley towns, and the work be-

24. Sylvester Judd, *History of Hadley* (Northampton, 1863), pp. 313–318.

gan.[25] The engineer in charge of the work, a Northampton man, ingeniously solved the difficulty of raising and lowering laden boats from the level below the falls to the level above by means of a pulley and an inclined plane.[26] Despite various setbacks, the canal, two and one-half miles long, and at its upper end an eleven-foot dam across the river were completed by 1794, and in April 1795 the first boats went through.

The impetus given to river commerce by the improvement was immediately felt. Timothy Dwight, a much-travelled American, wrote of the canal at South Hadley Falls during the early years:

A spectator standing about a quarter of a mile below the fall . . . is presented with the singular prospect of these works, consisting of the inclined plane and a number of buildings connected with it consisting of a sawmill, forge, etc., together with a handsome house, erected for the superintendent. In the river itself and on the shores, the numerous wharves, boats, fishermen and spectators amounting to several hundred in the month of May, together with the ascent and descent of the carriage loaded with the freight and full of people, impress on the mind very sprightly ideas of bustle and business.[27]

South Hadley Falls, or Canal Village, became thus for forty years a center of activity on the river. Over 250 men had been used in digging the canal and a small number were now regularly employed in poling the canal boats up-

25. *Ibid.*, pp. 306–308, 406–407; Forbes Library, Northampton, Judd MSS., South Hadley; *History of Conn. Valley*, I, 86–87. The canal enterprise was born of a real need, but was nurtured by the rivalry of the lower Connecticut Valley and seaport towns on the one hand and Boston and the eastern seaboard shipping centers on the other. The Connecticut towns were eager to keep the lines of commerce running north and south whereas Boston wanted to tap the upcountry for her own interest and divert commerce eastward. This situation stimulated interest in the building of the canal. See Edwin M. Bacon, *The Connecticut River and the Valley of the Connecticut,* pp. 312–324.

26. For description of the workings of this invention see Timothy Dwight, *Travels in New England and New York* (New Haven, 1821), I, 322.

27. *Ibid.,* I, 324–325.

stream. Passengers frequented the tavern in the village and helped bring prosperity. In 1802 the proprietors undertook the lowering of the canal bed four feet and the substitution of a modern lock system for the inclined plane and carriage. A freight rate of five shillings a ton prevailed, and "upwards of 7,000 tons of merchandize had passed through this canal in a season," wrote Dwight.

For the settlement on the left bank of the river the canal was a boon, but it brought no noticeable prosperity to Ireland Parish upon the right bank. The river boats and their merchandise passed Ireland by. A few individuals in the parish became interested financially in the river freight business and made in the thirties and forties what were for those days modest fortunes from it. But as a community it was Canal Village, not Ireland, that benefited. The vigorous attempts after 1826 to establish a regular steamboat service on the river from tidewater to Barnet, Vermont, were powerless to affect that situation. The Connecticut River Valley Steamboat Company, with its boats leaving the wharf in South Hadley for Hartford three times a week, whence freight was transshipped to New York, performed a service in the thirties to all the river towns in Massachusetts. But West Springfield and Ireland profited no more than Springfield and Northampton; and the advantages were incidental to being a river town, not to the particular settlement by the falls. Indeed the west bank of the river by the falls could hardly be called a settlement at all in the heyday of Canal Village. Ireland Parish presented little more activity along the river in 1827 than it had a generation, perhaps two generations, before. The population, as the town survey shows, had increased, but its distribution proved it to be still agricultural and not commercial.

Canal Village, on the other hand, boasted not only a busy commercial life but the beginnings of manufacture as well. Besides the usual grist- and sawmills there was established sometime between 1807 and 1818 between the canal and the river a mill for pressing oil from the flaxseed grown in the neighborhood; and in 1824 a more important enterprise—a paper mill. One of the local merchants, having bought in the first years of the century a strip of land along the river just below the canal, was able to build far out into the stream a wing dam which created ample power to supply his own saw- and gristmills as well as the oil mill and the two paper mills later to be erected on this land.[28]

The first paper mill built here was put up in 1824 by two prosperous Springfield storekeepers who purchased with the site the right to draw water from the millpond. Book, news, and writing paper were manufactured here of such quality that by 1830 the United States government printing office was buying Howard and Lathrop paper and the *Congressional Globe* was printed on it. Possibly this success was instrumental in bringing a rival firm upon the scene in 1831. The famous paper makers, the Ames family, bought land and water rights almost contiguous to the Howard and Lathrop property, and here David Junior and John Ames built their mill and set up their recently invented machinery for making paper in a continuous strip. The tremendous volume of water supplied by the Bardwell wing dam guaranteed adequate force to drive the Ames cylinder, and up to the panic of 1837 this was the largest paper mill in New England. Thus despite ultimate bankruptcy in the forties due to ruinous lawsuits and a destructive fire of the sort that was unhappily frequent in early New England factories, these paper mills gave to Canal Village for some years the air of an industrial community.[29]

The men and women employed here were not numerous by modern standards. Howard and Lathrop in 1832 em-

28. *A History . . . of South Hadley,* pp. 44, 76, 85–86, 104–106; Holyoke *Transcript,* Aug. 3, 1878; Plan of Ireland Parish, West Springfield, 1827, reproduced in *Early Maps of the Connecticut Valley in Massachusetts;* Contract between Josiah Bardwell and "Proprietors of Locks and Canals," September 1, 1806 (in possession of George Bardwell of Holyoke).

29. *Joseph Carew, A Memorial,* 1881, p. 36 (in possession of Carew Manufacturing Company, South Hadley Falls); *A History . . . of South Hadley,* pp. 86–87; *Paper World,* VI, no. 4 (Apr. 1883), 1–2.

ployed thirty women and twenty men while the Ames'
plant shortly increased that number considerably. By
1845 the number had grown appreciably. The wages seem
small: eighty-five cents a day for men and thirty-three
cents for women, "they boarding themselves," and where
the company arranged to board them, as was customary
in the case of the girls employed, the rate was twelve cents
a day.[30] The fact that this rate of wages existed in 1832
and in 1849 suggests that fluctuations in the business
world had little effect upon these local labor rates. It was
business on a small scale and an intimate relationship that
existed between employer and employed. A ferry established in the early years of the century from near the
mouth of the canal across to "the Fields" on the west bank
of the Connecticut made possible if still inconvenient regular intercourse between Ireland and Canal Village, and
after the invention and establishment of the swing ferry
about 1828 travel back and forth was easier. But it cost
two cents to cross by the swing ferry and employes in the
paper mills could ill afford a third of their day's earnings
for transportation. Any Ireland farmer's daughter who
went to work in the Canal Village mills lived at least during the week in South Hadley.[31]

After 1832 Ireland Parish also found itself with a mill
which could furnish employment to farmers' daughters
anxious to earn money of their own. Unlike the other in-

30. Pliny Jones Day Book (in possession of Mrs. William G. Dwight
of Holyoke); Carew Manufacturing Company Papers (in possession of
the company, South Hadley Falls; hereafter cited as Carew Mfg. Co.
Papers), 1848–1849, Receipts; *Joseph Carew*, 1881, pp. 39–40; *Report of
the Secretary of the Treasury, 1832, Documents Relative to the Manufactures in the United States, House Executive Documents*, 22d Cong.,
1 Sess., no. 308, I, 295; *Statistical Tables of Industry in Mass., 1837*, p.
81; *Statistics of Industry in Mass., 1845*, pp. 164–165.

31. *A History . . . of South Hadley*, p. 92; *Hampden Freeman*, Feb.
16, 1850; Pliny Jones Day Book. The swing ferry was a variation of the
cable ferry. From a pole in midstream a cable was suspended which was
attached to the bow of the ferry, while a shorter cable from the main
cable was fastened to the stern in order to make the boat head upstream
at an angle. The current then did the rest by pushing against a kind of
center-board. Two teams could cross at a time on this ferry.

dustrial undertakings of the parish the Hadley Falls Company was an incorporated concern. Apparently it was not made up of local stockholders, with the exception of the owners of the earlier fulling mill, but of Enfield men and perhaps a few others. The Hadley Falls Company was a modest enterprise, although its invested capital, $50,000, may have looked colossal to Ireland farmers. Twenty-seven hundred cotton spindles did not constitute a big mill even in the thirties and the value of the cloth manufactured in 1836–1837 was only $33,270. The factory stood on the river bank nearly opposite the Canal Village paper mills, and, as on the east bank, a wing dam brought water to the wheels. Following the Lowell example, the company built boarding houses to accommodate the New England girls who came to work as operatives so that their parents could feel sure of their daughters' being well cared for while away from home. Forty-six women and twenty-three men were employed here in 1837; eight years later slightly fewer persons were engaged. By 1845 nearly $60,000 worth of goods was manufactured in a year.[32] As testimony to the profitable nature of this business is the evidence of one of the stockholders: "In 1836 I left a farm and aged Father—at thirty years of age—with about $8000 to take charge of a small cotton mill at Hadley Falls. In 1847 when sold to the new Company my $8000 had grown to about $40,000 every dollar of which was put into the new concern."[33]

It is to be noted that not one of these mill projects at the falls either in Canal Village or Ireland was initiated by local landowners. Probably this circumstance was due to lack of fluid capital. Certainly money was not plentiful and barter was common in the thirties. But there may also

32. Caroline Ware, *The Early New England Cotton Manufacture*, p. 65; *Hampshire Gazette* (Northampton), June 6, 12, 1832, "Wanted by the Hadley Falls Company five or six Families to take Boarding Houses at their Village. Charles Eastman, Agent, South Hadley Canal"; *Statistical Tables of Industry in Mass., 1837*, p. 93; *Statistics of Industry in Mass., 1845*, p. 187.

33. Harvard Business School Library, Lyman Mills Papers, Edward Smith to George W. Lyman, Feb. 16, 1858.

have existed some prejudice against manufacturing, for
tradition has it that at a later date a farm owner of a desirable site threatened approaching negotiators with a
shotgun while he vociferated that he would have none of
the "cotton lords."[34] Whatever the basic reason for the
continued preoccupation with farming, the fact remains
that in 1845 Ireland Parish was still a rural community.

34. Deeds and Papers in possession of Mrs. E. W. Hastings of Holyoke; Edwin Kirtland, "The City of Holyoke," *New England Magazine*,
XVII (Feb. 1898), 732.

II

THE REGIME OF THE COTTON LORDS

WITH the coming of the Connecticut River Railroad a new era dawned for Ireland Parish. The slowly developing New England farming community was to be subjected to sudden violent changes. No longer evolution but revolution by exploitation of the water power was to be the new order and Ireland was to be swept along by forces the extent of which few could guess, least of all the farmers of the parish. In 1842 five Northampton men secured a charter to build a railroad from Northampton to Cabotville, as Chicopee was then known, there to meet the tracks of the Hartford-Springfield railroad. The routing of the new railway as originally mapped out would have taken the road across the river near Mt. Holyoke and thence down through Canal Village. But probably with a view to the development which was in fact effected two years later, the promoters changed the plan in 1845 and the tracks were laid along the west side of the river down to the lower rapids and then across at Willimansett to complete the three miles of the way to Chicopee Junction. South Hadley attempted to lay out a competing road but the scheme was abandoned and Canal Village resigned itself to its fate.[1]

The sponsors of the railroad, eager to secure a large freight business for the line, early envisaged the possibilities of industrial development in Ireland Parish. Before the completion of the road several endeavors were made to purchase the land on the right bank at the falls, but as most of it belonged to an inveterate enemy of manufacturing corporations, the negotiations came to nothing.[2] When

1. *A History . . . of South Hadley*, pp. 106–107; Moses F. Sweetser, "Traffic and Transportation," *King's Handbook of Springfield*, pp. 89–90.
2. "History of Holyoke," *Holyoke Directory*, 1869, pp. vii–xi.

in December 1845 the first train steamed across the bridge at Willimansett and puffing into Ireland Depot headed northward to Northampton, the farmer at the falls could still watch it with no misgivings about the revolution its coming was to bring.

The vision of an industrial city supplied with power by the Connecticut River falls had been glimpsed by George C. Ewing, among others, the New York representative of Fairbanks and Company, scalemakers of St. Johnsbury, Vermont. In the days when his journeyings up and down the valley still had to be done by stagecoach he had marked the West Springfield site as one for future development, and there is reason to believe that he had brought pressure to bear upon the Fairbanks brothers to attempt the preëmption of the water rights here in order to move their factory hither nearer the country's business centers.[3] In the fall of 1846, therefore, Ewing readily accepted the commission to accomplish if possible what others had failed of doing, namely the acquisition of title to the real estate and water rights at the falls. He acted not only for the Fairbanks brothers but for a number of Boston and Hartford men as well. Some of these men had capital invested in the Connecticut River Railroad and in the Western Railroad, the line running from Worcester through Springfield to the New York state boundary. Several of them had put money into cotton mills on the Chicopee River where a dam and a canal system had been built in the thirties.[4] Here on the Connecticut River was opportunity

3. Hadley Falls Company Papers, Directors' Records, July 17, 1849. (This collection, now located in the office of the Holyoke Water Power Company, is hereafter cited as H. F. Co. Papers.) See also A. J. Rand, "Early Life in this Locality," Holyoke *Transcript*, Aug. 27, 1923.

4. Lyman Mills Papers, James K. Mills and Ignatius Sargent to Stockholders of Connecticut River Railroad Company, Mar. 11, 1858; *Annual Reports of the Railroad Corporations in the State of Massachusetts for 1843*, p. 22. Among the prominent names associated with the Chicopee development are Edmund Dwight, Jonathan Dwight, George W. Lyman, Samuel A. Eliot, James K. Mills, and Thomas Perkins. Vera Shlakman, *Economic History of a Factory Town (Smith College Studies in History, XX)*, 24–27.

again to build up a great cotton textile city if only Ewing
could inveigle the Ireland farmers into selling their land.

It was a grandiose scheme. Ewing, after three months of
negotiating with the most obdurate owner, succeeded by
ingratiating manners and ready arguments in securing
the first transfer of about thirty-seven acres in March
1847. He promptly followed this by further purchases.[5]
The most important was that which secured title to the
real estate of the Hadley Falls Company, the first cotton
mill of Ireland Parish. The stockholders of this little
manufacturing concern were by no means unaware of the
value of their property and held out for a price of $95,000
and the privilege of taking stock in the new company to be
formed. Thus when the interested capitalists met in Boston in the summer of 1847 in the office of James K. Mills,
commission merchant, to organize and lay their plans,
Mills could report that Ewing had already overcome the
first difficulties confronting the enterprise. The names of
these eager investors included many of the big stockholders in Lowell and Manchester mills and in the Lawrence
development as well as in the Chicopee concerns.[6] Their

5. "History of Holyoke," *Holyoke Directory,* 1869, p. viii.

6. H. F. Co. Papers, Stock Records, pp. 6, 10, 13–18. Of the stockholders of the original cotton mill the Chapins of Ireland secured 60 shares,
while the Smiths of Enfield, Massachusetts, netted 360 shares in the new
company.

The greatest individual purchasers of the new company's stock were
Thomas H. Perkins and Edmund Dwight who each bought 200 shares, or
$100,000 worth. Perkins had originally made his fortune in the China
trade and had amplified it by investment in cotton mills. Dwight similarly
had expanded an inheritance thriftily acquired in domestic mercantile
enterprise. Both men were largely interested in the Chicopee mills. There
were ten subscribers of $50,000 each, all of Boston except Alfred Smith,
president of the original Hadley Falls Company, and William Wetmore,
a New York merchant. The Boston men were James K. Mills; Charles H.
Mills; Erastus Bigelow, the carpet loom inventor; Edmund Dwight,
Junior; Richard Fay; Theodore Lyman; and George Lyman. The investment house of James K. Mills also took 100 shares. The list of Boston
stockholders reads like a social register of that city in the forties. *Our
First Men, A Calendar of Wealth, Fashion, and Gentility* (Boston, 1846);
Wealth and Biography of the Wealthy Citizens of New York City (New
York, 1845). These pamphlets are both to be found among College Pam-
phlets, Yale University Library.

financial connections and far-reaching business dealings made them a well-defined group, a power in New England. Damming the Connecticut would be a more daring engineering feat than any the Boston associates had yet undertaken and would be costly. But if the project were adequately financed—and these optimistic, successful men were prepared to supply capital—there seemed to be reason on the basis of past experience to conclude that a great cotton manufacture could readily and profitably be built up at the Hadley falls. Why should not more cotton mills pay still more dividends?[7]

Thanks to the skill of Ewing, by the end of June 1847 most of the land necessary to the scheme had already been purchased, and the rest, at higher prices, was shortly acquired. At the same time the name, Hadley Falls Company, was released by the original cotton-mill stockholders for the use of their successors. The promoters deemed it necessary also to spend $70,000 for a controlling interest in the property of the "Proprietors of Locks and Canals," and to secure other extant water rights in Canal Village at a cost of $13,000. Measurement of the water in the river at the end of July, the driest time of the year, revealed a flow of 6,980 cubic feet per second, which with a fall of 60 feet meant the equivalent of 30,000 horsepower, or 550 mill powers.[8] A mill power, the basic unit by which water-power charges were made at Lowell and the usual standard unit of water-power measurement ever since the building of Lowell, is estimated at thirty cubic feet of water per second, where the head and fall is twenty-five feet. Even big mills in the fifties rarely used more than four or five

7. Dividends in the New England cotton industry had never been so high as in the years 1844–1846. Although manufacturers realized that long-continued expansion in the industry must be unwise, for the time being their confidence in prosperity was unshaken. Ware, *The Early New England Cotton Manufacture*, pp. 107–109, 152–158.

8. "History of Holyoke," *Holyoke Directory*, 1869, p. ix; H. F. Co. Papers, Stock Records, Sept. 21, 1849; Journal A, Aug. 1849; Ledger A, Real Estate, p. 1. Later measurements proved this estimate of powers greatly exaggerated. The official estimate in 1871 was 300 mill powers. *Holyoke Directory*, 1871, p. 4.

mill powers.[9] Hence by September of 1847 the subscribers to stock in the still unincorporated company found themselves owners of an enormous water power and of some twelve hundred acres of land bought for about $120,000. After a few necessary additional purchases, the new company at a total cost of $300,000 for real estate and water rights was in possession of the greatest potential mill development in New England.

Three million dollars was the sum tentatively suggested as needed ultimately to improve this property.[10] In view of the fact that at that time only one bank in Boston had as large a capitalization as $3,000,000, this was a large sum of money even for the Boston promoters.[11] Therefore, presumably to save delay in securing an added half million dollars in stock subscriptions, the company was organized with a capital of $2,500,000 in shares of $500 each. One hundred shares of stock were later cancelled before they were paid for, owing to a disagreement between Ewing and the company; so capitalization was fixed at $2,450,000, subscribed by 201 individuals and 15 business concerns. The stockholders promptly endorsed the plans as presented by their glib advocate, James K. Mills, gave the directors full rein, and vested Mills himself, elected treasurer, with authority to contract for surveys, excavations, construction, and machinery.

Henceforward most of the stockholders despite the mag-

9. *Report of the History and Present Condition of the Hadley Falls Company*, p. 16 (pamphlet in Holyoke Public Library; hereafter cited as *History of H. F. Co.*); Indenture of the Hadley Falls Company to Glasgow Company, May 2, 1856 (office of the Holyoke Water Power Company). A mill power was further defined as the amount of power needed to propel during sixteen hours a day 3,584 spindles for making cotton yarn into cloth. The standardized unit was reworded in 1856 to read: "the right during sixteen hours a day to draw thirty-eight cubic feet of water per second when the head and fall is twenty feet." History of the Holyoke Water Power Company (office of the Holyoke Water Power Company). Minor variations according to locality are listed in William Kent, ed., *Mechanical Engineer's Pocket Handbook*, 9th edition, p. 766.

10. H. F. Co. Papers, Stock Records, Sept. 21, 1847.

11. Shlakman, *Economic History of a Factory Town* (*Smith College Studies in History*, XX), Appendix A.

nitude of the investment, left the management of the enterprise unquestioningly to the directors. The directors in
turn largely relied upon the treasurer, James K. Mills,
and Mills, with his Boston affairs still to manage, had to
delegate much authority to agents and engineers on the
scene. But Mills had successfully conducted other ventures
and he was well connected. For the next ten years the two
treasurers of the company, Mills and George W. Lyman,
the engineers in charge of construction, and then the resident agents of the machine shop and the cotton mills hold
the center of the stage. The town was to be developed by
plan as a company town. With profits the dominant motif,
it is noteworthy that none of the providers of capital in-
vestigated with any care the question of the probable lapse
of time necessary to realize dividends.[12]

Mills acted with dispatch. Capable engineers who had already made a preliminary survey were engaged to survey
the land and to map the location of the dam, canals, mill
sites, streets, and boarding houses, and to indicate the
necessary change in routing and grading of the Connecticut River Railroad tracks where they cut through the
company's land. The treasurer completed purchase of additional water rights on the east bank of the river, and
then on terms which were highly advantageous to the Hadley Falls Company, leased to two South Hadley concerns a
part of the land with water sufficient under a head of forty
feet to drive ten thousand spindles and four paper engines.
The two South Hadley mills so contracting were the Glasgow Company, a newly organized cotton mill, and the
Carew Manufacturing Company, the paper concern
formed by the superintendent of the now defunct Howard
and Lathrop mill. These mills would utilize the power supplied to the transportation canal, control of which the
Hadley Falls Company now had, by a short connecting
canal cut through the eastern bulkhead of the dam. This
arrangement has persisted unaltered to the present day.

12. H. F. Co. Papers, Stock Records, Sept. 21, 1847; Directors' Records, July 19, 1849; *Our First Men.*

By means of the gate control at the dam, the canal could continue to be used for transportation. The fishing rights above the dam, a matter which had caused much trouble to the Proprietors of the Locks and Canals years before, were to be safeguarded by building fishways or by compensating purchase. Thus easily the problems arising from franchises and property on the left bank of the river were disposed of.[13]

Next, contracts were made for the construction of the dam, the excavation on the right bank of canals and raceways for at least two mills, for the building of two cotton mills and the machinery for one of them, and for necessary boarding houses and offices. A stone quarry at the foot of Mt. Tom had been purchased for $500, which, located nearby on the line of the railroad, could supply abundant stone for the masonry. Nothing was forgotten in these detailed plans. "Gentlemen are at the bottom of the enterprise," wrote a Springfield journalist, "who will soon make the place a beautiful village, and in five years the 'New City' will have a population equal to Lowell."[14]

Whether or no the promoters could be congratulated on the beauty of their village, certainly the engineers who planned the industrial layout of the town and the canal system deserve great credit. So admirable was the arrangement in all its technical details and so perfectly executed that no fundamental change or reconstruction has been necessary in eighty-eight years. The original plan as advertised by circular in 1850 was as follows:

In the construction of the canals, it is so arranged that the whole Connecticut River can be used over *twice* [by sets of mills upon two different levels]. Their arrangement will be seen by referring to the plan. The water is first received from the pond into a main canal through the gateway . . . on the

13. *Hampden Freeman*, Mar. 1, 1856; H. F. Co. Papers, Directors' Records, Jan. 17, 1848. The Carew Company in 1881, however, still held some water rights independent of the Holyoke Water Power Company. *Joseph Carew*, p. 38.

14. Springfield *Daily Gazette*, Jan. 3, 1848; H. F. Co. Papers, Journal A, Aug. 1848; Directors' Records, Jan. 17, 1848.

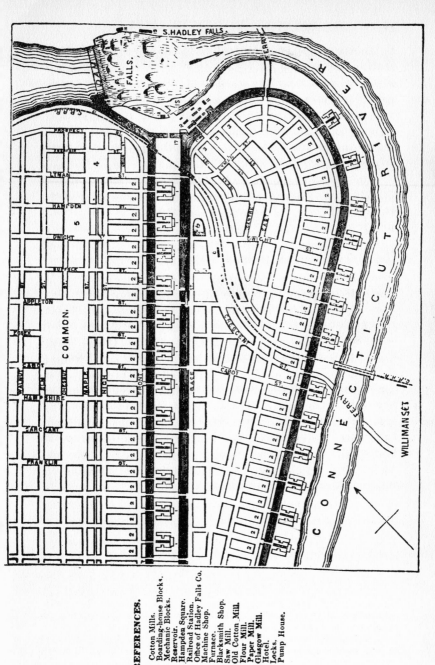

PLAN OF THE NEW CITY OF HOLYOKE

S. HADLEY FALLS.

CONNECTICUT RIVER

WILLIMANSET

[western] landward side of the dam. The length of this canal is 1013 feet. It then diverges to the South forming the upper canal, which is to be extended in a straight line to the length of 6,600 feet. Parallel with this canal [but on a level twenty feet below], at the distance of 400 feet, runs the raceway, which receives the water as it comes thro' the wheels of the factories, which are to be placed between the canal and raceway, at the rate of one factory to every 250 feet and carries it back to the head of the lower canal, to be used over again [by factories placed between this lower canal and the river], and then pass into the river. The length of the lower canal, which commences at the North end of the raceway, is to be 9,500 feet. The width of the main canal is 140 feet, and designed for 20 feet depth of water. The width of the upper canal, at the North end, is 140 feet; at the South end 80 ft. and is designed for 15 ft. depth of water. The fall to the raceway, which is of the same dimensions as the canal, is 20 feet. The lower canal has a fall [to the river] at the North end of 25 feet increasing at the South end to 30 feet. It will be observed by referring to the plan that there is a canal leading from the lower end of the main canal into the raceway opposite. In this canal there is a lock with a 20 feet lift, and an over fall with a granite face laid in cement. Between the gateway, at the dam and the bank navigation locks have been constructed, and by means of this canal, boats can pass from the river above into the lower canal, on which are built the machine shop, furnace and blacksmith's shop, with lumber &c. . . . A number of years will elapse, before the canals will be constructed the entire length proposed, and all the factories erected but the consummation of the grand design cannot be hoped for in vain.[15]

Such modification of this "grand design" as was planned in 1854 was undertaken to create additional mill sites by converting the raceway into a second level or middle canal.

15. *Plan of the New City of Holyoke* (in possession of Carew Mfg. Co.). The bracketed amplifications are mine. The mills at the northern end of the lower level canal have less fall than those at the southern end, as the former deliver the water directly into the river, which is higher just under the dam than below, because of the rapids.

Thus instead of a fall of twenty-five and thirty feet from the lower level to the river, a fall of twelve feet from a second level to a third was contrived and of twenty-three to twenty-eight feet from the third level to the river. But in essentials the original 1847 canal plan was followed. It has commanded the admiration of the most critical modern engineers. Other parts of the earliest scheme for developing the property, however, were soon rejected as being wasteful of mill sites. The first plan called for four cotton mills of 12,500 spindles, and the subsequent building and equipping of machine shops from the proceeds of land sales. So confident were the directors of the imminence of demands for sites that they thought it expedient to use mill sites "with economy to avoid the necessity at a future day of making land at a great cost in order to exhaust the water."[16] Therefore factories built into the air five stories high containing 18,500 spindles were agreed upon.

Work had to be suspended for a time in January 1848 because of a strike among the Irish day laborers at having their pay cut from seventy-five to seventy cents a day. Despite a brief display of violence the Paddies were soon persuaded to return peaceably to work by the arrival of militiamen from Northampton and, more effectual still, the counsel of the Catholic priest from Springfield who hurried to the scene. During the spring and summer the work was pushed ahead with what speed engineers, contractors, and several hundred Irishmen could make. In Canal Village building on the Carew paper mill and the Glasgow cotton mill went on simultaneously while at the "New City" sale of lots began.

By November the dam was completed. Crowds gathered from the surrounding countryside to see the gates close and the river pile up behind the dam. The structure was a colossal one for those days, from stone abutment to stone abutment a thousand feet long and thirty feet high, built

16. H. F. Co. Papers, Directors' Records, Jan. 17, 1848, Oct. 4, 1854; Ralph Smith, Development of the Holyoke Water Power Company (office of the Holyoke Water Power Company; hereafter cited as Ralph Smith, Development H. W. P. Co.).

of great hemlock timbers riveted to bed rock and faced with iron boiler plate. Cheers went up from the interested spectators as the last gates swung shut that November morning and the triumphant completion of the great work was viewed. But elation was short-lived. By noon leaks were appearing near the western bulkhead and about three hours later, when the water had risen to within two feet of the crest, suddenly with a thunderous roar the dam gave way in the middle. Timbers, boiler plate, and water swept downstream in one great flood.[17]

The disaster was greeted with less consternation than might have been expected. The story goes that Mills telegraphed to Boston: "Dam gone to Hell by way of Willimansett." The actual property loss was estimated at only $38,000, but the treasurer ruefully admitted that the resulting loss of time in getting the canals filled and the unhappy probable effect upon sales of land and power would bring that figure higher.[18] After careful study of the engineering problem a different type of construction was adopted for the new dam, and work began in April 1849. The second dam was made longer and much more substantial in every particular than the first. Gravel and concrete protected the foot and the foundation was packed solidly with stone to a height of ten feet. Solid timber planking eighteen inches thick along all the upper portion was completed by a rolling top of sheets of boiler plate.[19] With such energy was the construction driven forward that despite an epidemic of cholera[20] among the la-

17. *Hampden Freeman*, Mar. 1, 1851; Springfield *Daily Gazette*, Jan. 4, 11, 12, 13, 1848; Carew Mfg. Co. Papers, May 1848; *A History . . . of South Hadley*, pp. 108–110; H. F. Co. Papers, Journal A.

18. H. F. Co. Papers, Directors' Records, Jan. 2, 1849. Troubles with the lessees of power on the left bank soon developed, since both mills in South Hadley Falls—even now ceasing to be called Canal Village—were ready to operate in the spring of 1849 and found the water insufficient, because of the loss of the dam. Settlement was eventually effected by a remission of the water rentals to 1851. Carew Mfg. Co. Papers, Joseph Carew to John Chase, Mar. 3, 1849; C. B. Rising to Joseph Carew, Mar. 5, 1849; Memorandum to stockholders, Aug. 1849; Lyman Mills Papers, Letters, 1848–1849.

19. *History of H. F. Co.*, pp. 7–8; *Hampden Freeman*, Mar. 23, 1850.

20. It is impossible to ascertain whether or not this grim epidemic was

borers the work was finished before the end of October;
and eleven months after the failure of the first attempt a
watchful public could witness the successful damming of
the Connecticut.

Discouragements over delay notwithstanding, Ireland
during 1849 had assumed many aspects of a town. Provision and clothing stores had sprung up and land sales had
totalled a fair amount.[21] New Englanders with and without
savings came to try their fortunes in the new village—
storekeepers, carpenters, lawyers, doctors. A weekly newspaper had begun its career in September. A lodge of the
International Order of Odd Fellows had organized. Four
churches—Congregational and Baptist branches of the
old churches of Baptist Village, a Universalist group, and
a short-lived Episcopal church—had been formed. And
there were saloons. Cheerful persons had envisaged the
rapid growth and prosperity which was to come to the
village as soon as the dam was completed and had proved
its stability. But 1850 came, winter wore into spring, and
no rush to the New City took place. The most sanguine began to be discouraged. Complaints against the absentee
cotton lords began to be heard, not because they were successful lords of wealth, but illogically, because they were
not successful. Some of the population drifted away. Explanations that the country in general was facing hard
times, that manufacturing in particular was depressed,

truly Asiatic cholera or was rather bacillary dysentery, a disease which
had been brought by Irish immigrants to this country in 1848–1849. Local
outbreaks of cholera had possibly occurred in this country in 1849, but
the confusion of terminology and the notorious inaccuracy of the layman
in describing symptoms make it a fair guess that what has always been
called hereabouts "the cholera epidemic" was a spreading of bacillary
dysentery. Dysentery is usually transmitted by polluted drinking water.
Unsanitary living conditions could have spread either germ. Dr. Howard
Haggard to the author, Dec. 30, 1932. Whatever the label, the disease
for a few weeks took severe toll in the shanties of the Irish laborers.
Hampden Freeman, Sept. 8, 1849; Patrick J. Lucey, *History of St.
Jerome's Parish, Holyoke, Massachusetts, Diocese of Springfield* (hereafter cited as Lucey, *History of St. Jerome's Parish*), p. 24.

21. There were about thirty traders in the village by September, and
by the end of 1849 the company had sold fifty-nine lots. H. F. Co. Papers,
Stock Records, Feb. 20, 1850; *Hampden Freeman*, Sept. 8, 1849.

that people could not buy even at the New City when they had no money, and that the California fever was the true cause of the trouble—such explanations offered little consolation.[22] The year 1850 saw no brilliant beginning for the town.

With the dam functioning, the first cotton mill built and the water wheel installed, it needed only business revival to complete the transformation of the farming community and construction camp into a working mill village. In April manufacture began in a half-hearted way. Operatives were not wanting, since this was a mill for coarse goods, and highly trained help was not essential. Of the several hundred persons first employed, about one third came from the neighborhood, some 125 from the town itself and many of the others from Chicopee and Ludlow. But from the very beginning, the number of Irish people nearly equalled all the rest.[23] For Americans, working in a

22. Records of the First Orthodox Congregational Church in Holyoke, I; Records of Second Baptist Church in West Springfield; H. L. Foote, *Historical Sketch of . . . St. Paul's Church, Holyoke, Massachusetts,* pp. 4–5; G. C. Osgood, *Story of the Holyoke Churches,* pp. 55–65; *Hampden Freeman,* Sept. 8, Oct. 13, 20, 27, Nov. 12, Dec. 22, 1849, May 18, June 22, 1850; *Abstract of the Census of . . . Massachusetts . . . 1865* (hereafter cited as *Census of Mass.,* 1865), p. 248.

23. *Hampden Freeman,* Mar. 1, 1851; H. F. Co. Papers, Directors' Records, Feb. 19, 25, 1850; Stock Records, Feb. 20, 1850, Feb. 19, 1851, Feb. 18, 1852; Register. The register of employes, while unsatisfactory as a source of much exact information, gives some idea of the geographical distribution of nativity of the employes in the two Hadley Falls mills in 1849–1853:

Local		Foreign	
Holyoke	126	Ireland	419
South Hadley	11	Scotland	9
Springfield and West Spring-		England	8
field	10	Canada	8
Palmer	9	New Brunswick	4
Westfield	4	Nova Scotia	1
Chicopee and Ludlow	108		—
Lawrence and Lowell	4		449
All other Massachusetts	116	Unlisted but with English or	
	—	Irish names	167
	388		

Pennsylvania, 1; New York, 50; Maine, 19; Vermont, 49; New Hampshire, 51; Connecticut, 30; Rhode Island, 8.

five-storied mill beside Irish and English operatives was a
different matter from being mill girls in the old days of
the earlier Hadley Falls Company. Across the river in the
Carew paper mill the women were still American and an
educated, at least literate, class. But already in 1850 and
1851 here the native farmers' daughters were ceasing to
apply for mill jobs.[24]

It is an ironic paradox that Ireland Parish which for
one hundred and fifty years had been inhabited by straight
English colonial stock was now with a large Irish population no longer to be known as Ireland. The town was created
by the General Court in March 1850, but the name "Holyoke" was the choice of the directors of the Hadley Falls
Company who doubtless hoped that the Puritan label
would lend the place dignity.[25]

The new town government was in no enviable position.
For the most part the locality had been peopled in two and
a half years; and over many of its developments persons
living here had had no control. A fictitious legal person,
the Hadley Falls Company, represented by remote and
elusive Boston capitalists, and served here by well-meaning
but powerless underlings, owned much of the real estate,
controlled a water supply and a semblance of a sewerage
system, furnished its own means of fire protection, and had
the giving and taking of most inhabitants' livelihood. The
company had seen to the drafting of an ideal plan of industrial development, and streets and houselots had naturally been included. If the company built boarding houses
for its mill hands and paid taxes, what more could benevolence ask? The townspeople themselves must face every
other problem.

24. Carew Mfg. Co. Papers, Time Book, 1850–1866. A situation similar
to Holyoke's obtained in Chicopee where "foreign girls have been employed in such numbers that what American girls are employed there, experience considerable difficulty in finding society among their workmates
congenial to their tastes and feelings." *Hampden Freeman,* Mar. 13, 1852.

25. H. F. Co. Papers, Directors' Records, Feb. 19, 1850; *Hampden
Freeman,* Mar. 2, 1850. "Hampden" had been the name selected by the
residents.

But the influx of foreigners, mostly extremely poor, created complications. Ill fortune or indolence soon produced a large number who became a public charge. The cholera epidemic of 1849 left some persons dependent on charity, and accidents increased the number. The town on its incorporation in 1850, with a total population of 3,713, found itself with 120 persons to aid as state paupers. These persons without legal residence in this town or any other in the Commonwealth, were the charge of the state; but town expenses for their support outran the sums supplied from Boston. The selectmen in their role of Overseers of the Poor, purchased a poor-farm and by March 1852 had cut the numbers receiving public aid to sixty, six of whom were legal residents and thus properly town charges. Nevertheless the utmost economy of administration left the town overburdened, and had the Commonwealth not completed a State Alms House, whither in 1854 and 1855 the state paupers—mostly Irish—were removed, Holyoke might have been bankrupt before it was ten years old. Such a situation illustrates the defect of early immigration laws. As it was, in 1858 the town farm was sold and the few native paupers were boarded out.[26]

The School Committee also had a difficult problem. The schools in the rural districts of the township continued as in the days of Ireland Parish, but in the New City the number of foreign children whose parents could not or would not send them to school suggested the need of a campaign of parental education. One fourth of all the children in the town between the ages of five and fifteen failed to attend school at all in 1850–1851, and many others attended only part of the school year. The agent of the Hadley Falls Company promised to coöperate in enforcing the school laws so that every child under fifteen employed in a factory should have at least eleven weeks'

26. Holyoke Public Library, Holyoke *Town Records,* 1851, pp. 3–4, 10–12; 1852, pp. 4–5, 13; 1853, pp. 9–11, 13–14; 1854, pp. 8–11; 1855, pp. 11–17; Holyoke *Weekly Mirror,* Apr. 17, 1858 (hereafter cited as Holyoke *Mirror*); *Census of Mass.,* 1865, p. 298.

schooling in the course of the year.[27] But the School Committee felt uneasiness:

The system of *primary schools* is fraught with interests which should thrill the breast of every American citizen. The children now in a course of common school education in our country, are hereafter to guide the destinies of a great and growing nation! More, they are to exert a mighty influence upon the destinies of every nation on our globe! With what unspeakable importance, then is their moral and intellectual training stamped? Our *free institutions cannot be sustained by ignorant or vicious men, as the history* of all republics proves. *"Ignorance is the mother of vice."* It is only by *educating the masses, even all the people, that we can hope to perpetuate our republican form of government.*[28]

When in 1856 the percentage of children attending school in the industrial section was found to have decreased, the School Committee again pleaded helplessly for measures against selfish parents who placed their offspring in factories. Yet native American school children were well taught. In 1852 a high school was started in District Number One, and the next year one in the Baptist Village district, the old academy made into a public school. Thus for seven years the town boasted two high schools at a time when one was a distinction for a village.[29]

27. Holyoke *Town Records*, 1851, pp. 5–8; Records of the School Committee for the Town of Holyoke, Massachusetts, 1850–1876 (office of the Holyoke School Department), pp. 2–9. The Hadley Falls Company, so far from seeking to evade this law, presumably endeavored carefully to comply with it. James K. Mills in 1841, in response to a questionnaire sent out by the Secretary of the Board of Education, declared education for operatives in a cotton mill to be almost necessary; not only could they earn more, but common schooling kept them from indulging in vicious pastimes. The stress put upon the educational facilities in Holyoke in the circular issued by the company in 1853 indicates that the directors agreed with his pronouncement. Secretary of the Board of Education of Massachusetts, *Fifth Annual Report*, 1842, pp. 90–92; *History of H. F. Co.*, pp. 18, 22.

28. Holyoke *Town Records*, 1853, p. 8.

29. *Ibid.*, 1853, p. 4; 1854, pp. 2–5; 1857, pp. 18–20; Records of the School Committee, 1857; Holyoke *Mirror*, Dec. 6, 1856.

Fire protection was by means of volunteer companies. A fire district comprising just the New City, as the only section particularly in danger of fire, was organized in 1851, and special taxes were laid upon the property-owners. The steamer for pumping water belonged to the Hadley Falls Company, and water was supplied from the company's reservoir filled by pumping from the river.[30] Firemen were paid by the hour while on active service or drilling, but in their gay uniforms they also played a conspicuous part in the town's social life and were a source of civic pride when on parade or at firemen's musters in the neighborhood. Such high lights notwithstanding, the town found its financial and administrative problems many. The tax collectors were not above suspicion of malfeasance, the town debt was mounting, and there seemed to be little to show for it.[31]

Fortunately, pioneer faith in the future existed in New England as well as on the western frontier. A state bank with a capital of $100,000 was organized in 1851, chiefly as payroll accommodation, and soon paid small dividends.[32] Cotton manufacture raised its head slightly in the summer of 1851 and the directors of the Hadley Falls Company seized the opportunity to finish the second mill in their dormant New City, equipping it with machinery for the manufacture of sheer lawns, fabrics of a finer texture than had been attempted heretofore to any extent in this country. Much of the machinery was built in the company's own shop. In the early weeks of 1852 the demand for cotton goods rose to a point to justify full operation of mill No. One, which in 1850 had run at a loss and in

30. *Hampden Freeman*, Mar. 1, 1851, July 3, 1852. This 2,000,000 gallon reservoir and the piping to distribute the water had cost the company $40,738 by the end of 1850. H. F. Co. Papers, Stock Records, Feb. 19, 1851.

31. *Hampden Freeman*, Oct. 5, 1850, May 10, June 7, Oct. 11, 1851, Sept. 11, 25, 1852; Holyoke *Mirror*, Feb. 16, 1856, Mar. 20, 1858; Holyoke *Town Records*, 1853, pp. 12–18; 1854, pp. 8–11; 1855, pp. 13–17; 1856, pp. 4–8; 1857, pp. 8–11; 1858, pp. 8–9.

32. *Hampden Freeman*, Apr. 3, 1852; Hadley Falls Bank, Record Book A, 1851–1865 (in possession of Hadley Falls Trust Company, Holyoke).

1851 at half capacity. With the beginning of manufacture in mill No. Two in July 1852, prospects in Holyoke became brighter.[33]

But the next two years brought merely a repetition of the vicissitudes of the preceding years. The treasurer of the Hadley Falls Company declared that the work in Holyoke had been well done and at moderate cost, but that from the time of the organization of the company to February 1852 "manufacturing interest has been in a depressed condition and there has been no demand for this description of property."[34] Income accruing from the lease of water power to the South Hadley mills, from tolls from the navigation canal, and from tenement rentals was negligible compared to the company's outlay, and meanwhile unflattering reports of the town had begun to circulate. Certainly manufacturing concerns were not hastening to buy mill sites here. In fact a small flour mill, a wire factory, and a manufactory of cards and card clothing, the machines that clean and parallel the fibres before cotton or wool is spun, were the only new mills built other than the cotton mills of the Hadley Falls Company itself. One building housed the wire mill and the card factory and gave space to a maker of weaving reeds. The wire mill was put up by a concern which owned stock in the Hadley Falls Company, Woods Brothers and Company of Enfield. But the card manufacture employed only eleven persons while the other two concerns employed only four persons and one person respectively.[35] Even the completely successful operation of the second cotton mill could not make adequate returns on the $2,450,000 investment of

33. *Hampden Freeman,* June 28, 1851; H. F. Co. Papers, Stock Records, Feb. 18, 1852; Directors' Records, Mar. 3, Aug. 29, 1851. The fine roving machinery was bought from England. A few mule spinning frames were also bought, but the contract specified that the Hadley Falls Company might make the rest in its own shop.

34. H. F. Co. Papers, Stock Records, Feb. 18, 1852.

35. *Ibid.,* Feb. 18, 1852; Holyoke *Freeman,* Mar. 26, 1853; *Hampden Freeman,* Oct. 27, 1849, May 10, 1851, May 8, 1852; *Statistical Information Relating to . . . Industry in Massachusetts . . . 1855* (hereafter cited as *Statistical Information Rel. to Industry,* 1855), pp. 220–221.

the Hadley Falls Company. Clearly some steps must be taken to encourage the sale of water power.

First the company needed more active capital. So much money had been tied up in real estate and improvements that there was little left to carry on with until land-sales and rentals of power should release funds. So the directors voted to borrow $200,000 for three years at 6 per cent interest.[36] Efforts to find work for the machine shop were renewed, and meantime making equipment for a town gas plant kept it busy. The first definite encouragement came with the signing of a contract with Patrick T. Jackson and others in November 1852 for the erection of a "mill for fancy goods." Not only was this a step in the desired direction in securing a sale of land and lease of water power, but also it guaranteed the machine shop a large job in building all machinery and equipment for the new mill. P. T. Jackson, son of Patrick Tracy Jackson, one of the first great Boston merchants to interest himself extensively in cotton manufacture, was an influential person and a stockholder in the Hadley Falls Company. A new cotton mill in Holyoke meant work for builders, a large increase in population when manufacture began in 1854, and more trade.[37]

The Hadley Falls directors next undertook various publicity measures, and tried to convince the stockholders that expansion by one million dollars and another fine cotton mill of fifty thousand spindles was all that was necessary to earn large dividends on the whole investment. But the stockholders who had already waited for six years declared "that it is best to continue the careful management of the property as it is, obtaining what can be had for the

36. H. F. Co. Papers, Directors' Records, May 1852. Inasmuch as the stock was selling at 83 per cent of its par value at its highest on the Boston stock exchange in 1852 there is every probability that an issuance of new stock would have been futile. Joseph G. Martin, *Twenty-one Years in the Boston Stock Market*, p. 66; Holyoke *Freeman*, Jan. 15, 1853.

37. H. F. Co. Papers, Directors' Records, May 29, Aug. 29, Nov. 29, 1852, Feb. 14, Apr. 4, May 23, 1854; *Hampden Freeman*, Sept. 18, 1852; Holyoke *Freeman*, Apr. 16, 1853.

machine shop, and offering inducements for others to occupy more of the land and water power."[38]

Nevertheless, when men interested in starting a paper
mill in Holyoke attempted to purchase a site and lease
power, so determined were the directors to have a textile
city here that at first they refused to negotiate. Indeed had
the Parsons Paper Company not secured an option on the
gristmill the paper makers might never have secured a
foothold in Holyoke, since the Hadley Falls Company was
unwilling to encourage "any such small business as paper-
making." But rather than lose the flour mill, the directors
gave in and sold to Joseph Parsons and his associates a
mill site near the river, where in 1855 they began manufacturing.[39] There was more justification for the Hadley
Falls Company's attitude, however, than at first might appear. Until the lower canal was extended only one mill site
of any size was available, and, the treasurer maintained,
this lot should be kept open for a large cotton or woolen
mill which would employ many times the number of persons required to man a paper mill. The extension of the
second level canal was begun in 1854 to make more mill
sites ready.[40]

Still by 1854 prosperity had not come. A stockholders'
committee, appointed to investigate, declared:

Your Committee have been impressed . . . by the peculiar
condition of the affairs of this Corporation. The statement of
the Treasurer shows that the fixed or immovable investment
of the Company exceeds its capital stock by the sum of
$127,610.09, and that other expenditures are to be made to
complete the works, and that the Company are owing $1,154,-

38. H. F. Co. Papers, Stock Records, Feb. 16, 1853; Directors' Records, Feb. 22, May 18, Aug. 11, 1853; Journal B, June 1853. The most
effective advertisement was an elaborate brochure, published in 1853,
History of H. F. Co. It contained a map showing the town's railroad connections, an engineer's drawing of the dam, and a detailed analysis of the
town's advantages.

39. Scrap Book of Mrs. William Whiting, 1859–1891.

40. H. F. Co. Papers, Directors' Records, May 23, June 23, Oct. 4,
1854; *Statistical Information Rel. to Industry*, 1855, p. 220.

171.54; that the whole dependence of the Company for carrying on its large business is on borrowed means. This ought
not to be so. . . . [41]

The upshot of this report was the decision to divide the
company into separate corporations, one to continue as a
water power and real estate enterprise with the machine
shop appended, and the other to take over the cotton
manufacture and with added capital to operate as a textile
concern. Such division was customary in the earlier ventures of the Boston capitalists elsewhere.[42] More money
was the great need and this scheme promised to be the best
way to raise some $490,000 additional capital.[43]

The deed of property to the Lyman Mills, the new corporation, included an indenture for sufficient water power
to run all the machinery in the two cotton mills, namely,
fifteen mill powers, with provision for additional mill powers if needed later. This indenture became the pattern for

41. H. F. Co. Papers, Stock Records, Feb. 15, 1854; Holyoke Public
Library, *Report of the Committee appointed by the stockholders of the
Hadley Falls Corporation submitted March 1, 1854,* p. 5.

42. Shlakman, *Economic History of a Factory Town (Smith College
Studies in History,* XX), 36.

43. *Report of the Committee . . . of H. F. Co.,* pp. 8–12; H. F. Co.
Papers, Stock Records, Mar. 22, 1854. The new company, the Lyman
Mills, was to pay to the Hadley Falls Company $63,942.07 in cash and
$980,000 in Lyman Mills stock on which two thirds of the par value of
each share was to be deemed paid. Each Hadley Falls stockholder was to
receive a scrip dividend of $200 on each $500 share of Hadley Falls stock,
which should entitle him to subscribe for three $100 shares in the new
company, with one third of the par value of this new stock to be paid in
money whenever the directors should call for it. This device would raise
capital as painlessly as could well be since stockholders could sell part of
their subscription rights to raise funds to take up the remainder. An explanation of fixing the par value of the stock at the "unusual sum of
$100" was considered necessary: "It is, that thereby persons of small
means, operatives, overseers, and others engaged in the Company's service, may become interested, when if the par value was a large sum, they
might not have the means. And it certainly would be of great advantage
to have as many such persons as possible, to feel that they were partners
in the enterprise, and were deriving from their exertions some benefit
beside their mere wages. In this way, the jealousy so often existing between the employer and employee might be greatly allayed, if not entirely taken away." At the same time Hadley Falls' stock was reduced to
a like par value.

later sales and leases of power in Holyoke. The mill powers were conveyed under the form of a perpetual lease or
grant, record of which is kept in the County Registry of
Deeds, as if the power rights were real estate. Every grant
of mill powers carried with it title to the land necessary for
mill buildings, and the sale price was based only upon the
power indentured, not upon the amount of land conveyed.[44] Land sold in connection with the power rights
might include lots for tenements for the help, but such
tenement property might not be otherwise used and might
not be alienated except with the mill site. The annual
rental fixed was to be per mill power 260 ounces of troy
weight of silver of the then fineness of silver coin of the
United States, or the equivalent in gold, at option of the
grantee at the time of payment.[45] This rental was to be a
minimum for all succeeding grantees. At the pleasure of
the lessee he might be relieved of annual rent payments by
tendering to the Hadley Falls Company a sum of money
sufficient to produce at a rate of 6 per cent per annum an
amount equal to the annual rental. The Hadley Falls
Company must receive the sum so tendered and invest it as
a fund toward defraying the expenses of maintaining the
water power. This paragraph permitting commutation of
rental was omitted from later indentures. Otherwise,
though minor modifications were made in 1855 and in
1856 when new deeds were issued, this form was in essen-

44. H. F. Co. Papers, Directors' Records, Apr. 20, 1854; Lyman Mills
Papers, Deeds, Indenture to Lyman Mills, Apr. 28, 1854. A set of proposals was printed which contained the provisions applicable to any
mill site of the company. The indenture itself was the deed to a particular site. Ralph Smith, Development H. W. P. Co.

45. The silver clause, in later years the source of heated controversy,
was dictated by the high relative value of silver in that era of American
monetary history. Failure to pay this rent might result in forfeiture of
mill and mill powers to the grantor, although in case of deficiency of
water for any cause other than neglect on the part of the grantee, the
rent might be remitted and damages might be due to the injured grantee.
This last clause, allowing damages for failure of water, was altered in
1871 when some extenuating circumstances were recognized as releasing
the grantor from responsibility. Lyman Mills Papers, Deeds, Indenture,
Apr. 28, 1854, Paragraph VI, VIII, XI; Indenture to Brown and Whiting, 1871.

tials followed for fifty years.[46] The silver clause and the
tenement-property proviso were to lead eventually to
trouble, but for years the agreements here outlined served
adequately all purposes of power company and lessees
alike.

Under such circumstances the absentee promoters of
Holyoke ceased to be identical with the "cotton lords" of
the town. Many investors in the Hadley Falls Company
lost no time in subscribing the necessary cash to become
stockholders in the Lyman Mills also. Most of the stock
was taken up by August 1854, some by new subscribers,
although none by operative, overseer, or agent. The utter
necessity of getting the stock sold in order to finance both
companies was a matter of concern. Nevertheless this division of property made little difference in attitude and interests of the power company.[47]

In spite of all discouragements the directors continued
to believe in the growth in the near future of a textile town
with its teeming population. This conviction had sorry effects upon the town in causing the company to employ the
utmost parsimony in using land for dwellings. Because, in
the absence of transportation facilities, it was important
for mill operatives to live near the factories, real estate
promoters contended that adjacent tenement sites must be
used with economy and be closely built upon. The treasurer comprehended some of the difficulties involved in this
policy when he reported in 1854: "The want of houses and
consequent difficulty of placing work people in Holyoke is
probably one obstacle in the way of determining the set-

46. Lyman Mills Papers, Deeds, Indenture, Apr. 28, 1854, Paragraph
XX. In case of such outright sale a credit of $5000 for every mill power
was to be entered upon the company's books. The only active concern
ever to avail itself of the privilege of commutation of rental was the
Glasgow Company in South Hadley Falls. Three paper mills, built in the
seventies, also acquired outright title to permanent powers by purchase
of sites originally sold in 1856 to a prospective carpet manufacturer who
had bought the power. H. F. Co. Papers, Directors' Records, Aug. 3,
1854, Apr. 9, 1855, Nov. 18, 1856.

47. Lyman Mills Papers, Charter of Incorporation, Apr. 3, 1854; Stock
Certificates; H. F. Co. Papers, Stock Records, Mar. 22, 1854; Directors'
Records, Aug. 3, 1854.

tling there of persons who are engaged in various mechanical business and to whom a cheap and unfailing water power is necessary."[48]

This housing problem existed before and was to continue, making in an open countryside a crowded and unlovely spot. Gradually the townspeople began to express the feeling that the town's interests were being sacrificed to the financial welfare of the company. In 1855 there were only 514 dwellings to accommodate 778 families. In Chicopee, one complaint pointed out, small houses were the rule, while here brick blocks three and four stories high were the only available tenements; and for these less comfortable quarters higher rentals were charged than in either Chicopee or Northampton. The fundamental trouble, averred a shrewd observer, was that the real estate company was obsessed with the idea of Holyoke's impending rapid growth into a city where real estate would bring high prices, whereas the aim for the present might better be to create an attractive manufacturing village.[49]

Here was the typical company town. Non-resident stockholders had invested money in it for the purpose of deriving profits. But were they not also building up the state, furnishing support for workers, and utilizing their own talents like faithful stewards of the Lord? Certainly there was no evidence of the "public be damned" attitude. Lack of transportation was a controlling factor in the situation, and no American mill town had satisfactorily solved that problem in the fifties. A decade later a Hartford newspaper wrote: "The town is solidly and handsomely built, the ornamental brick houses, many of them boarding houses, three stories high, and with long rows of dormer windows roofed and slated, exhibiting the effects

48. H. F. Co. Papers, Directors' Records, Aug. 3, 1854.
49. *Ibid.*, May 18, 1853; Stock Records, Feb. 15, 1854; Holyoke *Freeman*, July 2, 1853; *Abstract of the Census of . . . Massachusetts . . . 1855* (hereafter cited as *Census of Mass.*, 1855), p. 144; Holyoke *Mirror*, Dec. 23, 1854, May 31, 1856, Apr. 24, 1858. The Hadley Falls Company derived from its ninety-four tenements in 1857 an income of $8,495. For these dwellings rentals varied from $24 to $150 a year. Lyman Mills Papers, Holmes to Mills, Feb. 14, 1857.

of Boston taste and capital employed when Boston capitalists controlled the place."[50] Here was the product of the American civilization of its day, which even Boston, the cultural center of the continent, accepted complacently.

Attractive the town was certainly not in the fifties in spite of the charm of the scenery of river and hills. The excavations for buildings and canals and the grading of streets had turned up loose earth which blew about in clouds in dry weather and made High Street even years later a dreary stretch of heat and dust in summer. The Hadley Falls Company in 1850 had set out maple trees around the brick tenements, and care was taken to keep the earthen sides of the reservoir well turfed. A public square was marked out on the company's plan of the town but it was little more improved than the vacant lots. The treelessness of the town for years lent it a bleak aspect.

In view of the sanitary conditions, however, it was probably well that the sun had free play. The few sewers that the company built in the early years debouched into the canals. Since it was customary to empty the canals once a week to clear them of possible obstructions, frequently the system amounted to having open sewers, although the upper canal could be flushed from the reservoir and the lower canal from the upper. But the staunchest defenders of the town bewailed the "filth and stench necessarily attendant upon thickly settled regions," and complaints over the lack of drainage of the streets were heard until in 1857 the company laid a sewer above and parallel to the first level canal.[51] The mill tenements all through the fifties were supplied only with outhouses. Irish immigrants living in board and turf shanties along the river bank in a squalid district known as the "Patch," to the north and west of the mill properties, had only an occasional cistern, and for years the outhouses there drained into the river at a point not far from the intake of the pipes from which

---

50. Hartford *Daily Times,* quoted in Holyoke *Transcript,* Jan. 23, 1869.
51. *Hampden Freeman,* June 22, Oct. 26, 1850, Jan. 25, 1851, May 29, 1852; Holyoke *Mirror,* May 3, Sept. 27, 1856, June 30, 1857; H. F. Co. Papers, Directors' Records, Aug. 3, 1854; *History of H. F. Co.,* p. 19.

the reservoir was filled. Why the much vaunted "salu-brity" of Holyoke failed to give way before a succession of pestilences became a mystery.[52]

The shanty-dwellers of the Patch and the "Flats," a similar section below the dam, were squatters for whom the Hadley Falls Company took no responsibility. The Irish occupants of these hovels were the poorest immi-grants, most of them utterly uneducated, their ignorance of elementary hygiene only exceeded by their poverty. A description of the Patch in 1854 reported twenty-five years later is probably only an exaggeration of degree. Said the visitor: "I was through here peddling maple sugar at that time. I stopped at one of the shanties to sell some sugar. First, the man and woman came out of the door, then six children came out, then six boarders came out, then a cow came out, and then a sow and ten pigs came out, all from the same door."[53] But the streets and tene-ments nearer the mills were little better. The germ theory of disease was not yet established even in the scientific world and the connection between filth and disease was only vaguely sensed by the more intelligent members of the community.

So shocking had conditions become by 1856 that the town created a Board of Health to investigate and to make regulations. The report of the committee presents an ugly picture.

Many families were huddled into low, damp and filthy cellars, and others in attics which were but little if any better, with scarcely a particle of what might be called air to sustain life. And it is only a wonder (to say nothing of health) that life can dwell in such apartments. . . . Although the Board have been unable to accomplish all they would desire, they feel that much has been done during the past year in removing sources of filth, uncleanliness and nuisances. . . . Yet in view of the conditions, habits and customs of very many of the inhabit-

52. Lyman Mills Papers, Davis to Lyman, Oct. 6, 1857; *Hampden Free-man,* Sept. 8, 1849, June 21, 1851.
53. Holyoke *Transcript,* Jan. 4, 1879.

ants of the town, they have . . . to say that their labors for the past year, are but the beginning of what is demanded by a well regulated community.[54]

Despite the glaring need of such supervision, so submerged in financial troubles was the town that no Board of Health was reappointed until 1859. The health regulations required underground water drainage whenever possible without unreasonable expense, but there were no means of enforcing the ruling.[55]

Yet the Hadley Falls Company and its offspring, the Lyman Mills, prided themselves on the wholesome living conditions in their town. They offered free vaccination to all employes "who have not had the kinepox." Water from the reservoir was piped to all the boarding houses. And in 1857 the agent of the Lyman Mills wrote to the treasurer in Boston that a "bathing tub" had been placed in the "W. C." of the office "for the use of the overseers and others connected with the works under circumstances which should be creditable to the company." The first bathroom in town in a private house was an innovation twenty years later. All mill employes who had no families here were expected to live in the boarding houses, where "respectable keepers," were to keep track of their boarders' conduct, "the doors to be closed at ten o'clock in the evening" and inmates not to be allowed "to collect on the front steps or sidewalk in front of their tenement."[56]

Nor were working conditions easy. Accidents in the mills were frequent, and fire risks were great in the crowded rooms where lint filled the air and oil lamps at first and gas later supplied the illumination, while sperm oil lubricated the machinery.[57]

Wages were little more than enough to live on. In stores,

54. Holyoke *Town Records,* 1857, p. 11.
55. *Ibid.,* 1860, p. 11; Holyoke *Mirror,* July 5, 1866.
56. *History of H. F. Co.,* pp. 11–13; Lyman Mills Papers, Davis to Mills, Mar. 5, 1857.
57. Holyoke *Freeman,* May 28, June 25, July 23, 1853; Holyoke *Mirror,* Apr. 10, June 26, 1858; Lyman Mills Papers, Davis to Mills, Mar. 4, 1857; Carew Mfg. Co. Papers, 1853, Survey of Mill.

clerks could be hired for $9 a month. In the Carew paper mill women's wages varied from about $2.98 to $3.00 a week without board, while skilled males might earn as much as $1.75 a day.[58] Although in these days South Hadley Falls was a distinct community, in the Holyoke cotton mills the rate was much the same. Girls in the card room earned generally $3.00 a week and in the spinning room slightly more. Weavers were on piece work. Bobbin boys, sometimes only nine or ten years old, were paid twenty-five cents a day. Overseers and skilled workmen such as mechanics were paid more generously than mill hands, but board cost a man $2.00 and a woman $1.50 a week, and the company, though demanding that boarding-house keepers extract the rent within three days of the operatives' payday, paid the help only once in four, sometimes once in six weeks. Wages were paid in bank notes, however, not as was true at the Glasgow Mill, in leather coins redeemable only at the company store.[59]

Hours were long as wages were small. In winter lack of daylight cut down the day's work, but in summer even children were worked nearly seventy hours a week. A law of 1842 forbade the employment of children under twelve in a manufacturing establishment for more than ten hours in any one day, but that was at least occasionally evaded here in Holyoke in the early fifties, whether through inadvertence or intention.[60] Bobbin boys whose job it was to replace the filled spools or bobbins with empty ones on the spinning frames were needed as long as the machinery was

58. Carew Mfg. Co. Papers, Time Book, 1850–1866; Letters, 1848–1849. Before 1850 each individual employe of the Carew mill signed a separate receipt for his or her pay and these receipts were kept clipped together. After 1850 the help were paid once every three months and signed their names in the book.

59. Holyoke *Freeman,* Jan. 15, 1853; Lyman Mills Papers, Davis to Lyman, Dec. 10, Davis to Mills, Sept. 29, Ranlet to Lyman, Oct. 5, 1857; H. F. Co. Papers, Letter Book, Mills to Holmes, Aug. 9, 1856, p. 89; John Fox (interview).

60. John O'Connell (interview); Lyman Mills Papers, Davis to Lyman, May 6, 1858. Agent Davis declared that the ten minutes after meals when the wheels were started up, though optionally employed, were generally utilized by a large part of the help for beginning work.

running, and unless an elaborate system of shifts was put into effect, as at a much later date, these children must be employed a full adult working day. The schedule was as given on the opposite page.[61]

Inspired presumably by the call of the New England Industrial League, in 1850 a Workingmen's League of Holyoke was organized, dedicated primarily to the securing of a ten-hour working day. Though the state organization was focussed on political action, the Holyoke League first of all attempted to obtain from local employers a voluntary reduction of hours. Reiterating that social reform, not violence, was their object, the four hundred League members declared themselves eager to build up good feeling between the capitalist class and labor, contending that time for education and self-improvement was necessary for the mechanic in order that he might thus achieve an effective voice in government. "We hold labor to be in every way honorable and dignifying, and it is for that dignity and honor we are now struggling that hereafter the mechanic, the artisan, and the laborer may assume that station in society which their importance to the civilized world demands."[62] It was the workman's political significance which was stressed. As was characteristic of the Massachusetts labor reform associations of the fifties, the League was confined to men, a circumstance in marked contrast to the agitations of the forties when the Female Labor Reform Associations had played an important part.

The endeavor of the League was at the time fruitless, but just before the fall election of 1852 these voters were tossed a sop by reduction of working hours in the Hadley Falls machine shop to eleven a day. No corresponding change in hours in the cotton mills was effected, however. There for the most part women, and largely foreign

61. Broadside formerly in the office of the Farr Alpaca Company of Holyoke.

62. *Hampden Freeman,* Feb. 16, May 4, 18, July 27, 1850; Charles E. Persons, "The Early History of Factory Legislation in Massachusetts," in *Labor Laws and Their Enforcement with Special Reference to Massachusetts,* edited by Susan M. Kingsbury, II, 62.

Time Table of the Holyoke Mills,

To take effect on and after Jan. 3d, 1853.

The standard being that of the Western Rail Road, which is the Meridian time at Cambridge.

MORNING BELLS.

First Bell ring at 4.40, A. M. Second Bell ring in at 5, A. M.

YARD GATES

Will be opened at ringing of Morning Bells, of Meal Bells, and of Evening Bells, and kept open ten minutes.

WORK COMMENCES

At ten minutes after last Morning Bell, and ten minutes after Bell which "rings in" from Meals.

BREAKFAST BELLS.

October 1st, to March 31st, inclusive, ring out at 7, A. M. ; ring in at 7.30, A. M.
April 1st, to Sept. 30th, inclusive, ring out at 6.30, A. M. ; ring in at 7, A. M.

DINNER BELLS.

Ring out at 12.30, P. M. ; ring in at 1, P. M.

EVENING BELLS.

Ring out at 6.30,* P. M.

* Excepting on Saturdays when the Sun sets previous to 6.30. At such times, ring out at Sunset.

In all cases, the *first* stroke of the Bell is considered as marking the time.

women at that, not voters, were concerned.[63] A year later several Lowell corporations, convinced apparently of the strength of public opinion in the state favoring shorter hours, voluntarily reduced the schedule in their mills to sixty-six a week. In Lawrence, Chicopee, Newburyport, and Fall River some concerns followed suit.[64] Not so in Holyoke. Here in Holyoke was no body of informed, intelligent public opinion to bring pressure to bear upon the corporation.

The foreign employes, Irish, Scottish, and English, were probably not unintelligent even if illiterate. To the Irish who mostly came from circumstances of abject poverty, living and working conditions in Holyoke could offer only an agreeable contrast, while to the Scottish and English mill operatives conditions could appear little worse than in Glasgow or Manchester. Other foreign nationalities were not represented in town before 1857 save for an occasional British Canadian and a handful of Germans and Swiss.[65] Toward the end of the decade the Lyman Mills' agent began to look for a supply of experienced power loom weavers; the Scottish girls were not sufficiently

63. *Hampden Freeman,* Apr. 10, 1852; Persons, "The Early History of Factory Legislation in Massachusetts," in *Labor Laws and Their Enforcement with Special Reference to Massachusetts,* edited by Kingsbury, II, 36–38, 87–88. The foreign population by 1855 totalled 2,015 out of a population of 4,639, and the number of foreign-born females, from whose ranks the mill operatives were largely drawn, exceeded the males by 40 per cent. *Census of Mass.,* 1855, pp. 24, 110; Lyman Mills Papers, Register II, 1853.

64. Holyoke *Freeman,* Sept. 24, Oct. 1, 1853; Shlakman, *Economic History of a Factory Town (Smith College Studies in History,* XX), 142.

65. *Census of Mass.,* 1855, p. 110. The Irish numbered 1,657 of the 2,015 foreigners in 1855. Few Irish women were employed as weavers, however. Their names are largely confined to the registers of the card rooms and spinning rooms. H. F. Co. Papers, Register; Lyman Mills Papers, Register I. In 1853 the Hadley Falls agent imported eighty-two Scottish women as weavers. Of these thirty-seven signed their names to the contract and forty-five made their marks. Two years later the mill paymaster was sent to England and Scotland to get an additional supply of these weavers. Contract between Jones S. Davis and the Female Workers for the Hadley Falls Company, March 12, 1853 (in possession of Mrs. W. F. Whiting); Lyman Mills Papers, Letter Book I, Mills to Holman, Aug. 14, 1855; Cash Book A, p. 75.

docile to suit him, proving according to his plaint "a source of expense and trouble rather than profit."[66] And thus a few Belgians from Ghent were brought to Holyoke. But until the invasion of French Canadians late in the winter of 1858–1859 the town had few working people who could not speak some English.

Common language could not render the population homogeneous. As the Workingmen's League could testify, from the town's beginning there was a gap between employed and employer, although it was not wide in a community like Holyoke of the early fifties, where the well-to-do of the capitalist class lived elsewhere. Deeper was the gulf between native American and immigrant, between Protestant and Roman Catholic. The occasional Irishman of education himself looked secretly askance at his uncouth fellow countrymen, and until schooling had given the immigrant children some boost in the social scale, social intercourse between New Englanders and foreign-born was rare. Irish boys were not even considered reliable enough to be given jobs as shop clerks or delivery boys.[67] A local branch of the Know-Nothing Party was established in 1854 and sent its candidate to the legislature. But it was short-lived, utterly discredited by the end of 1855.[68]

After the establishment in Holyoke of a Roman Catholic Church with resident priest in 1856 the distance be-

66. Lyman Mills Papers, Davis to Mills, Jan. 25, Feb. 13, Mar. 4, 1857.
67. William A. Prentiss, Fayette Smith, John O'Connell (interviews). So few were the persons of education among the Roman Catholics in town that two grown men, brothers, had to serve as altar boys at St. Jerome's in the early years until boys could be educated to respond properly in the Latin of the Mass. (Private information.) Yet Father O'Callaghan, himself a man of learning, declared in 1858 that he believed every Irish family in Holyoke had its own Bible. Holyoke *Mirror,* Feb. 6, 1858.
68. Holyoke *Mirror,* Aug. 26, Nov. 18, 1854. Local Know-Nothing adherents, though numerous for a few months, apparently took their stand less on an anti-foreign, anti-Catholic program than on the slavery and protected-industry issue to which they fell heir as a survival of free-soil whiggery. The unpleasant details of the conduct of the committee of the legislature appointed to investigate conditions in the nunnery at Roxbury were given full publicity in the *Mirror,* and this sufficed to annihilate any lingering Know-Nothingism. *Ibid.,* Aug. 25, 1855.

tween immigrant and native American widened. The first
priest of St. Jerome's parish, a saintly but uncompromising old man, was bitterly attacked for his criticisms of the
use of the Protestant Bible in the opening exercises at
school and was accused of seeking to discourage school attendance of his parishioners' children. There developed
later among the Catholics a sense of grievance which grew
into outright resentment. Among the more well-to-do
Americans, on the other hand, the Catholics were not generally regarded with actual hostility. In the ranks of the
native American workmen there may have lingered some
anti-foreign sentiment, but on the whole the adult American attitude was fundamentally one of indifference. While
the Irish Catholics were coming to feel set apart as mar-
tyrs to their religion, the New Englanders simply were
unaware of their existence as factors in the scheme of
things outside of the workaday world.[69] The Irish could
work, but as creatures from a different world they could
scarcely expect to mingle with the natives. At the end of
the first decade of village life the line was drawn not
between capitalist and laborer, well-to-do and poverty-
stricken, but between Protestant American and Catholic
immigrant.

The distinction was after all inevitable in a community
where the churches were the centers of what social life
there was. Church sociables and fairs were among the
principal gatherings of each season, and the newcomer in
town made his friends through the church. After the long
working day, long for merchant as well as for mill worker,
there was little time for play. Except for an occasional
professional entertainment—a play, a concert, an exhibi-
tion of animals, a sleight-of-hand or ventriloquist performance—there were few diversions other than the simple

69. *Ibid.*, Apr. 15, 1854, Mar. 8, Apr. 18, Aug. 20, 1856, Dec. 5, 1857 to
Apr. 30, 1858. Lucey, *History of St. Jerome's Parish,* pp. 34–35. Among
the school children a good deal of antagonism grew up. One jingle hurled
as a taunt at the American school children ran:
        "Yankee goes to meeting to hear the devil preaching!
        Paddy goes to chapel to get a rosy apple!"

festivities which were arranged by the church groups. To the Odd Fellows weekly meetings and annual "levee" and ball, and to the meetings of the Masonic Lodge might be added evenings at the "Lyceum" where debaters assailed each other with rhetoric. Firemen's musters and balls, the singing school or oratorio society, sleigh rides or picnics—there was virtually nothing else. Once a year the county fair and horse show aroused interest, but lucky were the adults who could find time to attend.[70]

An editorial in the Holyoke *Mirror*, deploring the restricted social life of the town, spoke in scathing terms of the role of the churches: because the town was new and the inhabitants were often transient, people made no effort to be neighborly; the churches, theoretically the source of Christian fellowship, were worse than useless in promoting any general social life, because of denominational clannishness; their exclusiveness of all save their own congregations warped "every man's social nature to a particular creed."[71] There was probably much truth in this indictment. Baptist and Congregationalist, Methodist and Universalist, each Protestant group was self-sufficient. As for the Roman Catholics, it was enough that they were tolerated, that a black-skirted priest should be allowed to raise money for building the little brick church dedicated to St. Jerome, and that the Sons of Erin should dance in New England and celebrate saints' days with Shamrock Balls.

Jones Davis, agent of the Lyman Mills, made a peri-

70. *Hampden Freeman*, Jan. 18, Sept. 7, Oct. 12, 19, 1850, Jan. 4, 11, Oct. 11, 18, Nov. 29, 1851, Apr. 3, July 3, Nov. 20, 1852; Holyoke *Freeman*, Feb. 5, 1853; Holyoke *Mirror*, Feb. 18, 1854, Sept. 6, 23, 1856, Jan. 31, Mar. 27, Oct. 17, 1857, Jan. 2, Feb. 6, 27, July 31, Oct. 2, 1858; Diary of Anna Fairfield, Sept. 1857, Sept. 16, 1858 (in possession of Mrs. W. F. Whiting); Diary of Chloe Ely, 1857 (in possession of Mrs. Edwin Chase of Holyoke).

71. Holyoke *Mirror*, Feb. 7, 1857. A decade later one might attribute this feeling to a sensing of different social levels in the different churches, the Congregational and Episcopal at the top of the ladder, Baptist and Methodist below. But there is little evidence of this situation in 1857.

The Universalists dissolved as a separate unit in Holyoke in 1857, ostensibly to lend their needed support to an older church in town. Osgood, *Story of the Holyoke Churches*, p. 65.

odic effort to create more community friendliness at least among the mill employes. But his Christmas parties at the Lyman Mills Cloth Room hall and his encouragement of the Lyman Mills Hose Company, like the sleigh ride in 1859 when all 758 employes in 53 sleds were treated to a whole afternoon's ride, smacked unmistakably of policy; while other kindnesses to the help, though prompted doubtless by genuine humanity, served to make surer his treasured position of "the big man in town." The company paid the bills.[72] Probably more comforting to most of his operatives was their church on one hand or the saloon on the other.

While the social life was simple, the intellectual opportunities of the community were meagre in the extreme. High school students had some books available which were procured by the school authorities, and a few boys went on to college from the Academy and to interest themselves in literature and abstract ideas.[73] But reading matter of any sort was scarce. There was no town library and no bookstore. The local newspaper was published only weekly and the Springfield *Republican*, the chief intellectual supply two decades later, though stimulating, was not generally subscribed to in the fifties. The better educated of the community got some mental exercise from the Lyceum debates upon topics such as: "Do the writings of Dramatic Poets have a tendency to corrupt the Morals of a people?" or "Does the pulpit or the bar offer greater opportunities for the service of mankind."[74]

72. Holyoke *Mirror*, Dec. 27, 1856, Jan. 10, Mar. 14, 1857, Jan. 2, 1858; Lyman Mills Papers, Davis to Lyman, Aug. 4, 6, Sept. 6, 1858, Feb. 3, Nov. 26, 1859; Agent's Abstract, July–Dec. 1859; Springfield *Daily Republican*, Feb. 5, 1859; Lucey, *History of St. Jerome's Parish,* pp. 35–36. It was an innovation in Holyoke to have Christmas observed in any way. Diary of Anna Fairfield, 1856–1858.

73. Lyman Mills Papers, Account Book and Receipts of Stephen Holman, 1851–1859; Diary of Oscar Ely, 1857, 1862–1863 (in possession of Mrs. Edwin Chase).

74. *Hampden Freeman,* Nov. 29, 1851; Holyoke *Mirror,* Dec. 20, 1856, Jan. 31, 1857. For nine months the Holyoke *Freeman* was published, "A Family Newspaper Devoted to Literature, Art, Science, Poetry, Agriculture, Amusement, Political, Commercial and General Intelligence."

Women had no share in the Lyceum programs, but the columns of the *Freeman* and the *Mirror* indicate their participation in the intellectual life of the town. Perhaps the nearness of Mt. Holyoke Female Seminary in South Hadley encouraged the younger women to faith in the capabilities of the feminine mentality. Certainly in the early fifties women in Holyoke took a more active interest in the feministic movement than was true a generation later. Pleas for more nearly equal economic chance, advocacy of the bloomer dress, faith in the wisdom of women suffrage, all imply an alertness to the possible role of women outside the home and factory. The pioneer spirit of this generation of women may have led them with their families to move from Holyoke to the West.[75]

In the winter of 1856–1857 the Second Congregational Society sponsored a course of improving lectures at the church, but attendance was so scanty that the series had to be given up after the first few lectures. "We must be content hereafter to let the idea go abroad that nothing will pay in Holyoke except some low burlesque concert or something akin to it, that appeals only to the lower passions of man's fallen nature."[76] People were too busy in earning a living to devote time or thought to mere ideas.

"Man's fallen nature" found more congenial outlet in the saloons. The liquor question was a persistent problem in the town. In the heyday of the "river gods," the local potentates of river transport, rum had flowed freely in Ireland Parish and public opinion had accepted it as a matter of course. But with the growth of an industrial community and a concentrated population, with the influx of foreigners whose temper was regarded as uncertain, and with the ever-spreading success of the temperance movement the country over, sentiment in Holyoke changed

---

75. *Hampden Freeman*, June 21, 28, 1851; Holyoke *Freeman*, Jan. 29, 1853; Holyoke *Mirror*, May 31, Oct. 18, 1856, Jan. 16, Feb. 13, 27, Dec. 25, 1858; Scrap Book of Mrs. William Whiting.

76. Holyoke *Mirror*, Feb. 14, 1857. Yet some distinguished lecturers had upon occasion been heard in the village. *Ibid.*, Jan. 14, Mar. 4, 1854.

somewhat.[77] In 1852 a state law like the Maine liquor law prohibited the sale of strong liquors for any purposes save medicinal and mechanical. Prohibition, however, did not eliminate the saloon. A situation on a small scale foreshadowing the difficulties of the 1920's promptly developed. Many of the foreign population had little enthusiasm for the new order and the American half of the town was not unanimous in support. "It may as well be understood," wrote one citizen, "that Holyoke is one of the Rumest places in the Rum County of Hampden. It has ever been so since the town was chartered, and unless powerful action is used to aid the law it will remain so for all time."[78] A prophetic pronouncement. A local enforcement league was active for a time, and gradually advocates of temperance in Holyoke multiplied. During the dreary winter of 1857–1858 when the effects of the panic were most acutely felt in the community, a Total Abstinence Society made efforts to organize a public library with a reading room where young people might find recreation outside the saloon. Nothing concrete came of the agitation, unless the library of some two hundred volumes at the Lyman Mills for the use of employes was built up as a response of the plea for a general town library. But the sale of liquor went on, unauthorized saloons flourished, and by the end of its first decade of existence Holyoke had established the reputation of being one of the "wettest" spots in Massachusetts.[79]

What was the attitude of the farming community of Baptist Village to this upstart manufacturing town at its doorstep? Some of the farmers' sons were themselves

77. *Hampden Freeman,* Oct. 29, 1849, Apr. 27, June 22, 1850, July 12, Dec. 13, 20, 1851. Some 650 persons, mostly Irish people, were reported as signing the temperance pledge when the venerable apostle of temperance, Father Matthew, campaigned here in 1849.

78. *Hampden Freeman,* May 29, July 24, Oct. 2, 1852; Holyoke *Town Records,* 1853, p. 12.

79. Holyoke *Freeman,* Jan. 1, 1853; Holyoke *Mirror,* Mar. 4, May 13, 27, Aug. 12, 26, 1854, Jan. 16, Feb. 20, July 24, 31, 1858; Lyman Mills Papers, Davis to Lyman, Mar. 4, Apr. 19, 1859; Treasurer's Cash Book A, p. 321.

drawn from the "Street" into town. The old Baptist and Congregational churches each dismissed a noticeable proportion of their members to make up new churches in the New City. But most of Baptist Village had little to do with the new arrivals down in the "Fields." Baptist Villagers were prone to look upon the interlopers of the factory district as inferior at best and irreligious at worst. Only gradually was the gap bridged as the younger generation grew up, and not until the street railway in the eighties shortened the two miles from the "Street" to town, did the two communities merge. In the fifties Baptist Village still held aloof and doubtless viewed the struggle for existence in the mill town as deservedly dubious.[80]

Even before the panic of 1857 Holyoke was growing with discouraging slowness. For a short time after the separation of the Lyman Mills from the Hadley Falls Company prospects improved. The power company completed an arrangement with Erastus B. Bigelow, inventor of the Bigelow carpet loom, whereby a site with fifteen mill powers was sold for $75,000 payable in stock of the company. That unwelcomed concern, the Parsons Paper Company, was ready by 1856 to expand and built a second mill which doubled its capacity.[81] And in 1857 the finisher at the Parsons mill combined with a few others to organize the Holyoke Paper Company. This company bought a mill site at the south end of the recently extended second level canal and contracted with the agent of the Hadley Falls machine shop to build a mill for five paper engines and necessary houses nearby. The machine shop netted thereby also a small order for machinery. The success of the Parsons enterprise had completely vanquished the doubts of the Hadley Falls Company directors about the desirability

80. Records of the First Baptist Church of Holyoke, I; Records of the First Orthodox Congregational Church in Holyoke, I; *Hampden Freeman,* June 22, 1850; Dr. Harry Hastings and Fayette Smith (interviews); Holyoke *Mirror,* Jan. 16, 1858.

81. Parsons Paper Company Papers, Directors' Records (office of the company, Holyoke); H. F. Co. Papers, Directors' Records, June 25, Nov. 18, 1856; Stock Records, Feb. 17, 1857; Holyoke *Mirror,* Feb. 21, 1857. Purchase of the mill powers of the Bigelow property was outright.

of the paper industry in Holyoke.[82] A second small iron-wire concern opened in 1857, locating in the old mill where the card manufacture and Clarke wire concern were already housed. Wire drawing required tremendous power, as did the operation of paper machinery. The available power explains the locating of wire and paper mills in Holyoke. Beyond these no new businesses came. Still the machine shop and the gas works of the company made a fair showing for 1856. That year the directors embarked on a regime of debt reduction to the exclusion of expenditures upon the fixed property of the company, and in 1857 were instructed by the stockholders to continue the frugal scheme.[83]

But the most Spartan economy could not tide the company over the panic of 1857. The treasurer, anxious to lower costs before the passage of the tariff of March 1857,[84] began to urge payroll cuts upon the agents in Holyoke. Davis of the Lyman Mills protested. The reduction of the labor force in the fine goods mill, No. Two, was out of the question since the supply had been insufficient to run all the looms there for some time past; and "a good supply of workers and a constant since uniformed stapled cotton" were essential for having the product run well. As to cutting wages, the Lyman Mills then were paying less than Lawrence or the Portsmouth Mill by 12 to 15 per cent, and Davis declared further reduction folly. Perhaps in response to this statement Davis gave notice two weeks later of an impending 15 per cent wage increase in the No. One spinning room. Instead of the grateful reception an-

82. Lyman Mills Papers, Holmes to Mills, Mar. 21, April 17, May 15, 1857.

83. *Ibid.*, Holmes to Mills, Jan. 6, 30, Feb. 4, Mar. 2, 1857. Land sales for 1856 and January 1857 totalled $9,684.39, including lots which were not industrial sites. The machine shop in 1856 turned out 1,319,926 tons of castings and $220,176.42 worth of machinery, while that year's sale of gas amounted to 2,696,600 cubic feet at a cost of $2.25 per thousand, with an average loss of 7.92 per cent from leakage, condensation, or other causes. At the Springfield gas works the loss averaged 20 per cent.

84. The rates upon cotton goods were not altered, but mills may well have apprehended downward revision of the schedule. Davis R. Dewey, *Financial History of the United States*, 8th ed., p. 262.

ticipated, nearly one hundred Irish girls demanded at once a flat rate of $16 a month, walked out at noon, and were joined the next day by others. The episode had no permanent effect upon the community. The ringleaders of the strike lost their jobs, the mill ran with other spinners until slackening demand necessitated curtailed operations later in the year, and the agent was not converted to any policy against yielding an inch lest the help demand an ell. Similarly the agent of the machine shop refused to reduce wages since he had trouble as it was in getting competent workmen at their prices.[85] This time management could not save itself at the expense of labor.

So matters stood until September. By that time the money market, following upon the failure of the Ohio Life Insurance and Trust Company, had tightened to a point where New York banks were suspending specie payment. The Hadley Falls Company and the Lyman Mills had trouble in securing money for payrolls and were nearly desperate over meeting their notes at the banks. On the nineteenth the failure of a big Boston selling house threw Holyoke into consternation, as the Hadley Falls Bank was known to do considerable business with the bankrupt concern, and the treasurer of the Hadley Falls Company and the Lyman Mills, and P. T. Jackson, the treasurer of the Hampden Mills, were members of the firm. Mill operatives gathered their bank notes and rushed to the bank to secure specie. The run was stopped for the moment and the local press attempted to belittle the seriousness of the situation. The Hampden Mill, it announced, would operate as usual while the Lyman Mill No. One would close for a week only and then resume its four-day a week schedule.[86] But by the end of September the treasurer of the Hadley Falls Company and Lyman Mills was obliged to acknowledge him-

85. Lyman Mills Papers, Davis to Mills, Mar. 4, 1857 (dated 1856 but obviously meant for 1857), Mar. 24, 26, May 18, 1857; Holmes to Mills, May 18, 1857; Springfield *Daily Republican*, Mar. 25, 26, 1857.

86. Dewey, *Financial History of the United States*, pp. 262–265; Lyman Mills Papers, Waln Leaming and Company to Mills, Sept. 8, 1857; Ranlet to Mills, Sept. 1, 4, 7, 1857; Holyoke *Mirror*, Sept. 26, 1857.

self defeated and, resigning his position, turned over to
the directors an appalling financial tangle.[87]

The Hadley Falls Bank had continued to meet payrolls
in spite of the drain of specie, but it now refused to do so
longer unless some check upon the call for gold and silver
could be arranged. Even mill overseers were demanding
coin and the cashier feared that suspension of specie payments must follow shortly. Furthermore, the bank warned,
unless the Lyman Mills' notes due in October were
promptly paid, the bank itself must "go to the wall." A
short-term loan at a high rate of interest was negotiated
for the Lyman Mills and by dint of promising to redeem
for the bank all notes returned for specie the company obtained money for the October payroll. The No. Two mill
and the repair shop were put upon two-thirds time, and
pay day was deferred until mid-November.[88] And so the
most critical days were weathered.

The Hadley Falls Company, however, its credit less secure than before the separation of the manufacturing
unit, was obliged to resort to more sweeping measures. To
prevent creditors from seizing company property, temporarily title was transferred by mortgage to the new treasurer, until a few weeks later he was enabled to issue notes
of the company, payable with interest in six months.[89] In
Holyoke already the force of machinists at the shop had

87. H. F. Co. Papers, Directors' Records, Sept. 24, 1857. Later Lyman,
in explaining the difficulties he confronted, declared that when he relinquished the position of treasurer of the company in August 1854, he
passed over to Mills, his successor, $24,014.73 and only a small debt.
When he, Lyman, resumed the office in October 1857 the debt was about
$488,652 and he had $250.04 cash on hand. *Ibid.*, Stock Records, Apr. 9,
1858.

88. Lyman Mills Papers, Ranlet to Mills, Sept. 29, 1857; Ranlet to
Lyman, Oct. 5, 7, 9, 17, 1857; Warriner to Lyman, Oct. 7, 1857; Davis to
Lyman, Oct. 16, Nov. 5, 1857; Morton and Grinnell to Lyman, Oct. 16,
1857; B. J. Howland to Lyman, Oct. 17, 1857. Pressure was brought by
other banks also. The mills in turn could not collect the money due them
from selling houses and jobbers for some weeks. *Ibid.*, Warriner to Lyman, Oct. 7, 1857; Waln Leaming and Co. to Lyman, Oct. 17, 1857; Holyoke *Mirror*, Oct. 24, 1857.

89. H. F. Co. Papers, Directors' Records, Sept. 24, Oct. 8, 9, 12, 1857;
Holyoke *Mirror*, Oct. 17, 1857.

been somewhat reduced, and Lyman instructed Agent
Holmes to sell property of the company—horses, lumber,
iron, whatever he could—in order to pay off the men and
discharge them when paid. But as long as machinery contracts were unfulfilled some men must be kept on. In mid-
October, Holmes wrote:

We pay none except those we discharge. It is almost impossible to collect a dollar, and as for selling anything now worth
naming for cash it seems to be out of the question for no one
seems to have any money. I shall have nine hundred dollars
tomorrow and discharge as many hands as it will pay. We
should have some eight thousand dollars paid to us this week,
but I can hardly say now that I expect to receive one quarter
of it.[90]

By the end of the year all jobs were finished and the machinists discharged. Gloom settled down upon the town.

In the textile mills not only was working time reduced
by one third but many employes were dismissed. In December Lyman Mill No. One, the coarse goods mill, was
shut down entirely. Though the market was more constant for fancy goods, specialties of the Hampden Mill
and of the Lyman Mill No. Two, these factories also were
obliged before spring to curtail operations, and the
Lyman Mill No. Two closed completely for a time. When
full time was resumed at the Hampden Mill at the end of
March 1858, a smaller force was employed and a lower
wage scale went into effect. And immigrant labor was
grateful for work at any wage. The paper mills, the Parsons at Holyoke and the Carew at the Falls, continued to
run, but with fewer employes, while the Holyoke Paper
Company, its mill not yet finished, proceeded slowly with
few workmen on reduced wages to complete its buildings.[91]

90. Lyman Mills Papers, Holmes to Lyman, Oct. 5, 19, Nov. 23, 1857;
Lyman to Holmes, Oct. 17, 1857.
91. *Ibid.,* Holmes to Lyman, Oct. 14, Nov. 23, 1857; Davis to Lyman,
Oct. 5, Dec. 10, 1857; P. T. Jackson to Lyman, Nov. 16, 1857; Mill Returns, I, 1855–1857; Carew Mfg. Co. Papers, Time Book, 1850–1866; Holyoke *Mirror,* Jan. 2, Mar. 20, 27, 1858.

The work people of the town faced the situation as best they could. Some lucky ones found temporary jobs on neighboring farms and able-bodied men were glad to work for $4 a month and their board. The town gave assistance to over one hundred persons. When wage cuts were first announced in the fall, operatives in the mills had been philosophical about their case. The workmen in the Lyman Mill repair shop with a touch of sardonic humor donned their most ragged clothes and marched through the streets saying that hard times meant wearing their old clothes over again. But as matters grew worse rather than better, many people left town. Of the ninety-seven members of the Second Congregational Church in January 1856 only twenty-five were still in Holyoke in October 1858, and of the twenty-one original members of 1849 only three remained.[92] So extensive was the exodus that in March 1858 Davis wrote in alarm to Lyman seeking authority to hold out hopes to former operatives of the mills' reopening soon.

Most of the best work people have left the place and others are following every day. . . . It will cost a large sum of money to supply the Lyman Mills with a new set of work people, particularly the No. Two Mill. We hope this matter of starting the mills and future relations to work people is receiving due consideration.[93]

But not mill hands alone were suffering. The proprietors of the big hotel, the Holyoke House, were unable to raise $400 in order to keep the house running. When opened in 1850 the Holyoke House had been acclaimed as ranking with the Revere and Tremont in Boston or the Irving House in New York. The cashier of the Hadley Falls Bank set forth the case to Lyman in the spring of 1858:

If you can assure Mr. Ross and Dillon of about $400, I think

92. Holyoke *Town Records,* 1858, pp. 6–7; Holyoke *Mirror,* Oct. 24, 1857, Oct. 30, 1858. New members were added to the churches even while others were dismissed.
93. Lyman Mills Papers, Davis to Lyman, Mar. 11, 1858.

arrangements can be made to keep the hotel open another year. Otherwise it must be closed. . . . It would be a local calamity to have the house closed and, in connection with other recent misfortunes here, would in my opinion add greatly to the discredit of the place and depress somewhat the hopes of its friends, if not the value of their property here. When you consider that $400 per year is only about *one-half* of the simple interest on the amount which Ross and Dillon paid *in cash* for the *lot* on which the hotel stands, may I not hope for a favorable answer?[94]

Yet the Hadley Falls Company had to refuse. Indeed the company found itself increasingly involved. Just before the annual meeting in February 1858 creditors made an attachment upon the property in Holyoke. Reorganization and recapitalization or bankruptcy were the alternatives confronting the company. The stockholders, perturbed and disgusted, at last agreed to attempt the launching of a new company which should buy out the Hadley Falls Company and, it was hoped, thereby secure $490,000 in cash, enough to meet the existing debt of $488,652.[95]

But the campaign to obtain subscriptions to stock in the proposed company went badly. Many Hadley Falls stockholders were weary of the struggle. The great venture had failed; why try to rebuild the ruins? "I do shrink," wrote one, "from renewed ownership in a concern that has been

94. *Hampden Freeman,* Oct. 12, 1850; Lyman Mills Papers, Ranlet to Lyman, Mar. 27, 1858; Boston Letter Book, Lyman to Ranlet, Mar. 30, 1858; H. F. Co. Papers, Directors' Records, Apr. 9, 1858.

95. Lyman Mills Papers, Protest of Hadley Falls Company Draft, Nov. 25, 1857; Martin and Smith to Lyman, Dec. 14, 1857, to James K. Mills, Dec. 24, 1857; H. F. Co. Papers, Directors' Records, Oct. 17, 1857; Stock Records, Feb. 17, 1858. One advocate of selling all property but the water privileges, dam, canal system, and mill sites reasoned that compared to the property assets the debt was not great. ". . . One or two years ago we should not have noticed it; now we were for paying our debts and closing up." By the scheme adopted the stock of the projected company was to be offered first to stockholders of the Hadley Falls Company who for every three shares of the old stock were to be given the privilege of subscribing to one one-hundred dollar share in the new company.

so annoying and vexatious."[96] More explicit were the criticisms of Alfred Smith, the venerable director whose interest in the Hadley Falls dated back to the thirties:

The property has cost nearly two million of dollars including the debt which is now about to absorb the whole. There was an original error of judgment on the part of the leaders in this enterprise, and also on the part of those who took the stock, as to the want of . . . such a mighty water power. From this error, if there had been no others a heavy loss of Capital or Interest or both, was unavoidable. But after due allowance for the losses arising from that original error of Judgment, I am far from thinking that the total loss was necessary, or that this result would have followed upon a more moderate scale of plans and expenditures, subsequent to the construction of the great dam, and the first canals.[97]

Under competent management Smith figured the investment worth easily $500,000 over and above the debts. Under Boston management he considered the property worth nothing. The prime requisite of competitive capitalism is good management. The Boston practice of appointing a Boston manager at a high salary, *who lived* in *Boston* and left only subordinates at the mill in the country, was uneconomical. Therefore, concluded Smith, he would not subscribe. And from this position the hard-headed old Yankee refused to move.[97] After six weeks of frantic effort to market the stock the most hopeful backers of the new project admitted defeat. The state Supreme Court appointed a receivership for the Hadley Falls Company and its property was put up for public auction in January 1859. A year later the company was dissolved after paying its shareholders $1.32 on each hundred-dollar share.[98]

Meantime the fate of the town hung in the balance. Who

96. Lyman Mills Papers, William Sturgis to Lyman, Dec. 4, 1858.
97. *Ibid.*, Alfred Smith to Lyman, Mar. 6, 11, 1858.
98. H. F. Co. Papers, Stock Records, Mar. 10, Apr. 9, 1858; Directors' Records, Apr. 28, 1858; Receivers' Cash Book, Jan. 1860.

was to control its destinies? Business in the spring and summer of 1858 began to pick up. The textile mills started on full time in April and by May were short-handed. Townspeople began to be more optimistic in spite of the loss by fire of some property in the summer. Yet general business improvement notwithstanding, so many persons had been hard hit that the winter of 1858–1859 again saw suffering. People flocked to town in search of jobs, and the selectmen reported giving assistance to sixty-one strangers who had come "in pursuit of work and had spent all their money." Davis with festivities at the Lyman Mills kept up what cheer he could for the working people.[99] But until the auction ended the uncertainty about the disposition of the Hadley Falls property, Holyoke dwellers could not be unfeignedly cheerful. Were an ownership concerned like its predecessor with the fostering of a cotton textile city to take command, the town must develop somewhat differently from what it otherwise might. And what might be the alternative?

The auction took place in Holyoke itself. A considerable crowd attended. The bidding was opened by Chester W. Chapin, once of Ireland Parish, now railroad magnate of Springfield, who was representing a group of associates—"Boston cotton lords," quickly ran the rumor. Confidently he offered $300,000, the total sum apparently which his friends had deemed needed to secure the property. Promptly a counter bid of $315,000 was heard. Chapin, professing to doubt the *bona fide* character of the rival offer, insisted upon delay to investigate the source of the bid. Presumably he used the hour's grace to communicate with his principals, for after a time he raised the bid $2,000. The immediate response was a bid of $325,000. Chapin gave up.[100] The whole of the real estate and water power rights of the Hadley Falls Company passed into the

99. Holyoke *Town Records,* 1859, p. 11; Holyoke *Mirror,* June 19, 1858; Lyman Mills Papers, Edward Smith to Lyman, Feb. 16, 1858; Davis to Lyman, May 6, 1858.

100. Springfield *Daily Republican,* Feb. 11, 1859; Scrap Book of Mrs. Whiting. This story comes also by word of mouth from James Burke of

hands of Alfred Smith, from whom, as president of the first Hadley Falls Company, part had once come. However unwilling Smith might be to reinvest in any Boston-managed enterprise, his belief in the soundness of a well-run power project brought the property at last into his own hands. His aims were more general than those of the cotton lords, and by his more flexible attitude the town was to benefit. Holyoke rejoiced.

The Holyoke Water Power Company was organized at once and bought the property of Smith for $350,000. The stone quarry at Mt. Tom and the swing ferry were purchased shortly at moderate prices, and by August the new company was in full possession. When the company was being organized Smith wrote: "I will take back the stock at cost and interest from all subscribers who are not satisfied after two years' trial."[101] And his faith was justified.

The regime of the Boston capitalists was done. Only their creation, the great dam and the industrial village, could not be undone. For weal or woe Holyoke must now push on its industrial path. The insolvency of the Hadley Falls Company was due partly to mismanagement. But largely the failure of the great Boston business men must be attributed to the "original error of judgment" as to "the want of such a mighty water power," to an exaggerated idea of the rapidity of New England's industrial expansion, to a variation of the American theme of manifest destiny. Manufacturing interests in the fifties had not yet been developed to an extent to create the demand for power which the sixties were to bring. Massachusetts industrialism was soon to embark upon a career of activity which would make the preceding era seem primitively limited. But for that the Hadley Falls Company had not the

Holyoke, last agent of the Lyman Mills, who had it in the nineties from the agent of twenty years previous, to whom, in turn, the account was told by Stephen Holman, in 1859 paymaster at the Lyman Mills and an eye-witness of the auction.

101. History of the Holyoke Water Power Company; Lyman Mills Papers, Alfred Smith to Lyman, Apr. 5, 1859; Holmes to Lyman, Oct. 15, 1859.

strength to wait. Holyoke bowed to new masters. The townspeople, underlings, had no choice. But the scene is still America and from the ranks of the underlings were to come some of the dominant figures of the next decades.

III

LOCAL INDUSTRIAL DEVELOPMENT
1859–1873

HOLYOKE in the spring of 1859 found itself with a new company in control of its destiny. The dam was built, the canal system fully mapped out and sixty per cent of it dug. The large machine shop was in existence. Three cotton mills, two paper mills, and several small manufactories, such as the wire and power-loom reed plants, had survived the storm of 1857. The Hadley Falls Bank and the Holyoke Savings Bank were still functioning. The local newspaper was still being published. A few stores—two or three groceries, two meat markets, dry goods and clothing establishments, a stove and hardware dealer's, and a shoe store—offered the necessaries of life to the town. Water and gas were sold to townspeople by the power company. Four churches, two schoolhouses, a railroad depot, several rows of brick tenements, a scattering of separate frame houses, and an array of turf and plank shanties along the river bank in the Patch, completed the physical layout of the place. The New City was a rather dreary spot.

But the prospects for the future were not unhopeful. Holyoke was no longer an outright company town. The Holyoke Water Power Company was headed by men familiar with the local scene. Chief of these was old Alfred Smith, whose connection with the Hadley Falls had begun in 1832, and whose shrewd analysis of the difficulties behind the failure of the Hadley Falls Company was guarantee against repetition of those mistakes. The agent and engineer in charge came to live in town. Although Alfred Smith himself resigned as president of the new company a few months after its organization, and his successor knew little of Holyoke at first hand, the fruits of Smith's long experience were embodied in the company's policies. To give permanence and stability to the town eventually new manufactures must be found. But for the time being a careful regime of patience and economy was inaugurated. The stockholders declared against any scheme of building mills or dwellings in order to effect sales or rentals. Income from the water power rentals, from leases of manufacturing space in existing buildings, and sale of gas and water sufficed to pay the investors a 5 per cent dividend on the investment the first year, and there seemed therefore no occasion for uncertain expansion. Capital was wary as a result of the panic of 1857, and there was no immediate prospect of further investment in the town.[1]

The first problem confronting the Holyoke Water Power Company and thus the townspeople in the spring of 1859 was the disposition of the machine shop and foundry. In spite of the potential business for so well equipped a shop as the Hadley Falls, the Holyoke Water Power Company, determined to function only as a power company, was reluctant itself to carry on the enterprise. That first summer the directors opened up the shop for the manufacture of heavy machinery, but only until the property could be otherwise disposed of. Though the Civil War was to introduce to the United States no new industries and no new methods of production such as had followed the war of 1812,[2] the demand for machine-made, standardized goods and so for the machinery to produce them was to be ever increasing. The making of machine tools, agricultural and mining machinery, locomotives, turbines, as well as machinery for cotton and paper mills, all opened up unlimited prospects to business enterprise. But to exploit this opportunity larger capital resources were necessary than Holyoke could at first find.

Although the old Hadley Falls shop had been closed from the fall of 1857 to the spring of 1859, many of the

1. Holyoke *Mirror*, Sept. 22, 1860; Ralph Smith, Development H. W. P. Co.

2. Victor Clark, *History of Manufactures in the United States* (hereafter cited as Clark, *History of Manufactures*), II, 12.

skilled machinists and patternmakers were still in town
and were endeavoring to raise money to set up in business
for themselves. Several small concerns were at length
launched, employing each a few men and renting space in
one wing of the machine shop, and in the summer of 1860
the Water Power Company succeeded in disposing of the
rest of the shop to J. C. Whitin, textile machinery manufacturer of Whitinsville, Massachusetts. It was a cheerful
day in town when the 250 men employed by Whitin began
repairing and improving the building preparatory to filling the contracts for machinery which Whitin had made.
Rumor had it that nearly $1,000,000 worth of contracts
had to be refused by Whitin in the first months. Thenceforward until the spring of 1863 this industry was regarded as permanent and one of fundamental importance
to the town.[3]

The two years intervening between the acquisition of
the Holyoke property by the Water Power Company and
the outbreak of the Civil War saw a steady recovery also
in the town's other industries. Business revived for concerns like the wire manufactures and the paper mills. But
most important for the general prosperity was the activity
of the textile mills, inasmuch as more persons were employed in the two Lyman Mills and the Hampden mill
than in all the other factories or shops in Holyoke put
together.[4]

Labor shortage in the spring of 1859 led to the first im-
portation of French Canadians to Holyoke. A few French
Canadians had been employed by textile mills in the neigh-
borhood, and therefore to French Canada the agent of the
Lyman Mills now turned. He made arrangements with a
French Canadian who had been in town to set forth with a

3. Holyoke *Mirror,* Apr. 16, May 28, July 2, Aug. 20, 1859, July 21,
1860; Holyoke *Transcript,* July 4, 1863.
4. Holyoke *Mirror,* June 11, Sept. 3, Oct. 15, 1859, Nov. 10, Dec. 22,
1860, Feb. 2, 1861; Holyoke *Transcript,* Aug. 15, 1863; *Statistical Information Relating to . . . Industry in Massachusetts . . .* 1865 (hereafter cited as *Statistical Information Rel. to Industry,* 1865), p. 253.

large wagon built specially for the purpose and with such persuasiveness as he could command to bring back from Province Quebec all the workers he could garner. Apparently Prue went from village to village in Quebec and spoke of the prospect of money wages which could be sent home or brought back in a few years' time to set up whole families in business in Canada. While his instructions were to secure skilled workers if possible, such were not to be had, and the forty-five girls and six men and boys comprising the first importation were habitants. The greater dexterity of women's fingers made girls rather than men Prue's objective. Even fifteen years later the French-Canadian men who came found jobs as laborers rather than as mill hands. With the allure of cash wages to be earned in the United States, Prue collected his wagon full in short time. He himself netted $4 for every operative he brought to the mills. Into the great omnibus the girls were packed, supplied from home with food for the trip. A smaller wagon followed with the baggage. Since the southward journey had to be broken, schoolhouses along the road served as sleeping quarters for the travellers. Despite the inevitable discomforts of the trip and the strangeness of a New England mill town, many French Canadians followed these first ones to Holyoke.[5]

The Hampden Mills as well as the Lyman secured additional hands by importation in this way. Thus supplied, both textile concerns ran full time for nearly two years.[6] In May 1860 the local press in alluding to the new repair shop building for the Lyman Mills declared: "Manufacturing is now at the hight of prosperity and the mills are

5. Lyman Mills Papers, Davis to Lyman, May 24, 1859; Agent's Abstract, Sept. 1859; *Hampden County History*, III, 110; *Holyoke Directory*, 1875–1876; Massachusetts Bureau of Statistics of Labor (hereafter cited as Mass. Bur. Labor Statistics), *Ninth Annual Report*, 1878, pp. 228–229; J. J. McCoy, "Diocese of Springfield," *History of the Catholic Church in the New England States* (hereafter cited as McCoy, "Diocese of Springfield," *Catholic Church in N. E.*), II, 674; *Census of Mass.*, 1865, pp. 66–67.

6. Holyoke *Mirror*, Aug. 20, 1859, Apr. 14, 1860.

earning more probably than ever before."[7] Operatives,
however, in Massachusetts cotton mills in this year earned
on the average only $202 per worker.[8] Province Quebec
could not have been greatly enriched by the savings sent
back from Holyoke.

Unhappily this boom in the cotton mills was short-lived
and was succeeded by a period of great difficulty for cotton manufacturers. The glutting of the cotton goods market as well as the continued increasing of spindleage in
England in the early months of 1861 pointed to the wisdom of curtailing production.[9] But Treasurer Lyman
wrote from Boston: "The tariff bill has passed, favorable
to our No. Two goods and ours are handsomely printed
and are selling in New York and South better than was expected some weeks since. . . . I still think that too many
goods will be made and if the goods are sold the prices obtained will be less than if the product of the . . . mills was
reduced in quantity. As the matter now stands, mills will
continue to run full time on all saleable goods." The threat
of war was not serious in Lyman's eyes. He continued:
"There is news here [Boston] understood as a thing settled that an arrangement will be made in Washington satisfactory to the business men of the country if not to other
persons, and that peace will prevail among the people."[10]
The firing on Fort Sumter upset these calculations and the
poorest immigrant mill hand in Holyoke had to suffer the
consequences. By the end of April after Lincoln's first call
for volunteers, Lyman, gloomy about the outlook, agreed
with the other directors of the Lyman Mills and of the
Dwight and Chicopee mills that curtailment of output by
one third was wisest. It was a question, Lyman contended,
of the best way of ensuring the continued running of the
mill for the longest possible time. "We want to enable the
help who remain with you to live decently well as long as we

7. *Ibid.*, May 12, 1860.
8. *Eighth Census of the United States,* 1860, *Manufactures,* III, xi.
9. Clark, *History of Manufactures,* II, 8, 26–28.
10. Lyman Mills Papers, Boston Letter Book, Lyman to Davis, Mar. 1,
1861; Holyoke *Mirror,* Feb. 23, 1861.

can, and to preserve as well as possible our organization,"[11] he wrote.

So, short time for the operatives began. But although Agent Davis in Holyoke protested, this regime was followed in the summer by a complete two months' shutdown, only men repairing machinery being kept on. Out of a population of about 4,600 some 700 were thrown out of work. For the new French Canadian arrivals the situation was particularly difficult. With the cessation of the publication of a local newspaper in July 1861 when the publisher departed to war, the miseries of life in Holyoke can only be surmised. They have no chronicler. Yet dividend payments to Lyman Mills stockholders were continued.[12] The Hampden mill, however, by the end of 1861 was operating full time. In fact the high grade cottonodes, ginghams, and tickings manufactured by this company were in such demand that "despite the conditions of affairs through the country" the mill had to be enlarged in the spring of 1863 and throughout the rest of the war ran full. But in 1862 the Lyman Mills' supply of raw cotton gave out and their mills which had resumed operations again had to be closed down.[13] Cotton manufacture alone could not ensure the industrial stability of the community.

Some mill hands doubtless enlisted in the Union Army. But in spite of state bounties to volunteers and in spite of generous efforts on the part of the more well-to-do citizens to lighten the distress of the rest, in the words of the town selectmen, it was a time of "trial and sacrifice to all." The Catholic priest eased the situation by urging his parishioners to coöperate with their American fellow-townsmen in accepting the draft, when bigger cities in the north were

11. Lyman Mills Papers, Boston Letter Book, Lyman to Davis, May 2, 1861.

12. Scrap Book of Mrs. Wm. Whiting; *Thirtieth Anniversary Holyoke Daily Transcript;* Holyoke *Mirror,* July 13, Oct. 26, 1861; Lyman Mills Papers, Boston Letter Book, Lyman to stockholders, Aug. 15, 1861; Dividend Books.

13. Holyoke *Mirror,* Jan. 4, 1862; Holyoke *Transcript,* Apr. 11, Aug. 1, 15, 1863, Apr. 9, 1864, Nov. 18, 1865; Lyman Mills Papers, Boston Letter Book, Mar. 12, 1862; Pay Rolls, 1861–1869.

faced with draft riots.[14] Thus though industrially the town was not prospering, the community met its difficulties with stout heart. The year 1862 marked the nadir of the town's fortunes.

The turning in 1863 which launched Holyoke at last upon an era of prosperity and growth was effected partly by a change in policy on the part of the Holyoke Water Power Company, partly by the demand for goods for the Union armies, and partly by the protection supplied to manufactures by the war tariff.[15] Stewart Chase, the resident agent of the Water Power Company, had lived in town some three years and had seen the paralysis of the enterprise. It was apparently to him that the adoption of a new policy was due. A shrewd promoter as well as a loyal citizen of the town, he realized that now the period of watchful waiting should end. In 1862, therefore, he persuaded the company to loan $20,000 to one of the two wire manufacturers in Holyoke to finance the building of a mill. The business had been started here in 1859 and was doing well, so that it was no speculative investment. But this loan marked a departure from the Water Power Company's initial policy. At the same time Chase had the company build in South Holyoke at the end of the second level canal a brick factory adapted to woolen manufacture, which he soon leased to a Hartford concern. Two other woolen mills were brought to South Holyoke not long afterward and the experiment which introduced woolen manufacture to town promptly proved justified. A thread mill and yarn mill also were established in this year, but in these instances causes other than concessions from the Holyoke Water Power Company brought about their location in Holyoke.[16]

14. Holyoke *Town Records,* 1863, p. 5; *Hampden County History,* II, 200–222; Holyoke *Transcript,* July 25, 1863, July 5, 1876.
15. Clark, *History of Manufactures,* II, 8–13.
16. Ralph Smith, Development H. W. P. Co.; Holyoke *Mirror,* Sept. 3, 1859; Holyoke *Transcript,* Apr. 11, June 20, July 25, Aug. 15, 22, 1863; Autobiography of Joel S. Webber (in possession of Fred Webber of Holyoke). Ground had been broken for the Beebe mill across the river when Chase persuaded Beebe and Webber to undertake their new ven-

Of the other factors working for the town's growth—
the war tariffs encouraging manufactures and the government demands for army supplies—both forces were equally
applicable to other manufacturing towns in the North.
But Agent Chase in his efforts to develop the power company's enterprise made the most of the opportunity thus
afforded. Still it was only in the field of woolen manufacture that the war boom was felt immediately. The manufacturer leasing the first new mill in 1863 had a large government contract for army overcoatings, and such was the
demand for warm uniforms that the two newer woolen
mills also had more orders than they could fill in months
even before the machinery was installed in the buildings.
Hence these three mills were enlarged and operations expanded as rapidly as possible during the next two years.

It was a war boom, an emergency expansion. For there
was not, as in the case of paper and machinery, any peculiar fitness for woolen manufacture in Holyoke, either
because of accessibility to raw materials or markets or because of labor supply. On the contrary, as far as labor was
concerned, the manufacturer brought with him most of his
skilled help and then was obliged to find living quarters for
them. Part of the expense of founding mills was the necessity of building tenements to house the operatives. Yet the
woolen mills prospered, even after the shift to a peace-
time basis of operations. In the summer of 1864 an unfore-
seen factor contributed to the town's development. An unusual drought dried up many New England streams and
shut down many water power mills. The Holyoke canals,
however, continued to have water and local "boosters" advertised the unfailing character of Holyoke's supply. The
immediate result was the building of a mill in Holyoke by
the Merrick brothers of Mansfield, Connecticut, for the
Merrick Thread Company. And at the conclusion of the
Civil War the realization dawned upon paper manufac-

ture in Holyoke. Local capital in the case of the warp mill and alignment with the Lyman Mills in that of the thread mill led to the starting
of these enterprises in Holyoke. See below pp. 79–80.

turers that the combination of ample power for running
the heavy Fourdrinier machines and the supply of chemically pure wash water for the half-stuff made Holyoke an
ideal center for making high grade papers. Seven new
paper mills were established here between the spring of
1865 and the end of 1866.[17] "The spirit of hustle and success pervaded the bustling town," wrote one chronicler.[18]
Holyoke began to grow.

Of the woolen mills only the first built was to be of great
permanent importance to the community. The lesser concerns carried on under varying conditions and furnished
steady employment for about 250 persons.[19] But the rôle
of leader in woolen manufacture fell to the Germania Mills,
so called after 1865, when two German brothers, Hermann
and August Stursberg, bought a half interest in the plant
which already had run for two years successfully. August,
a Rhineland manufacturer, established himself as the active head of the mill in Holyoke and promptly became a
person of importance in town. A devout Lutheran, kindly
in intent, but never doubting his own rightness, he dominated the German colony that grew up about the mill.
Some spinners and weavers had come with him from the
Rhineland and other experienced hands before long followed their fellow-countrymen to make their home in the
German colony in South Holyoke. The cohesiveness of the
colony contributed to the efficiency of the Germania Mills.

17. Autobiography of Joel S. Webber; William Mauer (interview);
Holyoke *Transcript,* Apr. 23, June 18, 25, July 2, 23, 30, Dec. 17, 1864,
Jan. 7, June 10, Nov. 18, Dec. 31, 1865, June 30, 1866.
18. Allyn, "Sketch of Holyoke," *Thirtieth Anniversary Holyoke Daily
Transcript.*
19. Holyoke *Transcript,* Jan. 7, Nov. 18, 1865, July 3, Nov. 6, 1869, Oct.
15, Dec. 17, 1870; Mass. Bur. Labor Statistics, *First Annual Report,* 1870,
p. 388. There were Beebe and Webber and the New York Woolen Company. Jared Beebe and his son-in-law, Joel S. Webber, had started on a
shoestring. Into their first mill in Willimansett Beebe had put $5,000 in
1860 and Webber $1,000. The Holyoke mill was started in 1863 with $40,-
000 capital, $14,000 in cash accumulated from the sale of the little plant
across the river, and the rest in still unfilled government contracts for
"army blues." Autobiography of J. S. Webber; Private information. The
capital of the New York Woolen Company, on the other hand, was listed
at $150,000 in 1869. *Holyoke Directory,* 1869, p. 99.

And Stursberg fostered this group consciousness. Backed by his expert knowledge of making high-grade, heavy fabrics, he quickly built up the reputation of the Germania beavers and doeskins, and in 1870 the mill had to be considerably enlarged. As was true to a lesser extent of the smaller woolen manufactures also, this branch of the Holyoke textile industry through these years throve steadily.[20]

Cotton manufacture in this period, 1863–1873, in Holyoke the old established industry, suffered greater ups and downs than woolen, largely probably because of unpredictable fluctuations in the price of raw cotton.[21] But even within the industry locally there were differences in the extent to which these fluctuations were felt. The contrast between the coarse goods mill and the fine of the Lyman Mills may illustrate this. The No. One mill, making shirtings, sheetings, and drills of heavy yarn, was built in 1850 and, a late-comer in this field of manufacture, found great difficulty in competing with mills with already established reputations and markets; the No. Two mill, on the other hand, was one of the very first in this country to make fine lawns and prints woven from mule-spun yarn, and the demand for these appears to have been as steady and the prices secured as profitable as the No. One mill's market was unsteady and dubious. Similarly the ginghams put out by the Glasgow Company, in 1854 one of two gingham mills in the United States, maintained such a reputation and market that it earned enormous dividends—50 per cent, 20 per cent even when times were dull—and in 1864 the directors invested some of its earnings in building a paper mill in the Falls.[22]

But the cotton industry, generally conducted by the old

20. Osgood, *Story of the Holyoke Churches;* Private information; Wm. Mauer (interview); *Holyoke Directory,* 1869, p. 99; 1871, p. 102; 1874–1875, p. 123; Holyoke *Transcript,* May 22, Sept. 11, 1872, May 7, 1873, Feb. 28, 1874. In 1872 the heads of the Springfield Blanket Company, a horse-blanket concern, bought a site and erected a mill. But production had scarcely begun when the panic checked prosperity.

21. Clark, *History of Manufactures,* II, 103–106, 117–118.

22. Lyman Mills Papers, Bush to Davis, May 6, 1869, Apr. 1870; Mill Returns, 1854–1858; Invoices, 1860–1870; Minot Hooper and Co. to Davis,

guard in Boston with close watching of the seasonal fluctuations, was in the Lyman Mills, and perhaps to a lesser
extent in the Hampden, carried on with perpetual readjustments of output. New England cotton manufacture
was still dominated by a not very large group of Boston
capitalists, so that Milk Street in the sixties and seventies
might well have had a connotation as definite as Wall Street
a generation later. Cotton manufacture was a great game
in which the moves were made by the players in the Boston
offices, a satisfying game which promised returns from one
investment if not from another. From Lowell, Lawrence,
Manchester, Chicopee, even perhaps Fall River and Pawtucket, New Bedford, Holyoke—if dividends failed from
one mill, they might be had from another. Still directorates while interlocking were not identical and jockeying
for position went on.

Mill operatives were far afield in Lawrence or Chicopee
or Holyoke. If need be, more could be had where they came
from. Thus the fluctuations in output were generally at
the expense of labor. For example, in the cotton industry
between 1865 and 1871 the succession of minor booms and
depressions was unvaryingly regular. In 1865 the mills
could not secure sufficient labor. Agents in Scotland dispatched some 200 skilled spinners and weavers to Holyoke,
but 1,000 girls were needed, it was said. Seven months later
cotton manufacture was pronounced not unusually brisk,
but the Lyman Mills managed to run full time. By the
summer of 1867 "dull times" were announced in trade
papers, and while the Hampden Mills ran one third less
than capacity the Lyman Mills utilized their 1,100 hands
full time but on wages reduced 10 per cent. By January
the *Transcript* observes that nearly all the mills are running on short time and are turning off extra help or are
reducing wages. Yet July 1869 saw business reviving
again and despite falling prices six months later, attrib-

Specifications, 1868–1872; Holyoke *Mirror,* Mar. 4, 1854; Holyoke *Transcript,* Feb. 6, 1864, Nov. 18, 1865, Feb. 2, 1867, May 23, 1868, Jan. 29,
1870.

uted to Congressional manipulations of currency, the summer of 1870 was once more a period of rushing business for the Lyman Mills. The No. One mill had to run both spindles and looms all night in order to fill its orders, and a special night force of four hundred was engaged and organized. The year 1871 found the additional hands dispensed with again and a new wage cut effected. And so it went for another thirty years. Operatives were employed, worked their full sixty-seven hours a week, were reduced to part time, or were dismissed, according to the market fluctuations.[23] Who pulled the strings? People in Holyoke could not be sure.

With nearly one and one half millions of capital the Lyman Mills might seem to have been in a position to equalize output over a period of months or years, particularly in the coarse goods or standard lawns where neither style nor weather could be expected seriously to affect demand. But the Lyman Mills' capital was so invested that its working capital was perhaps not very large, and it was easier to dismiss help or curtail costs by wage cuts than to produce for stock what the market would not immediately absorb. The company's taxes were high, double the assessment of any other taxpayer. Too great an accumulation of unsold goods might tie up overlong money needed for dividend payments. Yet, be it said, Lyman Mills' dividends rarely assumed the proportions of those of many New

23. Holyoke *Transcript,* Nov. 11, 18, Dec. 2, 1865, June 30, 1866, May 4, June 1, 1867, quoting the *Commercial Bulletin,* Jan. 11, 18, 1868, July 3, Dec. 4, 1869, Aug. 20, 1870, Jan. 21, 1871; *Holyoke Directory,* 1869, p. 97; 1871, p. 101; Lyman Mills Papers, Boston Letter Book, Bush to Davis, Nov. 16, Dec. 22, 1870. Senator Sprague of Rhode Island insisted that the slump was no ordinary down-turn, but was the result of hostile legislation and of the poverty of the United States resulting from spending $5,000,000,000 on the Civil War.

In 1872 the Lyman Mills directors undertook erection of a third mill as well as twenty-four additional tenements. The new mill was expected to employ 400 persons. The payroll in the summer of 1872 had already reached 1,200. The 192 tenements of the company added to the twenty-four new ones were able to house about 1,500 people. The No. Three mill went into operation in May 1873. Holyoke *Transcript,* June 5, 1872, May 28, 1873.

England mills, and by the standards of the day the employes were considerately treated.[24] But only the resident agent and his staff were on hand to witness the results of this policy of indifference, and after the retirement of Jones Davis in 1872 for thirty-five years no agent protested the effects upon the help of any given mandate from Boston.

Absentee cotton lords made one other investment in Holyoke. In 1863 some of the Boston associates organized the Hadley Company to develop thread manufacture in Holyoke. This was to become one of the town's great enterprises. But when in the thick of war difficulties daring Yankee capitalists with unwavering faith in Yankee manufacturing skill bought the J. C. Whitin Machine Shop building and its appurtenant eight mill powers in order to start thread manufacturing here, doubts about the success of the venture were many. Pessimists declared it impossible to spin in this country six-cord spool cotton of a quality to compete with British. American thread was labelled "coarse, weak and glazed on the surface." But patience, combined with $600,000 of capital, overcame the obstacles and by November 1864 an astonished public was greeted with the production in Holyoke of "the best thread in the market."[25]

Credit is due to obscure individuals, mechanics, careful and exacting overseers, long-suffering, painstaking spinners. The ability and readiness to pay "highest wages," as the agent advertised, was instrumental in securing good help, and with the best machinery American capital could buy and the finest Sea Island cotton, today it does not seem remarkable that the new mill turned out good thread. But in 1864 the achievement occasioned excitement akin to the triumphing satisfaction caused fifty odd years later by

24. Holyoke *Transcript,* July 4, 1863, July 30, Aug. 3, 1864, Feb. 2, 1867, July 30, 1870, Feb. 7, 1880; Lyman Mills Papers, Davis to Lyman, Nov. 4, 28, 1859; Shlakman, *Economic History of a Factory Town* (*Smith College Studies in History,* XX), 106. In 1867 for example when the Lyman Mills paid a 3 per cent dividend the Glasgow Mill across the river paid a 20 per cent.

25. Holyoke *Transcript,* Apr. 11, 1863, Feb. 13, Nov. 26, 1864.

the ultimate success of American chemists in rivalling German dyes.[26] There was immediate and constant demand for the product of the mill. Even in the last six months of 1867, when cloth manufacture was slack, the Hadley Company did a $400,000 business. By midsummer 1870 the directors had the plant enlarged so as nearly to double its capacity.[27]

In the Holyoke cotton industry there was only one important exception to the rule of absentee ownership. This was the Merrick Thread Company. The Merrick brothers completed their Holyoke mill in 1866 and, successful there, soon added to its equipment until by 1871 they employed some three hundred persons. Timothy Merrick came to live in Holyoke and so far from managing the mill on impersonal lines, this rock-ribbed, teetotaling Baptist felt it his duty to watch over the flock of operatives entrusted to his care like a faithful shepherd. However trying his zeal may have been to those who failed to agree with him about methods, his interest in the welfare of the community and the weal of his mill made him a public force to reckon with. Like the Hadley Thread Company the Merrick concern ran steadily without the variations of activity which characterized the cotton cloth mills.[28]

26. *Ibid.*, Feb. 20, Mar. 12, July 2, Dec. 3, 1864, quoting Springfield *Republican*, Nov. 11, Dec. 2, 1865, June 1, 1867, Aug. 27, 1870. A letter published first in the Boston *Post*, Dec. 26, 1864, gives an idea of the exaggerated degree of enthusiasm the new manufacture aroused. Having pronounced the Hadley Company's product as fine as English thread, the author, one of a committee of Boston women investigating Massachusetts manufactures, alludes to the success of an endeavor to have freedmen in Port Royal raise Sea Island cotton. With a market in Holyoke waiting, the imaginative author concludes: "So Massachusetts may become the pioneer in a great Free Labor movement. . . . She will grow her own cotton,—Erect the mills,—Build the machinery, and Manufacture thread. . . ." Thus there was "prospect of new work for white women, and profitable labor for black freed men, and a growing wealth for those who understand its best uses." Holyoke *Transcript*, Jan. 21, 1865.

27. Holyoke *Transcript*, June 1, 1867, Jan. 18, 1868, July 30, Aug. 20, 1870.

28. *Ibid.*, Oct. 17, 31, 1863, Apr. 23, May 24, July 23, Nov. 12, 1864, June 10, Nov. 4, 18, 1865, June 30, 1866, Oct. 24, 1868, Jan. 30, Apr. 3, July 3, Dec. 17, 1869; *Holyoke Directory*, 1871, p. 102. The Holyoke

New mills meant new machinery. Whitin sold his machine shop here in 1863 and the men who had tried unsuccessfully in 1859 to finance the shop were now able to seize the opportunity created by Whitin's withdrawal. Five of the old Hadley Falls Company machinists, still young, capable, and ambitious, abetted by Agent Chase of the Water Power Company, found $30,000, financed the building, and equipped the Holyoke Machine Company. The new shop set up in South Holyoke was only a third the size of Whitin's, but the capital was all local and the men concerned were vitally interested. The growth of Holyoke in 1865 brought large orders for castings and for cotton and paper mill machinery. Soon the company was to specialize in paper machinery and turbine water wheels; but its first jobs were principally making gearing and shafting for the new mills. The business grew steadily. A foundry and smithy were added and by 1873, with $150,-000 capitalization and over one hundred men employed, the Holyoke Machine Company headed a vigorous branch of the town's industry.[29] In a water power town naturally every new mill called for a new water wheel. Before 1870 only the steam-run saw- and gristmill and the steam-driven brick machines in the South Holyoke brick yard were using anything but water for power. Men at the Holyoke Machine Shop early built fairly efficient water wheels of several kinds, and in 1870 the company contracted with the Swain Turbine Company of Lowell to build all its forty-eight-inch turbines. Thereafter a number of designers, patternmakers, and skilled draftsmen in the shop devoted special attention to the perfecting of water wheels.[30]

Warp Company, a small enterprise dating from 1863, was owned by Holyoke and Springfield men, but it encountered severe ups and downs and was never an important industrial unit.

29. Sumner Whitten (interview); Holyoke *Transcript*, Apr. 11, July 11, Oct. 3, 17, Dec. 5, 19, 1863, Feb. 13, Oct. 8, Nov. 12, 1864, June 30, 1866, Oct. 3, 1868, Jan. 16, July 3, 1869, Feb. 5, Dec. 31, 1870, Feb. 25, 1871, May 8, 18, June 5, 1872; *Holyoke Directory*, 1869, p. 105; 1871, p. 105.

30. Holyoke *Transcript*, June 12, 22, 1872; History of the Holyoke Water Power Company.

There was more business than one company could carry, and other shops shared the local jobbing and developed specialties of their own. One characteristic of the tool and machinery industry in Holyoke was its organization on a small scale. Although important, it was an offshoot of the textile and paper industries rather than an independent development. With the exception of the Holyoke Machine Company which itself down into the eighties was no great, impersonal company, the producing unit was a small shop. Doubtless the very nature of the manufacture made for this system because the jobs gave scope to the inventor. The day of the great commercial laboratory or workshop where invention was subsidized was still far in the future. In this period several separate concerns sprang up where a handful of workmen, sometimes the owners of the business among them, turned out the product, evolving improvements as they worked.[31]

The only other line of metallic-goods manufacture in Holyoke was wire. Although the necessity of great power to draw wire made the unfailing supply of water power in Holyoke an obvious inducement to the wire maker to locate here, the more important wire company moved to Worcester in 1865. But the lesser wire maker, George W. Prentiss, continued in town, steadily developing and enlarging his lines of business, piano wire, broom wire, wire for card clothing, and other textile machinery. By 1873 he had built his own mill, doubled his output, and founded a family concern of enduring character.[32]

But contrary to the expectations of the founders of the town, it was not textiles or any concomitant machinery-making but paper which after the Civil War took the lead

31. Some of the original investors of the Holyoke Machine Company themselves withdrew to start up new, more specialized enterprises. Holyoke *Transcript,* Apr. 16, Nov. 5, 1864, June 1, Nov. 2, 1867, Oct. 10, 1868, Apr. 17, 1869, Sept. 24, Dec. 3, 1870, Jan. 28, 1871, May 18, June 15, 1872; *Holyoke Directory,* 1874–1875, p. 125.

32. W. A. Prentiss (interview); Holyoke *Transcript,* Apr. 11, Sept. 12, 1863, Mar. 11, 1865, Jan. 9, June 21, 1869, Dec. 31, 1870, Feb. 18, Mar. 25, 1871; *Holyoke Directory,* 1869, p. 105; 1871, p. 105; John Nelson, "Wire Company Seventy Years Old," reprint from *The Iron Age,* Mar. 3, 1927.

of all other manufactures here. The story of the rise of the paper industry in Holyoke takes on color from the circumstances attending the starting of the first paper mill in 1853 when J. C. Parsons and his associates were refused a mill site by the Hadley Falls Company because paper manufacture was deemed too insignificant an undertaking to sell power for. There is a certain humor in the situation in 1857 and 1858 whereby the Hadley Falls Company collapsed while the once spurned paper company went on to ever increasing profitable production. Moreover, the character of the men who developed the new industry furnish peculiar interest to the tale. Parsons, the Newton brothers, O. H. Greenleaf, and William Whiting, founders or heads of what might be called the four stem dynasties of Holyoke paper making, these men and their associates, or their competitors—most of them young, determined, and able, widely differing in disposition, yet all possessed of a vast enthusiasm—these were the men who made Holyoke the great paper center of America. The capitalists of the Holyoke cotton mills were non-residents—not even names to the people working in their mills. To a less degree was this absenteeism true also in the woolen mills. But in paper making nativism prevailed. The paper-mill men of Holyoke were no shadowy persons without local associations. On the contrary, they were the vitalizing element, and with the paper industry Holyoke's industrial history takes on the living force of personalities.

Joseph Parsons was the first paper manufacturer on the scene. Direct descendant of one of William Pynchon's pioneer associates in settling the Connecticut Valley in 1636, a tight-lipped, shrewd, self-contained Yankee, Parsons himself seems at first view a colorless person. Save for his daring in projecting and successfully developing the Parsons Paper Company there is little in his career to make him live as an interesting and powerful individual. He kept himself consistently out of the public eye. Universally respected, an unpretentious gentleman, he was not deeply beloved. Rather, his immediate associates found him hard to get on with. But it was his very obstinacy which built up the Parsons Paper Company. Refusing to be defeated by the Hadley Falls Company, he secured his site by devious means and built a mill equipped to produce two tons of paper a day.[33] Since in 1854 there were only six paper machines in the Connecticut Valley altogether with a daily output of about 9,700 pounds, Parsons encountered the charge of headstrong folly at the Gargantuan proportions of his enterprise. Wiseacres prophesied that such quantities of writing paper could never be sold at a profit, that here was only a sure method of swamping the market with an unsellable surplus. Yet a decade later the mill had more orders than it could fill, and it had become the largest writing- and envelope-paper establishment in the United States. The company earned huge dividends, 50 per cent on its $60,000 of capital stock, sometimes more. Envelopes were a new development of the writing-paper trade. Before 1863 Parsons sent off envelope paper by four-horse team to Rockville, Connecticut, but in that year an envelope company was organized in Holyoke and with five Duff machines and some twenty-two operatives the new concern, to the marvel of observers, turned out 120,000 envelopes a day made from Parsons paper. The quality of paper and perfection of finish of the envelope made the product much sought after, and boxed writing paper of this company became a well-known Holyoke commodity.[34]

The Holyoke Paper Company was the next launched. It was projected by a man who had been a foreman for Parsons, and the mill was well laid out. In 1865 control was sold to Oscar H. Greenleaf of Springfield and his brother. Greenleaf had started his career as a tin pedlar, trundling his pack through the Berkshire hills, taking rags from the farmers' wives in exchange for his tinwares. Through

33. See above, p. 37.
34. Parsons Paper Co. Papers, Directors' Records, I; *Paper World,* XII, no. 3 (Mar. 1886), 1–3; Holyoke *Transcript,* Aug. 15, 22, Nov. 7, 1863, June 11, 1864, Sept. 9, 1865; *Statistical Information Rel. to Industry,* 1865, p. 253; *The Red Envelope,* Feb. 1921, pp. 21, 30 (published by the United States Envelope Company, Hartford, Conn., 1915–1925).

marketing the rags he first made connections with paper-stock merchants, and soon finding capital for a small business of his own he formed a partnership, Greenleaf & Taylor, dealing in paper-makers' supplies. The price of paper stock soared during the Civil War and by 1865 Greenleaf was in a position to buy into the Holyoke Paper Company. He refused to move from Springfield to Holyoke to live and perhaps for this reason played no part in the social scheme of the town. But for all his dour, rather ungracious personality, as head of the great Holyoke Paper Company he was an important person in Holyoke. Under his management the mill was at once enlarged so as to increase the output to four tons of fine writings a day.[35] Greenleaf set the example to a considerable group of Springfield men who organized and built paper mills here in the course of the next few years.

The third dynasty of Holyoke paper manufacturers stems from the Newton family, since theirs was the third paper mill here. Of the Newton brothers, Daniel and John, the builders, Moses, the inventor, and James H., the brilliant and unstable promoter, each made his own particular contribution to Holyoke and to the development of its paper industry, building mills and selling them, devising effective technical improvements in the processes of paper manufacture—inventions never properly patented or safeguarded from exploitation by competitors—and finding ways to utilize by-products. Always at variance among themselves, these four presented to the outside world a united family front. Daniel sank his profits in repeated efforts to mine gold in the Vermont hills; Moses lost the benefit of his inventions by trying to save lawyers' fees by drawing up his own patents; James H. threw away a fortune, began again, made another, and lost that. In Holyoke the Newton brothers played the Jacobean rôle of the "wisest fools in Christendom." This family's first interest in Holyoke had been as builders, and since in 1863 they

35. *Paper World*, XIII, no. 5 (Nov. 1886), 2; Holyoke *Transcript*, Nov. 18, 1865, June 30, 1866. See below, p. 92, note 49.

bought Ely's steam sawmill to expedite their building operations, there seemed to be indication that as contractors and carpenters they would continue. In 1864 when Daniel and John Newton put up a frame mill on the second level canal not far from the old swing-ferry landing it was as a building speculation rather than as a paper manufacturer's undertaking. But by the beginning of 1865 when the mill had been running a few weeks they organized the Hampden Paper Company and at once found themselves with a rushing business manufacturing paper for the paper collars and shirt fronts quite universally used at this time in place of linen.[36]

The implications of this performance were obvious: anyone with a little capital and a little courage could make money manufacturing paper in Holyoke. In the case of the Parsons and the Holyoke Paper Company observers might attribute the phenomenal success of the mills to the expert skill and knowledge of paper making of the men at the head. Parsons himself had had a long initiation in paper making in the thirties and forties at the Ames mill in South Hadley and at the Eagle Mill in Suffield, and Butterfield, one of the originators of the Holyoke Paper Company, had been Parsons' foreman. But the Newtons were building contractors, not paper makers; and yet their enterprise also was money-making. Doubtless additional paper mills would have come to Holyoke in the course of the post-war boom even without this example, but the profitable career of the Hampden Paper Company must have lent encouragement to hesitating investors. The tariff was high enough to make profits nearly inevitable and capital was being attracted into the paper industry everywhere.[37] But Holyoke was recognized as a favored site. In the

36. Holyoke *Transcript,* May 16, June 13, Oct. 10, 17, 1863, July 2, Sept. 3, Nov. 5, 1864, Feb. 4, Sept. 9, Nov. 18, 1865.

37. *History . . . of South Hadley,* p. 86; Lyman Mills Papers, Holmes to Mills, Mar. 21, 1857, Holmes to Lyman, Oct. 14, 1857; Holyoke *Transcript,* July 14, 1866; *Paper World,* XII, no. 3 (Mar. 1886), 2; Clark, *History of Manufactures,* II, 132–133.

course of the next eighteen months six new paper concerns
were launched and mills for them started.

The first and the most important of these new companies
was the Whiting Paper Company organized by William
Whiting in March 1865. Whiting, ingratiating and debo-
nair, was very different from the heads of the older paper
mills. With the engaging charm of his Irish mother, coupled
with the hardheadedness of his New England father, he was
always in evidence, quite ready to have his name linked with
any prospering project, business, or civic, whether of his inception or not. His openhandedness always proved a good
investment, perhaps through calculating prevision, possibly by chance. In the sixties the gay, athletic, horse-lov-
ing, young Whiting was an attractive and compelling
figure. He had begun his career as a bookkeeper at the age
of seventeen in the office of the Holyoke Paper Company,
but at the first opportunity to show some of his wider capabilities he had demonstrated his salesmanship as well as
his knowledge of paper and had been promoted to the position of a salesman for that company. In his business travels, therefore, he was able to make a wide circle of contacts
in the paper world and had chances to impress his shrewd-
ness and knowledge upon the moneyed men with whom he
had dealings. Thus it was no great surprise to Holyoke
people to learn in the spring of 1865 that Whiting had enlisted $100,000 of capital to start a new company and a
new mill.

Instead of building a new mill Whiting succeeded in
purchasing the wire mill, a well built brick structure with
four mill powers appurtenant to the site on the first level
canal. Although public opinion in town deplored the negotiation which sent the thriving wire company to Worcester, the arrangement had for the Whiting Paper Company
the great advantage of enabling it to begin manufacture
in August of that same year and thus to make the most of
the boom. The design was to manufacture the fine grades
of writing paper, the line with which Whiting's experience
with the Holyoke Paper Company gave him most famili-

arity, but the immediate demand for collar paper was such that for nearly a year the mill ran exclusively on this cheap grade. Four beater engines and one hundred employes were turning out two tons of collar paper a day.[38]

The other new companies were not able to begin manufacturing until 1866. It was Parsons stockholders who backed the Holyoke Manilla Company, James H. Newton and Worcester associates who organized the Franklin Paper Company, and Butterfield and South Hadley Falls men who launched the Valley Paper Company. The other two new paper mills built in the first years after the war, the Bemis and the Riverside, were founded by Springfield money. Holyoke prided itself on having its paper mills largely developed by Holyoke capital. The continued Springfield residence of such few mill owners as preferred to commute was rather resented as an unwarranted slur upon Holyoke. But until after 1871 there was scarcely a paper mill in town that did not originate with or soon link up in ownership or management with one of the four original concerns, the Parsons, the Holyoke, the Newtons' or the Whiting companies. Capitalization was not large as compared to the cotton mills. The maximum was $100,000 until the Holyoke Paper Company was sold to Greenleaf when he and his associates put up $300,000. In South Hadley Falls the Glasgow Company sold its paper mill in 1866, and the new Hampshire Paper Company was capitalized at $200,000.[39]

To make high-grade paper, rags, after sorting and cutting, had to be bleached and washed. In this process the chemical purity of the wash water was of importance. After the rags had been boiled, the pulpy fibre was put

38. William F. Whiting, Charles C. Jenks (interviews); Holyoke *Transcript,* Mar. 11, May 13, Sept. 9, Nov. 18, 1865, May 26, 1866.

39. W. A. Prentiss, Thomas Humeston (interviews); *Holyoke Directory,* 1869, pp. 101–105; 1871, pp. 103–104; 1874–1875, pp. 124–125; Hampshire Paper Company Papers, Journal A, Box 1867; Holyoke *Transcript,* Nov. 18, 1865, Jan. 20, May 19, June 30, July 14, Aug. 4, 18, Dec. 8, 1866, June 1, Dec. 28, 1867, Feb. 1, Sept. 12, 1868, Jan. 15, Apr. 9, Nov. 19, 1870, Apr. 6, June 22, 1872; Typescript compiled from Franklin Paper Company Directors' Records (office of Franklin Paper Company, Holyoke).

into the beaters, china clay, rosin, and other ingredients were added to give cohesiveness to the stock, and the mixture was beaten for some hours. Water was pounded into the fibre until the "half-stuff," so called, was ready to pump into the Jordan engines for refining. From the Jordans the "stuff" was fed through a chest and thence pumped to the Fourdrinier or cylinder machine. The Fourdrinier with its fine wire meshing vibrated the watery stuff until the fibres firmly felted, and then the wet paper was run through rollers and driers to press and partly dry it. As it emerged in one long piece it was cut into strips, immersed in a tub of sizing to give a hard, nonabsorbent surface, and then hung over poles and carried off to finish drying in lofts at the top of the mill. Most Holyoke mills of this time installed Fourdrinier rather than cylinder machines which, working on a somewhat different principle, would not make so fine a grade of paper as the Fourdrinier.

The new mills generally started with the manufacture of cheap papers, manilla, collar, or inexpensive envelope paper. Although Holyoke's peculiar advantage for the paper maker lay rather in the producing of high grade paper where the chemical qualities of the wash water were most essential, still the more customary procedure was to work up to making fine writings. Of course some companies never changed over. The three mills built and run by the Newton brothers all ran on collar papers down to 1869. In that year part of one mill was converted to make book and writing papers, and one was sold to the Taft family. The Tafts continued to produce collar and cloth-faced papers until the paper collar fashion subsided in the early seventies. Then the Albion Paper Company, as the Taft organization was called, took up book papers.[40] Only James H. Newton, profiting by his own special patented process, carried on the manufacture of cloth-faced papers.

40. Holyoke *Transcript,* Jan. 16, 23, Feb. 20, Nov. 13, 1869, Sept. 24, 1870; *Holyoke Directory,* 1869, p. 101; 1871, p. 103; 1874–1875, pp. 123–124. The three mills first built and run by the Newtons were the Hampden, the Franklin, and the Ferry.

Generally the paper manufacturers aspired to branch into the making of fine writings.

The course of Whiting's company was typical at least of the larger and more successful concerns. After nine months of making collar papers, Whiting, assisted by the able young son of one of his backers, E. C. Jenks, succeeded in producing a cheap line of writing paper, foolscap and letter cap, made from the trimmings of collar papers bought from the collar manufacturers. Whiting also purchased quantities of old army tents and canvas from the government, presumably at low cost, and by the summer of 1867 the mill, though running only twelve hours of the twenty-four, was turning out three and one half tons of writing paper a day. Gradually the cheaper grades were discontinued so that by 1869 nothing but writing paper was produced. Charles Jenks, the young superintendent, carried on experiments for improving the quality, and before the end of this period Whiting writing papers were beginning to be recognized as high grade. So profitable was this first mill that a second Whiting mill was built in 1871, a unit separate from the first but dedicated to the same general line of papers.[41]

Not all the companies ran so smooth a course as this. Some mills changed hands and underwent reorganization, and even the best managed faced some difficulties. The inrush of capital immediately following the war resulted in considerable overexpansion of the paper industry. By 1868 the daily output of writing paper in Holyoke was over twenty tons with an additional five or six tons of collar, envelope, and tissue paper, whereas fifteen years before less than five tons of paper had been the total daily production of all the mills in the Connecticut Valley.[42]

41. C. C. Jenks (interview); Holyoke *Transcript*, May 26, June 30, 1866, June 1, 1867. In Whiting No. Two the stock was even more closely held than in the original company. The Jenks family had no share in this enterprise, and L. L. Brown and William Whiting himself, already as the result of the past five years a person of means, controlled the property.

42. Holyoke *Transcript*, July 14, Aug. 18, 1866, Apr. 27, May 11, 1867, Jan. 18, 1868, Jan. 23, May 1, June 5, 1869, Jan. 28, 1871; W. F. Whiting

Therefore early in 1869 all the fine writing concerns save the Carew in South Hadley Falls agreed to run on short time in order to curtail output and did not resume full operation until summer.[43]

But as in other lines of business, 1870 saw a revival. From 1871 to 1873 again paper-mill building proceeded. Three times within the three years the Newtons built, equipped, and sold paper mills, so that 1873 found the brothers with no mill of their own.[44] James H. Newton, to be sure, kept his large share in the Franklin Paper Company, and in September 1873 Moses Newton and James Ramage organized a partnership for the manufacture of sheathing paper and carpet linings. With that ingenuity which characterized many of the doings of Moses Newton the partners developed their product chiefly from the waste of the rag rooms of other mills, linty dust and rubbish, so called, which still gave the necessary felting quality for building papers or carpet linings, a by-product which before that time had been dumped into the river.[45]

Meanwhile the general prosperity brought other extensions to the Holyoke paper industry. Parsons, having secured a four year government contract for envelope papers, built a new mill to take twenty-nine engines. The Bemis Paper Company was sold in 1870 to the Union Paper Manufacturing Company of Springfield and the owners of the newly consolidated company added to the Holyoke mill a sixty-two inch Fourdrinier installed for fine writings and a three cylinder machine with ten driers for collar papers. Only the three great high-grade paper mills,

(interview); Clark, *History of Manufactures*, II, 133; Joel Munsell, *A Chronology of Paper and Paper-Making*.

43. Holyoke *Transcript*, May 29, July 3, 1869. Carew refused to adhere to this arrangement out of consideration of his help.

44. The purchasers were the Crocker Manufacturing Company, Beebe and Holbrook, and Warren and Dickinson. Holyoke *Transcript*, Mar. 28, Sept. 24, 1870, Apr. 1, 1871; *Holyoke Directory*, 1871, p. 103; 1874–1875, pp. 123–125; *The Paper Mill*, Feb. 26, 1927.

45. James H. Newton also showed enterprise in developing new methods; the Franklin, in 1869 trying esparto grass, was the first Holyoke mill to venture into the use of new fibres. Holyoke *Transcript*, Aug. 7, 1869, Sept. 24, 1870; Herbert Newton (interview).

the Parsons, the Holyoke, and the Whiting, exceeded the Union in importance. The last big writing paper mill to be built in this era was the Massasoit mill, owned by an old established Springfield firm, and operated for many years in conjunction with a Huntington mill belonging to the same group of men. Since they had ample capital they were able to purchase a site, the mill powers appurtenant to which the company owned outright, without annual rental, making thus the Massasoit one of three concerns in Holyoke to have that advantage.[46]

The spring of 1873 for the writing-paper manufacturers was a period of depression severe enough to induce an agreement of half-time operations similar to the curtailment compact of 1869. New mills were headed into the manufacture of book papers for which the demand was steady. By such devices prosperity was restored and by summer Holyoke mills were again running full.[47]

Thus the Holyoke paper industry before 1873 was peculiarly a local undertaking. At least half of the capital invested in the paper mills belonged to Holyoke people and most of the rest came from Springfield, a situation in marked contrast to what obtained in the textile industry. The sources of the local capital can be traced only in a general way. Some of it came direct from the land, as in the case of the Bagg family, stockholders in the Parsons Paper Company, who had owned a prospering farm in West Springfield for generations. Some capital had been extracted from commerce in the heyday of river traffic in the thirties and forties, capital which was invested in industrial enterprise in Holyoke when opportunity presented itself. So Whiting Street and Broughton Alvord, also Parsons stockholders, had netted capital. Some money had been made in small industrial ventures, such as the money the Newtons derived from the family sawmill in Greenfield

46. See above, p. 55, note 81. Scrap Book of Mrs. Wm. Whiting; Holyoke *Transcript*, Nov. 10, 1866, Jan. 15, Feb. 5, Oct. 15, Dec. 10, 1870, Apr. 13, 1872; *Holyoke Directory*, 1871, pp. 103–104; 1874–1875, pp. 124–125; *The Paper Mill*, Aug. 10, 1929.

47. Holyoke *Transcript*, Feb. 22, 26, Mar. 8, June 7, July 5, 1873.

or the sums Joseph Parsons made in his little paper mill in
Suffield before Holyoke existed. Whence came the original
nest eggs which made possible small investment or speculation during the Civil War, capital which with luck grew
to proportions to reckon with? In most cases again the
primary source seems to have been land from the improvement or sale of which a small cash sum was realized to be
invested in some industrial undertaking. Thus Parsons
himself, E. C. Jenks of the Whiting Paper Company,
Jared Beebe and his son-in-law, and many another Holyoke paper maker, all originally got a financial start from
landholding. At least after 1850 there is no indication of
capital's deriving from mercantile ventures. Of the Springfield money invested in Holyoke paper mills, on the contrary, not a little had been made in commerce, such as that
of the Taylors or Greenleaf or Stephen Bemis.[48]

Capital in Holyoke cotton mills was another story. The
Lyman and the Hampden mills both were of the old order,
owned and managed like the rest of the New England cotton mills of the preceding generation by a well defined
group of Boston capitalists beside whom the local paper
manufacturers in the sixties were small fry. But in the paper industry not for another thirty years was absentee
ownership to play any part. Even where the heads of the
paper mills lived in Springfield they were daily at the Holyoke plants since commuting by the Connecticut River
Railroad was easy.[49] The most important paper companies
were scarcely more than family concerns and the numbers
of the stockholders were few.[50] When the owners became

48. Charles W. Chapin, *Sketches of the Old Inhabitants and Mansions
of Springfield*, p. 45.
49. See above, pp. 19, 20–21. The Holyoke Paper Company, after 1865,
the Riverside, the Union, and the Massasoit were stock companies,
Springfield-owned and run. Greenleaf had the principal share in the Holyoke, the Appletons in the Riverside, the Dickinsons and Powers in the
Union, and E. C. Rogers and Taylor in the Massasoit. Jared Beebe and
his son-in-law, George Holbrook, owners of the Beebe and Holbrook mill
after 1872, both lived in Springfield, and Holbrook commuted by train to
Holyoke, as did Greenleaf, Rogers, the Appletons, and Dickinson.
50. The Parsons stock was controlled by four men, the Whiting by

prosperous enough to invest in other enterprises in Holyoke or elsewhere, the family paper mill was still recognized as the goose that laid the golden egg and was cherished accordingly.

The growth of the town gave a tremendous boom to building and so to contractors and merchants dealing in building supplies. Lumber yards and sawmills flourished; brick kilns and stone masons' works were kept busy. The Irish mason who had directed the stone work on the canal walls in 1848 had managed to build up his business until in 1871 when his men began on the foundations of the new town hall he was a citizen of some importance who had passed from the rank of workman to that of the small capitalist. From brick yards, opened just before the Civil War, E. T. Bosworth was turning out 10,000,000 bricks a season in 1873, with three hundred men at work and a monthly payroll of $10,000. Still more prosperous were the lumbermen, for although mills and tenements were of brick, practically all other buildings in town were frame. In 1871, as the dam impeded great log drives down the Connecticut River, a boom and sawmill were built at Holyoke. Here the Connecticut River Lumber Company, a powerful organization of New England lumbermen, established its distributing headquarters, and every summer the river above the dam near "Dead Man's Curve" teemed with logs and lumberjacks while sawmill operators sweated at the mill. The sawn lumber was shipped thence by flatcar over the tracks of the Connecticut River Railroad and distributed to merchant and contractor like any other Holyoke commodity. But the retail lumber dealer and the builder had more immediate connection with the town's development and there was room for several.

Sometimes an interest in building supplies led directly to contracting and might thence lead to an interest in manufacturing projects. Such was the general course of the Newton family career, and such in modified form was

three, the Valley by four, the Franklin by five, the Felton by three, the Albion by three, etc.

the history of the Chase family, who, though they never undertook building, dabbled in paper manufacture before 1873.[51] In 1871 Asa Willard, Holyoke contractor, embarked upon another variation of builder's investment when he purchased of the Water Power Company a mill site with one mill power appurtenant, erected a factory with rooms and fractions of the one mill power to rent, and so provided place for the small or experimental manufacturing enterprise, such as the old gristmill building had housed.[52] From lumber merchant supplying building materials or contractor constructing the mill or renting space and power, to owner of shares of stock in a new manufacturing venture, might be a short step. The builder thus occupied in these years a middle position between the industrialist and the tradesman.

For although in some communities the merchant as he prospered invested some of his accumulating capital in new industrial enterprises, in Holyoke such was not the case. Indeed large mercantile businesses failed to develop here and capital in any sizeable amounts, therefore, was not to be extracted for reinvestment. Years later a few farsighted merchants found money to put into the Farr Alpaca worsted mill when the price of the stock was low. But as a rule the first generation of merchants found that their drygoods stores, their groceries, or their meat markets absorbed all their available capital. Real estate prices for stores and dwellings were frequently pronounced disproportionately high as compared to the cost of industrial sites. Furthermore owing to the geographical setting of

---

51. George Lewis (interview); *Holyoke Directory,* 1871, pp. 88, 91, 105–106; Holyoke *Mirror,* Apr. 6, 1861; Holyoke *Transcript,* Jan. 16, June 25, 1864, May 27, 1865, Jan. 11, June 27, 1868, Jan. 7, 1871, May 1, June 15, 1872, May 14, Sept. 6, 1873; *Thirtieth Anniversary Holyoke Daily Transcript.*

52. Holyoke *Transcript,* Feb. 11, 1871. Before 1865 there had been eight different concerns manufacturing different commodities in the old gristmill building. When the Mt. Tom Paper Company bought the building this kind of establishment was hard pressed for space and power. After Willard's speculative investment the next mill built was made bigger than its occupant needed in order to have space to lease to others. *Ibid.,* May 6, 1865, Apr. 12, 1873.

the town between river and confining hills and the consequent lack of any extensive radiating lines of communication, it was nearly impossible for Holyoke merchants to build up anything beyond the local retail trade. And Springfield, a city of established stores, competed with this. Hence the tradespeople remained small-scale business men whose profits had to go back into the business or perhaps be deposited in the savings bank.

A merchant with a few hundred dollars to invest found no ready way of putting it into a local manufacturing enterprise. Once the town began to grow the Holyoke Water Power Company ceased to encourage industrial ventures of small scale and, unless the prospective manufacturer could afford to purchase a whole mill power with its site on the canal, there was no place before 1871 where new manufacturing enterprise could find a foothold. Frequent were the protests of the *Transcript* over this situation which drove the little fellow to start his mill elsewhere. Even after Asa Willard's successful experiment proved the feasibility of his scheme the Holyoke Water Power Company still refused to foster the little manufacturer. Any ambition on the part of the merchant for more rapidly profitable investment than his business afforded must find other outlet, most often in real estate speculation. Here was a tempting venture between 1865 and 1873 when there seemed to be no limit to the town's capacity for expansion and new "block" building.[53] Such money as was made in Holyoke in the years before 1873 was derived either from the mills or from the juggling of real estate. Thus the local merchant, socially the equal of the local industrialist, was financially, and so as an economic factor, an unimportant inferior.

Banking which might have proved a stepping stone to industrial investment for the tradesman in these years had not developed to any great proportions. The two savings banks, the Holyoke Savings dating from 1855, the newer Mechanics' from 1872, were sponsored by the most con-

53. Holyoke *Transcript,* May 8, 22, 1869, Aug. 6, 20, Sept. 10, 1870, Feb. 11, 1871, Mar. 29, 1873.

servative business men of the community and could not
lend money for any but established enterprises, while the
commercial banks, the Hadley Falls Bank reorganized in
1865 as a national bank, and its young rival, the Holyoke
National Bank chartered in 1872, were only less careful.[54]
A young manufacturing community which lacked many of
the essentials of a future metropolitan economy could not
aspire to the role of financial center. The banker as such
occupied no special place in the business hierarchy of Holyoke.

Manufacturer and merchant alike faced one problem as
the sixties wore on, namely, high freight costs. In the fifties
shipping by flatboat down the Connecticut to Hartford
was not unknown, but such a method could not successfully compete with rail transport and was abandoned in
the sixties.[55] In 1869 the newly formed Holyoke Manufacturers Association secured data proving that the Connecticut River Railroad was subjecting Holyoke to discrimina-
tory and unjustifiably high freight rates. Freight from
Springfield to Holyoke cost $8.50 a carload more than
from Springfield to Northampton, a haul of twice the distance. Since appeals to the railroad directors for lower
rates fell upon deaf ears, the leading citizens of Holyoke
undertook to secure a competing line which, as in Northampton, would force down freight charges. By dint of the
unflagging efforts of some half dozen men special town
meetings were called, the legislature was besieged with petitions, and, though opposed by the Connecticut River
Railroad as an unwarranted luxury, the Holyoke and
Westfield Railroad was chartered.

The new road was chiefly financed by the town itself, a
loan of 7 per cent on the town bonds supplying $166,500
of the $200,000 needed, while individuals subscribed the
rest. The directors, a board elected in town meeting, con-

cluded an arrangement with the New Haven and Northampton Railroad to build, equip, lease, and run the road
for half the gross annual income accruing. The very first
year, 1872, the freight passing over this road far exceeded
its projectors' hopes. Inevitably with the spur tracks now
built to the very doors of most of the mills on the first and
second level canals cartage costs dwindled, competition
forced down freight rates over the Connecticut River Railroad also, and Holyoke business men found themselves in a
favorable position in regard to transportation facilities.[56]
Hence by 1873 Holyoke's industrial future was assured.
Despite minor business setbacks and some differences of
opinions about the policies of the Holyoke Water Power
Company, investors in Holyoke could look forward confidently to a steady profitable growth. The capitalistic
form of industrial organization was entrenched, the incorporated company supplying the money for plant and
equipment, the management distinct from the workmen,
and the producers at bench and machine wage-earners set
apart from both. This was not the only form. The small
workshop where part-owners worked beside their employes
was not unknown.[57] But inevitably the power rental arrangements with the Holyoke Water Power Company in
this period tended to eliminate all but big, strongly financed mills. The Water Power Company preferred to see
the mill sites and power utilized by a few large corporations in big brick buildings. Presumably this layout lent
an air of greater stability to the community. Certainly
these same consolidating tendencies were incipient everywhere in the American business world, and men called the
result progress. While in Holyoke men's first preoccupation was with earning their own living, enlarging their

56. Holyoke *Town Records,* 1872, pp. 47–48; 1873, pp. 41–42; Holyoke
Transcript, May 15, 22, June 12, 1869, Aug. 27, 1870, Dec. 2, 1871, Sept.
28, 1872.

57. The Whittaker Reed manufacture, in the early sixties the little machine shop from which the Holyoke Machine Company was in part made
up, Pattee and Fairchild, Coghlan and Mullen, and in 1873 at the very
end of this era, B. F. Perkins, all are examples.

own businesses, and widening their own fields of activity, whether as wage-earners, tradesmen, clerks, or mill owners, their enthusiastic faith in the future of the town was invigorating to the community as a whole. The local origin of Holyoke's paper manufacture was giving the town a stability which cotton manufacture alone could not maintain. Fortunes were only dimly foreshadowed, and the contrasts between the lot of capital and labor were not yet sharp. The great game was just beginning.

IV

COMMUNITY PROBLEMS, 1859–1873

H ERE was a new community with no tradition of its own. Some of its many problems were inherent in the industrial development of the town; some were born of the rapidity of the shift from an agrarian to an industrial community; and most of the rest were brought by the influx of foreigners. Men with a little capital who were familiar with the modes of American life were able to invest in Holyoke in these early days and find it good. But what of the other elements of the population? From the very beginning of the town and increasingly as the industrial boom gathered force at the end of the Civil War, a large proportion of Holyoke dwellers were laboring people with no savings and no means of livelihood other than what was offered them in the mills through the capital investment of others. Although Marxian terminology was practically unknown in America before 1873 and unfamiliar for a generation thereafter, labor was already distinct from capital and recognized to be so, not immutably and inevitably but generally and normally. And yet the fourteen years which elapsed between the organization of the Holyoke Water Power Company and the panic of 1873 brought to Holyoke a prosperity of which all classes partook somewhat and bred an atmosphere of neighborliness and common interest in the community life.

The character and conditions of labor in Holyoke differed to some extent from industry to industry. In the machine shop the scope for invention and mechanical ingenuity coupled with the individual craftsmanship required by the very nature of the industry gave the workman a position of some dignity, not unlike that of the skillful garage mechanic in the 1930s.

In the paper mills labor was fundamentally affected not

only by the peculiar circumstances attending paper manufacture everywhere, but also by the fact that here the mills
were nearly all owned and run by local men. Paper-mill
hands were self-respecting and had a friendly sort of independence. The machine tender, the man in charge of the
Fourdrinier or cylinder machine, was always the most important workman in a paper mill, with his assistants and
the engineers handling the beaters and Jordan engines
next in rank. The machine tenders, the aristocrats of labor
in the industry, skilled workmen who took pride in the performance of their machines, were more eager to prove their
prowess in their art than to fight a wage-earners' battle
against capital.[1] And at first there was no reason to assume
that the progression for the intelligent and conscientious
worker might not be from machine tender to foreman to
superintendent and so perhaps to stockholder and employer. What matter that such ambitions were rarely fully
satisfied, in this pioneer era never? The mere aspiration
was a unifying factor in the personnel of a mill. Although
management was known to be usually drawn from the
office force, still here workmen, foremen, superintendents,
office force, agents, and owners were closely associated. A
semblance of camaraderie grew up. Holyoke paper-mill
owners personally knew their help. The result was an unusual degree of stability, with labor turnovers exceptionally small for the paper industry. Whiting, to be sure,
complained good-naturedly of the impossibility of keeping
girls in his finishing room because of the rate at which they
married. But that fact doubtless did not detract from the
attractions of jobs there.[2]

In every community, however, paper-mill employes in
these days were confronted with situations different from

1. Matthew J. Burns, History of the International Brotherhood of
Paper Makers (typescript in possession of the author).
2. Mass. Bur. Labor Statistics, *Third Annual Report*, 1872, pp. 156–
157, 347. Compare the evidences of paper makers' constant shifting of
location in the brief biographies of early paper makers published in the
pamphlets, Ralph Snell, ed., *Superior Facts*, 1926–1933, published by the
Paper Makers Chemical Corporation; e.g., *Superior Facts*, IV, no. 10
(Apr. 1931), 1–6.

those of textile operatives. In the first place, there were comparatively few workmen in the paper mills. In 1869 all eleven Holyoke paper mills together employed fewer persons than the Lyman Mills alone with its 1,100 hands.[3] In the second place, there was little employment of minors in paper plants, either girls or boys, and of the young girls between sixteen and twenty employed many had the most desirable jobs, those in the finishing rooms. In the third place, paper making was largely a man's job. The female employes were mostly rag-sorters or cutters, and in the sixties and early seventies a system of circulating rag-sorters was common. About half the rag-room workers were employed as a permanent force in a mill and for the rest the supply consisted of women who moved from plant to plant, preparing enough rags to run the machinery of one mill for a time and then progressing to the next in town. But while no job in a cotton mill could be so unpleasant as the task of women sorting over the none too clean rags in a paper mill, the fate of the female paper-mill hand elicited no special comment. Irish women, unprotesting over the distasteful chore, did the rag-sorting; American girls were largely employed in the finishing room. Otherwise all the departments used only males.[4]

In the textile mills the number of women greatly exceeded the number of men, and nearly as many children as women were employed in some departments. After 1863 the number of French Canadians in the Lyman, Hampden, and Hadley mills increased rapidly, and it was a commonplace among overseers that the French Canadian parents put their children to work as soon as possible and kept them there by outright falsehood, if need be, to evade the state school laws. But the school laws were not very

3. *Holyoke Directory*, 1869, pp. 97, 101–105. In 1865 with four mills in operation 93 males and 237 females are listed in the official census as the total employed in the paper industry here. *Statistical Information Rel. to Industry*, 1865, p. 253.

4. Mass. Bur. Labor Statistics, *Second Annual Report*, 1871, pp. 318–319; *Third Annual Report*, 1872, p. 347; *Ninth Annual Report*, 1878, p. 229.

seriously regarded by most mill people in town, whether mill agents, overseers, or parents. Jared Beebe reported in 1870 that there were thirty-three young persons under fifteen years of age employed in his woolen mill, all of whom worked the full sixty-nine hours a week. And this was despite the law of four years' standing that no minor might be employed in a factory more than sixty hours in any week. The disregard of the school laws gave pause only to more thoughtful citizens. It may well be due to this irresponsible attitude that in 1877 24 per cent of the Holyoke textile mill employes under twenty years of age were illiterate while 15 per cent in the paper mills were.[5]

Except for the laws requiring some schooling for minors employed in a manufacturing establishment and limiting their hours of labor, laws revised and elaborated several times but still ineffective in Holyoke, there was no legal regulation of hours or conditions of labor in Massachusetts before 1874.[6] It was a person's privilege, an inherent liberty, to work as many hours a day as he chose. At least he was free to starve if he preferred to refuse to work long hours, five days a week eleven and one quarter hours with a short eight-and-three-quarter-hour day on Saturday in the textile mills, or in a paper mill perhaps even longer. There was no universal schedule of work. The paper mill owners had not as yet evolved a regular two-shift system whereby the machines ran day and night for six days of every week. Before 1873 Holyoke paper makers worked seventy-two hours a week at the maximum and fifty-eight hours at a minimum, although the hours for the women employed were not so long. Textile-mill hands were far more likely to find themselves not working at all several days a week during one of the periodic business slumps, because, as a candid Yankee manufacturer explained at a

5. Mass. Bur. Labor Statistics, *First Annual Report*, 1870, pp. 135, 388, 391, 397; *Third Annual Report*, 1872, p. 350; *Fourth Annual Report*, 1873, p. 391; *Fifth Annual Report*, 1874, p. 5; *Ninth Annual Report*, 1878, pp. 229–230, 258; *Holyoke Directory*, 1869, p. 99; 1871, pp. 101–102.

6. Mass. Bur. Labor Statistics, *Seventh Annual Report*, 1876, pp. 270, 271, 276, 280.

later time, it was more economical to run a textile mill eleven hours a day for a few days than to spread out the work over a greater number of days. The time lost in starting up and stopping the machinery was too costly to be worth the convenience to the help. But interest in securing a state ten-hour law was not keen in town, and a local labor reform association organized in 1869 languished despite the efforts of a few philanthropists to arouse the working people to zeal for the cause.[7]

It was not customary in the Holyoke cotton mills to reduce the hours in winter, as was sometimes done elsewhere, to lessen fire hazards by avoiding as many hours of work by gas or lamplight as possible. With the lint in the air of those close rooms and the feeble flare of gas jets, the crowds of operatives, young girls and tired children, it is a miracle that fire or accidents were not the rule rather than the exception. No requirements were put upon factories to supply fire escapes and only the insurance regulations made obligatory some precautions. Yet few losses by fire occurred and until the Hampden Paper Company's mill burned to the ground in 1870 Holyoke had a proud record.[8]

Less a source for congratulation were other features of working conditions. Ventilation and sanitary arrangements in general were primitive. Water in the mill raceways flushed the sewerage from the mills out into the canal or river. In the Hadley Thread mill though the rooms were "clean and pleasant," as the phrase went, the air was so bad as to be nauseating, and in the spinning room where many children were employed a state Bureau of Labor investigator reported: "We were so oppressed with the heat as to be obliged to retire."[9] Girls frequently fainted at the

7. Mass. Bur. Labor Statistics, *Third Annual Report,* 1872, pp. 156–157, 164–166, 175–176; *Tenth Annual Report,* 1879, pp. 156–157; Holyoke *Transcript,* Aug. 14, Sept. 11, Oct. 16, Nov. 6, 1869, Sept. 24, 1870.

8. Holyoke *Transcript,* May 29, 1869, Jan. 29, 1870; Lyman Mills Papers, Davis to Lyman, Nov. 4, 1859. The Lyman Mills did not use gas for illumination until after July 1859.

9. Mass. Bur. Labor Statistics, *Third Annual Report,* 1872, p. 350.

spinning frames and when belatedly the mill was equipped
with ventilators it was a source of pride to the management that women no longer collapsed at their work. Some
mills of course were better ventilated than others.[10]

Only wage rates were commonly uniform. Cotton-mill
wages were determined in Boston where rates were kept in
line with what was paid elsewhere, and paper manufacturers in Holyoke agreed informally among themselves
what wages should prevail. At best they were not high.
Joseph Parsons writing in 1870 declared the great need
of the working people of Holyoke to be a higher standard
of living:

Usually there is an understanding among our manufacturers
as to the wages we will pay employes; but when a man comes
to us and says he can't well live on what we are paying him,
we raise his wages as much as is necessary. Our company would
be willing to pay women $2 as $1 and men $4 as $2, if others
would do the same. As now situated, we could afford to do so.
Have never had strikes or trouble of that sort. Would look
with favor on any of those changes in taste or habit that
would create a demand for higher wages. Twenty-five years
ago there were only foreigners in the trade; then everyone
knew the business as a whole; now only part is learned. There
is considerable room for promotion, but it comes more through
managing capacity than through the knowledge of a variety
of parts.[11]

Much of the help was paid by piece work and a quick capable girl could earn fair amounts. In 1867 a woman at
the Holyoke Paper Company mill was reported to have
made in one month $51 in addition to her board, a sum not
often cleared by a man in the same length of time. "We
understand," concluded the *Transcript* reporter, "that
many of the girls earn $2 a day and stop work at four

10. Mass. Bur. Labor Statistics, *Fifth Annual Report,* 1874, pp. 128,
130.
11. Mass. Bur. Labor Statistics, *Second Annual Report,* 1871, p. 319.

o'clock."[12] But this was scarcely typical. Average piece-work earnings of a woman in a paper mill were about $36 a month and the wages by time amounted to between $27 and $29.25 a month. Men on a time basis netted from $39 to $91 a month.[13]

Small though these sums may seem, they were princely compared to the pay in the cotton mills. The wage average there was cut down by the number of children employed who were paid from thirty-seven cents to eighty cents a day. The Lyman Mills, employing, to be sure, only 53 minors out of a total of 1,100 persons for 1871, reported its average wage per employe to be fifty-four cents a day or $163.63 a year.[14] Yet a few years before Holyoke wages were not only pronounced "comfortable" but higher than elsewhere in Massachusetts.[15] In the thread mill women rated from seventy-five cents to $1.60 a day and men from $1 to $2.25. The woolen mills generally paid by piece work but the average daily wage was listed at $1.52 in 1871.[16]

Working people were not likely at those rates to emerge rapidly into the investing capitalist class, no matter how frugal they might be. Still, living costs were not high as manufacturing towns went. Board for women in company boarding houses was $2.50 a week in 1867, $3.50 for men. As most mill hands lived within half a mile of their work and were allowed forty-five minutes or an hour for dinner, it was usual for operatives to go home at noon instead of

12. Holyoke *Transcript,* Oct. 26, 1867.

13. Carew Mfg. Co. Papers, Pay Roll Book, 1866–1882; Mass. Bur. Labor Statistics, *First Annual Report,* 1870, p. 384; *Holyoke Directory,* 1869, p. 101; 1874–1875, p. 125.

14. Mass. Bur. Labor Statistics, *Third Annual Report,* 1872, pp. 164–166. These averages are probably misleading. The calendar of working days was theoretically supposed to have 308 days. Fifty-four cents multiplied by 303 totals $163.62. The true number of working days was less.

15. Holyoke *Transcript,* June 1, 1867, quoting *Commercial Bulletin,* "Nowhere else can operatives live more cheaply. Dressers on fine goods earn about $2.50 per day and frame spinners about six shillings which are comfortable wages, and proportionately higher than paid by many Eastern corporations."

16. Mass. Bur. Labor Statistics, *Third Annual Report,* 1872, pp. 175–176.

resorting to a lunch pail. Rents were high owing to the cost of tenement sites. Yet in the face of all these circumstances saving went on and most of the $40,000 in the Holyoke Savings Bank was put there by thrifty mill hands. In 1872 there was even room for a second savings bank.[17]

All the hard work and discomforts, long hours in the mills at meagre pay, notwithstanding, the working people of town were not dissatisfied. Was it merely that they were inarticulate? More probably it was because conditions here were on the whole less trying than what these immigrants had known before in Ireland or in Canada. Strikes were almost unheard of. Day-laborers and workmen in the building trades tried once or twice to strike for better pay, but the hordes of unskilled immigrant laborers pouring in every month made the attempt futile.[18]

Within the mills only twice were there strikes before 1874, both times in the woolen mills.[19] The fact that these two strikes were launched by skilled German workmen who doubtless had had a comparatively high standard of living in Germany is suggestive. Neither contest was long-drawn out. In 1866 the weavers at the Germania mills rebelled at the reduction of the piece rate from eighteen cents to sixteen cents a yard, but as jobs at the Germania were considered desirable, other weavers hastened to apply for the vacancies and thus the first strike quickly came to nought.[20] Again in the fall of 1870 forty Germania weavers struck. The mill was rushed with orders and had been running overtime so that it seemed reasonable to suppose that the

17. Holyoke *Transcript,* June 1, 1867, quoting *Commercial Bulletin; Holyoke Directory,* 1874–1875, p. 121; Mass. Bur. Labor Statistics, *First Annual Report,* 1870, pp. 376, 388; *Third Annual Report,* 1872, pp. 175–176, 304, 306, 310, 314; *Second Annual Report,* 1871, pp. 318–319. For example Parsons' tenements rented for $8 a month to employes or to others for $12.

18. Holyoke *Transcript,* Apr. 7, 1866, Feb. 11, 1871.

19. This number amounts to four if the two-day strike in March of 1857 in the Lyman Mills and an announced strike among the dyers in the Hampden Mill in 1864 are listed. In the second instance there is no evidence that the strike took place. For the former, see above, p. 57.

20. Holyoke *Transcript,* Aug. 11, 1866.

corporation could afford better pay to wage earners as
well as to stockholders. But rather than give in to the
strikers, Agent Stursberg shut down the whole plant. Public opinion strongly condemned the weavers:

There is no dissatisfaction in the other departments, and the
two hundred other employees of the mill are united in their
denunciation of the course pursued by the weavers. In passing through the mill yesterday, we found but one sentiment
prevailing. All cordially support the agent, acknowledging
the necessity and justice of his action, and regret the folly
that has imposed so much hardship upon the innocent and
well disposed operatives who are willing to work at regular
prices, or give honorable notice of their intention to quit
service.[21]

Although weavers in the New York woolen mill, inspired
by the Germania workmen, also went out on strike and
shortly won an increase of a cent a yard in rates, the Germania weavers after ten days admitted defeat. Only a few
of the ringleaders in the trouble were refused their jobs.
"All experience in this country and Europe," proclaimed
the *Transcript*, "proves that strikes are a curse to the
working man."[22] So Holyoke workers perhaps believed.

But life for the workingman was not merely a dreary
round of tasks calculated just barely to keep the wolf
from the door. It had its brighter moments. Unquestionably the general tone of relations between employer and
employe was friendly. In the cotton mills where superintendents and overseers were themselves merely more highly
paid employes of non-resident owners, kindly feeling was
particularly noticeable. The overseer in each department
did the hiring and firing of his help, and thus upon the
character and temper of the individual overseer much of
the serenity of life for the worker depended. In the Lyman
Mills there was rather an unusual group of men, and the

21. *Ibid.*, Oct. 8, 1870.
22. *Ibid.*, Oct. 7, 15, 1870; Mass. Bur. Labor Statistics, *Second Annual
Report*, 1871, p. 290.

shift in personnel in this period is remarkably small.[23]
Many are the newspaper accounts of the surprise parties
contrived for an overseer by his help. Frequently elaborate
presents were given him with flowery speeches, but with
obviously genuine feeling. Typical was the performance in
1865 when Isaac Berry was shifted from the post of overseer in the No. Two mill weave shed to that of the No.
One mill. After the weavers had invaded his house in the
evening and presented him with an easy chair and a pipe,
and his wife with silver forks and knives and a castor costing $35, Berry was called upon for a speech. "We would
here say," announces the *Transcript*, "that although Mr.
Berry is of course exceedingly happy at receiving such
generous keepsakes from his employes, he still does not feel
any ways aristocratic, and will continue to 'fiddle' himself
into the good grace of all that give him a call."[24] Equally
characteristic was the occurrence at the Hadley Thread
Company's mill and the comment of the *Transcript*: "The
affair [the presentation of a desk] was quietly carried
through, and expresses a liberality on the part of the girls,
besides showing that they know when they have a pleasant
occupation with pleasant and gentlemanly overseers."[25]
Instances of this sort could be readily multiplied. This
situation endured as long as the first generation of overseers and local executives were on the scene. Holyoke for
all its growth was still a mill village.

While there were thus breaks in the monotony of Holyoke's workaday world, leisure for the mill hands six days
a week was non-existent. And over half the population was
estimated as employed in or about the mills. But neither
was there leisure for tradesmen or housewives. The stores
were ordinarily kept open evenings till eight or later. Because of the dearth of domestic help, women of all ranks
were obliged frequently to man the kitchen themselves, and
as ready-made clothing for women was unheard of except

23. Holyoke *Transcript*, Aug. 27, 1870; Mass. Bur. Labor Statistics,
Third Annual Report, 1872, pp. 164–166.
24. Holyoke *Transcript*, Oct. 19, 1865.
25. *Ibid.*, Jan. 5, 1869.

for shoes, stockings, and corsets, the amount of sewing which women had to do is staggering.[26] Even with a sewing machine it was a time-consuming task. For a time balmoral skirts were to be purchased ready-made, those heavy woolen petticoats purporting to be of the kind Queen Victoria wore while sojourning at Balmoral Castle. But for the most part women who could not afford to employ a dressmaker had to make their own clothes and most of their children's. For the householder two generations ago in New England even simple living involved an amount of labor which precluded the possibility of leisure most of the year. Woodboxes to fill and fires to tend, oil lamps to clean and trim, wash tubs to fill and to empty, preserving in summer, and breadbaking all through the year—there was little time left over for either man or woman to devote to pleasure-seeking.

The opening in 1870 of a town library with some 2,500 books available for the 300 subscribers made possible wider reading, but reading for pleasure was considered unworthy. As the *Transcript* declared in 1864: "Reading for amusement, merely, tends to weaken the intellect. If good books are not furnished for the young, they will read novels and sensational newspapers which intoxicate the brain and lead to pernicious results."[27] There was church of course. Twice on Sunday and at least once during the week, much of Holyoke's American population expected to go to church. And on Sundays and feast days the Catholics, Irish, and French Canadian, went to Mass. Perhaps twice a year, at Christmas and St. Patrick's Day or New Year's and St. John the Baptist's Day, each fraternal organization, the Fenians, the German Benevolent Society, St. Jerome's Temperance, Benevolent, and Literary So-

26. *Census of Mass., 1875, Population and Social Statistics,* I, 512. In the summer of 1873 an experiment was made by one clothier in town in carrying ready-made linen suits for women. It occasioned some astonished comment. It was the day of ruffles. One dressmaker's bill itemized a charge for hemming by hand two hundred yards of ruffling. Holyoke *Transcript,* June 11, July 19, 1873.

27. Holyoke *Transcript,* Apr. 16, 1864, Feb. 26, 1870, Feb. 11, 1871, May 15, 1872.

ciety, or the Société de St. Jean Baptiste after its organization in 1872, celebrated with a ball or a big picnic and
parade. The native American refreshed himself with firemen's musters, a Lyceum debate or lecture, and perhaps
attendance at the Masonic gatherings. But, as had been
true in the fifties, diversion outside of the church group
was not general.[28]

Only in the realm of sport was there a new departure.
A brief but vehement craze for velocipede riding had its
day in the late sixties, a pastime costly, a little dangerous,
and not adapted to pursuit outdoors on the uneven roads
of Holyoke. Still it was an indication perhaps of the rising
interest in sport. Where an occasional sleigh ride in winter
or picnic in summer had been the chief outdoor interest in
the fifties, there now developed a vast enthusiasm for baseball. As early as 1860 there were formed two rival ball clubs,
but the game played was not baseball. With the vanishing
of those organizations during the war the field was clear
for the introduction of modern baseball. High school versus grammar school, Lyman Mills cotton team versus
Lyman Mills repair shop team, Meteors versus Monitors,
Flats versus the Hill—the number of teams and clubs and
the heat of the rivalry varied from month to month and
year to year, and general interest was unflagging. In winter skating on the canals was a favorite pastime and at the
southern end of the first level canal in 1873 enterprising
youths contrived a rink which provided entertainment to
performers and watchers alike. For the more well-to-do
horse-racing came increasingly to be a diversion, in winter
occasionally on the ice on the river well above the dam, and
at other times of year along the "Street," the old county
road through Baptist Village. But this was sport for the
few only.[29]

28. W. A. Prentiss (interview); Holyoke *Transcript*, Mar. 19, 1864,
Aug. 12, 1865, Mar. 21, 1868, June 26, Nov. 16, 20, 1872, Jan. 11, 1873.

29. Dr. Hastings (interview); Holyoke *Mirror*, June 30, July 14, 28,
1860; Holyoke *Transcript*, Jan. 21, Dec. 9, 1865, June 9, 23, Aug. 25, Sept.
15, 1866, June 1, July 27, Aug. 24, 1867, Jan. 4, Apr. 4, 1868, Jan. 30, Feb.
20, 27, Mar. 13, Apr. 24, Sept. 4, 1869, Aug. 27, 1870, May 8, 1872, Dec.

Meanwhile the town grew. The census of 1860 reported 4,632 inhabitants as compared to 3,713 in 1850, and by 1865 the number was 5,648. It was therefore the next eight years that brought the rapid growth in population and the many resulting problems to the town. The year 1870 found a population of 10,722 and 1873 approximately 14,000. Over 43 per cent in 1865 were foreigners and by 1870 the proportion was well over 50 per cent foreign. Of these immigrants the Irish were most numerous, the French Canadians after 1867 next, and the Germans third. Some English and some Scottish people were here and two German Jewish families arrived in the late sixties. There were virtually no other nationalities represented.[30]

Among the three numerically important national groups colony-living was the rule. The others, too few to form true colonies, accommodated themselves wherever they could find place. Since in the status of transportation before 1880 it was only practical for workpeople to live within a mile or at most two of their jobs, occupation largely determined the location of these colonies. The Germans were concentrated in South Holyoke near the Germania mills, where for forty years the Saxons and Rhinelanders and any later-coming Prussians lived apart from their neighbors. As skilled workmen, devout Lutherans, and people of some cultural background, the Germans rather despised the uncouth "Paddies" and poverty-stricken French Canadians about them, and the Catholicism of these unwelcome neighbors cut them off sharply. Through the Lutheran church, the Turnverein, and the German Benevolent Society the Germans were self-suffi-

10, 1873; Allyn, "Sketch of Holyoke," *Thirtieth Anniversary Holyoke Daily Transcript.*
30. *Census of Mass.,* 1865, pp. 66–67, 248, 298; Holyoke *Transcript,* Sept. 17, 1870; *Holyoke Directory,* 1874–1875; *Census of Mass.,* 1875, *Population and Social Statistics,* I, 288–336; H. M. Marks (interview). Holyoke's percentage of foreign population in 1865 was larger than that of any other town or city in the state. Lawrence ranked next with 42.48 per cent. *Ninth Census of the United States,* 1870, *Population and Social Statistics,* I, 166.

cient, enjoying their "Kaffeeklatch," taking pride in their homes with their window boxes or gardens, and maintaining exacting standards of cleanliness. The Lutheran parochial school where children were taught German further kept the colony apart.[31] The Irish in South Holyoke had been there before the Germans, and "Tigertown" took its name from the rough Irishmen who located there in the late fifties to work in the Holyoke Paper mill or in the nearby brickyard. As the sixties wore on a number of French Canadians also came, so that the first French Canadian priest chose South Holyoke for the location of his parish church. Thus by the seventies, Tigertown was polyglot, although German, Irish, and Canadian did not mingle. The last two also were grouped in other sections, in the Flats near the Hadley Thread mill and the paper mills beyond, and upon the "Hill" where Irish lived in mill tenements or in the Patch and French Canadians herded together in "Frenchville."[32]

In the Patch lived the poorest Irish, the newly arrived, unskilled day-laborers. Here when the dam was building and in the fifties, it was customary for the new arrival to construct for himself with the help of his neighbors a crude shelter, generally half board, half dug-out, often consisting of one room and a loft without windows. As the thriftier of the firstcomers rose in the world these shanties were abandoned to be in turn occupied by the then newcomers. Only squatters on the land to begin with, on terrain owned chiefly by the Water Power Company, the families who moved to better quarters left these huts standing for their successors. It was inexpensive kindliness. The prospering

31. Sumner Whitten (interview); Osgood, *Story of the Holyoke Churches*. Only once in 1870 did the Germans come into direct conflict with Irish and French Canadians. It was while celebrating the Prussian victories at Sedan. The Irish and Canadians tore down the improvised Prussian flags, proclaiming it an insult to their adopted land that the Stars and Stripes had not been unfurled above the other. Holyoke *Transcript*, Sept. 20, 1870.

32. The natural terracing of the river valley created a plateau above the dam, the "Hill," and the level low-lying plain between the second level canal and the river, the "Flats."

Irishman usually invested in a plot of land of his own as soon as he could, built a dwelling upon it when his savings warranted, and perhaps later pulled it down to replace with a better, a "neat frame house."[33] But meanwhile neighborliness developed in the Patch a community spirit. One pump and one oven served many households jointly, and firewood salvaged every spring from the river by the men of the Patch was divided evenly among all. They shared what they had and in illness and trouble cared for each other with rare tenderness. Only as time went on and the firstcomers, Irish from County Cork, encountered an ever-growing group of County Kerry immigrants, jealousies and petty feuds grew up within the colony of an intensity which only Father Harkins of St. Jerome's could keep in check.

The French Canadians, first numerous in the later sixties, never resorted to the kind of community shanty building to which the Irish had been driven in the earlier years. Tenement blocks had been built in the interim which by a hideous process of crowding, crowding, and still more crowding, were made to house the accumulating foreigners until the town fathers were obliged to interfere. By 1870 "Frenchville," located near the dam, was a distinct separate colony, marked off from the Irish settlement adjacent by an invisible but once well-recognized line.[34]

However neighborly and kind to the newcomer of his own nationality, neither Irishman nor French Canadian wasted any cordiality upon the other. The French Canadian usually spoke little or no English and so was at a disadvantage, although many was the County Kerry man whose brogue was so broad that it could scarce pass muster as English even in Holyoke. Until the Catholic hierarchy created a French Canadian parish in 1869 and appointed

33. Mass. Bur. Labor Statistics, *Second Annual Report,* 1871, pp. 318–319; Michael Bowler (interview).

34. Michael Bowler, Thomas Carmody (interviews); Lucey, *History of St. Jerome's Parish,* p. 97; Holyoke *Transcript,* Apr. 17, 1863, Mar. 21, 1868, Apr. 10, 1869, July 22, 1872; Allyn, "Sketch of Holyoke," *Thirtieth Anniversary Holyoke Daily Transcript.*

a resident Canadian priest, the French colony had little
to do with the Catholic church in Holyoke. What became
of these people, at home devoted to their religion? Theirs
was a sorry plight. Irish Catholics discovered in 1869, to
their horror, that a number of the French Canadian girls
in town were receiving instruction in English in a Protestant church.[35] The ill-feeling engendered by such a circumstance was not easily soothed. Common religion so far
from acting as a bond served as a source of antagonism.
Furthermore, there was first the indignation of the Canadians at the little concealed preparations of the Irish Fenians in town for the conquest of Canada in 1870, and
then later the ridicule meted out to the ingloriously returned band after its fiasco. The other foreigners in town
were more prone to sympathize with the French Canadians
than with the Irish, if only because of the preponderance
of the Irish.

The story of the Fenians of Holyoke is rather a tale
apart. Among the native Americans in the sixties there
was a good deal of sympathy with the brotherhood. There
were two chapters here, the Irish Lion Circle and the
O'Neil Circle. During 1868 and 1869 the Fenians drilled
regularly in Exchange Hall behind locked doors, employing their rifles saved from war service or secretly acquired
afterward. A number were Civil War veterans, and the
Holyoke company was joined by men from Westfield and
a delegation from Springfield. In addition to secretly drilling they openly paraded on St. Patrick's Day in gay uniform, "green jacket trimmed with orange braid, and blue
pants, with cap," arousing thereby more interest than disapproval.

The projected invasion of Canada, to be sure, was by
no means a purely local undertaking. General Sweeney of
the United States Army was proclaimed to be one of the
leaders of an army that was to cross the border in several
sections. And in 1869 one or two raids actually took place.
But the O'Neil Guards of Holyoke were part of the last

35. Holyoke *Transcript,* Feb. 27, 1869.

contingent to set forth. When in May the signal was given to march for the border, the local band, some thirty-five strong, set forth valiantly on foot. At White River, Vermont, they made junction with other companies, and there entrained for the border. Five miles this side of the Canadian line the train was stopped by the United States regulars, instructed by President Grant to turn back the conquering army of nearly five hundred fighting Irishmen. Protest proving futile, the companies accepted from Uncle Sam a free train-ride home. The O'Neil Guards sneaked back into Holyoke as inconspicuously as they could, less than two weeks after their confidently heroic departure to twist the British lion's tail in Canada. The bloodless defeat of the expedition was the theme of every gibe in town for many a day. Hereafter the Irish were viewed with less favor by American-born Holyokers.[36]

As numbers multiplied housing became increasingly a problem. In 1856 the first Board of Health had reported shocking conditions but fifteen years later overcrowding was far worse. Most of the manufacturing corporations had built tenements for their own working people, but these accommodations were not adequate for mill hands alone, while for day-laborers, clerks, merchants, or professional people there was no such provision. Individuals put up blocks as a speculative venture after 1870, and the well-to-do of the community built houses for themselves. Still the supply lagged far behind demand. The demand for housing of any sort opened the way for the erection of wretchedly constructed blocks where the first consideration was the number to be packed in rather than health or comfort. Although the town Board of Health was empowered to remove families from overcrowded tenements, there was no place to move them to, and the ruling remained a dead letter. In 1866 the health officers found a block on High Street with seventeen rooms above the first floor

36. *Ibid.*, Aug. 12, Sept. 23, Oct. 28, 1865, Mar. 21, 1868, Mar. 27, 1869, May 28, June 4, 1870; Thomas Carmody (interview).

where 105 people were living, in some of the rooms ten persons.[37]

Not only the lack of dwellings but also the poverty and ignorance of a large part of the population entered into this housing situation. The squalor and filth in which Irish and French Canadian immigrants lived in these years is partly attributable to their lack of any knowledge of the most elementary rules of sanitation. Shanties in the Patch sometimes had no windows, and plumbing was an unknown luxury. Indeed the town sewers were not extended to the Patch until after 1873. At the rear of the shanty a pig sty was often appended as the family grew more well-to-do. Only later another room or a window might be added to the dwelling. Unsavory though these shanties were, the lack of ventilation, sanitary arrangements, or fire protection was worse in the "beautiful" brick blocks near the mills.[38] The report of the Bureau of Statistics of Labor in 1875 describes these:

Holyoke has more and worse large tenement houses than any manufacturing town of textile fabrics in the state, and built in such a manner that there is very little means of escape in case of fire. The sanitary arrangements are very imperfect, and in many cases, there is no provision made for carrying the slops from the sinks, but they are allowed to run wherever they can make their way. Portions of yards are covered with filth and green slime, and within twenty feet, people are living in basements of houses three feet below the level of the yard. One large block, four stories high, and basement, has eighteen tenements, with ninety rooms, occupied by nearly two hundred people; and yet there are only two three-feet

37. Holyoke *Transcript*, June 25, 1864, Dec. 9, 1865, May 5, 1866, May 1, 15, June 12, Aug. 14, 1869, July 9, 1870, Apr. 10, May 25, Dec. 4, 1872, Apr. 26, May 29, Aug. 2, Oct. 1, 1873. The number of carpenters and masons in town in 1875 is testimony to the uninterrupted building program Holyoke's growth necessitated. Between January 1872 and October 1873 there were 280 new buildings put up. *Census of Mass.*, 1875, *Population and Social Statistics*, I, 512.

38. W. A. Prentiss, Michael Bowler (interviews); Holyoke *Transcript*, Sept. 25, 1869, Apr. 10, 1872.

doorways on the front, and none on the back, with an alley-
way at back only six feet in width. At present there is some
spare room at the front, but it is uncertain how long it will
remain so. There are also quite a number of six and eight
tenement houses, with only one door at front and none at
back, over-crowded, dirty and necessarily unhealthy. Our
agents visited some tenements having bedrooms into which
neither air nor light could penetrate, as there were no windows and no means of ventilation, and some of them were
actually filthy. It is no wonder that the death-rate, in 1872
was greater in Holyoke than in any large town in Massachusetts, excepting Fall River, and if an epidemic should visit
them now, in the state they are in, its ravages would be great.[39]

Such was the hell-hole that industrial development had
created in the open countryside where twenty-five years
before cattle had browsed. Who was to blame? Had transportation been easier so that people could have lived at
greater distance from their work, overcrowding with its attendant evils could not have been so acute. It was for
years the hopes of many people that the building of an
inter-county bridge across to South Hadley Falls, by
making accessible the cheaper real estate in the Falls,
would relieve the housing problem. But while the completion of the bridge in 1872 was a convenience to both communities, the prophesied migration of working people to
the east shore did not follow. Until the trolley line was extended across the bridge to the Falls in the eighties there
was no such exodus. Instead working people continued to
huddle together in the Flats and on the Hill.[40] The igno-

39. Mass. Bur. Labor Statistics, *Sixth Annual Report*, 1875, p. 392.
40. Thus the fears which Holyoke Water Power Company directors
were accused of harboring, that the ease of transit, once the river was
bridged, would reduce to a nullity all profits from Holyoke real estate,
proved ill-founded. But the long-standing opposition of the Water Power
Company to the building of the bridge was unfortunate because of the
resentment engendered in the breasts of many public-spirited citizens
and the inauguration of an enduring hostility between the company and
the town. While the company directors could point to generous gifts to
the community, many persons felt that such donations were merely sops
and that the best interests of the town were constantly sacrificed to the

rance of the victims of the existing arrangements was partly to blame. Education and a vision of a higher standard of living might in time help eliminate that factor. And a good deal was due to the general lack of knowledge of the medical profession of the time.[41]

But the town as a whole failed to realize that here was a community problem which the doctors and the overworked Board of Health could not solve unaided. The Board of Health, which was composed of the three town selectmen, devoted themselves faithfully to their task. Specially appointed first in 1866, they made regulations undertaking to cut down sources of disease. They published rules for keeping alleys and streets free from offal and garbage, for cleaning vaults, for building drains and sewers, and, backed by the State Board of Health, they announced their right of entry into premises for purposes of examining into and destroying nuisances and causes of filth.[42] But it was an uphill fight. The connection between public health and fresh air, an adequate sewerage system, and a supply of pure water, was not sufficiently understood to insure general coöperation.

Between 1870 and 1873 Holyoke faced two smallpox epidemics. There had been a few cases in earlier years but first in 1870 did the appearance of smallpox induce the selectmen to build a "pest-house" where victims could be segregated. Spreading apparently from infected rags in the paper mills, the disease made rapid inroads in the com-

immediate financial welfare of the company stockholders, a policy of short-sighted greed. In fact the whole policy of the company in the matter of real estate prices has been a bone of contention between town and corporation almost from the beginning. Allyn, "Sketch of Holyoke," *Thirtieth Anniversary Holyoke Daily Transcript;* Holyoke *Mirror,* Feb. 4, 18, 1854; *History . . . of South Hadley,* pp. 112–114; Ralph Smith, Development H. W. P. Co.; Holyoke *Transcript,* Nov. 5, 1864, May 19, 1866, Apr. 20, 1867, Oct. 23, 1869, Jan. 15, Mar. 26, Nov. 26, 1870, May 4, 1872.

41. Diagnoses of deaths as reported to the town clerk by the doctors reveal this lack of knowledge, e.g., Holyoke *Transcript,* Feb. 20, 1869.

42. Henry I. Bowditch, *Public Hygiene in America,* pp. 350–357; Holyoke *Transcript,* Nov. 18, 1865, Mar. 17, Apr. 7, 21, May 5, 1866, June 1, 1867, Mar. 14, Aug. 1, 1868, July 27, 1872.

munity. Physicians administered vaccine to some 1,500 persons in April, to the poorest at public expense. But while vaccination was recognized professionally as the only means of halting the epidemic, the terror and anger of the French Canadians and the poorest Irish at being inoculated presents a pitiful picture. In November the town fathers banned public entertainments and exhorted people to stay away from funerals and wakes. Yet twenty-two new cases of smallpox developed in one week, nine in one tenement of the Lyman Mills. When in December the superintendent of the Lyman Mills contracted the disease and died, panic seized the community.[43] Although the chances of recovery of patients removed to the town pest-house were proved to be greater than of those staying at home, the opposition to removal thither was strong among the classes most needing help. The outright refusal of many of the immigrants to be vaccinated led at length to the enactment of compulsory vaccination of every person in town, whether or not he had been directly exposed. The Board of Health divided the town into districts, assigned a doctor to each, and issued instructions that every attempted evasion of vaccination was to be punished with a fine. Such measures proved efficacious, but in less than four months there had been 147 cases of smallpox. Fortunately only twenty-three deaths had resulted.[44]

But two years later came a more severe form of the disease. With living conditions foul as they were the rapid spread of the contagion was inevitable, unless further vaccination could be effected. Yet it was even more difficult than before to enforce. Red flags hung in front of tenement houses as warning that there was smallpox the in-

43. Holyoke *Transcript,* Feb. 18, 1865, Mar. 12, 19, 26, Apr. 2, Oct. 1, 8, Nov. 19, Dec. 3, 1870; Holyoke *Town Records,* 1871, p. 15; Lyman Mills Papers, Boston Letter Book, Bush to Davis, Dec. 16, 1870; Davis to Bush, Jan. 6, 1871.

44. Holyoke *Transcript,* Dec. 17, 24, 1870, Jan. 21, Feb. 11, Mar. 18, 1871. The local health officers had called upon the State Board of Health to abet them in enforcing the vaccination decree. Free vaccination was undertaken in the police station. About 300 smallpox victims were attended by the town officers in the course of the year.

mates tore down. The Irish fought to hold their wakes and funerals as usual and resorted to deliberate concealment of illness. Occasionally the health officer and the town policeman had to remove a patient by sheer force to the pesthouse lest infection be spread by utter carelessness.[45] Compulsory vaccination or revaccination was carried on but still the epidemic did not subside. At length by careful inquiry town officers learned that among some of the population there prevailed the practice of inoculating well children with the virus obtained from the scab of a child sick with smallpox.[46] To combat such ignorance was difficult, but armed with pity, patience, and vaccine, the Board of Health aided by cold weather finally brought the epidemic to an end.

Mortality from all sources ran high, from diphtheria, measles, scarlet fever, and consumption and cholera in particular.[47] In 1868, a healthful year for the town, the death rate was about thirty-three per thousand. New York City at its worst in the sixties had a death rate of thirty-eight per thousand. Holyoke's infant mortality in summer was particularly great and the oppressive heat of the summers of 1871 and 1872 made matters worse than usual.[48]

The summer of 1871 brought to a head the question of the town water supply, when the pumps broke down which filled the reservoir from the river. Water had to be hawked through the streets in barrels. Thereupon the town pur-

45. Holyoke *Town Records,* 1872, p. 13; 1873, p. 15; Holyoke *Transcript,* Jan. 25, June 14, July 5, 26, 30, Aug. 2, 13, 23, 30, 1873. In one case, the health inspector, having been told by the milkman that there was smallpox in a certain tenement house, examined the premises without finding any stricken, while the inmates of the building denied that there was anyone ill there. But returning at an unexpected hour, the officer found in the absence of his informers, a twelve-year-old boy, very ill, lying on a chest in a tiny closet. One instance is reported in which the straw was emptied from the bed upon which a patient had lain, and dumped in the alley where children played.

46. Holyoke *Transcript,* June 11, 28, Aug. 13, Nov. 15, 1873, Jan. 5, 1874. The town doctors had vaccinated 2,670 persons by August of 1873.

47. This was clearly not Asiatic cholera. Holyoke *Transcript,* Oct. 24, 1863, Apr. 14, 1866, May 11, 1867, Apr. 24, 1869, Jan. 7, 1871, June 19, July 3, 17, 1872, Feb. 12, 18, July 30, Aug. 2, 1873, Feb. 4, 1874.

48. *Ibid.,* Feb. 20, 1869; Stephen Smith, *The City that Was,* pp. 20–21.

chased terrain in the western section of the township where
two ponds commanding a watershed of over three square
miles offered an ample supply of pure water. The necessary permissive state legislation secured, bonds were issued, and the work of impounding these waters and piping
them to the town was begun in the spring of 1872. The
town vested the administration of the waterworks in a
board of six commissioners who were able soon to announce that water rentals would more than meet the interest on the bonds and provide for a sinking fund. When the
mains were connected in August 1873, 2,163 families were
supplied with pure running water, where before scarcely a
dozen had running water at all. Henceforward whatever
other ills might attend the growing community, an inadequate or impure water supply would not be one of them.[49]

Equally vital to the public welfare was a satisfactory
system of sewage disposal. In the fifties the Hadley Falls
Company had laid down sewers from the Hill to empty
into the first level canal, but as the town expanded these
could serve only the corporation tenement houses and the
mills of that one section. In 1868 the town extended the
system by adding to the number of lateral sewers draining
into the first level canal and by building two sewers to
empty into the river, one above the dam, the other below,
draining the Flats. Nevertheless by 1872 over one half of
all the sewerage from the most crowded sections of the Hill
was still draining into an open cesspool without outlet located less than a quarter of a mile from thickly populated
districts. To this arrangement the high mortality rate in
summer was partly attributed and partly to emptying the
canals of water every Sunday and four days usually of the
week of July 4 every year. The noxious fumes arising
from the cesspool and muddy canal bottoms where sewage

49. Allyn, "Sketch of Holyoke," *Thirtieth Anniversary Holyoke Daily
Transcript;* Holyoke *Transcript,* Mar. 22, June 14, Aug. 9, 1873, Jan. 24,
Aug. 22, 1874. With the opening of town waterworks, the Water Power
Company reservoir was abandoned and the square later sold for building
lots. In later years additional sources of water had to be secured for the
city, but the water board was always prepared.

lay lent force to the pleas of concerned citizens to safe-
guard public health by extending the sewerage system to
all parts of town and in such way as to empty waste into
the river. But even with the abutters paying two thirds of
the expense of constructing sewers it was costly, and New
Englanders felt bound occasionally to hesitate. However,
with a complete system of main and lateral sewers mapped
out, the town in its last year carried on construction at a
creditable pace.[50]

Interest in fire protection was much more general than
in public health. With fire losses non-resident investors in
Holyoke mill property as well as inhabitants were concerned, and so the community paid special attention to
having capable fire companies. As in earlier years these
were all volunteer organizations, and the fire department,
efficient though it was, cost the town less than $1000 a
year.[51] Care of hydrants, first set out in 1860, came within
the jurisdiction of the chief engineer, a salaried town officer, as did street lamps after their installation a few
years later. Street lamps, gas and naphtha, were increased
in number year by year as the town could afford them, and
proved a convenience to pedestrians in those days of cinder
and gravel walks.

Street lighting was an aid also to the night watchmen in
the maintenance of public order, a difficult task as population grew after 1865. Drunkenness, rowdyism, petty thiev-
ery, and vice made the original force of four night watchmen utterly insufficient and by the end of the sixties a chief
and a permanent police force were necessary. Chief of
Police Ham, honest and conscientious, with two hundred
pounds of muscle to throw into his job, kept trouble-makers
in check throughout his years of service down to 1882. But

50. Holyoke *Transcript*, Mar. 26, 1864, Apr. 4, 1868, July 7, 1871, June
19, Feb. 15, July 6, 13, 17, 27, 1872, July 2, 1873; Holyoke *Town Records*,
1865, p. 6; 1866, p. 14; 1867, p. 7; 1868, pp. 6–7; 1870, p. 10; 1872, p. 7;
1873, pp. 9–11.

51. Holyoke *Transcript*, Jan. 25, Mar. 14, 1868, Jan. 31, Feb. 5, 12,
Mar. 5, 1870. Only two serious fires occurred in all the years of the town
regime: one which burned two business blocks on High Street, the other
not long after which destroyed the Hampden Paper mill.

neither he nor his force could eliminate the fundamental social maladjustments which kept the police court full. As was probably to be expected, most of the court charges were brought against the foreign-born.[52]

The police court cases dealt mostly with drunkenness, and illegal sale of liquor. Between 1867 and 1873 a variety of state liquor laws were enacted, revised, and rescinded, but under state prohibition or under license, modified local option or unrestricted, Holyoke remained wet. In 1857 there were here some hundred "dram shops"; by 1870, with a population of less than 11,000, the town under a regime of state prohibition for everything but beer and ale counted eighty-nine known liquor shops, with more rumored to exist. Temperance societies, notably that of St. Jerome's parish, probably did more to cope with Holyoke's liquor problem than attempts at legal restraint. But drunkenness was always a familiar vice here. The immoral or indifferent newcomer was quick to discover that in selling liquor he had a commodity always in demand. Many were the families that were helped on the way to prosperity by selling over the grocer's counter "a can of kerosene" in which a potato served as a stopper, the unofficial insignia of an intoxicating fluid within. In the days of a state prohibition commissioner and a local agent it was impossible to put a stop to this traffic just as later it was to be impossible by means of the local police. But during the regime of the selectmen, there was none of that undermining of government by the corruption of the liquor interests that was later to be the despair of upright citizens.[53]

52. Holyoke *Town Records,* 1864, pp. 6, 12; 1866, p. 8; 1868, p. 20; 1869, p. 4; 1870, p. 9; 1871, p. 8; 1872, p. 8; 1873, p. 13; Allyn, "Sketch of Holyoke," *Thirtieth Anniversary Holyoke Daily Transcript;* Holyoke *Transcript,* Nov. 14, 1863, Mar. 19, July 23, Sept. 3, 10, 1864, May 27, July 24, Aug. 12, Sept. 16, Dec. 16, 1865, Aug. 15, Sept. 12, 1868, July 30, 1870, Feb. 25, Mar. 4, 1871, Feb. 26, 1873. See also weekly Police Court records as published in Holyoke *Transcript,* 1872–1873.

53. Mass. Bur. Labor Statistics, *Tenth Annual Report,* 1879, p. 175; *Twelfth Annual Report,* 1881, pp. 86, 112–113, 118; Holyoke *Mirror,* Aug. 20, 1859; Holyoke *Transcript,* July 23, 1864, June 27, July 4, 1868, May 29, June 12, 26, 1869, Feb. 26, Apr. 9, 16, 23, 1870, May 4, 8, 11, 15, 1872.

The problem of poor relief in town was greatly enhanced by the widespread intemperance, for it was extensive among the very poorest families where public aid was often required. Money given the needy by the Overseers of the Poor found its way to saloons, and grocery orders were transmuted into rum.[54] The inflooding immigrants brought Holyoke many a problem but none more acute than that born of their extreme poverty. Calls upon the town for help for the destitute were constantly mounting. The state contributed to the support of helpless newcomers, those who had no settlement in the town and who therefore had no right to town help. But quite apart from legal responsibilities, citizens of Holyoke could not leave newcomers to starve. Even though there was work in the mills for immigrants, the problem of poor relief was greater in the sixties and seventies than in the fifties. Yet immigration restriction was not regarded in Holyoke as any answer. On the one hand the mill owner wanted the cheap, albeit untrained, labor, and on the other hand the immigrant himself was eager to help his family and friends to follow him to America. The native American workman who bore the immediate brunt of this policy of exploitation was in a hopeless minority.

In 1869 the Overseers of the Poor in desperation protested at the relief burden put upon the town by the indigent foreign element. In earlier days in New England the churches were expected to care for the needy of their own congregations. Neighborliness did most of the rest. But after the Civil War the numbers of nearly destitute immigrants made this impossible. In these years Holyoke had the largest percentage of foreign-born population of any town or city in Massachusetts. Furthermore, a large proportion of the foreigners were Catholic and the priests were primarily concerned with the spiritual not the material welfare of these parishioners. Good works might include alms-giving, but only incidentally. The parishes, St. Jerome's and the French Canadian parish of the Precious

54. Holyoke *Transcript*, Mar. 27, 1869.

Blood, were poor to begin with, but the policy of the hierarchy of buying land and erecting church buildings and
schools rather than doling out financial assistance to the
needy parishioner made the situation more difficult than
otherwise. The difference in point-of-view about Christian
duty rendered relations between Protestant and Catholic
more troubled, the more pressing the problem of charity
became. In the words of the town officers:

We believe that the truest and best interest of a church con-
sists in making provision for its own poor, and if the Roman
Church would give attention to this important element of
living christianity, by following the christian rule adopted by
every other religious denomination in town, in providing for
its own poor, it would not only relieve a vast amount of sor-
row and suffering, cheer the sick and helpless, and in the hour
of death save many a body from a pauper's grave, but it
would secure a more abiding and heartfelt respect for their
religion.[55]

The coming of the Sisters of Providence to open an orphanage and hospital in Holyoke in November 1873 eased
the situation. But meanwhile the plight of the destitute
was distressing.

The number of widows in town with children was enough
to create a problem. And still the town debt was mounting.[56] No better picture of the conditions of poverty and
squalor is needed than the description given in the pages
of the *Transcript* in August 1873, at a time when business
was booming and the town was regarded as prospering:

There is one pitiful and miserable sight which we have seen
night after night in front of the fruit and vegetable stands,
since green and ripe fruit came into the market. It is a drove
of poverty stricken children, often girls, clad only in one or
two ragged and dirty garments, down on their hands and

55. Holyoke *Town Records*, 1869, p. 9.
56. Holyoke *Transcript*, June 1, 1867, Aug. 1, 1868, June 22, 1872, Nov.
17, 1873; Holyoke *Town Records*, 1857, p. 11; 1872, p. 20; 1873, p. 23.

knees in the gutters, greedily picking out of the mud and dirt
and eating the bits of spoiled and decaying fruit which have
been thrown out as worthless. No danger that it will be left
there to mould and decay, and rise up again in our noses.
Nothing is so far gone, but that some child will be found hun-
gry enough to eat it. A day or two ago we watched some little
girls who had lit upon a spot where a few mouldy berries had
been thrown out. They clawed in the mud with their fingers,
and wrangled over the possession of a berry as if it had been
a lump of gold. One of them finally fished out a stalk of spoiled
rhubarb and seemed to find it a great dainty. If driven away,
they troop back again like a flock of famished vultures to
pick up refuse coated with dirt that a pig would reject. Judg-
ing by the famished looks and actions of the children we are
sure there must be poverty and misery and destitution in
their wretched living-places that only the sufferers know.
They are growing up brutalized by neglect, and there is no
need to wonder over the long criminal lists and the never failing police court record, when we see what training for crime
and misery these children are receiving, as their miserable
fathers and mothers received before them. They are dirty and
vile and profane perhaps, but what else can we expect? Will
the cholera take them off and half the city with them, as the
result of this neglect and abuse; or are they designed to swell
the ranks of the dangerous and degraded by and by?[57]

To many of the most acute problems of community-liv-
ing general education seemed to be the only answer. So,
feeling powerless to help the first immigrant generation,[58]
responsible native American citizens devoted their attention to education of the second generation. In this campaign the public schools inevitably played the most important rôle.

The years from 1859 to the inauguration of city government saw considerable change in the schools of Holyoke.
Earlier in the fifties the School Committee had urged the

57. Holyoke *Transcript,* Aug. 2, 1873.
58. Of the population over twelve years of age in 1870, 2,201 could
neither read nor write. *Ibid.,* Sept. 17, 1870.

need of all-embracing education. But the schools like everything else in town suffered during the lean years, the community was discouraged—at least ready to wait for business improvement before spending money—and even the general upturn of affairs in 1859 and 1860 brought no immediate help. As the agent of the State Board of Education later described the situation: "The school houses were poor, ill-furnished, and unventilated. The schools were overcrowded, ungraded, disorderly and backward." Nine school districts were supporting twenty-seven teachers and fourteen schools for about seven hundred children.[59] Most of these teachers were untrained and inexperienced. Although the School Committee valiantly announced: "Even in war, we find an argument in favor of popular education,"[60] it was 1863 before the distraught little town acted upon these convictions. Until then the old district system obtained whereby the town School Committee apportioned among the nine districts the money appropriated by the town or granted by the state but left to each district's separate prudential committee the expenditure of such sums and the hiring of the teachers. By further unfortunate division of responsibility, to the town committee fell the duty of examining the qualifications of teachers presented by the district prudential committees for ap-

59. Holyoke *Transcript,* Aug. 6, 1864; Holyoke *Town Records,* 1862, p. 17. It must be borne in mind that no clear distinction was made between separate schools and grades within a school. One building was frequently described as housing several schools.

60. Holyoke *Town Records,* 1862, pp. 14–16. This report concludes: "In those States where education is diffused and the people have access to our common Schools, the Flag of our Country waves triumphantly. In those States only, where common Schools are neglected or not established, does rebellion find its devotees. Ignorance is a fruitful source of crime, vice and poverty; education is the friend of virtue, peace and plenty. When, too, we *are* obliged to defend our country from invasions, or protect it from irruption and dissolution, how much better to depend upon an army of educated and moral soldiers than upon one composed of the vicious and ignorant. Even in war we find an argument in favor of popular education: for the Northern soldier has not his equal in education as well as bravery. Our common Schools have furnished the material to protect and preserve the best Government on earth. Do all you can, then, to sustain and improve them."

proval, an arrangement inefficient and wasteful. In 1863 the townspeople, awakened to the inadequacy of the schools, vested full authority in one committee, increased appropriations, and sanctioned the appointment of one member of the committee as superintendent.[61] Henceforward the school administration was centralized.

The new regime was a vast improvement upon the old. The School Committee, elected in town meeting, had full control of expenditures for schools, supervision of buildings and equipment, examination and appointment of all teachers. But in practice the committee turned over increasingly all responsibility of administration and direction of policy to the superintendent of schools. By 1872 the superintendency had become a job of such importance that it was made a full-time, salaried position. As numbers of school children increased and the community became more ambitious, the school system had to be extended. Expenditures jumped from $3,491 in 1859–1860 to nearly $20,000 in 1866–1867 and to over $30,000 in 1871–1872.[62]

What kind of schools resulted is not easy to estimate. Superficially the layout after 1866 was complete enough, a high school,[63] a grammar school, and intermediate and primary, ungraded schools scattered over the old nine dis-

61. The abandonment of the district system was urged by the governor of Massachusetts as a wise measure for all towns. In his earlier capacity of secretary of the State Board of Education, Governor Boutwell had had ample opportunity to judge of the comparative advantages. His findings in this matter were presented at length by the Holyoke School Committee in 1863 and convinced the town. Holyoke *Town Records,* 1863, pp. 12, 25–29; 1864, pp. 15–19.

62. Confining this superintendency to one of the committee unfortunately necessitated a shift of superintendents at least every two years, the term of the school-committeemen, so that experience counted for little, since committeemen were rarely reëlected. Up to 1868 the salary was extremely modest, less than $525. Boosted to $800 and then to $1,200, the salary in 1872 was set at $1,600 when the post was made a full-time job. Holyoke *Town Records,* 1860, p. 9; 1866, p. 11; 1867, p. 10; 1872, p. 29.

63. When in 1862 the high school of District No. 1 was converted into a town high school, the old Academy in Baptist Village which had served as a high school for District No. 3 was closed. All advanced studies thenceforward were carried on in the town high school. *Ibid.,* 1854, p. 4; 1864, p. 17.

tricts. The buildings were sufficiently numerous and well equipped to compare well with those of neighboring towns. But what was the quality of education to be had here? Was it such as to be most useful to a mill population? Did it reach the persons who most needed it? When the state agent who had once so condemned Holyoke public schools spoke in 1864 of "the truly admirable condition of the schools of which the citizens of Holyoke may justly be proud," and when again four years later a similar official pronounced Holyoke schools excellent,[64] the flattering phrases probably did not refer only to the physical aspects of the schools. Nominally at least the breadth of education was notable.

Beginning at the top of the pyramid, with the high school, superintendent and principal in 1864 mapped out a graded curriculum of some flexibility. Before then there had been no definite, prescribed progression from one study to another. Although there had been a village high school since 1852 the first class to be formally graduated was one of six young women in that summer of 1864. Boys and girls with no intention of graduating were still encouraged to enter the high school and pursue studies at random for a time rather than to forego further schooling altogether. The first curriculum was revised at intervals. Latin was required and "the study of General History, Constitution of the United States and Moral Philosophy" introduced in 1865. A year later the range of subjects included also arithmetic, algebra, physical geography, English analysis, English literature, rhetoric, Greek, mental philosophy, natural philosophy, chemistry, astronomy, reading, spelling, and writing, and in 1871–1872 vocal music was added.[65]

64. Holyoke *Transcript,* Aug. 6, 1864, Sept. 19, 1868.
65. *Ibid.,* Dec. 1, 1866; Holyoke *Town Records,* 1865, pp. 28–30; 1866, p. 31; 1872, p. 37; *Report of the School Committee,* 1868, p. 10. Penmanship, cherished art before the day of the typewriter, was carefully fostered. In 1867 the senior class, in recognition of their superior penmanship, were presented with a stand of stuffed birds under glass, which the class, in turn, gave to the school.

The question of the relative emphasis to be put upon the teaching of the classics and of natural science early concerned the School Board. "In a manufacturing town," stated the report of 1865, ". . . mathematics and the natural sciences ought to be extensively studied and thoroughly mastered in the schools. A knowledge of these branches is indispensable to success in manufacturing or the mechanic arts, and in some form of one or the other, most of our youth will pass their lives."[66] Doubtless in consequence of this point of view in 1868 the school authorities added new scientific courses, geology, natural history, and surveying.[67] There remained, however, the problem of training students who in order to go to college must have a classical education, Greek as well as Latin. Furthermore, through the sixties girls outnumbered boys in the high school so that a strictly utilitarian, scientific education seemed undesirable. The principal attempted three distinct courses of study, "a regular and a classical of four years each, and an English department of two years," the last to be a "thorough, practical business course." Unfortunately the classical course soon proved too superficial to give that "admirable preparation for Collegiate education"[68] hoped for, and not until 1873 were the classics taught here with a thoroughness which enabled boys to go direct to college from the Holyoke High School. Nor is it likely that the scientific courses were better taught in the sixties. Only a small proportion of each entering class completed any four-year course.[69]

66. Holyoke *Town Records,* 1865, p. 16.

67. *Ibid.,* 1869, p. 35. How thorough the course in geology was may be questioned, but there was an occasional field trip. In 1866 Professor Gunning of Amherst took a group of adults and high school students to see the dinosaur tracks north of the town and lectured to them on the glacial theory. Where the Baptist fundamentalist was so strongly entrenched, perhaps this speaks well for the high school administration. Holyoke *Transcript,* May 5, 1866, Aug. 22, 1868.

68. Holyoke *Town Records,* 1869, pp. 22–23, 34, 35; 1872, pp. 26, 39–41; 1873, pp. 39–40.

69. Of the class of 1868, two out of twenty-six were graduated; of the class of 1869, six out of twenty-two; of the class of 1870, six out of seventeen. *Ibid.,* 1869, p. 36; 1870, p. 42; 1871, p. 34.

In the grammar school, the course of studies included the three "R's," English grammar, some American history, and geography. Gymnastic exercise and singing were added in 1871. Anxious to make the grammar school as effective as possible, the School Committee laid out in 1870 a curriculum designed to cover four years, with spelling, reading, and writing, arithmetic to decimal fractions, and "Geography—through New England," as the first year's work.[70] Since the grammar school principal himself noted that most pupils left the school at the end of one year, such education as they had by then achieved was all they would ever get. Were opportunities to make more intelligent citizens needlessly lost here? A great proportion of Holyoke school children were taught only to read, write, and spell, to memorize multiplication tables, to solve simple arithmetic problems, and to have an idea of New England geography. After 1871–1872 they were taught a little singing. An ingenious teacher might occasionally impart fragments of other knowledge, incidentally, by way of illustration, or through directed reading. But for wider general information children must rely upon the excerpts in the Graded National Series of *Readers* and in Parker and Watson *Readers*.[71] Yet seven years of schooling were allotted to acquiring these tool subjects,—two years in the first primary, two in the second primary, two in the intermediate grades, and one year in the grammar school. The pace set seems intolerably slow. In the grammar school a class in

70. *Report of the School Committee,* 1867, pp. 10–15; Holyoke *Town Records,* 1870, p. 47. Following this year's work besides arithmetic, writing, and spelling, children were to study in the second year, "Geography completed," "History—through American Revolution"; and in the fourth, "Physical Geography," "Grammar—Analysis of Sentences," "History—through Civil War and Review," weekly exercises in composition and declamation, drawing lessons twice a week; and daily singing and "gymnastics, physical and vocal" were included for every grade. Holyoke *Town Records,* 1870, *Course of Study for the Public Schools of Holyoke,* adopted Aug. 8, 1870, pp. 1–7.

71. Holyoke *Town Records,* 1870, pp. 46–47; 1872, p. 37. The average age in the grammar school in 1868 was thirteen years and six months. *Report of the School Committee,* 1868, p. 15.

American history succeeded in covering only eighty pages of the text in the course of a whole year.[72]

But the fundamental problem of educating Holyoke's future citizens had to be met in the primary grades, for comparatively few got beyond the fourth grade. Of 1,100 children of school age in 1865 only about 100, of 2,000 in 1870 only 159, were registered in the grammar school, while high school enrollment averaged near 50. The superintendent of schools, without precedent to guide him, devised a general pattern of work for these elementary pupils. The amount of work planned for these first six grades had to be meagre, for many pupils labored under a language handicap, coming from homes where English was scarcely understood, where Gaelic or German or the French Canadian patois was habitually spoken.[73] Moreover the primary grades were badly understaffed and in some schools at some periods there were as many as seventy or eighty pupils for one teacher to instruct. Such congestion hurt the whole school system, for to relieve the lower grades pupils were promoted who were not ready. Nevertheless there was some excellent teaching. Many teachers brought the gentleness and patience of the home missionary to give to their rough little immigrant pupils a conception of civility as well as letters. And improved methods of instruction were constantly sought. As early as 1871 the superintendent was encouraging the use of the word method of teaching reading, an innovation in many public schools fifty years later.[74]

Despite many capable teachers discipline was frequently

72. Holyoke *Transcript,* Mar. 19, 1870.

73. *Ibid.,* Jan. 28, 1865, Aug. 27, Sept. 24, 1870; Holyoke *Town Records,* 1864, pp. 25–27; 1865, p. 20; 1866, pp. 28, 35; 1871, p. 39; *Course of Study,* 1870, pp. 1–6. A high school entrance examination required after 1866 was instrumental in cutting down numbers. *Report of the School Committee,* 1867, p. 21; Sumner Whitten (interview).

74. Holyoke *Town Records,* 1864, pp. 15–16; 1865, p. 19; 1866, p. 24; 1870, p. 46; 1871, p. 37; 1872, p. 35. *Report of the School Committee,* 1867, pp. 4–6; 1868, p. 2; Holyoke *Transcript,* June 1, 1867. There were reported to be 120 more pupils in the Chestnut Street School than there were desks for in the spring of 1867. Holyoke *Transcript,* Apr. 27, 1867.

hard to maintain. The School Board reluctantly permitted teachers to resort to corporal punishment where moral suasion proved vain, because the alternative of turning out the offenders to roam the streets threatened to create a worse problem than it solved. More acute was the question of irregular attendance and of truancy. Irregularity in attendance, frequent because of parental thoughtlessness or ignorance, was accentuated by health problems. In the year of the first smallpox epidemic school attendance was so broken up as to cause the loss of nearly a whole term in every school. Truancy was a greater difficulty. Its prevalence led the town to enact a by-law empowering the Overseers of the Poor to send to school any child of school age who was found wandering about the streets without lawful occupation. But so vague an authorization was useless and truancy continued to grow. The superintendent of schools in 1872 listed 538 cases among 1,600 school children. But his plea for regular truant officers and a special school for truants went unheeded.[75]

Even more discouraging was the number of children of school age who never attended school at all. Some of these the superintendent described as "students in the public or private haunts of vice and crime,"[76] but many were employed in mills and shops. A state law of 1867 stipulated that all children under fifteen years of age must be sent to school at least three months out of every year under penalty of fine to be collected from the employer, but a survey conducted by the Commonwealth in 1869 revealed a general disregard of that law. In the 151 mill towns where child labor was used, between 5,000 and 6,000 children under fifteen were estimated as employed in mills and shops, of whom about 60 per cent could read and write. Not only mill-owners' cupidity or indifference but the poverty of the parents brought about the frequent evasion of the law.

75. Holyoke *Town Records,* 1860, p. 14; 1866, p. 33; 1871, pp. 32, 37; 1872, pp. 43–44; 1873, pp. 36–37; *Report of the School Committee,* 1867, p. 5; 1868, p. 2; Holyoke *Transcript,* Sept. 16, 1865, June 1, 1867, May 30, 1868.

76. Holyoke *Town Records,* 1872, p. 44.

Holyoke was probably no worse than other mill towns in this respect. When parents lied about their children's ages in order to get them employment, it was nearly impossible to improve matters greatly. Yet many children under age were known to be at work in the mills here with no regard to schooling.[77] The figures of the superintendent of schools in 1873 listed 2,318 children between the ages of five and fifteen with an average registration in the public schools of 976 and an attendance averaging spring, fall, and winter of 767. Misleading as these statistics are until we add the 700 children by this date enrolled in the Catholic parochial schools, still it was plain that the schools were not reaching a large number. Considering that school appropriations were generous, the results were not satisfactory.[78]

Evening classes for mill hands were opened one winter, since many persons viewed it as an opportunity and a duty to educate the ambitious illiterate, even if adult. When in 1869 some twenty mill girls paid out of their earnings $2 for tuition in an informally organized night school, need of a free public evening school was manifest. The next year a staff of eight teachers carried on classes three evenings a week for nine weeks. Their pupils used whatever books they owned or could borrow. Although attendance averaged 111, the town voted to abandon the evening school in order to devote the $500 to reducing the town debt. Fortunately evening classes for girls were organized by the nuns in the Catholic Convent School.[79]

To the public schools of Holyoke in the fall of 1869 was added a Catholic parochial school. In many ways it was a

77. Holyoke *Transcript,* Mar. 20, 1869. The Bureau of Statistics of Labor in 1874 commented that the law was bound to be a dead letter since parents refused to coöperate. Mass. Bur. Labor Statistics, *Fifth Annual Report,* 1874, p. 5; *First Annual Report,* 1870, p. 319; *Third Annual Report,* 1872, pp. 350, 175–176.

78. Holyoke *Town Records,* 1873, p. 37. In 1869 Holyoke held first place in the county and seventy-second place out of 340 in the state for amount of school appropriation. Holyoke *Transcript,* Apr. 24, 1869.

79. Holyoke *Transcript,* Apr. 11, 1868, Feb. 20, Mar. 13, Apr. 3, Oct. 23, 1869, Jan. 8, 15, Mar. 5, 26, 1870; Holyoke *Town Records,* 1869, p. 28; 1870, p. 29.

boon to the town, for it instantly relieved some of the crowding in the public schools at no public expense. Father Harkins of St. Jerome's had long been determined to have Catholic children given a more thorough religious education than they could receive from instruction after regular school hours and on Sunday. Thus he arranged to bring from Cincinnati four sisters of the Order of Notre Dame to establish a convent and conduct a girls' school. It was a big undertaking for a poor parish, but the school was opened in September with 207 girls entered. This number increased rapidly and in December two more nuns came. Four day-time classes were soon in full running order and an evening school and a Sunday School at St. Jerome's started. The regular pupils ranged in age from five to seventeen. Although Protestants may have been predisposed to deplore the establishment of a school where religion was to mark off one group of future citizens from the rest, Protestant and Catholics alike recognized the good quality of the teaching and the discipline which the Sisters offered. In the fall of 1872 Father Harkins carried farther his plan of Catholic education in his parish by opening a school for boys in charge of two of his own sisters aided by graduates of the Convent School. Three hundred boys attended the Institute, as it was called, the first parochial boys' school in the diocese to be taught by lay teachers. Whatever the ultimate result, for the time being the parochial schools eased matters for the School Board.[80]

Such were the problems confronting this growing industrial town. To solve many of them community action was clearly essential, and yet common action was difficult to achieve. The job of selectman, entailing as it did also the post of Overseer of the Poor and member of the Board of Health, was anything but easy, and $3 a day while on duty was small compensation in view of the perpetual

80. Holyoke *Transcript,* Apr. 24, Aug. 28, Sept. 11, Oct. 23, Dec. 4, 1869, May 11, June 29, Sept. 11, 21, 1872; Lucey, *History of St. Jerome's Parish,* p. 58; McCoy, "Diocese of Springfield," *Catholic Church in N. E.,* II, 670; Holyoke *Town Records,* 1873, p. 33.

criticism to which his acts were subject. The town debt was on an upward curve, and still schools, public health, poor relief, and police protection were not sufficiently provided for. When troubles loomed large on the horizon busy citizens were prone to shift the blame upon the shoulders of one town officer or another. Even town meetings came to be ill attended as years went on and private affairs grew more absorbing. Important town business had to be dispatched by a mere handful of men and some large sums of money were perforce appropriated by a few. If the townspeople themselves were not going to carry their joint responsibilities with attention, it was time, many felt, to invest the government of the community in the control of a few who would be solemnly bound to act for all. A population of 10,000 sufficed for a city charter, and Holyoke had passed that mark in 1870. Put to a vote, the town overwhelmingly favored applying for a charter; the petition was made and was granted in the summer of 1873.[81]

Some people doubtless voted in favor of a city charter because, with the kind of unreasoning megalomania characteristic of America of the seventies, they thought an added prestige would derive from living in a full-fledged city rather than a town. A few may have hopefully smelled paying jobs not accessible under the administration of the selectmen. But most of the 377 who cast votes for the charter were convinced that Holyoke had outgrown the town meeting and that her community problems henceforward could be better solved by city government. In December 1873 the town of Holyoke ceased to exist and the proud citizens proclaimed the city.

81. Holyoke *Town Records,* 1869, p. 13; 1871, p. 21; 1873, pp. 22–23; Holyoke *Transcript,* Mar. 14, 1868, May 8, 1872, Mar. 22, Aug. 2, 20, 1873, Aug. 22, 1874.

V

THE PAPER CITY, 1873–1893

THE business depression following the failure of the Great Northern Railroad in September 1873 at first occasioned no profound disturbance in Holyoke. Despite the restraining effect of the panic elsewhere, business continued active here for some weeks, mills running full and employes being paid promptly. The newly built Newton and Ramage paper mill began operations, the negotiations for bringing to Holyoke a new alpaca mill were concluded, and the Germania Mills continued to run overtime.[1]

Not until November did any manufacturers act to curtail production and so costs. And here the movement was launched by the fine writing-paper manufacturers whose markets for months had shown signs of being oversupplied. It is not improbable that, panic or no panic, part-time operations would have been inaugurated in these mills just as in June 1873. The sixty-day half-time agreement from November first on did not extend to mills making book, manilla, or coarser papers, and in most of these production and wages were kept at the summer's level. Among the textile concerns only three took alarm; one small woolen mill stopped some machinery, while the Lyman Mills and the Hampden cut wages about 15 per cent. The thread companies, the other woolen manufacturers, the wire and most of the iron workers carried on full time without wage reductions. In fact the Holyoke Machine Company and all the machinery repair men in town for a time were rushed with orders for overhauling machinery of mills on part time. In the building trades and in the sawmills the slackening of business was felt, but here a reduction of force and at most a 10 per cent wage cut sufficed to meet changed

1. Holyoke *Transcript,* Sept. 27, Oct. 1, 11, 22, 25, Nov. 5, 1873.

circumstances. The store-keepers naturally felt the pinch some months after the manufacturing part of the community, when short hours and lowered wages told in the purchasing power of the mill hands. But although the weavers in the Lyman Mill No. One and some seventy of the weavers in the Hampden Mills struck in December at the pay cuts until forced nearly three months later to find jobs elsewhere or acquiesce, wage earners were on the whole stoical and employers considerate.[2]

As 1874 turned into 1875 competent observers agreed in pronouncing Holyoke's business record for 1874 unequalled by any city of its size in New England. A number of new stores were opened and there were few failures among the merchants.[3] The mayor's inaugural address in January 1875 announced "while inactivity in business has prevailed in the country we have been flourishing and prosperous."[4] Manufacturers managed to keep the mills running and people employed enough to prevent widespread suffering even though the mill orders were sometimes hand-to-mouth affairs. As the *Transcript* suggested, the uncertainties of business in 1874 were more by way of contrast to the boom years preceding than any indication of real distress in Holyoke. Real estate prices fluctuated little, and building went on, if not at the rapid pace of pre-depression years, at least at an encouraging rate. Hordes of job hunters invaded the city all through the spring of 1875, confident that here was work for all. In May, one paper-mill superintendent reported, thirty or forty persons applied at the mill for work every day.[5] Mill heads and mill hands, builders and store-keepers, all could be grateful for having fared so well.

In fact Holyoke encountered only one real disaster, the

2. *Ibid.,* Nov. 5, 8, 19, Dec. 6, 1873, Jan. 3, Feb. 11, 14, 28, May 4, 7, 18, 25, 1874; Lyman Mills Papers, Agent's Letter Book, Bush to Lovering, Nov. 1, 4, 11, 18, 1873, Mar. 6, 1874.

3. Holyoke *Transcript,* July 15, Aug. 19, 26, Dec. 9, 16, 1874.

4. *Municipal Register,* 1875, p. 4.

5. Holyoke *Transcript,* Apr. 29, June 10, 1874, Jan. 2, Feb. 24, Mar. 31, Apr. 3, May 8, 1875.

shut-down of the Hampden Mills in midsummer of 1875. The concern, one of P. T. Jackson's last ventures, had been the first independent company to build a mill in Holyoke, and for years it had been highly successful. Its failure and the subsequent sale of the mill property eighteen months later was disturbing, first because many of the six hundred operatives were out of work for months, and secondly because this was the first great Holyoke mill to go to the wall, the first large enterprise to fail since 1858. Holyoke learned that her factories for all their power advantages were not invulnerable. Perhaps here was another example of the kind of "Boston management" which had brought the Hadley Falls Company to grief eighteen years before in the face of a somewhat similar business slump.[6]

It was a problem in times like these even for skilled spinners and weavers to find work and the fall and winter of 1875–1876 saw unemployment in Holyoke reach a height unknown since 1857.[7] Thanks to developing the manufacture of ducks and of drills for the China trade, the Lyman Mills were able to continue operations, although omitting dividends in 1876 and at reduced wage rates. Some of the trained help of the Hampden Company gradually secured jobs there and in other Holyoke textile mills, or else drifted away to Fall River, Rockville, Connecticut, or other textile towns. Some immigrants returned to Scotland or to French Canada.[8] Well might the Water Power Company congratulate itself on having rejected the plan of its predecessor of making Holyoke primarily a cotton textile city. Still the thread mills increased production steadily, installing additional machinery and expanding the plants.

6. In 1877 the purchasers of the plant began operations as the Hampden Cotton Mills. But a year later it was necessary to reorganize the company and the concern was never highly successful although by 1883 it employed 500 hands. Holyoke *Transcript,* Feb. 17, May 19, 1877, Mar. 30, 1878; *Paper World,* VI, no. 2 (Feb. 1883), 11.

7. Holyoke *Transcript,* July 10, 28, Sept. 8, 22, Nov. 10, 1875, Jan. 22, 1876, Jan. 3, 1877.

8. *Ibid.,* July 28, Sept. 29, 1875, Jan. 26, 29, Feb. 19, 26, Mar. 15, June 14, Aug. 16, Sept. 9, 1876; Lyman Mills Papers, Dividend Books; Payroll Books.

The woolen mills for the most part had orders enough to keep the machinery running full time, and while each of the four established concerns had ups and downs, nevertheless local woolen manufacture like cotton thread suffered little in the depression.[9]

Furthermore, two new textile concerns, destined to be enormously important to the city, were added to the industrial category in 1874, the Farr Alpaca Company and the Unquomonk Silk Mill. Both the alpaca mill and the silk mill were producing goods in their newly constructed Holyoke factories before the end of 1874 and both were thus directly helpful to the community in creating jobs for unskilled day labor and for skilled operatives alike. Here several hundred persons found work.[10] Both textile ventures merit further analysis.

The manufacture of alpaca wool[11] had been introduced into England in the fifties and at the end of the sixties into Canada. There in Hespeler, Ontario, Herbert Farr had invested in an alpaca mill, but when he had learned the essentials of handling the long fibres of alpaca wools he decided to manufacture within the United States where a low tariff on the raw wool was many times offset by a high tariff upon the finished fabric. Farr's negotiations with men in Holyoke began just before the panic in September 1873. Some fifteen citizens met with him to hear his presentation of the case for alpaca manufacture in Holyoke. He proposed to provide two thirds of the necessary capital from his own resources and that of his Canadian associates. If the mill building and power rights could be supplied by local capital, his money could most profitably be put into working capital, machinery, and raw materials. Some of the English help in Hespeler would immigrate to

9. *Holyoke Directory,* 1874, p. 6; Holyoke *Transcript,* Feb. 28, 1874, June 30, 1875, Apr. 8, 15, June 7, July 19, Sept. 2, 27, 1876, Apr. 28, Aug. 1, 15, 18, Nov. 3, 1877.

10. *Holyoke Directory,* 1874, pp. 112–113.

11. The alpaca is a species of llama that lives only in the high Andes of Peru. The fibres of its wool are from nine to eighteen inches long and have a silky lustre once greatly admired. But the supply of alpaca is small.

Holyoke, enough at least to train operatives here. It would cost, Farr estimated, about 10 per cent more to manufacture in the United States than in Canada, but there would be a saving of 60 per cent in customs duties on the finished cloths.

The listening citizens, a representative group of manufacturers and professional men, were impressed. Jared Beebe, as a textile expert, went to Canada to investigate, and meanwhile a committee of three undertook to interest local investors. Money was hard to raise despite the favorable reports from Beebe's Ontario trip and Farr's assurance. The upshot was that when the company was organized, capital was set at $250,000 of which Farr and his brother-in-law put up $135,000 and Holyoke business men about $100,000. The Holyoke Water Power Company financed the building of the mill and allowed the company ten years in which to extinguish the debt.[12] The Newtons built the mill on the first level canal south of the Beebe and Holbrook and Massasoit paper mills.

By spring 1874 the mill was ready for the machinery brought down from Canada and by May weaving was in process in the new saw-tooth weave sheds. About half the employes, including all the overseers with whom operations were begun, had come from Canada or England; the remaining hundred were found and trained on the spot. By June the treasurer could announce an output of about 11,000 yards of alpaca cloths, the finish of which was already better than of the Canadian product, and, predicted as soon as the new machinery ordered from England was running, a probable production of about 25,000 yards a week. This cheerful report brought in bids for the unsold 186 shares of stock. Farr departed for England to study finishing methods and soon imported a machine designed to give the goods a permanent, perspiration-proof finish. Much experimenting perfected the process; so at the Cen-

12. Farr Alpaca Company Records (office of the Farr Alpaca Company; hereafter cited as F. A. Co. Records), I, 23, 27, 71, 86; John Hildreth, Frank Metcalf (interviews); Holyoke *Transcript,* Sept. 13, Oct. 8, 11, 22, Nov. 29, 1873.

tennial Exposition in Philadelphia in 1876 the goods displayed by the Farr Alpaca Company took the highest award and elicited specific comment from the English judge. The manufacturing success of the Holyoke company was assured. A first dividend of 7 per cent was paid for 1876–1877, and with earning power thus proved the stock could no longer as in 1875 be bought for fifty cents on the dollar.[13]

A quite different type of enterprise was the Unquomonk Silk Mill, from its beginning a family-owned undertaking. William Skinner's first mill had been located upon a small stream above Haydenville, Massachusetts. In the spring of 1874 the dam of the Mill River reservoir burst, sweeping away the mills and the industrial village at Skinnerville. Skinner was then hesitating between rebuilding there and setting up in Worcester. James H. Newton's persuasiveness, however, led to a generous offer from the Holyoke Water Power Company which Skinner decided to accept. The Water Power Company allowed Skinner a $6,000 mill site, ground and power rent-free for five years, and lent him enough to pay the Newtons for building the mill and connecting the machinery to the shafting. From January 1, 1875 on Skinner was to pay the Holyoke Water Power 7 per cent interest on the investment, and was given the privilege of buying the mill and site in five years' time at the original cost. On such terms Skinner began spinning silk for spooled twist in Holyoke in December 1874.[14]

A dyer who had received his training in England, Skinner had built up his spooled silk business gradually. The loss of the Haydenville mill he put at $200,000. But a $20,000 endowment life insurance policy which matured that year gave him some working capital and the courage

13. Holyoke *Transcript,* Mar. 21, May 2, June 3, 1874, Mar. 11, Oct. 18, 1876; F. A. Co. Records, I, 22–24, 28, 34–35, 43–45, 59, 66, 118. The dumping of British goods in American markets and the fall in the price of wool had combined to make operation for the year 1875–1876 unprofitable.

14. Holyoke *Transcript,* July 1, Dec. 12, 1874; Wm. Skinner (interview). In addition, the power company presented him with a house lot to which he moved his own house down the valley from Skinnerville.

of his family ran high. The Holyoke plant was soon equipped with braiding machines which turned out a good quality of silk braid used by New York and Boston custom tailors for binding men's suits and frock coats, a product which proved instantly profitable. Thus encouraged, Skinner installed looms for weaving in 1876 and thereby began the manufacture of the silk linings which were to be so large a part of his business in a few years' time as to lead to his dropping the spooled silk line altogether. The silk mill was an important source of employment in the hard years of 1875 and 1876, for only a few employes moved to Holyoke from Skinnerville and the rest of the two hundred were Irish and American men and women trained to their jobs here.[15]

To the untiring zeal of the Newton brothers as well as to the liberality of the Water Power Company under its new agent, William Chase,[16] is due much of the honor of keeping Holyoke growing during these years. About 1872, when the Water Power Company had definitely committed itself to encouraging paper and diversified manufacture instead of cotton, D. H. and J. C. Newton entered into a deal with the company which gave to them the right to develop the then unbroken tract of land along what was to be the continuation of the first level canal between Appleton and Cabot Streets.[17] The details of the negotiation were never made public, but clearly it was beneficial to the city. The Newtons not only later proceeded to build a series of block houses—ugly, but liveable—along the stretch above and paralleling the canal, on land once reserved for tenements and warehouses appurtenant to the cotton-mill sites, but they kept watch for manufacturing enterprises which

15. William Skinner Sons Cash Book, 1875–1879.

16. Stewart Chase, the first agent of the company, died in May 1873, and was succeeded by his equally able and more genial brother. Whether the new policies of the company were the result of the change in agents or in the business conditions is conjectural only. Holyoke *Transcript,* June 3, 1873; *Thirtieth Anniversary Holyoke Daily Transcript.*

17. The arrangement appears to have been in the nature of a long-term option on the mill sites. See F. A. Co. Records, I, pp. 86–87.

might be brought to Holyoke and successfully developed here.

Thus the Newtons first organized the Massachusetts Screw Company and built the factory where manufacture began in the summer of 1874. It was no great business, employing only some fifty hands, but it fitted well with the builders' interests. At about the same time they erected a woolen mill for the Connor brothers whose small flock or shoddy manufacture had been carried on for some months in a spare room of an old paper mill by the dam. The four-set woolen mill took another corner of the Newton land on Cabot Street.[18] After the Farr Alpaca and Skinner mills were put up, a cutlery establishment, and one for file-cutting, a brace-bit manufacture, a rubber goods factory and later another cutlery concern, all helped fill the "Newton plot." In launching most of these enterprises in Holyoke the Newtons had a hand, in several of them a considerable interest, and while some of the smaller undertakings proved impermanent, they still gave to the city a variety of industry during years when it was most advantageous.[19] Neither a Fall River nor a Gary could well develop where many sources of livelihood existed.

This program of promotion and expansion redounded to the benefit of the machinery makers and jobbers. That branch of industry had not been able to maintain throughout the high pitch of activity of the fall of 1873; and midsummer of 1875 found the Holyoke Machine Company cutting its force in half. But patternmakers and inventive draftsmen used the slack season to work upon improvements of machinery to effect better methods of production,

18. Holyoke *Transcript,* July 15, 1874, Jan. 2, 1875; *Holyoke Directory,* 1874, pp. 125–126. A fire in the Connor mill not long after production began forced the Connors to suspend operations for a time. The Newtons re-leased part of the mill to a newcomer for satinet manufacture. By 1878, however, the Connors were reëstablished and doing well. Holyoke *Transcript,* Sept. 25, 1875, Dec. 9, 13, 1876, Jan. 13, Mar. 3, 10, 1877, Apr. 27, 1878, Sept. 24, 1879.

19. Holyoke *Transcript,* Apr. 10, Oct. 27, 1875, Jan. 12, May 10, 1876, Jan. 27, Feb. 14, Nov. 14, 1877, May 11, 1878, Jan. 24, 1880; *Holyoke Directory,* 1877.

and within five years' time a multiplicity of patented labor-
and money-saving devices were being manufactured in
Holyoke. Chemical pulp digesters were not in demand in
the middle of the seventies, but their use was coming and
inventors and machinery makers were at work upon them.
Meanwhile the Holyoke Machine Company began to make
several new pieces of paper machinery. In 1875 part of
the shop was rented to George Deane, the inventor of a
newly perfected steam pump, the manufacture of which was
soon to take on large proportions. While orders for small
jobbers and machinists were hard to secure, failures were
few and each machinist tended to find specialties which he
could pursue—rotary bleachers and other paper-makers'
equipment, Fourdrinier wires, bars, plates, and patented
parts, and, after the introduction of the Bell telephone in
1876, improved switchboard signalling devices.[20]

It was the fine paper makers who felt most keenly the
problem of adjusting prices and output to demand. This
branch of the paper industry was clearly suffering from
overproduction, the result of expansion in boom times. As
a considerable proportion of the fine writings manufactured in the United States was produced in Holyoke and
South Hadley Falls and the Berkshire towns to the west,
manufacturers met to discuss what to do. During most of
1874 by agreement among the producers, writing-paper
mills had run at half-capacity. Nevertheless, supply outran demand again as soon as such checks were dispensed
with, and so again writing-paper manufacturers at the end
of 1875 and through much of 1876 pledged themselves to
half-time operations.[21] But all concurred that such arrangements could afford no permanent basis for a healthy
industry. Upon increased consumption at home or export

20. Holyoke *Transcript,* Feb. 20, Apr. 28, July 7, Oct. 20, 1875, Jan. 27,
May 12, 1877, Mar. 2, Aug. 21, Dec. 28, 1878, May 7, 1879; Sumner Whitten
(interview); *Paper World,* VI, no. 2 (Feb. 1883), 8–11; J. Roy Lewis, History of the New England Telephone Company (in possession of the
author).

21. Holyoke *Transcript,* Feb. 22, 26, Mar. 8, June 7, Oct. 29, 1873, Jan.
3, Mar. 28, 1874, June 26, Nov. 20, 1875, Jan. 15, May 26, Aug. 19, Dec.
23, 1876.

or both must depend the answer to this problem of over-production.

Paper manufacture had been built up under a Republican tariff; costs were higher for American producers who consequently could not readily compete with European in the foreign market. Nevertheless, in the fall of 1876 twelve Holyoke paper manufacturers committed themselves to promoting the paper export movement, and in December of that year the *Boston Journal* reported a small shipment marketed in England at a fair price. Encouragement also was given by the Whiting Paper Company's winning an award and much publicity at the Centennial Exposition, and again in 1878, together with the Holyoke, and the Union Paper Manufacturing Company, prizes at the international exposition in Paris. Thus foreign manufacturers and dealers were made aware of the superior quality of these Holyoke papers. It was not only the prestige attaching to these awards which now enabled Holyoke manufacturers to compete more successfully with foreign, but also the fact that the increasing use of wood pulp by the end of the seventies had lowered the price of rags. American prices on fine papers need no longer be out of line because of the greater cost of raw materials. The American Association of Paper Manufacturers, formally organized in 1877 to watch over the developing trade, opened up some useful discussion of general trends. But until technical improvements in manufacturing processes further reduced costs, the agitation for developing export was bound to be futile. For another twenty years imports of paper were to exceed exports the country over, and in the seventies Holyoke paper manufacturers, like the other American producers, could find no sure outlet abroad.[22]

More desired than foreign markets, however, for the Holyoke writing-paper maker was the home market on high-grade papers. It was not easy to convince the American stationer that quality could be had in American sta-

22. Holyoke *Transcript*, Feb. 9, May 7, Sept. 27, 30, Dec. 6, 1876, Aug. 7, 17, 1878, citing the *Boston Journal*. See below, pp. 193–194.

tionery comparable to European. When Tiffany and Company of New York in the early eighties placed their contracts for wedding stationery with Whiting of Holyoke rather than with Alexander Perry of Aberdeen, Scotland, it was the culmination of a long struggle on the part of American manufacturers for recognition on a quality basis. Nevertheless, the plight of the Holyoke writing-paper manufacturer was not so serious as might appear. Reduced production notwithstanding, the Parsons Company was able to declare 100 per cent dividends in 1875 and in 1876, and the Carew Manufacturing Company in South Hadley Falls paid over 25 per cent dividends in those years.[23] By 1877 the fine quality of Holyoke papers was already creating a demand which put an end to prolonged production curtailment, and, the reputation once established, abundant cheap power plus the important asset of chemically pure wash water indicated that Holyoke could maintain her advantage in the American market for high-grade papers.[24]

Meanwhile cheaper papers had been coming to the fore. Moses Newton and James Ramage early proved in their mill for making roofing, sheathing, and carpet-lining papers that money was to be made in other lines than fine writings. Organized in 1876 as the Newton Paper Company they continued to turn out their product at such highly profitable prices that the other Newton brothers were inspired to emulate the performance. The Connecticut River Pulp Mill for supplying wood pulp by the soda process was put up in 1876 by the indefatigable John C. and D. H. Newton, and in 1880 the four brothers jointly established a much larger enterprise than any of their

23. *Paper Trade Journal,* Sept. 5, 1874; *Paper World,* VI, no. 2 (Feb. 1883), 12; VIII, no. 1 (Jan. 1884), 6–7; C. C. Jenks (interview); Parsons Paper Co. Papers, Directors' Records; Carew Mfg. Co. Papers, Directors' Records. The Parsons Paper Company alone of all the Holyoke paper companies antedating 1880 has records available for this period. It is fair to point out that the original capital of the company, $60,000, had never been increased.

24. Holyoke *Transcript,* Nov. 17, 1877, July 10, Aug. 31, Oct. 26, Dec. 25, 1878; W. F. Whiting (interview).

earlier, the Chemical Paper Company. In the interim
James H. Newton seized the first moment of pronounced
improvement in the paper business to build in 1878 a mill
devoted to book papers. This, the Wauregan Mill, was kept
out of the field of fine writings by the prevailing conviction
that Holyoke's eight existing high-grade paper mills had
preëmpted that limited line. Sulphite pulp and the development of machine-dried writings were shortly to revolu-
tionize the manufacture of cheaper writing papers, but until then the additions to the Holyoke paper industry after
1873 were in the realm of the less competitive book papers,
manillas, or the Newton building and carpet paper.[25]

How had other New England cities survived the depression? A survey of Massachusetts industrial towns undertaken by the State Bureau of Labor in 1877 showed that
manufacturing communities on the whole had not suffered
as much as might have been apprehended. Unemployment
had not been excessive in most industries using skilled labor; and in fact between 1875 and 1877 in most branches
of textiles, paper, and metallic goods the number of employes and the number of days employed—albeit at reduced wages—had actually increased.[26] Fall River had
been crippled by a long and embittered strike in the cotton
mills and Lynn and Brockton had been affected by a boot-
makers' strike. Yet in most of the mill cities population increased at a pace to imply industrial expansion. Fall River
itself grew from 26,766 in 1870 to 45,340 in 1875, and
49,006 in 1880; Lowell from 40,928 to 49,688 to 59,485
in the same time and Lawrence from 28,921 to 34,916 to

25. Herbert Newton (interview); Holyoke *Transcript*, Apr. 22, 1874,
Feb. 23, Apr. 15, May 6, 1876, Nov. 20, 1878, Mar. 21, 1879; Newton Paper Company, Directors' Records (office of the Newton Paper Co.); *History of Conn. Valley*, II, 921; *Paper World*, VI, no. 2 (Feb. 1883), 9–11;
Private information; *Holyoke Directory*, 1880, pp. 43–45.

26. Mass. Bur. Labor Statistics, *Ninth Annual Report*, 1878, pp. 1–9;
Holyoke *Transcript*, Aug. 4, 1875. In Chicopee, however, the great
Dwight mills not only cut wages 30 per cent between 1874 and 1876 but
reduced their staff materially. Holyoke *Transcript*, Aug. 7, 1875, Feb. 26,
Mar. 11, 1876.

39,178. Holyoke's population increased from about 14,000 in 1873 to 16,760 in 1875 and to 21,961 in 1880, a 50 per cent increase during the seven years which included the panic. Boston, Massachusetts' metropolitan center, however, increased proportionally rather less except through annexation of neighboring towns.[27] It is probably inferring too much from scanty data to conclude that manufacturing communities fared better than commercial centers. Or was it that the manufacturer dared to produce for stock against the moment when markets to supply the still unpeopled west should demand goods? Certainly though prices and wages declined, volume kept up.[28]

Holyoke from the standpoint of capital investment had done well. She had added two important new textile industries, a new paper mill, a pulp mill, and several lesser manufactures,[29] and to offset these gains had suffered only one serious failure. A few merchants had been forced into bankruptcy in 1877 by having to bear too heavy inventory losses, but that situation had no effect upon the city as a whole.

The main body of wage earners, however, from 1875 to 1879 had no great cause for gratitude. In 1876, 557 assignments of workmen's pay were made. In regard to wage rates and steadiness of employment, Holyoke's average was below that for the state as a whole, so that despite numerical growth her record was not so notable as her pro-

27. Mass. Bur. Labor Statistics, *Thirteenth Annual Report,* 1882, p. 197; *Census of Mass.,* 1880, *from the Tenth U. S. Census,* pp. xii, 19, 25. Boston's population in 1870 was 250,526; in 1880, with 41,973 persons added by annexation, it was 362,839.

28. Mass. Bur. Labor Statistics, *Fourteenth Annual Report,* 1883, pp. 348–373.

29. *Holyoke Directory,* 1871, p. 56; Holyoke *Transcript,* Oct. 4, 1873, Dec. 11, 1878. By the end of 1878 a cotton dye-house and bleachery, opened in the fall of 1873, was proving itself a most successful enterprise. D. Mackintosh and Son was to be a considerable establishment in the last decade of the century. Mackintosh, so the story runs, had been a dyer at the Hampden Mills. Discharged in 1872 he had the courage to start up his own dye-house, little more than a cleaner's establishment, and from that beginning he built up his plant even during the depression to a business handling one and a half tons of goods a day.

moters liked to think.[30] Perhaps William Whiting in his
mayoral inaugural speech in 1878 summarized the case
fairly when he said: "If we were not so fortunate as appeared, neither are we so impoverished as some profess to
believe."[31] After the hopeless strike of the Lyman Mill operatives at the beginning of 1874 there were no labor troubles for mill owners. When some of the employes at the
screw mill protested the 30 per cent cut in wages within a
six months' period in 1876, their places were filled so
quickly from among eager applicants that workers thenceforward quietly accepted what they could get. Unskilled
day-labor was less docile. Several times contractors had
strikes to face out.[32] And in 1876 a mass meeting of unemployed heard leaders urge a march upon the City Hall
to demand of the Board of Aldermen the building of a new
sewer to supply work. "We did not come to this country to
starve," cried one.[33] In the fall of 1878 women who had
supported families on their earnings as rag-sorters in the
fine writing-paper mills had also to resort to the city for
help when their hours of employment were cut down.[34] Unquestionably there was misery and want which was never
told. But when the boom came people forgot as quickly as
possible the pinch of the hard times gone by.

So came the lush years of the eighties. The upturn in the
business cycle began in 1879 and was so marked by midsummer that in Holyoke the Water Power Company was
reported to have sold more real estate in six months than
in the preceding five years. There was more building in the
city than at any other one time in the thirty years of its
life. All lines of manufacture boomed. Demand had more
than caught up with supply, and the investing capitalist
must look with favor upon a site which until 1881 offered

30. Holyoke *Transcript,* Mar. 31, 1875, Jan. 13, 24, 1877; Mass. Bur.
Labor Statistics, *Ninth Annual Report,* 1878, pp. 7–9; *Fourteenth Annual Report,* 1883, pp. 365–375. Employes in Holyoke in 1875, however,
averaged higher wages than in Chicopee, Newburyport, or Lowell.

31. Holyoke *Municipal Register,* 1878, p. 6.

32. Holyoke *Transcript,* Dec. 18, 1875, June 7, Aug. 2, 1876, July 28,
1877, Oct. 9, 1878.

33. *Ibid.,* Sept. 16, 1876.   34. *Ibid.,* Dec. 25, 1878.

unlimited cheap water power. So many opportunities to rent space and power to infant industries of considerable potential growth presented themselves to the Water Power Company that in 1881 the directors decided to erect a large mill on the first level canal to house such new enterprises. The rooms of the Cabot Street mill, as it was called for twenty-five years, were quickly leased, an envelope company, a publishing firm, manufacturers of card and glazed paper, of blank books, and in 1882 of imitation sealskins, being the first of a series of occupants.[35] As was hoped, the companies thus inexpensively started were again and again to grow to the point of moving into mills of their own, and the space was then released to newcomers.

So great was the expansion in the local paper industry that suddenly the Holyoke Water Power Company awoke to the fact that its power resources might be exhausted before its real estate was bought up. In 1880 the company had employed a hydraulic engineer to check the amount of water used by manufacturers leasing power. Gauges installed in the wheelpits registered the amount of opening at the gates and the head on the wheels so that readings twice every day revealed the drawing of any water used in excess of what the user paid for. These measurements and insufficiency of water in the canals that summer of 1880 resulted in several drastic revisions of earlier arrangements.

In the first place, the company, realizing that its permanent power was already nearly all sold, made ready a new form of lease, namely, indentures for what are called nonpermanent mill powers, rights to power only after the permanent mill powers have been supplied. Such non-permanent powers were, of course, less satisfactory, and for manufacturers who might wish to expand in Holyoke here

35. *Ibid.*, July 26, Aug. 9, Nov. 8, 12, 19, 1879, Jan. 3, 1880, Feb. 2, 1882; *Holyoke Directory,* 1884, pp. 319–325. It seems probable that the success of the Newtons in the preceding years in developing the land along the first canal between Appleton and Cabot Streets by bringing in new industries influenced the Water Power Company to embark for itself upon similar development of the adjoining sites.

was sad news. Rumor had it that the power company was definitely discouraging the building of further paper mills in town, and the *Paper World*, a widely read trade journal published in Holyoke after 1880, prophesied that the new paper mill then rising on the second level canal would be the last of its kind in the city.[36] Converters, blank book or envelope makers, and makers of sundry subsidiaries might find place here, but mills manufacturing paper required too much water. To make the 150 tons of paper turned out daily by the twenty-three paper mills an amount of water was used that had already proved taxing to the supply.

In the second place, the company urged upon lessees the installation of the most efficient water wheels to be bought, and to promote knowledge of these built beyond its Cabot Street mill an elaborately equipped testing flume where accurate hydraulic power tests could be made.

Most important of all, in August 1881 the company published regulations whereby users of water power in excess of what their indentures entitled them to were to pay at a much higher rate for the use of these surplus powers. Instead of $300 a year per sixteen-hour-day mill power and $150 additional for night power, lessees of surplus powers must pay $4 a day for twelve-hour use per mill power up to 50 per cent of the amount allowed by their indentures and for the remaining 50 per cent $8 per mill power. The gauges in the wheelpits would register data from which would be computed the exact amount drawn. Paper manufacturers protested in vain.[37] Even if they had to use considerable surplus water, they were getting power cheap. Steam power was estimated in 1880 as costing at least $19.89 per horsepower a year, over four times the cost of water power, and three years later the difference was

36. *Paper World,* II, no. 1 (Jan. 1881), 21; Holyoke *Transcript,* Feb. 25, 1880, July 16, 1881; History of the Holyoke Water Power Company.

37. Holyoke *Transcript,* Aug. 13, 20, 24, Nov. 5, 1881. Manufacturers admitted that charges for extra water were just when the river was low. But when water was going over the dam and so wasted, opponents of the new regime considered the rates unfair. As a minor concession, the company agreed for six years to lower the surplus rates for night use from $8 to $5 per mill power.

figured to be much greater. The *Paper World* estimated
the cost per horsepower if coal were used ten hours a day to
be nearly $20 a year, whereas for indentured twenty-four-
hour mill powers the rate in Holyoke amounted per horsepower to only $6.93. As 84 of the 140 water wheels in Hol-
yoke ran continuously from Sunday midnight to Saturday
midnight, the economy is clear.[38]

Still, any limitations on the use of power notwithstanding, Holyoke increasingly was coming to be known as the
Paper City. Four new paper mills were erected in 1880.
Besides these a fifth company was launched in that year
and began manufacture in the old wooden mill bought of
the Crockers. Henceforward, save for the enlarging of
plants or buildings for concerns already established here,
no significant additions to the manufacturing interests of
the city were to be made in any field not connected with
paper. Of the manufacturing phases of the industry two
features are noteworthy about the development here at this
time—one, the rise of mills for making cheaper writings,
machine-dried, engine-sized papers; the second, the technical changes brought about by the growing use of wood
pulp. Indeed perhaps one is the corollary of the other.

The older methods of making paper had called for final
sizing with glue made from rawhide after the sheets of
paper had come from the machine. Writing paper was
dried by hanging on racks in lofts, and the labor of handling the sheets this way was considerable. The innovation,
therefore, of drying the paper on the machine, generally
by steam, insured reduction of costs. Adding rosin sizing
to the fluid half-stuff in the beater engines also eliminated
a process, and while no one pretended that the paper so
made was as fine, as strong, or as white, as what could be
produced in the old way, still it was reasonably satisfactory for school pads and many other ordinary purposes. A
third method combined the use of some rosin engine-sizing

38. *Holyoke Directory*, 1881, p. 9; *Paper World*, VI, no. 2 (Feb.
1883), 5. State census figures list somewhat fewer wheels, but as the
Paper World was published in Holyoke it is more probably right.

with additional animal tub-sizing. Further cheapening of quality could be achieved by using part wood pulp with rag stock and eventually by eliminating the rag content altogether. The possible variations on the theme of cheapening were many.

Up to 1880 most Holyoke paper makers had made high grade writings, envelope, book, or collar papers only. The policy of the old guard, headed by J. C. Parsons, was to continue the established lines, to limit output somewhat if need be but to sell at a good profit. But a new school of paper men was growing up in Holyoke, among the foremost J. S. McElwain, since the early seventies virtually the manager of the Parsons Paper Company. With difficulty the younger man had persuaded Parsons to bid for and accept the government contract for stamped envelope papers and later for government postcard papers. The profit per ton was not what Parsons had been accustomed to, but the volume was great and the free advertising given by securing the contract enormous.[39] Now, as the eighties dawned, again new fields opened up with the possibilities of manufacturing machine-dried writings for a rapidly growing public demand. The uses for paper, the editor of the *Paper World* announced, increased fourfold between 1870 and 1880.[40] Some of the older Holyoke companies elected to eschew the cheaper lines. McElwain, despairing of getting Parsons to seize this opportunity, undertook himself to start a new concern dedicated to machine-dried writings. So the Nonotuck Paper Mill was built. Very soon thereafter four other new enterprises were launched, three of them upon the manufacture of machine-finished papers, the fourth upon book paper. So successful were these cheaper lines that the part-owner of three plants built a

39. Private information.
40. *Paper World,* II, no. 1 (Jan. 1881), 13; VIII, no. 1 (Jan. 1884), 4–5; Private information; Holyoke *Transcript,* Oct. 15, 1870; Parsons Paper Co. Papers, Directors' Records; *Holyoke Directory,* 1880–1881, pp. 10–12. The government built in 1879 on Race Street a plant for printing the government envelopes and postal cards and for nearly three years this was operated here. Holyoke *Transcript,* Sept. 13, Dec. 10, 31, 1879, Jan. 3, 1880, Apr. 16, June 1, Aug. 31, 1881.

fourth mill in 1882, also devoted to machine-dried lines. The Parsons Company, on the other hand, as if to emphasize its adherence to a regime of quality, bought the old mill next to its own and began the manufacture of ledger and bond papers of the best grade.[41]

Fundamentally there was little change in methods of production, save in the introduction of wood fibres. But a number of improvements were made in the eighties which reduced manufacturing costs of rag papers too until American producers could sell at prices to compete abroad. Labor-saving devices, such as rag-cutters, more economical trimming machines, better dandy rolls, cut costs, and, more important still, the improved machines could be run so much faster than before that skillful tenders could put through in a week amounts of paper previously undreamed of. Thus again overhead charges were brought down.[42]

To what extent the Holyoke mills in the eighties could be said to be producing fine writing papers rather than cheap papers might be a question of controversy. It is partly a matter of definition of terms. The answer also must depend upon the exact moment to which one refers, as most of the manufacturers changed their lines somewhat from time to time, dropping collar paper, for instance, to concentrate upon engine-sized writings, or shifting from book to envelope papers. Few are the companies which never varied their type of output, at least experimentally. When it came time to replace machinery or to contrive an addition to floor space it was not difficult to change the quality of product. But if, by definition, fine papers are to be differentiated not by processes of manufacture but by percentage of rag content, then the problem becomes still harder to solve. Sulphite, wood pulp derived chemically by cooking the spruce or other chips with sulphurous acid,

41. Private information; *Holyoke Directory,* 1880–1881, pp. 43–45; 1884, p. 320; *Paper World,* III, no. 4 (Oct. 1881), 3; Parsons Paper Co. Papers, Directors' Records.

42. *Paper World,* VI, no. 3 (Mar. 1883), 25; VIII, no. 1 (Jan. 1884), 4–5, 7; Holyoke *Transcript,* Nov. 16, 23, 1881, Dec. 22, 1882, Apr. 8, 1884, Aug. 1, 1885; *Holyoke Directory,* 1884, p. 386. South America was one of the chief foreign markets for United States paper at this time.

was little known in Holyoke before 1884. But the Newton soda pulp mill had been turning out four tons a day as early as 1876 and the trick of mixing soda pulp or mechanically ground wood pulp with some stronger fibre was perfectly familiar by 1880.[43] Which mills first resorted to partial use of soda pulp, ground wood, or sulphite, in what proportions they were used at any given date, and how the mixing of fibres was worked out, no one today, in the absence of records, can be sure. One concern, so the story goes, anxious to preserve its name as a producer of high grade papers, had its sulphite delivered to the mill at night so that passers-by might not see the tell-tale evidence of cheapened quality.[44]

But whether or no according to most exacting standards Holyoke manufacturers specialized in fine papers, such was their reputation. In 1883 the city, already recognized as the greatest paper-making center in the world, saw 177 tons produced daily and most of it pronounced fine writing paper. A year later tonnage had risen to 200 tons daily. Thanks, however, to the extending of the government postal service the yearly consumption of paper in the United States had increased by about 2,400 tons and Holyoke mills continued to run profitably.[45] The last four new mills built in the city were given over to making the best grades of paper only.

Such tremendous increase in production inevitably resulted in a reaction, and 1884 and 1885 caught Holyoke paper manufacturers in a new period of depression. But

---

43. *Paper World*, IX, no. 3 (Sept. 1884), 12; *Holyoke Directory*, 1880–1881, p. 12; *History of Conn. Valley*, II, 921; Ralph Snell, Sumner Whitten (interviews); Private information.

44. Private information; Holyoke *Transcript*, Aug. 4, 1880.

45. Here, the *Paper World* declared, paper makers encountered no competition because they could always sell more than they could make. "It is no boy's venture when a paper mill is built here; it can hardly be termed a venture at all. There is a surety about the future of the mill that says in unmistakable language; I shall build a paper mill; I have plenty of capital and shall not owe a cent; my experience is of the very best; I know before I make the paper where I can sell it." *Paper World*, VI, no. 2 (Feb. 1883), 14; VIII, no. 1 (Jan. 1884), 8–9; IX, no. 1 (July 1884), 12–13.

this was short-lived, though connected in manufacturers' minds with the Democratic national administration. Business men inclined to agree that the election of Cleveland after twenty-four years of Republican party control in Washington had a noticeably depressing effect upon manufactures. Nevertheless early in 1885 Holyoke paper mills ran full time on orders and by 1887 the paper trade was again booming, in Holyoke even as markedly, so far as volume went, as in 1881.[46] As soon as Harrison's election in 1888 could be safely anticipated, markets improved everywhere. Tariff legislation had no immediate bearing upon these facts, as changes in schedules had been minor. Like the White Queen, Holyoke manufacturers rather suffered from apprehensions than from actual injuries.[47]

In 1888 mills again increased their output, until by the fall of 1889 an estimate placed the increase in the local tonnage on loft-dried writing paper at twenty-five tons a day, or 20 per cent over what it had been in 1887. And when machine-dried writings were included in the figures the increase could be put at 85 per cent. Rumors began to float about that a trust was to be formed to control output and prices, based perhaps on news of several informal meetings of manufacturers held in Holyoke. But there was no serious effort to bring about any such combination. By 1890 business in fine writings was unusually good, owing, it was declared, to the new paper tariff, and so far from curtailing production Holyoke paper makers saw two new mills begun the next year which were materially to add to the total.[48]

46. Holyoke *Transcript,* Oct. 23, Nov. 18, 1884, Jan. 11, 18, Mar. 16, July 25, Aug. 1, 1885; *Paper World,* IX, no. 6 (Dec. 1884), 18; XIV, no. 3 (Mar. 1887), 4; XIV, no. 6 (June 1887), 10, 20; X, no. 4 (Apr. 1885), 16.

47. Sentiment notwithstanding, the state statistics for the paper mills in Massachusetts show that, out of forty-nine reporting, twenty-seven mills ran full, and 67 per cent business was the lowest reported for 1887. Massachusetts Bureau of Statistics, *Statistics of Manufacture* (hereafter cited as *Statistics of Mfg.*), 1886, 1887, p. 69.

48. Holyoke *Transcript,* Oct. 19, Nov. 30, 1889, May 13, Aug. 31, Nov. 22, 1890. Besides the Norman and the Linden mills, and a new Riverside

Nevertheless not all of the added tonnage of the Holyoke mills came from the new book and writing-paper plants. The Chemical Paper Company mill of the four Newton brothers was the largest in the world when it was built in 1880. Here was the example, par excellence, of quantity rather than quality output. Its production of first fifteen, soon twenty-five, tons a day of cheap manillas, wrappers, "manilla writings," as the papers made for telegraph blanks were called, cardboards, and rope papers tended apparently to discourage the small producers. There had been several attempts to manufacture manillas, boards, and wrappings in Holyoke in the years following the Civil War. The old gristmill building by the dam had been fitted up as a manilla mill in 1866 and in South Holyoke about the same time another manilla mill had been started. Both mills changed hands several times and produced several variations of coarse papers; but none of the companies were markedly successful, and the Chemical Paper Company soon commanded the field.[49] It was characteristic of the Newtons that this new venture, like many of their others, was linked with their sawmill interests. Just as the soda pulp mill used spruce and poplar chips, so the Chemical was able to utilize some of the by-products of the sawmill, although most of the pulp was sent down from the family plant in Readsboro, Vermont, after 1887 and by the middle eighties a large proportion of jute was being used.[50]

mill, there were additions to three existing mills in 1891–1892. *Statistics of Mfg.,* 1891, p. 305; 1892, p. 452.

49. R. F. McElwain (interview); *Paper World,* II, no. 1 (Jan. 1881), 21; *Holyoke Directory,* 1881, pp. 43, 45. The Mt. Tom mill, as the gristmill building was called after 1866, was occupied successively by six different companies until the Parsons Paper Company in 1881 bought the property in order to have room for expansion. The manilla mill at the end of the second level canal had an only less checkered career, and after a severe fire in 1877 was finally made into a warehouse. Holyoke *Transcript,* Dec. 8, 1866, Dec. 28, 1867, Apr. 9, 1870, Mar. 21, June 27, 1874, June 19, Sept. 15, 19, 1875, Oct. 28, 1876, Feb. 10, 28, Nov. 5, 1877, Oct. 2, 1878, Oct. 15, 1881.

50. The two builders of the family erected a new sawmill on the first level canal in 1877. Holyoke *Transcript,* Mar. 17, 1877; Herbert Newton, Ralph Snell (interviews).

Before the Readsboro plant was well begun the Newtons, urged on by

The ingenious Moses was quick to see the beauty of the builder's by-product. It was to the inventive twist of Moses Newton's tortuous mind that much of the success of the Chemical, as of earlier Newton ventures was due. In the newer plant with its sixteen mill powers and its powerful machinery for producing both chemical and mechanical wood pulp papers, a series of new papers and boards were turned out, any one of which, properly patented, would have netted the inventor a fortune—newsboard, variations of strawboards, and the like.[51] As it was, the company prospered and by 1891 was ready to buy another mill.

The Newtons had no monopoly even in Holyoke of the manufacture of some of these boards. Three glazed paper and cardboard concerns grew up here in 1880 and 1881 within a few months' time. One soon moved across the river into Springfield; but the other two from modest beginnings expanded rapidly and became not unimportant additions to the city's industry. It was largely the development of wood pulp manufacture that made these businesses possible.[52]

their able young bookkeeper, George Gill, called a halt there while they undertook negotiations together with the Holyoke Manufacturers Association to buy out the Holyoke Water Power Company. Gill argued that could Holyoke manufacturers control the power system themselves, the Newtons might more efficiently build a new pulp mill in Holyoke and have their manufacturing interests centered in one locality. The moment was favorable, as Water Power Company stock had dropped in price owing to the defalcation and flight of the president of the company. Stockholders were ready to sell cheap during the weeks in which the exact amount of the defalcation was uncertain. Only one block of shares held up the deal, that of a large Hartford stockholder who lay too ill to transact business. Days dragged by, until John C. Newton, unable to bide his time, dropped the scheme and turned back to push on the Readsboro venture. Without the Newtons the Holyoke Manufacturers Association could not proceed and the opportunity passed, never to come again. To dwellers in Holyoke it is an interesting speculation whether the course of the city's development thereafter would have been profoundly altered had the power been owned here. George C. Gill (interview); Holyoke *Transcript*, Sept. 20, 1893.

51. The soda pulp mill property was sold in the middle eighties to the Beebe and Holbrook Paper Company and the pulp manufacture was removed to the Chemical. Holyoke *Transcript*, July 31, 1883; Private information.

52. *Holyoke Directory*, 1880–1881, p. 13; 1884, pp. 320–322; 1887, pp. 351, 353.

Capital for this tremendous expansion in little over a decade derived mostly direct from the existing local industry. Newton money made in one mill was periodically put into another. Dickinson, of the Excelsior, put profits between 1880 and 1883 into three new mills. William Whiting and Parsons stockholders sponsored others, while J. S. McElwain, for years Parsons' right-hand man, in 1880 organized the Nonotuck Paper Company.[53]

Perhaps the story of McElwain and the Nonotuck deserves greater attention since it illustrates characteristic features of the expansion in the industry, namely, the small amount of capital necessary, and the way in which new companies gave openings into the employer class for employe, in mill or office, of established concerns. McElwain, in 1866 a mere boy without means of his own, had been sent to Parsons by a large stockholder in the Parsons Paper Company. McElwain soon proved himself invaluable but was unable to persuade the owners of the company to permit him to purchase any financial interest in the concern. In the Valley Paper Company, however, reorganized in 1867 practically as a subsidiary of the Parsons, he secured some stock and so from the dividends of that prospering business had a means of building up capital. When after some fourteen years devoted to the service of the Parsons Paper Company he found himself still with only one tenth of a share of its stock and encountered the adamant refusal of Parsons to enter the field of machine-dried writings, McElwain determined to branch out for himself. Such capital as he could not himself supply was provided by a few friends, among them Dwight Bradburn, to whom the management of the new mill was to be entrusted. Sixty thousand dollars in cash sufficed although the mill cost $250,000 in building. The difference between these two sums, as well as working capital, had to be borrowed from

---

53. *Paper World,* III, no. 4 (Oct. 1881), 33; *Holyoke Directory,* 1881, pp. 43–45. Much of this material here and in following paragraphs was obtained from persons qualified to speak with authority but unwilling to have their names used.

banks in Springfield and Holyoke. But bank loans were made on the basis of faith in the individual and McElwain's integrity and ability were well known.

Bradburn's share in the Nonotuck Paper Company typifies the other aspect of financing new concerns. Familiar with paper making from boyhood up, Bradburn had risen from lesser jobs to machine tender and then to superintendent of one of Holyoke's fine mills. Beyond that, head of the manufacturing, but an employe still, he could not go. Shares of stock in the successful, established companies were rarely to be had. But when McElwain, knowing Bradburn's manufacturing skill, offered the latter an opportunity to take stock in and run the Nonotuck, Bradburn at once accepted. The great and immediate success of the new company justified the faith of its founders.[54]

The prosperity of the Nonotuck had other consequences. It gave McElwain a weapon with which to fight his battles at the Parsons Paper Company where he continued to serve. The Parsons, having begun the manufacture of ledger and bond papers in 1881, extended this phase of its business until, despite rebuilding and enlarging the existing structures, a new mill with more space and additional mill powers had to be built, if the expansion was to go on. Then in 1888 came McElwain's chance. Again as years before he urged the directors to allow the superintendent and office staff of the company to have a stake in the business, if not in the original company, then in a new one. Then as the stockholders were still loath to permit any partition of the stock of the original, McElwain insisted upon the incorporating of a separate unit, the Parsons Paper Company No. Two, in which the Parsons Paper Company and a few of its servants of long standing might buy stock. Any objection to this arrangement was overcome by the realization that selfish obduracy now on the part of the original owners might result in McElwain's withdrawal altogether to put his knowledge and reputation

54. Holyoke *Transcript*, Dec. 14, 1881; *Paper World*, II, no. 1 (Jan. 1881), 22.

at the disposal of the Nonotuck. He was too useful a man to lose. Of the $300,000 capital of the Parsons Paper Company No. Two, $200,000 was provided by the parent company, the rest by men in its employ.[55]

The last additions to Holyoke's array of paper mills were all born of the profits of older firms. In 1892 McElwain's ambitions for his son led the older man to withdraw from active connection with other concerns and throw his energies into building a new mill. Here father and son together as heads of the Linden Paper Company should create a fine mill by means of McElwain experience and McElwain profits. But permanent mill powers were no longer to be leased and the new mill had always to struggle against unfavorable power costs. Furthermore, the downward sweep of the business cycle was almost at hand and the Linden, built too late to benefit by the dying boom, nearly brought the McElwain saga to a disastrous close. Similarly another Newton mill, built by James H. Newton and his son, and the Riverside No. Two were expansions financed from profits, and both beginning manufacture just before the depression set in also came close to catastrophe. Yet there was only one failure in these years, that of practically the only Holyoke paper mill without Holyoke backing. Poor management alone was to blame for its insolvency in 1891. When the property then came into the hands of George Gill, who had been a protégé of and bookkeeper for the Newtons, the mill ran with astonishing success.[56]

In these years of prosperity before 1893 a number of realignments of ownership of paper companies took place. Where a man had owned stock in several companies he now tended to exchange his interest in all save one or two in order to concentrate his holdings. This shuffling back and forth was carried on in friendly fashion simply for the

55. *Paper World,* VIII, no. 1 (Jan. 1884), 4–5; Holyoke *Transcript,* Feb. 9, 1889.

56. Holyoke *Transcript,* Jan. 19, 1881, Mar. 8, 1882, Feb. 12, 1887, May 13, 1890; *Statistics of Mfg.,* 1892, p. 452.

purpose of consolidating the expanding interests of this new generation of paper manufacturers.[57]

In marketing there were few changes. Most companies sold as before through wholesale merchants in the commercial centers, in Springfield, New York, and Philadelphia chiefly, or by direct sale to large customers or converters. But the rise of local jobbers in the early eighties was testimony to the ever increasing importance of Holyoke as a paper city.[58]

Just as the expansion of paper manufacture was accompanied by the growth of various subsidiary manufactures, blank books, pads, paper boxes, envelopes, and boxed stationery, so the development of paper mill machinery and parts went on at rapid pace. Paper trade journals began to abound in advertisements of Holyoke-made machinery and devices used in well-known Holyoke paper mills. Three new machine shops were opened between 1879 and 1882 as well as a brass foundry and one for ordinary castings. The building of new mills and extensions of old made constant demands upon these shops.[59] Furthermore the Water Power

57. Holyoke *Transcript,* Oct. 20, 1888, Jan. 19, 26, 1889, Jan. 25, 1890, Nov. 21, 25, 1891; *Paper World,* XII, no. 1 (Jan. 1886), 16; XXIV, no. 1 (Jan. 1892), 18; *Holyoke Directory,* 1890, p. 459; 1893, p. 509; *Statistics of Mfg.,* 1892, p. 452.

58. *Paper World,* X, no. 1 (Jan. 1885), 11; XII, no. 3 (Mar. 1886), 2. The jobber started here selling to the mills wrappings and papers not made in Holyoke, and later perhaps added paper-makers' supplies. Gradually the more enterprising wholesalers secured odd lots of Holyoke writing paper to market, and one of the most successful began business practically as a pedlar. Private information; *Holyoke Directory,* 1881, p. 210; 1884, pp. 255–262; 1887, p. 294; 1892, pp. 410–411; Holyoke *Transcript,* July 11, 1885, June 22, 1886; Hampshire Paper Company Papers, Letters, 1892–1893.

59. Holyoke *Transcript,* Dec. 4, 1880, May 20, Aug. 26, 1882, Apr. 9, June 26, Aug. 7, 1883, June 6, 1885, Aug. 31, 1889; *Paper World,* VI, no. 6 (June 1883), 25; *Statistics of Mfg.,* 1890, p. 402; *Holyoke Directory,* 1880–1881, p. 48. Aside from the introduction of pulp grinders and boilers for sulphites there were no fundamental changes in papermaking machinery from the fifties down into the twentieth century. Improvements were minor. When the Parsons Paper Company, sparing no expense, rebuilt and expanded its plant in 1884 the machinery which replaced the old was improved only in that it took less floor space and could be operated at greater speed. *Paper World,* VIII, no. 1 (Jan. 1884), 4–5.

Company flume tests of water wheels were giving well-earned publicity to the wheels made by the Holyoke Machine Company although after 1881 only parts were manufactured here. Besides paper machinery and its accessories, other machinery makers and workers in metallic goods developed important lines. Most notable probably was the Deane steam pump which early commanded a wide market in this country and abroad. Wire manufacture also expanded.[60]

For a time the lull in paper manufacture of 1884–1885 likewise affected the local machinery makers. The Holyoke Machine Shop in 1885 for the only time in the company's history down to 1930 had to reduce its running schedule to four eight-hour days a week. But meanwhile inventor and patternmakers were perfecting the design of a new turbine while others drafted designs for pulp machinery.[61] Henceforward to the smaller shops fell most of the local business, and the small shop continued as in the sixties to be characteristic of the industry here. Frequently foremen of an established plant undertook to invest their savings in enterprises of their own, thus capitalizing their experience in doing repair work and making parts. Before 1893 only three shops and foundries in the city employed over fifty men; most shops had under thirty.[62] Such enterprises as proved permanent grew gradually. While numerically, therefore, the founders and machinists were not significant parts of Holyoke's industrial population, their importance is to be gauged by the facts that in 1890 the capital investment in thirteen shops and foundries nearly equalled that of the woolen mills, and that total wages of the 1,048

60. *Paper World*, II, no. 1 (Jan. 1881), 21, 25; VI, no. 6 (June 1883), 6. After 1881 the Holyoke Machine Company built its water wheels in its Worcester shop. *Statistics of Mfg.*, 1890, pp. 403–404; 1891, p. 305; *Holyoke Directory*, 1884, pp. 324–325; 1887, pp. 355–356; Holyoke *Transcript*, Nov. 12, 1879, Jan. 15, Feb. 23, Nov. 16, 1881, May 13, 20, Aug. 26, Nov. 25, 1882, Dec. 26, 1883, July 4, 1885, Nov. 19, 1887.

61. *Paper World*, XV, no. 2 (Aug. 1887), 7.

62. *Holyoke Directory*, 1884, pp. 324–325, 379–391; 1893, pp. 514–515; Holyoke *Transcript*, May 5, 6, 1885, Nov. 12, 1887, Apr. 6, 1889, June 19, 1890; *Statistics of Mfg.*, 1891, p. 305; 1892, pp. 452–453.

woolen-mill employes was a fifth less than the pay of the 837 shop- and foundrymen.[63] Here was a skilled and exacting craft.

In the realm of cotton manufacture the fifteen years of prosperity down to 1893 marked fewer changes in Holyoke than in most other fields. The Lyman Mills, the largest taxpayer in Holyoke, added to the plant in 1882, bringing the spindleage up to 80,000 and the number of employes to 1,500, and in 1891 built another mill. The second generation of overseers were less outstanding than their predecessors as citizens, and remained more aloof from the help. French Canadian and a few Polish operatives largely supplanted the Irish hands of the fifties and sixties. The company carried on its business much as before, and stockholders received regular dividends.[64] The other cotton-cloth mill, however, endured only to 1885, to be replaced by a firm of dyers and dealers in colored cotton.[65] In South Hadley Falls the gingham mill, for years the pride

63. The woolen mills did not include the worsted establishment. The comparative figures of the 1890 *Census* are as follows:

Establishments	No. Employed	Yearly Wage	Capital Investment
5 woolen mills	1,048	$ 400,719	$1,533,731
5 cotton mills	2,989	1,027,847	5,554,356
20 paper mills	3,260	1,607,077	9,833,640
13 foundries & machine shops	837	530,418	1,406,594

Eleventh Census of the United States, 1890, *Report on Manufacturing Industries in the United States*, XII, Part II, "Statistics of Cities," pp. 246–253.

The metallic goods industry is listed separately and by 1895 had some twenty-eight different establishments in Holyoke with, however, only 439 employes in them all. *Census of Mass.*, 1895, *Manufactures*, V, 599–600. Of the twenty-eight, a bicycle manufacture organized in Holyoke in 1891 was expected to prove a most profitable undertaking. The failure of the enterprise was a severe blow to many individuals. *Statistics of Mfg.*, 1891, pp. 305–306; 1892, p. 452; 1897, p. 222.

64. Holyoke *Transcript*, Apr. 14, 1875, Aug. 18, 1877, Feb. 7, 1880, Nov. 23, 1881, May 26, 1888; *Paper World*, VI, no. 2 (Feb. 1883), 6; *Statistics of Mfg.*, 1891, pp. 305–306; *Holyoke Directory*, 1893, p. 512; Lyman Mills Papers, Parsons to Lovering, July 22, 1891; Dividend Books. Dividends, however, were omitted from the summer of 1884 to 1886.

65. Holyoke *Transcript*, Nov. 28, 1885, July 21, 1888, Dec. 3, 1891; *Holyoke Directory*, 1890, p. 516. See above, p. 149, note 29.

of that village, was allowed to run down, apparently bled for dividends, until it was ill-prepared to meet the depression of the nineties.[66]

But the Holyoke thread mills boomed. The older company, dropping thread as its chief line to concentrate upon warps, seines and twines, added to its mill, declared a stock dividend of $150,000 in 1882, and paid 20 per cent cash dividends at that time.[67] The Merricks had a still more spectacular development. Having completed in 1882 a large new mill where English mules and the best American machinery could produce a good six-cord thread, they built a new plant for finishing the output of both their spinning mills. With this model equipment the company successfully invaded the field of quality threads, so that in markets where Merrick 200 yard six-cord spool cotton had been a negligible factor, in five years' time it was important. Competitors began to feel the pressure and in 1888 the Thread Trust, so-called, consisting of J. & P. Coats, two Clark companies of New Jersey, and the Willimantic Linen Company, attempted to bring the Merricks into line on prices. When the Holyoke concern refused to enter into any "combine" or binding price agreement the trust threatened to cut prices till the Merricks were ruined. A sudden drop of 10 per cent in price on Coats and Clark thread was followed by another cut of 6 per cent. The Merricks met the lowered prices and yielded no jot. Rather, they added to their dye-house, increased staff, payroll, and production, and held to their course. By 1893 the stubborn Baptists were winning.[68]

66. Holyoke *Transcript,* Sept. 4, Nov. 27, 1875, May 20, July 22, 1876, Dec. 21, 1878, Nov. 17, 1890. The plant was leased to the Farr Alpaca Company for two years. Then it was renovated for cotton manufacture and changes in personnel attempted. By the nineties a cotton mill of 18,500 spindles and 386 looms was a small plant. Much of the machinery in this mill was antiquated even then and the new agent was considered brutal by the working people of the village. Bankruptcy came later. F. A. Co. Records, II, 65, 101; *South Hadley Falls Directory,* 1893, p. 480.

67. *History of Conn. Valley,* II, 924–925; Holyoke *Transcript,* Feb. 16, 1881, Feb. 18, 1882; Edward Lamb (interview).

68. Holyoke *Transcript,* Nov. 19, 1881, Mar. 4, Apr. 5, 1882, Feb. 1,

No such struggle took place in the other branches of the local textile industry. By purchasing Japanese reeled silk, Skinner found that his help could produce good quality yard goods, and Chinese silk could be used for sewing twist. The dyeing he had done in Paterson, New Jersey.[69] For the big woolen mills the eighties were generally prosperous. Although Congressional dickering with the wool and woolen goods schedules of the tariff, or rather the fear of radical revisions, gave the woolen manufacturers uncomfortable moments, the changes in rates before 1894 were not enough to trouble any concern with sufficient capital to buy raw wool when the market was favorable. A tendency was developing through the eighties, however, for selling houses to urge manufacturers to produce cheaper lines; and Holyoke woolen men all felt the pressure in greater or lesser degree. The bigger the scale of manufacture, apparently the less this pressure hurt. Only the Germania Mills continued to operate successfully on fine quality, high-priced goods. While the smaller concerns maintained production through the decade, by the nineties they were reduced to partial operation. Where quantity production was possible the local woolen manufacture did well.[70]

No enterprise in Holyoke so well exemplified the profit-

1890, Mar. 13, 1891; *Statistics of Mfg.,* 1890, pp. 389, 403; *Holyoke Directory,* 1887, p. 354; 1890, p. 462; 1893, p. 513.

69. Holyoke *Transcript,* Nov. 7, 14, 1885; William Skinner Sons Cash Book, 1879–1895; Wm. Skinner (interview). Silk-hosiery manufacture, a comparatively new industry in the United States, was begun in Holyoke in 1888 by Alexander McCallum of Northampton and a few associates. French silk workers were brought over to operate the machines. The business throve, but although McCallum kept a small branch here in the Cabot Street mill the main factory he later set up in Northampton. Holyoke *Transcript,* Aug. 11, 1888, Jan. 25, 1890; *Holyoke Directory,* 1893, p. 513.

70. *Twelfth Census of the United States,* 1900, *Manufactures,* IX, Part III, "Special Reports on Selected Industries," p. 77; Arthur H. Cole, *The American Wool Manufacture,* II, 24; Fred Webber (interview); *Holyoke Directory,* 1887, p. 354; 1893, p. 513; *Statistics of Mfg.,* 1890, p. 401; 1891, p. 305; Holyoke *Transcript,* May 26, 1880, Mar. 4, May 3, 13, June 3, 1882, Feb. 2, 1889, Aug. 25, 1891. In 1880 when Germania "beavers" for the China trade were in demand the mill ran two shifts for a time. But

able nature of quantity production as the Farr Alpaca
Company. From 1878 on the concern expanded rapidly.
Having proved its alpacas as good as English, the company embarked upon a long period of nearly unchecked
prosperity. It bought in 1878 a mill site and mill powers
for future expansion and paid for this out of profits by
1885. In 1879 the plant was greatly added to, in 1882
capitalization was increased by $50,000, and in 1890 when
a second mill was built another $100,000 of stock was of-
fered the stockholders and taken up at once. Even before
that later date the company had the largest payroll in the
city, some $4,000 more per month than the Lyman Mills.
The Farr Alpaca by 1893 had become more vitally important to the city as a whole than any other one concern
except the Merrick Thread Company.[71]

This expansion was made possible by creating step by
step during the eighties the beginning of a practical monopoly of the business in alpaca dress goods and suit
linings. The tariff was an essential feature in this development since the protective duties reduced European competition.[72] But there were other worsted mills in this country that had all the advantages of tariff protection which
the Farr enjoyed, concerns like the Pacific Mills of Lawrence and the Arlington Mills which made the cheap cot-

the price was too high to endure and the agent was obliged to cheapen
the quality somewhat. Wm. Mauer (interview); Holyoke *Transcript,*
Jan. 29, 1876, July 3, 1880, Feb. 11, 1881.

71. F. A. Co. Deeds; Records, I, 86–87; II, 8–10, 41, 47, 55, 144, 150;
Holyoke Directory, 1887, pp. 353–354; 1893, pp. 508–516.

72. F. A. Co. Records, II, 97–98. The treasurer's report for the year
ending May 31, 1886 illustrates the extent to which protection sometimes
was nullified. "The consumption of goods during the year has been large
and our sales are the heaviest we ever had, but the struggle for business
was never so severe, owing to foreign competition. Foreign manufacturers have made our market a slaughter market, without regard to cost
of goods in order to keep their mills running. In such a competition we
are of course at a serious disadvantage, for we not only have to pay
wages ranging up to 100 per cent more than our French and English
competitors, but we pay duties on our raw materials higher in some instances than the duties on goods, and of course under such conditions it
is impossible for us to retaliate on the foreign manufacturers by entering
their markets with our goods."

ton warp worsteds or alpaca and mohairs.[73] The success of
the Holyoke company was determined by two factors,
shrewd financial management, and the evolving of a few
staple fabrics of genuinely superior manufacture.

In addition to skillful purchasing of the raw wools, a
matter of vital importance in the development of the company's financial strength, the able management extended
to building up reserves of capital from earnings in good
years to use in harder times to offset such losses as inevitably resulted sometimes from drops in the price of wool
in process, from "dumping" of foreign goods, or from
changes in fashion influencing the company's markets.[74]
The treasurer insisted upon a frugal policy of writing off
for depreciation ample sums yearly out of the gross profits
and maintaining working capital regardless of dividends.
But in fact after 1877 only once, in 1882, did the company pass a dividend. The periodic expansions were financed without borrowing, and a very small margin of
profit per loom paid dividends.

The manufacturing features of the company's development were even more fundamental in its success. To create
a monopoly line required constant vigilance in details of
manufacture and intelligent adapting of product to
changes in market and fashion. By 1880 Farr and his help
had perfected a lining better finished than English, color

73. There were 10 worsted mills in Massachusetts when the Farr Alpaca was organized and 102 in the United States in 1870. *Compendium of
Ninth Census of the United States,* 1870, p. 810; Mass. Bur. Labor Statistics, *Twentieth Annual Report,* 1889, p. 307; A. H. Cole, *The American
Wool Manufacture,* I, 332–335; II, 159.

74. F. A. Co. Records, II, 43, 56, 58, 71, 73, 85, 98, 123, 164, 171, 179–
181; Cole, *The American Wool Manufacture,* II, 61–67. Judgment in the
purchase of wool was particularly important because although neither
alpaca nor enough lustre wool nor suitable mohair was raised in the
United States, the import duties upon these wools existed and were not
always compensated for in the duty on the finished goods. To manufacture worsted, the raw wool must be "aged" for a time to render it workable. Hence, since it was essential for the worsted manufacturer to keep
on hand a large stock, fluctuations in the price of raw wool were bound
to affect him particularly. Every Congressional revision of the tariff or
every proposal touching the wool and woolen goods schedules might cause
him serious miscalculation or ruin.

fast, and perspiration-proof. Other firms could not learn
the secret of its low-cost manufacture.[75] Farr in person
kept careful watch over the process of manufacture and
finishing, and worked out with the overseers and help in
the weave sheds methods of speeding up the looms so that
yardage could be greatly increased without affecting the
quality of the materials. This quantity production facilitated the capture of the lining market. When the new mill
was built in 1890–1891, Farr pushed the manufacture of
mohair, a fibre little used by other American manufacturers, and concentrated production on better-grade, higher-
priced goods, using the older cheaper lines simply as fillers.

More looms, more weave sheds, greater and greater volume of output—if the Farr Alpaca Company was to have
a monopoly its own mills must supply demand. Even by
1885 the plant had grown so that its founders no longer
could have close personal contacts with all their help. Farr
still made his daily round of the mill but inevitably to his
trusted overseers fell more and more responsibility for the
smooth functioning of their departments. Where twenty
fifty-yard pieces of cloth were made a week in 1875, by
1885 three thousand pieces were manufactured. After the
additions of 1890–1891 volume again jumped, and still
demand exceeded output. A New York commission house
served as selling agent, but as the mill's product was increasingly sought for selling became a matter of equitable
distribution to eager customers. The rapid growth of the
company occasioned no jealousy in Holyoke. Mill help
might hope for advancement in a plant which extended operations at frequent intervals, local merchants obviously
benefited by an increase in the purchasing power of the
mill people, and stockholders were fairly widely scattered

75. F. A. Co. Records, II, 10, 59, 65, 85, 111, 157. For example in 1875
Musgrave, who had been a dyer at the Farr Alpaca, set up his own little
alpaca mill across the river in Chicopee Falls. His experience was of the
best and his product at that time better finished than Farr's. But his
capital was limited, alpaca wools were expensive and hard to purchase at
any price, and the better financed Holyoke company had thus an advantage which soon eliminated the little fellow as a competitor. John
Hildreth (interview); Holyoke *Transcript,* May 5, 1875.

in the city.[76] More than was true of any other one enterprise, this was regarded as a concern in which all the community had some stake, a source of profit and employment
to a large local public.

Banking in Holyoke continued to be comparatively unimportant, a convenience to industrialists rather than a
necessity. To some extent this situation was the result of
the Water Power Company's itself acting as banker, lend-
ing money and extending credit to new concerns it brought
here. Moreover, practically every corporation had banking connections outside the city, partly for the sake of not
having neighbors or competitors know its finances and
partly because Holyoke banks were not strong enough to
lend large sums.[77] Nevertheless banking facilities did increase during this era of prosperity until by 1893 the city
boasted five commercial banks, three savings banks, and
two coöperative savings banks. Successful mill men invested in bank stocks in Holyoke, supplying capital for
the banks rather than having local banks supply it for the
mills. The banks expected to serve big mills for payrolls
and to furnish loans for small ventures, builders', store-
keepers', and private individuals'. The savings banks, fostered by substantial and public-spirited men of various
walks of life, were a boon to less well-to-do, thrifty persons, as depositors and also as borrowers. As elsewhere,
loans on real estate constituted a large proportion of the
savings banks' investments and proved in general wisely
placed.[78] The coöperative savings banks, one opened in
1880 to finance home-building on a small scale, and the

76. John Hildreth (interview); F. A. Co. Records, I, 1–10; II, 131, 134,
145–146, 151, 156, 164, 170, 200–201, 264, 335–336.

77. George C. Gill, head of City National Bank, 1902–1926 (interview).
It is significant that a private banking firm which opened its doors in
Holyoke in 1876 found in three years' time that its business was centered
in Springfield and accordingly moved its headquarters thither. Holyoke
Transcript, Apr. 22, 1876, Mar. 22, 1879.

78. Hadley Falls Bank Papers, Record Book A; Holyoke Directory,
1890, pp. 329, 481–484; 1893, pp. 364, 380, 521–524; Holyoke Transcript,
May 13, 1876, Jan. 14, 1877, Nov. 23, 1878, Aug. 27, 1879, July 12, 1882,
Feb. 6, 1884, Jan. 17, 26, 1885, Feb. 24, 1891. The oldest savings bank in
the city, for example, with $1,333,877 in deposits in 1881 owned no real

second a somewhat similar venture confined to French Canadians of the community, fulfilled their purpose effectively by enabling workmen to own their own homes
through paying on a monthly installment plan.[79] It was
thus always the impecunious mill hand, store-keeper, clerk,
or professional man, to whom the Holyoke banks were of
greatest service.

Not only the small home-builder but also the person
building tenements as an investment made use of the local
banks. Every period of industrial expansion and hence
rapid growth of population, such as took place in the late
sixties and first years of the seventies and again between
1879 and 1884 and from 1890 to 1892, saw tenement
blocks spring up, many of them as speculative investment.
Company housing for mill help had been the rule in the
sixties, but after 1873 the Holyoke Water Power Company abandoned the policy of selling tenement sites appurtenant to and inalienable from the mill sites, and thereafter the contractor-builder and the individual investor
found openings. Land for dwellings became easier to buy
because the working population was able to spread out,
particularly after the laying of a street railway in 1884.[80]
Thus contractors built small blocks for others, or for themselves, and the number of building contractors increased
greatly during the eighties. People of many occupations
and stations in life put their savings into building, sometimes in the form of block houses, often into three- or
four-story tenements. Customarily these small investors
themselves occupied one apartment and rented the rest for
enough to pay interest on the mortgage and net some cash
return.[81]

estate at all, and was able to pay a 5 per cent dividend annually. *Ibid.,*
Jan. 15, 1881.

79. *Holyoke Directory,* 1893, pp. 503–504; Holyoke *Transcript,* Aug. 7,
Sept. 25, 1880, Jan. 8, Nov. 16, 1881, Nov. 11, 25, 1882, Nov. 30, 1883, May
12, 1886, June 8, Nov. 2, 1889, Jan. 25, 1890.

80. Possibly the reduction of working hours for textile hands made
many working people willing to live farther from the mills than before
the passage of the state law of 1874.

81. *Holyoke Directory,* 1880–1881, p. 205; 1884, p. 232; 1890, pp. 336–

But as the eighties turned into the nineties, the small-scale builder-landlord began to be supplanted by the professional contractor who bought lots, built cheap five- and six-story tenements of second-hand brick and rubble, sold the building if he could, or himself acted as landlord if need be. In a measure this type of building operation had long been known here, but with the rise of the large, professional building contractor "jerry" building began to predominate in the poorer sections of the city. The bridging of the river to Willimansett in 1890 brought that part of Chicopee into easy reach of the Holyoke working-man and so checked somewhat the extent of profitable investment in tenement building here.[82] Construction, however, was not as yet carried on by incorporated companies. Lumber dealers and brick makers still played their part in the life of the business community, and the great sawmill above the dam on the river continued its activity.[83]

As the city grew, retailing expanded also. In 1883 a Grocers' Association was formed which undertook to lay down rules of fair play and common practice in matters of giving credit. Fruit stores and butcher shops multiplied. In the latter case methods of marketing were affected by the establishment first of a well-run abattoir down in Ward One on the river bank and after 1880 by the coming into the city of refrigerator cars from the west. Where the meat dealer in the early seventies had frequently bought

337; 1893, pp. 372–373; Sumner Whitten, John Hildreth (interviews); Holyoke *Transcript*, Jan. 1, 1879. The Holyoke Water Power Company itself built rows of small brick houses along streets beyond the business section of the Hill. The Newtons similarly built up a section near the "Newton plot," while doctors, lawyers, merchants, machinists, and textile hands all took a turn at building and acting as landlords. *Thirtieth Anniversary Holyoke Daily Transcript.*

82. Holyoke *Transcript*, May 2, June 11, 1890. In 1886 land east of the second level canal had sold from twenty-five to fifty cents a foot. Across the river in Willimansett lots sold at a rate of five cents a foot. *Ibid.,* Feb. 15, 1886.

83. *Holyoke Directory*, 1893, pp. 371–373, 515–516; Holyoke *Transcript*, Mar. 28, 1877, June 14, July 24, 1883, Sept. 7, 1889. The brick yards were moved across the river in the eighties. Only one lumber dealer also undertook contracting for building.

cattle on the hoof and slaughtered them himself the butcher now bought from the slaughter house or wholesaler. Milk and green vegetables in season were peddled direct by the farmers of the vicinity, and many a small householder had his own vegetable garden in his back yard. Flour and stock feed was milled in the city. But apart from the retailers of foodstuffs, the local merchants were not able to compete with Springfield on a quality basis. People who had no time to go to Springfield depended upon Holyoke stores, but it was the persons with least money to spend who spent it here. As Holyoke merchants had limited trade with the more affluent citizen their stocks were adjusted in quality and price to a poorer class.[84] Holyoke's utmost ambitions to play the commercial center were foredoomed to failure.[85]

For twenty years through depression and booms Holyoke had grown as a manufacturing community, from a village where one could greet by name every householder to a city of unfamiliar faces in which a mill head could scarcely know by sight all his own help. Capital investment in the manufacturing enterprises, and the total of wages paid out between 1880 and 1890 had nearly tripled and the number of employes risen from 8,794 to over 13,000.[86] Numbers alone and the size of the plants began to interfere with the personal relationship between mill owners and mill hands, and while feeling might still be friendly

84. *Holyoke Directory,* 1874, pp. 103, 105–108; 1880, pp. 206–209; 1893, pp. 378–406; Holyoke *Transcript,* Apr. 12, 1873, Sept. 4, 1875, Aug. 2, 1876, Feb. 1, 1879, Jan. 10, 1880, Feb. 9, Nov. 23, 1881, Nov. 11, 1882, Apr. 30, May 17, 1883; Allyn, "Sketch of Holyoke," *Thirtieth Anniversary Holyoke Daily Transcript.*

85. Another business which developed here in the eighties seems to have arisen without any particular local fitness, namely publishing. By 1885 there were eight publications printed here. Of these only two survived to 1900. *Census of Mass.,* 1885, *Manufactures, the Fisheries and Commerce,* II, 1348. In 1890 a group of business men, anxious to encourage the city's growth, formed a Board of Trade. But, as William Whiting pointed out, such an organization could not induce new stores or industries to locate here or prevent others from leaving. Holyoke *Transcript,* Sept. 13, 1890.

86. *Eleventh Census of U. S.,* 1890, *Report on Manufacturing Industries in the United States,* XII, Part II, "Statistics of Cities," p. 4.

and the skilled and conscientious workmen could still believe in their chances of promotion, the earlier intimate contacts were gone. In 1895 Holyoke ranked eighth of the cities of Massachusetts in producing value.

Outwardly the form of organization had changed very little over the whole span of years since 1873; the corporation with its mill on the canal bank always the producing unit, save in the field of machinery and metallic goods where it was the small shop. The stock of the companies was still owned by comparatively few persons, and of these the greatest number were stock owners of the Lyman Mills, the Hadley Company, and the Farr Alpaca Company. In the paper industry, the most important interest of the city, the stockholders were far fewer, some 569 names listed as owners of the thirty-two companies.[87] The number of different persons owning these stocks was obviously only a fraction of that figure, because the newer companies generally were chiefly backed by part-owners of the older. Only by inheritance were the numbers of paper company stockholders multiplied.[88] Thus for all the 63 stock companies counted in the city in 1895, 1,489 original stockholders had become 2,107.[89] As in the initial period of growth, paper manufacture continued to be controlled by mill men who lived right on the scene in Holyoke. The Springfield commuters daily were at their plants and the only case of a paper mill run by outside money and experience had been that of the bankrupt Winona. In all the in-

87. *Census of Mass.*, 1895, *Manufactures*, V, 354, 599–600. Eight hundred ninety-four stockholders owned the shares of the four cotton mills. By subtracting the handful owning the Merrick Thread Company and the Mackintoshes the remainder are to be found as owners of the Lyman Mills and the Hadley Company.

88. *Paper World*, XII, no. 3 (Mar. 1886), 3. Thus the seventeen original shareholders of the Parsons Paper Company had become thirty-seven but thirteen of these held only half shares.

89. *Census of Mass.*, 1895, *Manufactures*, V, 21, 158. The Holyoke and Westfield Railroad was included in this enumeration. In 1885 thirty-four corporations were listed as having 1,598 stockholders. *Census of Mass.*, 1885, *Manufactures, the Fisheries and Commerce*, II, 522. Unfortunately data for the holdings immediately before the depression of 1873 is not to be had.

dustries only the Lyman Mills and the Hadley Thread
Company could be said to be absentee owned, other, that
is, than the Holyoke Water Power Company itself. Most
manufacturers put profits which were not left as capital
reserves back into their plants, into other Holyoke mills,
into local real estate, and into bank stocks.[90] Whatever the
explanation—a kind of entrepreneurial provincialism, a
belief that investment in Holyoke was sounder than in
most places, the fruit of civic pride and ambition, or mere
chance—noteworthy is the extent to which Holyoke's business enterprises were locally financed with an increasing
network of intertwining interests.

90. *History of the Conn. Valley,* II, 935–937; Hampden County Registry of Probate, Inventory of Estates of representative Holyoke manufacturers.

VI

THE RISE OF THE TRUSTS, 1893–1903

WHEN Grover Cleveland took office for his second term in March 1893, business men were already expecting catastrophe. The McKinley tariff of 1890 had been offset by the concessions to the Silver senators of the West in the Sherman Silver Purchase Act, and industrialists were uneasy. Since the failure of the British firm of Baring Brothers in 1890, the financial interests of the country had been gradually feeling the effects of the withdrawal of gold to Great Britain, and coupled with the agrarian distress of the West, general economic depression was inevitable. Political emphasis on currency problems diverted public attention from industrial overexpansion. Yet the course of manufacture in Holyoke indicates that while the gold question was the immediate occasion of the slump, overproduction was an important factor in the situation. Long after the gold balance in the Treasury had been restored, business drooped in Holyoke and in spite of the victory of McKinley, the gold standard bearer in 1896, it was not until 1898 and the war with Spain that manufacturing resumed its full speed. It took five years to catch demand up to the oversupply of goods.

In a city in which economic life was as closely tied together as it was here any financial disturbance must take severe toll. The collapse of business the country over in the spring of 1893 took effect in Holyoke gradually, somewhat as after the 1873 panic. When, however, the full force of the depression struck it was more severe than it had been in the earlier slump. Here it was not unanticipated in 1893, and production in most lines had been slackening since 1892. But the monetary situation and the scarcity of coin gave a turn to affairs that alarmed people. The currency problem, gathering momentum during the early summer, became acute by August 1893. Merchants in a frantic effort to maintain trade advertised their willingness to accept checks in payment for goods. A manufacturing city with few mills running full time and little cash with which to meet payrolls presented a sorry sight.[1] But in spite of the relieving of the situation and restoration of confidence in government credit after the repeal of the Sherman Silver Purchase Act in the fall, textile mills were without orders and obliged to operate at best on part time. Fortunately perhaps the paper industry, subject as always to a lag in following the business curve compared to other industries, was not much affected until the depths had been plumbed by others. When local textiles were beginning to recover, the paper industry was just descending to its low. Only the heavy machinery makers escaped the depression, because cancelling of contracts for machinery when once placed was too costly for customers to contemplate. Still the smaller shops and plants producing metallic goods suffered somewhat like the rest of Holyoke. Building was checked and with its setback the means of livelihood of a large number employed in the building trades lapsed.[2] And as always the merchants were directly affected by the drop in purchasing power of the large proportion of their customers.

The woolen and cotton mills first shut down.[3] At the Farr Alpaca plant in June the company's product was

1. *Statistics of Mfg.*, 1893, pp. 293–295; Lyman Mills Papers, Agent's Letter Book, Lovering to Arnold, Aug. 19, 1893. Old men reminiscing in the 1930's declare the depression of 1893 to have been much more acute than today's because no one then had money. Yet they agree that farm work and food was to be had readily.

2. Lyman Mills Papers, Agent's Letter Book, Lovering to Parsons, Dec. 3, 1894; Holyoke *Transcript*, Dec. 4, 1894. The largest single contract the Holyoke Machine Company ever secured was filled in 1895. It called for the manufacture of forty-eight water wheels.

3. Of the nine leading industries of Massachusetts, a state survey undertaken for the years 1889 through 1893 showed woolen manufacture to have declined most sharply in value of product. The average decrease for the five-year period was 8.65 per cent, whereas in woolen manufacture it ran over 17 per cent. *Statistics of Mfg.*, 1893, p. 293.

sold ahead into October, but with the convening of Congress in special session in August trade broke down, orders were cancelled by every mail until it was necessary to close down the mill entirely for two weeks and thereafter start up only part of the machinery. At partial operation the mill continued through the first half of 1894, and sales dropped off 47 per cent as compared to the fiscal year of 1892–1893. A new tariff bill which went into effect in August 1894, putting wool on the free list and reducing rates on fabrics after January 1895, forced readjustments. But the Farr dividend was cut only to 6 per cent with an additional interest payment of 4 per cent on the $200,000 set aside for working capital from profits of other years. The directors wrote off a large sum from the valuation of the plant and prepared for still harder times ahead. Wage rates were not cut after October 1893, but with only three days of work a week, whether pay was by the hour or by the piece, the income of the help was painfully curtailed. Where whole families worked in one mill, as Farr had encouraged, the reduction of the family income was serious. From the capital standpoint, however, the Farr Alpaca Company fared better than most textile concerns, and with the development of new lines and the importation of grey goods to be finished at the No. Two mill in 1895 the plant ran full and profitably, despite the tariff and the greatly reduced profit per piece.

The expected renewal of hard times came in 1896 and again the mill was run on part time. In fact from March 1896 to March 1897 the company encountered the worst business in its history, and its volume of production for that twelve months was one third its capacity. But while this part-time operation was hard on the "Farr families" where father, mother, and all worked in the mill, stockholders received ample dividends partly because a higher quality goods made larger profits per piece possible and partly because of a new selling policy which saved to the stockholders the sum set aside for sales guarantee. Although curtailed output continued down into the summer of 1898, 10 per cent dividends also continued.[4]

Other woolen manufacturers faced more serious depression. Between 1893 and 1897, the Germania mill successively reduced working time and wage rates, shut down altogether, resumed on cheaper lines of goods, and operated short-handed. Once the help struck at the wage cuts, only to be forced by starvation into accepting what they were offered. In 1897 the management resorted to running the plant even if goods had to be shelved as stock, and to bring down costs per piece the number of looms was gradually increased. Fortunately heavy-weight overcoatings, the staple line of the Germania, were still in demand, although better-heated houses were bringing about a fashion for lighter-weight suitings. Thus the change of styles which embarrassed local mills manufacturing suitings did not affect the Germania till after the World War.[5]

No two textile mills in the city ran quite the same course, but all were subject to the problems of changes in fashions. Such a shift contributed to a partial shutdown of the Skinner silk mill for a while when in 1894 silk braid for binding men's cutaways and frock coats ceased to be marketable. The business man of the nineties no longer stepped forth to his office in top hat and braid-bound cutaway as his leisurely predecessors of the seventies and eighties had done. The whole Skinner mill operated in 1894 only thirty-five hours a week of the legal fifty-eight. Yet such were the fluctuations of demand that in the next year Skinner added a new building to his plant.[6]

4. *Ibid.*, 1893, p. 374; F. A. Co. Records, II, 171, 179–181, 189–191, 196–197, 200, 206, 214–215. The treasurer admitted that the Wilson tariff was in actual operation far more favorable to this particular company's manufactures than had been expected.

5. *Statistics of Mfg.*, 1893, p. 374; 1894, pp. 270–271; Holyoke *Transcript*, Oct. 1, 5, 6, 8, 1894, Apr. 5, 1897; Wm. Mauer (interview); A. H. Cole, *American Wool Manufacture*, II, 158. The Germania bought American wool ordinarily, so that the tariff affected the concern differently from the Farr Alpaca, for example. For the effect of the tariffs see *ibid.*, II, 14–28, 32–33.

6. *Statistics of Mfg.*, 1894, pp. 270–271; Holyoke *Transcript*, Oct. 10, 1895.

Cotton manufacture, while not subjected to such radical vagaries of style, was always sensitive to adversity in the business world in general.[7] Many cotton-yarn spinners found the depression years of the nineties hard to survive. The Hadley Company, in the sixties and the seventies one of Holyoke's most flourishing enterprises, was reputed to be in difficulties, the result of long continued laxity on the part of the management, the too familiar outcome of absentee ownership. A shutdown in midsummer of 1893 was followed by a wage cut and later by only part-time operation.

Even the Merrick Thread Company, able to boast in 1893 that its payrolls as always were met in cash, and the help kept on full time till the end of the year, saw fit to leave unfinished the interior of the great new building which had been begun in the spring of 1893 opposite its old South Holyoke plant. There it stood empty for six years—mute evidence of hard times. The rest of the mill was operated for only a forty-hour week in 1894. Meanwhile two events took place which had immediate bearing upon Holyoke thread manufacture, namely, the death of Timothy Merrick, and a general conference of Eastern yarn spinners upon means of securing uniform rates among mills. Four years later, from a series of such conferences the American Thread Company, the "thread trust" in new form, was to emerge. Presumably the death of the old opponent of the trust made this "combine" easier to effect, for certainly there had been no change in his company's policy before his demise. But the depression altered the aspect of business, the Merrick estate became slightly involved, and the younger generation were not of the stern stuff of the elder. In 1898 they sold out to the combine at a price of $350 in cash per $100 share. Holyoke knew the

7. It might seem that thread manufacture at least should be immune to changes in style. Yet such is not the case. The displacement by lighter garments of the old heavily boned corset, which had to be stitched and restitched with yards of thread, threatened disaster to the thread mills in the 1920's. The call for fine yarns for lastex in the 1930's has again revived the afflicted industry.

Merricks as cotton manufacturers no more. The Hadley Company, on the other hand, welcomed the invitation to join the American Thread Company as a safe way out of troubles.[8]

The Lyman Mills, like other cotton mills, faced keener competition as time went on. A considerable expansion in 1891, 250 new looms and an addition to the manufacture of fine yarns, meant added burden when the sag of business came in 1893. The varieties of fabrics manufactured had multiplied many times in the preceding fifteen years and increasingly the mill depended for its success upon the flexibility with which its output was varied. The nineties saw still greater acceleration of the shifting of looms from one line to another, as fashion changed. Weights, widths, weaves, patterns—the layman must marvel at the ingenuity with which the management met the ever-changing demands of the sales agents. To keep 2,100 looms operating with a minimum of loss in resetting for new weaves, to keep them supplied with just the needed amount of warps and filling of the right quality, and to have spinners, loom-fixers, and weavers trained to produce these variations required judgment. Disappearing were the days when certain fabrics could be considered standard and always sure of a market.[9] In 1893 already southern competition in coarse goods was being felt. In August 1893 the Lyman Mills, following the cuts of other New England cotton mills, cut wages but ran full time. For the next three years the mill continued to run with gradually increasing payroll.[10]

8. Edward Lamb, clerk and office manager of Merrick Thread Company, 1887–1931 (interview); *Statistics of Mfg.*, 1893, p. 374; 1894, pp. 270–271; Holyoke *Transcript*, Mar. 20, Dec. 28, 1894, May 24, 1897.

9. Lyman Mills Papers, Minot Hooper & Co., Letter Books, Letters to Agent, 1889–1900, Jan. 19, 1898 and *passim;* Agent's Letter Book, Lovering to Minot Hooper & Co., June 9, 1892, Jan. 20, 1894; Treasurer's Letter Books, Parsons to Lovering, Oct. 23, 1890, July 22, 1891, Oct. 6, 1893; Lovering to Parsons, Sept. 11, Oct. 10, 1893, Dec. 21, 1894. The Glasgow mill in South Hadley Falls was shut down in 1896 and no more was heard of its resuming operations. Holyoke *Transcript*, Apr. 16, 1896.

10. Lyman Mills Papers, Agent's Letter Book, Lovering to Arnold, May 16, Sept. 15, 1896; Lovering to Parsons, Dec. 4, 1894; *Statistics of Mfg.*, 1894, pp. 270–271.

But markets were uncertain and stocks accumulated. In 1896 the company succumbed to a complete shutdown, the first since the Civil War. When the mill doors reopened pay cuts followed, then short-time operation. Desperately in December some twenty-eight mule-spinners, the only unionized group of work people in the mill, struck for a return to the former wage scale. The agent retorted by closing the mill down altogether, leaving eight hundred hands without work. The strike was soon called off but "the condition of the trade" through much of 1897 permitted only alternate weeks of operation and then a five-week shutdown. Fortunately for the operatives the management refused to follow other New England mills in still further wage cuts the next year.[11]

To reduce production costs the treasurer undertook instead to secure a lightening of the company's city taxes. The great corporation with its long array of brick buildings stretching along an eighth of a mile of the best mill sites in the city gave an appearance of affluence which tax assessors could not ignore. The property had always paid the highest taxes in town and city and there seemed no reason to reduce the valuation now even though the mill management was for the time being unable to make money.[12] The case dragged on for several years and was finally settled in favor of the city. By then general prosperity was returning and the corporation could resume full operation and pay its taxes without uneasiness on the score of dividends. Wage disputes did not again occur until the mulespinners conducted successfully a ten months' strike for

11. Lyman Mills Papers, Agent's Letter Book, Lovering to Parsons, Sept. 15, Nov. 10, 1896; Minot Hooper & Co., Letter Book, Minot Hooper & Co. to Lovering, Dec. 10, 30, 1896; Holyoke *Transcript,* Aug. 14, Dec. 9, 12, 29, 1896, July 31, 1897, Jan. 1, 1898.

12. The plea for abatement of taxes had been considered seriously since 1892 and postponed from consideration of policy only. The case presented interesting features, since it hinged in large measure upon the question of whether the property could be taxed on the value of the water power appurtenant, in this case twenty-one and one half permanent mill powers. Lyman Mills Papers, Agent's Letter Book, Lovering to Parsons, Nov. 10, 1896; Holyoke *Transcript,* Apr. 15, 1897.

pay increase. The granting in 1903 of over 16 per cent wage increase proved the prosperity of the corporation in spite of business fluctuations.[13]

Paper manufacturers weathered 1893 without serious troubles,[14] though prices dropped sharply before the year was out, and mills, many already operating on part-time, met their payrolls by check. At the end of three or four months currency little by little came back, until once again mills could pay in bank notes and coin. Then in the early months of 1894 the paper business fell and for some three years paper makers faced depression. Prices dropped 40 and 50 per cent; yet most manufacturers ran their mills, four days a week being an average. Three great new plants were ready for business by 1894 and there was little business to be had.[15]

Only one mill ran steadily, that of George Gill, the hard-working, hard-bargaining Yankee who had wrested his mill from the Newtons. Gill, his business acumen warning him that the depression was sure to find the paper industry eventually even though belatedly, made ready. Calling all his help together into the finishing room he put the case squarely up to them. Paper mills, he said, were already beginning to run short time, and he must follow suit unless by lowering costs he could undersell competitors and secure their business. If his help would acquiesce in a 10 per cent wage cut he would agree to keep the mill running full time. The bargain was struck, Gill fared forth, and, as he had

13. See below, p. 216.

14. The correspondence of the Hampshire Paper Company in South Hadley Falls can be regarded as giving fair indication of business conditions for the writing-paper manufacturers of this locality. An examination of the company's letter files by a sampling process revealed no upset condition of business down to 1894. Hampshire Paper Company Papers, Letter Files 1891–1893, Box L–M. Similarly the Newton Paper Company records indicate the undisturbed course of events in cheap lines. Newton Paper Co., Directors' Records.

15. *Calendar Record and Log Book of the No. One Mill of the Aga-wam Paper Company,* Jan. 1885, to May 1911, copied and published by Ralph M. Snell (pamphlet in possession of John Gardiner of Valley Paper Company of Holyoke); Holyoke *Transcript,* Apr. 22, Aug. 19, 1893, Jan. 16, 1897. Both the Linden and the Norman began to manufacture before the depression. See above, p. 162.

anticipated, was able to secure such orders as were being placed. With invincible courage and no cash he embarked in the summer of 1894 upon the installation of a steam plant so that water shortage need not shut down the mill, and though he lost money for some months it was a smaller amount, he could figure, than the loss of not running at all. His help, seeing many of their fellows in other concerns walking the streets jobless half the week, felt an enthusiastic loyalty to their own outfit. The wrath of other paper manufacturers in Holyoke at Gill's methods smacked somewhat of irritation at having been outwitted rather than indignation at his unrighteous failure to adhere to an unwritten business code.[16]

By 1896 the strain for the paper manufacturer had reached its peak. Many well-financed companies managed to pull through by drawing on the surplus profits of earlier years, convincing testimony to the wisdom of setting aside large reserves of undivided profits.[17] The failure to pursue this course led in 1896 to the financial embarrassment of the Albion Paper Company, the great book-paper concern of the Taft family. Taft, son-in-law of J. C. Parsons and brother-in-law of James H. Newton, had been a prominent figure in Holyoke since the Albion was organized in 1869. The Albion mill had been rebuilt and enlarged in 1878 and from then on had maintained an unshakeable position in the front rank of booming book-paper concerns. The fine-

16. *Paper World*, XXX, no. 1 (Jan. 1895), 25. "Today," Gill reminisces, "they'd say I was a chiseller—Well, I did; I chiselled."

17. For this statement I have been obliged to take the word of paper manufacturers in Holyoke today, only one of whom was connected at that time with a company where this situation obtained. Testimony, however, of men of a later generation familiar with local conditions in general, supports the contention. The president and treasurer of the Parsons Paper Company today asserts positively that that great enterprise was only brought through the stormy years by means of reserves built up by the frugal policy of the directors of the preceding forty years.

The Newton Paper Company, as a concern manufacturing special patented coarse papers, was not in identical case with most Holyoke paper manufacturers. In 1896, the Newton mill volume of production reached a new high for twenty years, but the company had pared profits down to an eighth of a cent a pound on paper inventoried at one and one half cents a pound. Newton Paper Co., Directors' Records.

looking, dashing, sport-loving man at the head of the business seemed to have no cares other than securing the most dazzling span of black horses with which to drive through the streets, the finest steam yacht upon which to entertain at sea customers and admiring Holyoke friends, the most exquisite and exotic plants for the greenhouse to be attached to the great cut-stone mansion rising on the hillside looking over the river, the crenelated turrets of that castle designed to represent American baronial estate. No one else in Holyoke attempted entertainment on the lavish scale of the Tafts—Taft of the Albion.[18] It was costly. Notes were signed at the bank, an easy matter to arrange in flush times when Taft's mill was running full and he and his relatives were bank directors. But when the banks in the hard times of the nineties began to press for the extinction or reduction of Taft's notes, the picture changed. Profits that had been consumed were not available for capital. The fate of the Albion Paper Company was a salutary warning to Holyoke.

The suspension of payment at the Albion was more than a lesson in frugality. It threatened real trouble to Holyoke paper manufacturers. Banks were wary of carrying their notes, for the Albion had been regarded as sound as the dam itself and if a debt of $254,000 embarrassed that concern how could lesser companies carry on? Only two other companies did collapse subsequently, both comparatively small and one a rather recently organized concern. The Albion was reorganized without great difficulty and the necessary additional capital found, since the plant had been well kept up and the superintendent was known to be a capable paper maker. Nevertheless, such was the shock of Taft's failure and the consequent shakeup that three years later the company was glad to consider proposals from the projected paper trust.[19]

The nineties was a decade of far-reaching changes for

18. *Paper World*, XXVII, no. 1 (July 1893), 2–4; Holyoke *Transcript*, Feb. 22, 1879, July 28, 1888, Dec. 22, 1894.

19. Holyoke *Transcript*, May 20, Sept. 9, Nov. 11, 1896, Mar. 9, 21, 27, 28, May 14, 1897.

the American paper industry everywhere. The demand for newsprint and cheap wood-fibre paper for the multiplying magazines was being met by great pulp and paper mills, but to achieve this output more and more capital had to be poured into the plants. The number of paper-making establishments in the United States increased by 17.6 per cent between 1890 and 1900, but the increase in capital invested was 86.5 per cent. Here was no longer a game for the small fry. Four great consolidations took place before 1900, one comprising thirty-one mills, one twenty-five, one fifteen, and one nine.[20] Holyoke, still primarily making high-grade papers, was caught up by the tide.

The depression, begun with currency problems of 1893, endured in most fields of Holyoke's industry nearly till the declaration of war with Spain. The length of duration and the severity of recurring "hard times" in the nineties contributed largely to the change in form of industrial organization at the end of the century. The trend toward consolidation of competing or similar enterprises had been observable in Holyoke in the realignment of control in the paper companies.[21] Whether or not this movement would have proceeded further, had the four years of depression not weakened the position of the independent manufacturers, is a futile speculation. For depressions were the successors of booms with a cyclical regularity which enabled William Whiting in 1894 with thirty-five years of experience in the paper industry behind him to predict the course of business for the ten years to come with nearly exact accuracy. Mill owners who in 1890 might have rejected any proposal for a "combine" were glad by 1898 to consider the idea.

The first of these consolidations, the United States Envelope Company, effected in 1897–1898, made little change

20. *Twelfth Census of U. S.,* 1900, *Manufactures,* IX, Pt. III, "Special Reports Selected Industries," p. 1023. These four combines controlled 10.5 per cent of all the paper-making establishments, 24.1 per cent of all the capital, 23.3 per cent of all employes, and 24.1 per cent of the total value produced in the United States.

21. See above, p. 162.

in Holyoke because the Holyoke Envelope Company, the thriving venture of some eighteen years' duration, was the only local company concerned. But the success of this trust was the inspiration of the writing-paper combine which markedly changed the character of Holyoke's industrial organization. The "thread trust" had taken over the Merrick and Hadley companies in 1898 and to all appearances was functioning smoothly. The International Pump Company was organizing and about to include Holyoke's Deane Steam Pump Company.[22] Could not a similar consolidation of writing-paper mills make savings advantageous to all? Any thought of "combination in restraint of trade" was necessarily suppressed, nor is there reason to suppose that the converts anticipated anything beyond effecting economies in purchase of raw materials, in distributing and selling the manufactured product, and in eliminating price-cutting with which as individual producers they could not compete. The original promoters, and later the agents of Lee Higginson & Company of Boston, were not manufacturers, but brokers interested in marketing the stock. With the cessation of the independence of sixteen of Holyoke's great paper companies, one era of Holyoke's history—the period of vital growth—comes to an end.

How was the combine brought about? A classic example of the unsuccessful trust, created toward the end of the era of trust building, the American Writing Paper Company has a story in its organizing and launching that is illuminating.[23] Competent paper manufacturers familiar with conditions in the local mills declare that the combine as consummated was disastrous for the best interests of Holyoke, and in the same breath they pronounce the organization a needless failure. There was no reason save one, they say, why the American Writing Paper Company should

22. Holyoke *Transcript,* Jan. 16, 1897, June 11, July 22, Dec. 29, 30, 1898, Feb. 7, 1916.

23. The account as here given is compiled from information given me by a number of different persons, themselves immediately concerned with events at that time. Their stories supplement each other in detail and agree in broad outline. It has seemed wiser not to use names.

not have been in its own field as successful a trust as the United States Steel Corporation. That one factor, incapable management, was, however, inherent in the scheme nearly from the beginning.

Unlike the successful steel trust, the combination was not initiated from within the industry, but by outsiders, financial promoters unfamiliar with the requirements of this particular business. Consequently in the initial stages the organizers made commitments which were vitally to affect the course of events. Holyoke writing-paper manufacturers had long felt the unwisdom of the kind of cutthroat competition which had undermined some branches of the paper industry,[24] and there is reason to believe that a combination of manufacturers of the high-grade papers under trusted leadership would have met with enthusiastic approval and coöperation. Long before definite proposals were made to Holyoke mill owners, preliminary soundings were taken. Had one suggested organization materialized, with William Whiting, now reported to be weary of politics and ready to resume an active business career, as president, and George Gill as next in command, doubtless the combination formed would have been quite different from that achieved in midsummer of 1899. Perhaps the unwary promoters approached the wrong men first. By the time news of specific offers leaked out, heads of well-run mills discovered that the projected company was committed to the management of men at the Riverside paper mill. Apparently as the price of the support of a group of the Springfield men owning Holyoke paper mills, the organizers had promised a post of responsibility to W. C. Caldwell, protégé of Appleton of the Riverside.

It was an injudicious initial move. Appleton as a man of some importance in Springfield banking circles was a useful person to have supporting the proposed combine, but he made no pretense of being a practical paper manufac-

24. *Paper World,* IX, no. 6 (Dec. 1884), 18; X, no. 4 (Apr. 1885), 8–9; XIV, no. 6 (June 1887), 10; XV, no. 4 (Oct. 1887), 12; XV, no. 5 (Nov. 1887), 8.

turer. The second Riverside mill built at the peak in 1892
had begun to produce in the slump of 1894. Caldwell had
been a salesman for the original company and, having
found favor in that capacity in the eighties, was given a
chance to own stock in the Riverside No. Two. It is a fair
guess that the new mill was a burden in a falling market,
and that the heads of the Riverside would have gladly sold
out on any reasonably inviting terms. Be that as it may,
the choice of Caldwell as head of the new company inspired
uncertainty if not actual distrust where confidence was
necessary. Whiting refused to have anything further to do
with the scheme.[25] The heads of the Parsons decided to sell
only the old mill and keep the property and organization
of the excellently equipped Parsons No. Two. The hard-
headed Yankees at the Valley and in the South Hadley
Falls mills, the Carew and the Hampshire, eschewed the
combine. Was after all the whole project to collapse?

In order to have a sufficient control of the supply of writing paper to ensure monopoly prices, Holyoke manufacturers figured that ownership of mills making 75 per cent
of the country's total output was necessary. Obviously they
would not all be located in Holyoke. Exact information
about the status of the "combine" in the spring of 1899
was hard to get in the city, but rumors were rife that the
more powerful companies were holding out. It soon was
common knowledge that to secure added sources of production, the promoters were having to approach the heads
of book mills; and the projected American Writing Paper
Company by the technician's standards was becoming a
book and writing-paper combine. As the summer of 1899
wore on it became evident that the combination must fail
unless a few of the companies still hesitating or refusing to
join be persuaded to sell. It was a game for the strong and
cool-headed. Where screws could be applied they were used
by both sides.

The story of George Gill is significant. Gill by his own

25. *Paper World,* XXX, no. 1 (Jan. 1895), 25; XXX, no. 3 (Mar.
1895), 102; Holyoke *Transcript,* Apr. 6, June 2, 1899.

statement was ready, in fact eager, to throw in his lot with a company which by its make-up and management could successfully pool the resources of the writing-paper industry and put an end to the competition becoming increasingly ruthless. Conversely, into any combine which did not hold every promise of shrewd management he was determined not to go, unless at his own price. As Lee Higginson's agent pursued the business, Gill became convinced that the project was not hopeful. When at length approached for his coöperation, he announced his willingness to sell his mill to the new company, but at a price which he deliberately set unreasonably high. Higginson, nettled, summoned him to Boston to discuss the matter. Gill went, explained his position in clear but unflattering words, refused to sell for less than one and a half million dollars, and much of that in cash, and departed, unmoved by the wrath of the brokers. Gill had paid only a small amount in cash for his mill, and carried the rest by personal notes held by Springfield banks and by a $200,000 mortgage owned by the Massachusetts Mutual Life Insurance Company.[26] Among the directors of the Massachusetts Mutual were men deeply concerned with the success of the American Writing Paper Company. These men, therefore, determined to bring Gill to terms. Notice was sent him that he must reduce his mortgage by $100,000 in thirty-one days. With unshaken nerve, Gill pocketed the notice without showing it to anyone, and by cool negotiating succeeded in the specified time in having the Ware Savings Bank take over the whole mortgage.[27] The promoters, hoist with their

26. Gill had reduced the mortgage by $3,000 since 1892.

27. Gill's mode of procedure in this emergency illustrates the man's courage. After receiving the notice from the Massachusetts Mutual demanding the reduction of the mortgage by half he bided his time, waiting for two weeks of the month until he could contrive a seemingly casual encounter with the president of the Ware Savings Bank. The Ware Savings Bank was a sound country bank ably managed. Gill induced the president, and a few days later, the directors and expert accountants brought in by them, to examine his books and his mill. He showed them his whole plant, considerably improved and expanded since 1892, his order book, and his commitments. The upshot was that the Ware Savings Bank undertook to take over Gill's whole mortgage provided that the directors

own petard, were themselves obliged to accept Gill's terms
or risk the failure of the whole combine. Gill got his price.
He paid the Ware Bank for the mortgage it had held only
a month, met his other indebtednesses, and with a surplus
of cash, a block of the new company's stock and some of its
bonds, accepted the title of one of its vice-presidents. He
could afford to lend the company his name for a time.

Other companies in Holyoke also sold out on highly advantageous terms. For mills which had been in deep waters
the trust promised a life-saving means of escape, and there
were several in that situation. On the other hand, there were
others which could wait until the owners could practically
dictate terms. Thus the owner of old Union mill built thirty
years before, by holding out to the last day, netted a price
far out of line with what newer, much better-equipped mills
had brought. So the last day of July 1899 wore to a close
and the American Writing Paper Company with fifteen
Holyoke mills included was completed. At that last minute
James Newton decided to sell the Wauregan and so the
number was brought to sixteen.[28]

The American Writing Paper Company, incorporated

could convert into cash the necessary $197,000 in the few days of the
thirty-one still remaining. The money was found, the Massachusetts Mutual mortgage was paid up—to the infinite consternation of many of its
directors—and the George C. Gill Paper Company, its mortgage safe in
friendly hands, was able to defy the American Writing Paper Company.

28. James H. Newton under shrewd advisement had steadfastly refused to sell the Wauregan mill to the combine, although the Norman, his
newer mill, he had relinquished, somewhat as the Parsons Paper Company had sold one mill and kept one. With characteristic impulsiveness,
overcome perhaps by sudden panic, he now reversed his course. For the
organizers of the American Writing Paper Company it was a stroke of
unexpected and rare good fortune. Too late to secure the terms which he
might have commanded earlier, Newton professed to be satisfied with
payment in nothing but preferred stock of the new company. And thus
to the other mills brought into the combine was added this great, finely-
equipped, prospering mill at a cost of nothing but stock certificates.
Many were the incredulous head shakings over the folly of the performance when other paper manufacturers heard of Newton's act. So generally was Newton's sudden change of decision condemned as rash even
by associates who had themselves sold out to the new company, that the
inference is clear that these newly constituted business colleagues had
doubts about the future of the consolidated enterprise.

in New Jersey, comprised twenty-five mills, sixteen of them in Holyoke.[29] Of these, four were book-paper mills and had no real place in a writing-paper company. All save the Holyoke had been well kept up, the oldest mills having been rejuvenated and improved in the eighties. Despite the heavy price paid for some of the plants, the consolidation might well have produced the economies prophesied by its organizers and proved the boon to the industry promised. Unfortunately, differences immediately arose among the managing heads in matters of policy. The abler manufacturers soon shrugged their shoulders, accepted their salaries, and departed on vacations in a fashion hitherto unheard of in business-minded Holyoke, leaving the responsibility of the plants to others.[30] The concern made some money at first. But within two years' time the shrewdest of the original group of Holyoke paper manufacturers were selling their interest in the American Writing Paper Company and either withdrawing into other fields or embarking upon their own paper-making ventures. Thus the men at the Parsons expanded their fine paper plant; Esleeck built a mill in Millers Falls; Gill went into banking.

In 1901 the company faced a strike on the part of the firemen. The men won out. Again in 1903 there were labor troubles. Informed public opinion, while not ready utterly to accept labor's contentions, felt that the company was managing matters badly in having allowed trouble to arise. A few of the independent concerns were also involved. Here was indication of the new order in Holyoke that the trust had helped to bring about.[31]

Meanwhile the McKinley boom was at last taking effect. After 1897 exports of paper for the first time in the his-

29. These were the Riverside One and Two, the Connecticut River Paper Company mill, the Linden, the Holyoke, the Parsons No. One, the Nonotuck One and Two, the Massasoit, the Beebe & Holbrook, the Norman, the Wauregan, the George C. Gill, the Albion, the Crocker, the George R. Dickinson, and the Excelsior.

30. Holyoke *Transcript*, July 11, 1899, Apr. 14, 1900.

31. *Ibid.*, June 7, 15, 28, July 8, 1901; Matthew Burns, History of the International Brotherhood of Paper Makers.

tory of the United States exceeded imports in value. While prices of paper declined steadily during the decade of the nineties, so also did the prices of ground and chemical wood pulp. Profits per pound were shaved closer than in the seventies and early eighties but less wasteful methods of manufacture and increased production still netted money for the able. The independent paper companies of Holyoke, whether writing paper, board, or book mills, found business profitable. For other than newsprint, where the forests of Maine gave an impetus to manufacture near the source of pulp supply, the cheap power of Holyoke gave an advantage more noticeable as time went on.[32] And as if the American Writing Paper Company had cleared the scene for action, the old established concerns were ready to make the most of their opportunities and recognized prestige. The machinery plants took on new lease of life, and the Deane Steam Pump, now part of the great International Pump Company, carried on in Holyoke outwardly as before the trust was formed. The "thread combine" and the cotton mills throve, and the silk and the worsted manufactures revived. The American Thread Company with its new organization kept its personnel in the local mills quite largely intact, so that the mill help felt little difference in the running of their departments. Only a few hands were supplanted by machines as the end of the century approached. The new mill which had been begun in Timothy Merrick's lifetime was filled with machinery and put into full operation. Woolen manufacture in general had faced great difficulties in the nineties and many old concerns elsewhere had gone to the wall or been absorbed into great consolidations. In Holyoke the existing establishments carried on over the turn of the century but not long afterward two were eliminated. The Farr Alpaca Company, on the other hand, found itself with its monopoly entrenched and its business expanding. The improved finish of the com-

32. *Paper World*, XI, no. 1 (July 1887), 1; *Twelfth Census of U. S.*, 1900, *Manufactures*, IX, Pt. III, "Special Reports on Selected Industries," 1018, 1022, 1023.

pany's product enabled the mill to command an income which led to 96 per cent dividends in 1901. Although operatives benefited only indirectly by the declared policy of the company to pay higher wages than elsewhere, places at the Farr were sought for and the number of employes by 1903 exceeded 3,000.[33]

Yet in spite of the general prosperity, the slowing down of the city's industrial growth was observable by 1903. While the full effects of the substituting of one consolidated paper company for sixteen independent concerns was not yet widely felt, merchants and dealers in mill supplies had already begun to complain of a falling off in business, attributing it to the American Writing's purchase of supplies elsewhere and to the loss of working time in the combined Holyoke mills.[34] In the decade since 1893 stores had, to be sure, multiplied, and there were even two department stores. But still here was a purely local trade depending for growth upon the city's industrial expansion and concomitant population increase. Now permanent mill powers were no longer to be leased for the asking, and desirable purchasable mill sites on the canal banks numbered only two or three. Must the city cease to grow? Perhaps in electrical power transmission might lie the answer for the water-power city.

33. *Twelfth Census of U. S.*, 1900, *Manufactures*, IX, Pt. III, "Special Reports on Selected Industries," 77; F. A. Co. Records, II, 237; Lyman Mills Papers, Agent's Letter Book, Lovering to Parsons, July 27, 1899.
34. Holyoke *Transcript*, Feb. 26, 1901.

VII

LABOR, 1873–1903

WITHOUT an adequate supply of labor, power resources and capital alike would not suffice to build a manufacturing city. The most important period for Holyoke in developing the power was that of the years from 1846 to 1851; the significant era for the bringing in of capital was the decade before the panic of 1873. But not until the eighties did labor come to the fore as a self-conscious unit in the general scheme.

In the fifties and sixties mill heads had imported such help as could be found and trained—Irish, Scots, English, French Canadians, Germans—and had worked them as hard as the law of supply and demand permitted. But despite the shortage of trained help, particularly after the Civil War, manufacturers had an ever-renewing source of supply in the hordes of the unskilled who came pouring in year after year presenting numbers from which to select those to be taught.[1] Many of the newly arrived immigrants found working and living conditions here at worst better than what they had known before. Under such circumstances there was little reason to expect anything for work people but long hours at low wages. The Workingmen's League of the fifties had died an early death in Holyoke[2] and until the middle seventies there was no association of work people of any sort.

Mutual Benefit Societies had existed by national grouping as early as the sixties,[3] but in 1874 an endeavor was first made to organize on trade lines. A number of paper makers formed a Protective Union the funds of which were

1. Mass. Bur. Labor Statistics, *Third Annual Report*, 1872, p. 158. See above, pp. 106, 111.
2. See above, p. 46.
3. Most powerful and active of these societies were perhaps the Turnverein and the German Benevolent Society.

to be used for benefits for sickness, injury, and unemployment. But the income was so scanty and the pressure upon the members so severe during the five weeks' shutdown of the fine writing mills in the winter of 1875–1876 that the society broke up some three years after its founding and nothing of the sort was again seen in town until the eighties.[4] Following upon the interest aroused in the British coöperatives, two coöperative stores were opened in Holyoke, a grocery store in the fall of 1873 and another in 1875. But they were short-lived and gave no basis for any more permanent organization.[5]

The problem for labor during much of the seventies was not one of securing better pay and shorter hours, but rather one of keeping steady employment under almost any conditions. Unorganized though labor in Holyoke was, wages had gradually risen here as elsewhere in the boom of 1870–1871 and 1872. But soon after the panic of 1873 wage rates were cut and short-time employment became general. A number of the spinners and weavers at the Lyman Mills protested the cut in pay by striking in December 1873, but it was impossible by such means to accomplish any improvement, since all New England cotton mills had reduced wages and there were no better jobs for textile hands than Holyoke itself offered. The corporations preferred curtailed operations when markets were doubtful, and textile operatives were obliged to accept the situation.[6]

Labor conditions in the seventies were rendered unstable not only by the business depression but also by the undiminishing supply of hands available. Unskilled labor continued to flow into Holyoke; and migratory laborers,

---

4. Holyoke *Transcript*, Jan. 17, Feb. 18, 28, 1874, Feb. 3, Apr. 7, 1875, Mar. 15, Nov. 1, 29, Dec. 6, 1876. As a kind of shop coöperative sickness insurance the Farr Alpaca Company attempted in 1879 to work out for its employes a fund to which each worker contributed regularly and the company paid in monthly 10 per cent of the employes' fund. It was abandoned after some six months of trial. *Ibid.,* Oct. 4, 1879.

5. *Ibid.,* Dec. 6, 1873, Mar. 7, 1874, Mar. 31, 1875; Mass. Bur. Labor Statistics, *Sixth Annual Report,* 1875, p. 460; *Eighth Annual Report,* 1877, pp. 115–116.

6. See above, pp. 138–139.

"tramps" particularly numerous in spring and fall,[7] put their brawn and sometimes even considerable skill at the disposal of the casual employer. The city had some call for workmen for laying sewers, putting in curbing, paving streets, and extending the water system. But the common laborer's best hope for permanent employment lay with the master builders or in the mills, perhaps in the yard gang. A carefully regulated system of apprenticeship could not be enforced in the building trades until unions were formed, but it was self-created to some extent by the demand of contractors to have work done principally by experienced workmen, whether masons, carpenters, brick layers, or painters. In the textile and paper mills the same demand for trained help obliged the boss of each department frequently to teach inexperienced hands. Here a tacit understanding prevailed long before union regulations were heard of whereby a certain period of time must elapse before the learner earned full pay, if on time rates; and if on piece rates inevitably he earned less until he became adept.[8]

Gradually, however, as the decade wore on, conditions for the workmen improved. The state in 1869 had created a Bureau of Statistics of Labor to investigate working conditions chiefly in factories. The agitation in the thirties and forties calling for the limiting of child labor had resulted in a prohibition of factory labor for children under ten; and statutes, revised in the fifties and again after the Civil War, stipulated a minimum of schooling for children under twelve employed in factories.[9] But even these laws, people knew, had not been enforced. Children were taught to hide when the inspecting constables came into the mill, and all were schooled in putting their ages high enough to

7. For example in 1874–1875, 1,225 tramps were housed in Holyoke at public expense. In April 1875 alone, 225 men were lodged. Holyoke *Transcript,* Apr. 3, May 1, June 19, Dec. 25, 1875, Dec. 2, 1876.

8. Lyman Mills Papers, Pay Rolls, 1868–1880.

9. Persons, "The Early History of Factory Legislation in Massachusetts," in *Labor Laws and Their Enforcement with special reference to Massachusetts,* edited by Susan Kingsbury, II, *passim.*

pass the legal requirement.[10] Massachusetts abolitionists
and reformers of conditions in the South could not now
with dignity or conscience fail to turn their eyes upon conditions at home. Socially-minded people throughout the
state looked at the manufacturing towns and cities and
saw there much that was not good. But before specific legislation was attempted, it seemed wise to collect data on
existing conditions and their social effects in order that
any law put upon the statute books might fairly cope with
facts, not with imaginary social ills.

The Bureau set to work with vigor at once, and in 1870
published its first report. Treasurer Bush of the Lyman
Mills, fearing perhaps the outcome of such investigation,
instructed the agent in Holyoke to pay no attention to the
questionnaires of the Bureau. But obstructionists notwithstanding, sufficient information about conditions throughout the state was forthcoming to lead to the passage in 1874
of a law restricting the hours of factory labor for women
and minors under eighteen years of age to sixty a week. In
most textile mills the actual schedule adopted provided a
short day on Saturday. It was chiefly the textile mills
which were affected because here the largest proportion of
the help were women. The rag-sorters and girls in the finishing rooms of the paper mills could work their ten hours
a day without forcing the closing of the whole plant when
their day was done. Not so in the textile mills.[11] The result
was a revision of the hours of the whole textile industry in
Massachusetts, of men as well as of women. Various sched-

10. In Chicopee in 1872 John Bleasius, aged nine, was instructed by the
superintendent of the Chicopee Manufacturing Company to hide in the
spool box if the inspector came by. Bleasius, now secretary of the Central Labor Union of Holyoke, had been forced, together with his brother,
to work in the mill by the threat of the superintendent to discharge his
father if the boys were not sent to serve as bobbin boys.

11. Lyman Mills Papers, Bush to Davis, Nov. 29, 1869. Again and
again over a period of sixty years Massachusetts cotton or woolen manufacturers have experimented with training men to do women's jobs in
order to keep machinery running after the women's day was ended. Men's
fingers are not sufficiently dexterous to do the careful work of spinners
and warpers.

ules were tried in Holyoke. In 1877 the usual hours for textile mills became six-thirty to twelve in the morning and one to six-fifteen afternoons five days a week, and from six-thirty to twelve-forty-five on Saturdays. There is no indication that in Holyoke the ten-hour law was evaded, as it was in Fall River, for example, and the revising of the statute in 1879 and the providing of ten state inspectors to enforce the child labor regulations made small difference in Holyoke.[12]

This legislation in no way affected the stores. When merchants agreed in 1878 to close two evenings a week at six o'clock and nine years later on a third evening, it was considered sheer generosity.[13] After the passage of these factory bills, the Massachusetts labor code stood for a time. A law was enacted in 1887 supplementing the old common-law employers' liability with more adequate legislation, but otherwise there was no important change in Massachusetts' labor laws until the nineties.[14]

The eighties saw the true birth of labor organizations in Holyoke. For some three years before the first labor union was formed there had been much discussion in the newspapers about the workman's lot. Heads of families who could earn only seventy-five cents a day in the mills were bound to be restive and uneasy. "Just listen to their hosannas in favor of law and order as at present constituted," cried one.[15] Indignantly some working people wrote letters to the *Transcript* protesting the hypocrisy of the temperance forces which would lay all the evils of the social sys-

12. Holyoke *Transcript*, Sept. 30, 1874, Apr. 28, 1877, Jan. 18, 1879.

13. *Ibid.,* May 8, 1878, Jan. 29, 1887.

14. The enactments of 1886–1887 were not regarded in Holyoke as significant. One created a State Arbitration Board in labor disputes, but its findings were to be in the nature of advice only, which did not need to be followed by either party. The other principal act of 1886 specified that wage payments must be made weekly. This aroused no loud opposition, as several Holyoke manufacturers had already voluntarily adopted the method of weekly payment to employes. Holyoke *Transcript*, Jan. 31, Feb. 3, 28, 1877; *Acts and Resolves of Massachusetts*, 1886, ch. 87, 263; 1887, ch. 270, 433. An extension of the Child Labor Laws in 1887 provided means of teaching all minors employed in mills to read and write English.

15. Holyoke *Transcript*, Sept. 1, 1877.

tem upon the saloon. Why should the laboring man give up his navy clippings and mug of beer in order to put every cent into the savings bank?[16] What was the use? The cost of living had risen by 1878 as compared to 1860 in every item, groceries by 9.9 per cent, provisions by 27 per cent, fuel by 5.5 per cent, rents by 41 per cent, and board rates by 58 per cent. Wages as compiled from data for about three quarters of the Holyoke mill population in 1875 had over the same period risen on an average of 21 per cent.[17] But if employment was not steady or sure, what enduring satisfaction could lie there? In the fall of 1877 two delegates from Holyoke attended a workingman's convention in Boston where a platform was adopted projecting a workingman's political party for Massachusetts. The platform, noteworthy for its reasonableness, listed six measures which were realized in time and some of which were later taken up by Benjamin Butler as national issues.[18] But such means brought no immediate relief to workmen's families at home, and in spite of the upswing of the business cycle in 1879 New England workmen began to fear that there lay ahead no permanent improvement for them.

The spring of 1879 brought into Massachusetts a great wave of French Canadian immigrants, lured by rumors of jobs to be had. The *Transcript* described the scene in Holyoke:

They come with all their worldly goods packed in boxes and bundles and the gents' room at the Connecticut Railroad depot is packed with their effects till it looks like a wholesale warehouse. Leaving the bulk of articles at the depot, they

16. *Ibid.*, Aug. 25, 1877.
17. Mass. Bur. Labor Statistics, *Tenth Annual Report,* 1879, pp. 78, 84.
18. The platform demanded in Massachusetts: 1. the repeal of the law trusteeing the pay of workmen in debt; 2. the naturalization of the foreign-born without expense to the foreigner; 3. the substitution of a graduated income tax for indirect state taxation; 4. the reduction of the hours of labor in state and city jobs; 5. the elimination of competitive prison labor by securing the payments of 50 per cent of the prisoner's earnings to his family; 6. the creation of half-time schools for working children under sixteen years of age. Holyoke *Transcript,* Oct. 3, 1877.

start out with their arms full of bundles to find a place to
stop. Some have friends or relatives here. Many have spent
their last cent to get here, expecting to find plenty of work
on their arrival. A crowd of emigrants [*sic*] arrived Thursday, having seen an advertisement of a paper company for
100 rag-cutters, and clamored to be directed to the mill.
Failing to find tenements, lodging rooms or work, some of
them have gone on to Providence, Pawtucket and other
points, but many have no money to go further. Some have located at South Holyoke, and many have crowded into
"Canada Hill." The working people view their coming with
some apprehension, fearing that the effect will be to over-
crowd the labor market, and cheapen wages still further. In
appearance and dress the Canadian comers resemble those already settled in the States, with the exception of the dress of
the men, many of whom are clothed in homespun gray. A
troop of them, big and little, are seen starting out on foot
from the depot after the arrival of nearly every through
train from the North.[19]

Holyoke workmen were apprehensive with cause, for
these French Canadians would work for fifty cents a day,
and their numbers seemed inexhaustible. How could the
American workman maintain a decent standard of living
in the face of such competition? While it is true that these
newcomers were rarely skilled workmen, their very numbers made them a menace for the skilled.

Hastened in its creation perhaps by fear of the effects
of glutting of the labor market, a first labor union was
formed in the city early in the next year. The immediate
occasion of the organizing of a bricklayers union was the
difference in wages paid here and in the neighborhood.
About one hundred men joined and by their joint demand
secured the higher rate from contractors. Then nothing
more is heard of this or any union for several years. Other
groups in the building trades were organized, carpenters,
masons, and painters, and a cigar makers union, and in

19. *Ibid.,* Mar. 29, 1879.

1885 a weavers union. But only the fact of their existence is known. The vitalizing force behind these units was a lodge of the Knights of Labor.[20] In 1884 also a lodge of paper makers was started, Eagle Lodge, from which some years later the International Brotherhood of Paper Makers was to evolve. But before the publicity attending the 1885–1886 developments of the Knights of Labor the country over, the formal organization of labor in Holyoke went on slowly. In the spring of 1885 suddenly the movement came to the fore.

The most conspicuous features of the movement in Holyoke at this time are first its lack of connection with factory labor and secondly the rapid growth and equally sudden evaporation of the Knights of Labor. The strikes which had in earlier years taken place in the textile mills had been more or less spontaneous affairs, not backed by organization. In each case wage rates had been the bone of contention. The *Transcript* bragging in 1880 of Holyoke's freedom from labor disturbances attributed this partly to the preponderance of women mill operatives, since they were more patient, milder, and less organized than men.[21] Certainly where unions of factory operatives were at length formed they were chiefly of men, first the weavers in 1885, and in 1891 a branch of the mule-spinners. Machinists and moulders, typesetters, paper makers, all were men. But with the exception of the weavers, none of these were organized until the nineties. In the preceding decade such force as Holyoke's labor movement had, took form outside the mills, in the building trades, in political or fraternal groupings. So Eagle Lodge, the machine tenders' association, was no trade union.

The speeches, labor rallies, and public discussions about the workman's place in an industrial society were directed in the middle eighties at political action, the forming of parties and the securing of legislation. The connection of

20. *Ibid.,* Apr. 5, 1879, Feb. 14, 1880, Mar. 23, 1885. In view of the predilection for secrecy among the Knights at this time it is inevitable that scant material about them is to be found today.

21. See above, pp. 106–107; Holyoke *Transcript,* Feb. 7, 1880.

the Knights of Labor with the political movements is fairly
direct. In April of 1885 the Holyoke Knights were reported to have had 240 applications for admission, and the
next month a Workingmen's Union, made up of all the labor organizations in the city, was formed, not, however,
like the later Central Labor Union as a clearing house for
local labor questions, but rather as a preliminary alignment for political education. All through that year laboring men held frequent mass-meetings in the Knights of
Labor Hall, the Turnhall, or the City Hall, sometimes
with speakers imported for the occasion, sometimes with
general discussion from the floor. State ownership of the
means of production, the eight-hour-day philosophy, now
claiming general attention in the state under the advocacy
of Ira Steward and George McNeill of Boston, the justice
of a redistribution of wealth—all came in for mention.
And again and again speakers urged *organization* upon
their listeners, organization into unions, perhaps, but also
organization to send labor representatives to the state legislature and to put labor men into office in the City Hall.
A Holyoke labor candidate was in fact elected to a seat in
the State House.[22]

Meanwhile the general public was becoming increasingly aware of this great new force in America, labor,
headed by the Knights of Labor, self-conscious, probably
self-seeking. Who were these Knights of Labor? What did
they want and were they dangerous? Holyoke hardly knew
what to think. The early months of 1886 saw the movement gaining momentum. Massachusetts manufacturers,
professing alarm at the prospect of extensions to the state
labor laws,[23] prepared a memorial to the legislature:

22. "Eight Hour Day," *New Encyclopedia of Social Reform;* Holyoke
Transcript, Mar. 23, Apr. 25, Oct. 3, 17, 24, 31, Nov. 21, 1885, Jan. 30, 1886.
23. Massachusetts manufacturers had made strides in adjusting their
views to a social standpoint during the business slump of 1884–1885. The
Cotton and Wool Trade commenting on the impending wage reductions
in Lowell, Lawrence, and Fall River cotton mills declared, "There is no
longer a disposition on the part of manufacturers generally to pay a
dividend to their stockholders at the expense of the operatives." Cited in
Holyoke *Transcript,* Jan. 28, 1884.

We are firmly of the conviction that the supremacy of the
State as a manufacturing community is already jeopardized;
that well-intended, but ill-advised so-called "labor reform"
agitation has already touched the danger line, and that a renewal of confidence which will secure adequate investments in
new enterprises can only be reached by the most conservative
statesmanship.[24]

It was true that other manufacturing states were slow to
follow Massachusetts' lead in enacting laws restricting
hours of labor for women and children, and that often
Rhode Island, Connecticut, and New Hampshire investors
appeared to profit considerably at Massachusetts' expense.
Consequently the indictment of avarice made occasionally
by labor leaders had an unjust sound to Massachusetts
capitalists' ears.

The first labor trouble in Holyoke which involved any
organization outside the city came at this moment, in February 1886. In this instance it was a strike within a mill,
the weavers at the Skinner silk mill, in protest chiefly at
injustice on the part of the overseer in distribution of the
warps and payment for the pieces when woven. Of the 120
weavers, 95 struck, and later appealed to the Knights of
Labor in Boston for aid, arbitration, or a boycott. Six
weeks later the overseer was dismissed for other reasons
and the strike came to an end. But Holyoke had been dis-
concerted, perhaps a little frightened. April saw continued
accounts of labor agitations in the country. Where would
trouble next strike at home? Rumor went out that a club
of Socialists existed in South Holyoke which drilled regularly in preparation for armed revolution.[25] Then in May
the Chicago anarchists and the Haymarket riot gave apparent justification for general panic. The press shut
down on further news of these disturbing labor elements.

24. Holyoke *Transcript,* Jan. 23, 30, 1886.
25. *Ibid.,* Feb. 5, 8, 13, 27, Mar. 13, 18, 24, 30, 1886; Allyn, "Sketch of
Holyoke," *Thirtieth Anniversary Holyoke Daily Transcript.* No memory
of any such scare has survived among old residents of the city. But the
fact that a reputable citizen in 1912 spoke of the tale as current in 1886
indicates that more persons believed it at the time than later recalled it.

One whole-hearted condemnation of what were labelled outrageous abuses of the liberties vouchsafed by America and then the *Transcript* dropped the topic. Such sympathy with the cause of labor as had clearly been in evidence in the city vanished. The Knights of Labor lodge, in April a force to reckon with in Holyoke, by midsummer was heard of no more.[26] It continued to exist for a time, but it played no further role in public life.

The whole labor movement was temporarily checked. The small radical group of workpeople in town, newly arrived Germans deeply imbued with a sense of social injustice, was quickly submerged, repudiated by their fellows in the German Benevolent Society who had lived longer in America. In the course of the next year in fact the differences within the German Society became so strong that the older conservative group expelled forty of the newer radical members. In the nineties, the braver Socialists again raised their heads, urging the folly of strikes, announcing the futility of hoping for better business or working conditions under Republican than under Democratic party government, arguing in letters and articles the inevitability of state socialism. But the party made little headway. The sanctity of private ownership and individual enterprise was strongly entrenched, and consideration of state ownership of the means of production most men regarded as uncalled for, dangerous, anarchistic.[27] Working people in Holyoke were not ready to toy with anarchy.

Few people in Holyoke indeed had any thought-out social philosophy.[28] Some way or other the great mass of working people ought to have more abundant life, but

26. Holyoke *Transcript,* Feb. 20, Mar. 29, Apr. 1, 5, 24, 1886, May 7, 1887.

27. *Ibid.,* Jan. 30, 1886, Nov. 12, 1887, Dec. 23, 1893, July 10, Oct. 9, 1894; Urban Fleming, President Holyoke Central Labor Union (interview); Edward Robinson (interview). The *Transcript* in describing the quarrel within the German Benevolent Society alluded to the disturbing element as "slow to comprehend that they are under the best government ever known among men." Holyoke *Transcript,* Nov. 12, 1887.

28. In 1891, the rector of the Episcopal Church suggested to his fellow members of the Book Club, the magazine club of the elite well-to-do, that

how? The Knights of Labor had built upon the belief in
the solidarity of labor of all kinds in all parts of the country. The weaknesses of that great centralized organization
had been revealed by the aftermath of the Chicago anar-
chist disaster. If the community of interest of working
people everywhere was no sound basis of organization,
what was? The Labor-Greenback party, the Anti-Mo-
nopoly party, later the Populist party, Holyoke workmen
viewed as being as ineffectual and as visionary as the Socialist party itself. How could political action solve the
workingman's immediate problems? Few thought that it
could.

In the paper industry the leading workmen in Holyoke
undertook rather to cope with their problems direct by open
discussion and coöperation with the mill owners. It is significant of the high character of the men involved and of the
kindly relationship existing between owners and workmen
that the leading machine tenders in the eighties felt confident of their ability to convince their employers of the justice and wisdom of the proposals. Paper making to this day
requires skill and judgment on the part of the man in
charge of the machine. For fourteen or sixteen hours of the
twenty-four he has little supervision. His importance is recognized by the intelligent employer. Consequently the need
of coöperation between management and workmen seemed
obvious. The early eighties had seen important changes in
Holyoke paper making. The average weekly wage had
fallen abruptly in the paper mills between 1881 and 1883,
largely owing to the increase in unskilled labor with the
advent of cheaper papers. In 1882 the loftmen in the fine
writing mills had requested an increase in wages because
of the increased cost of living and apparently the petition
was granted.[29] In the interests of Holyoke paper making

a Socialist periodical be included in the list of magazines subscribed to
for the year. The suggestion fell on arid soil. Minutes of the Book Club,
1873–1909.

29. Mass. Bur. Labor Statistics, *Fourteenth Annual Report,* 1883,
p. 241; *Thirteenth Annual Report,* 1882, p. 424; *Fifteenth Annual Report,*
1884, p. 415; Holyoke *Transcript,* May 24, 27, June 10, 1882.

in 1884 a group of machine tenders and beater engineers organized Eagle Lodge, a society founded on the ground work of the older Paper Makers Protective Union of the seventies. This society composed of able men undertook to sponsor the movement for shorter hours in the paper mills.

The paper industry had always known longer hours than any other. Two shifts, or tours, of workmen had sufficed to keep the paper machines in steady operation night and day from midnight Sunday to midnight Saturday of every week. In some mills a paper maker worked eleven hours a day in alternate weeks or thirteen hours a night.[30] The campaign launched by Eagle Lodge in the middle eighties was directed at gaining Saturday evenings or early Monday mornings without loss of pay. It was a reasonable demand in view both of the overproduction constantly proclaimed or prophesied in the industry and of the hours which obtained in other industries. Sixty hours a week had been the standard factory week in the Massachusetts textile mills for over a decade.

Eagle Lodge presented the case to the convention of American Paper Manufacturers at Saratoga in midsummer of 1886 and again in 1887 after considerable discussion had already taken place in Holyoke. The Newton Paper Company in April 1886 inaugurated the shorter week by closing early Saturday evening, reopening at seven o'clock Monday morning, and not reducing wages. Whiting took the lead among writing-paper manufacturers in agreeing to a sixty-hour week instead of seventy-two for machine tenders, by dint of engaging an extra tender so that each man had one day a week out. A similar schedule of hours was offered to Whiting's backtenders but they chose the alternative of 15 per cent increase in pay with the old seventy-two hour week. James H. Newton at the Wauregan and the Franklin, Esleeck managing the Valley, and somewhat later J. S. McElwain at the Parsons, fol-

30. Matthew Burns, History of the International Brotherhood of Paper Makers; *Pulp and Paper Investigation Hearings,* II, 1374–1375, *House Documents,* 60th Cong., 2nd Sess., 1908–1909.

lowed suit, making six of the great mills in Holyoke to close down Saturday evening and not to start up the machines again until six o'clock Monday morning. But that was all. The Saratoga convention agreed to the general principle but failed to arrange to put it in practice, in spite of all arguments of Whiting and Newton. The tour workers, disappointed, issued notice that henceforward any paper-mill employe might join a lodge of the Knights of Labor and have the Knights fight out the battle of hours.[31] Unfortunately mill owners well knew that the power of the Knights was already spent and that the threat was empty.

At this point the workers at the Winona mill in Holyoke resolved to call upon the State Board of Arbitration in Boston to examine this question of hours. The hearings received some publicity and the public was sympathetic with the tour workers. But as the decisions of the Board were not binding upon the mill management, the emphatic condemnation of the seventy-two-hour week in the paper industry netted nothing.[32]

Holyoke tour workers now decided to resort to political pressure; and several bills were brought before the Massachusetts legislature in the course of the next few years. But Massachusetts manufacturers made a determined stand against the proposed legislation. It was not, they argued, that they were prepared to deny the desirability of the shorter working week for the whole industry. But Massachusetts could not alone make the change, and unless paper manufacturers the country over would subscribe to a sixty-hour week, Massachusetts workmen must acquiesce. Some manufacturers contended that American paper makers were already far better paid than European and that here was merely a concealed drive for increase in

31. *Paper World,* XIII, no. 2 (Aug. 1886), 20; XIV, no. 2 (Feb. 1887), 10; no. 3 (Mar. 1887), 4; no. 5 (May 1887), 12; no. 6 (June 1887), 10; Holyoke *Transcript,* Apr. 27, Oct. 23, 1886, Feb. 5, Mar. 5, Apr. 9, 10, May 14, Aug. 6, 1887.

32. *Paper World,* XV, no. 3 (Sept. 1887), 32; no. 5 (Nov. 1887), 11, 12, 13; no. 6 (Dec. 1887), 10; Holyoke *Transcript,* Oct. 15, Nov. 19, Dec. 17, 1887.

wages.[33] But the report of the Bureau of Statistics of Labor showed that paper-mill workers of Holyoke in the depression year, May 1884 to May 1885, had been unemployed approximately four months of the twelve, so that their annual income became seriously reduced. Intelligent workmen, however, when confronted with the alternative of lowered wages or part-time employment argued forcefully that short time was greatly preferable to reduced wages. Some Holyoke mill owners professed to have run their mills in 1885 solely for the benefit of their employes. Yet even in the boom year of 1887, $409.80 was an average yearly earning for a paper-mill hand and five years later in 1892 the Bureau was to list the paper industry as having the highest percentage of profit and the lowest percentage of wages of any industry in the state. The example of the Holyoke mills which worked profitably on the shorter schedule was cited without avail.[34] Not until after 1900 did a three-tour system supplant a two-tour in the paper industry.

Holyoke paper manufacturers were eventually to pay the penalty of their failure to act upon the machine tenders' plea. As James Newton pointed out, care and knowledge were the essentials of success in paper manufacture rather than long hours at low wages, and a loyal, intelligent force of work people had long distinguished the paper industry in Holyoke.[35] Machine tenders were expected to progress to posts of superintendents, and there was every reason for mill owners to consider and respect their help. With the manufacturers' refusal to grant the tour

33. Manufacturers lost no opportunity of emphasizing the benefits of tariff protection to the American workman. Holyoke *Transcript,* Nov. 16, 1881, May 7, 1887; *Paper World,* XIII, no. 2 (Aug. 1886), 19.

34. Mass. Bur. Labor Statistics, *Eighteenth Annual Report,* 1887, p. 184; *Statistics of Mfg.,* 1886–1887, pp. 74, 109; 1892, pp. 425–426; Holyoke *Transcript,* Jan. 18, 21, 1884, Apr. 5, 1886, Oct. 15, 1887, Mar. 7, 1891; Burns, History of the International Brotherhood of Paper Makers.

35. *Paper World,* XV, no. 5 (Nov. 1887), 11–13. The state arbitrators spoke in 1887 of "the spirit of mutual forbearance and respect which have hitherto characterized in a remarkable degree the manufacturers of Holyoke and their employes." *Ibid.,* XV, no. 6 (Dec. 1887), 10, 15; Holyoke *Transcript,* Nov. 19, 1887.

workers' petition for Saturday evenings off, a kind of hostility between capital and labor found root such as had not existed before in Holyoke paper mills. Mill owners, as if uneasy, began to adopt an autocratic attitude in dealing with their help which was later to breed trouble.[36] Where Eagle Lodge had felt confident of the community of interest of work people and owners, now there developed a feeling of fundamental opposition. The immediate reaction of the tour workers was the formation of a paper-makers' union.

The organization of the International Brotherhood of Paper Makers with a national charter from the American Federation of Labor in 1893 was the direct outcome of the defeat of Eagle Lodge's efforts to get shorter hours for the tour workers in Massachusetts. As early as 1887 the tour workers in Holyoke had launched a labor weekly, *Paper Makers Record*, which, lasting for six months, carried news of interest to paper makers far beyond the local scene. Two years later the secretary of the local Brotherhood of Paper Makers undertook to correspond with paper makers elsewhere in an endeavor to keep workmen informed of good jobs available. And in 1890 there was held in Holyoke a secret convention of this new Brotherhood of Paper Makers with forty delegates representing all the largest paper mills in New England. With the defeat of the bill for a shorter working week a few months later, agitation for a national union became widespread.[37] Eagle Lodge by assessing its members a small amount weekly built up a fund which was devoted to sending an organizer

36. Private information. In the nineties only at one mill did labor troubles occur, namely at the George R. Dickinson mill, once in 1891 and again in 1894. The chief importance of those strikes lies in the indication of change in mutual attitude. Holyoke *Transcript,* Sept. 28, 1891; *Paper World,* XXX, no. 1 (Jan. 1895), 11.

37. *The Paper Mill,* Dec. 21, 1887, p. 6; Holyoke *Transcript,* May 14, 1887, July 6, 1889, Dec. 13, 1890. The following account is derived principally from the manuscript compiled by Matthew Burns, once Secretary, now President of the International Brotherhood of Paper Makers, from the official union records. The occasional citations from the *Transcript* or *Paper World* merely supplement this main source.

to other paper-mill towns in New England and in New York state and Wisconsin. The national union thus launched, affiliated with the American Federation of Labor, was a union of the skilled men of the trade, the machine tenders and the beater engineers.

The International Brotherhood of Paper Makers, abandoning political action, undertook to organize mills for winning the fight for Sunday night closing. Eagle Lodge and a brother organization of backtenders, Ivy Lodge, simply sent notices to their employers in Holyoke and South Hadley Falls, that after July 9, 1893, no mills would operate on Sunday nights. Since the non-union paper makers of the community had joined in the open meetings urging the change there was little room for argument. Only three mill owners refused the arrangement. Most Holyoke manufacturers accepted the situation with good grace.[38] Here, they saw, was a just cause, and many of them doubtless ruefully viewed the result of earlier injustice in this forging of a weapon to force the manufacturer's hand, a national union. Here was evidence of the truth of a labor man's pronouncement forty-odd years later that the wrongs permitted by Holyoke manufacturers organized more unions than the whole American Federation of Labor. A union never grew up or endured without grievances.

The history of the paper-makers' union hereafter ceases to be a local story. The hostility of helpers, workmen not considered sufficiently skilled to be union members, and the opposition of employers created many difficulties. But just as Holyoke machine tenders had been pioneers in forming the national union, so in 1897, when dissensions bade fair to end its existence, it was the Holyoke local which together with two other locals petitioned the American Federation of Labor for an extension of the jurisdiction of the charter and thus by timely action saved the organization.

---

38. Holyoke *Transcript*, June 28, 1893. The tour workers won their fight in all the mills in Holyoke two years later. *Paper World*, XXVII, no. 1 (July 1893), 15; XXX, no. 5 (May 1895), 178.

A more democratic constitution was inaugurated offering equality of membership in the union to workers of all branches of paper making, and backed by the solid wisdom of veterans of Eagle Lodge, the Brotherhood carried on.[39] The preamble of this constitution of 1897 expressly repudiated any conception of a necessary antagonism of capital and labor: "We rather believe that we, who labor, have more interest in common with our employers than we have in separate or hostile action. This Brotherhood aims for peace and good will and to lessen friction rather than to increase it." Holyoke paper makers by the end of the century were avowedly anxious for peace.

A successful strike in the paper mills in 1901 which netted the firemen an eight-hour day and guaranteed the machine tenders and their help a maximum sixty-six-hour week was followed by a large increase in membership and prestige for Eagle Lodge.[40] Two years later, however, disastrous dissension within the Lodge developed. The finishers in the coarse mills contended that they had not shared in the benefits of recent wage increases, and demanded that voting on the issue of striking be confined to members not affected by the new schedules. Thus the 1,050 hands employed where the higher rates had already been accepted were not allowed to vote. Less than a thousand workers in the American Writing mills, the Parsons, and the two South Hadley Falls mills voted the strike which shut 3,500 out of work. The American Writing Paper officials insisted that the $50,000 increase in annual wages involved

39. A rival organization sprang up in 1898 in New York State, made up of machine tenders who, having never belonged to the original brotherhood, contended that only machine tenders had any influence upon conditions in paper mills and only machine tenders therefore had any right to a voice in union affairs. The ensuing split in the forces of paper mill employes greatly weakened the older union until the two groups were brought into one at a convention in Holyoke in 1902.

40. Through all the earlier struggles the firemen had never been included. Longer hours and less pay than for other workmen had been the rule. A separate union was formed in 1901. Holyoke *Transcript*, Dec. 17, 1887, July 8, 1901; Mass. Bur. Labor Statistics, *Thirty-second Annual Report,* 1901, pp. 143, 207–208.

would put the company in an impossible position competitively; yet a month after the workers called the strike off the company did advance pay rates.

Meanwhile not only had the help lost $300,000 in wages, but Eagle Lodge, the stronghold of union labor in Holyoke, had all but gone to pieces. Membership fell off and interest in labor organizations flagged. The stalwart old guard of paper makers, feeling that selfish, irresponsible elements in the International Brotherhood had betrayed them, abandoned active participation in labor's cause.[41] Not for fifteen years was organized labor again to be a powerful force in the paper city.

The paper makers were representative of the most intelligent element in the labor group. A number of the leaders in Eagle Lodge were men of unusual ability. But just as they found the problem of organization with the question of apprenticeship and rank difficult to work out, so it was in most of the unions. In nearly every case it was a specific issue and special occasion which gave rise to a new union. After the immediate conflict ended the tendency was for the union to peter out. The weavers organized fairly early in 1885 when the Connors' plant was found to be paying wages below that of other woolen mills. After the successful outcome of that fight for higher wages and then the struggle of the silk weavers the next year at the Skinner plant, the weavers' union apparently drifted out of existence. Not until 1899 again does a weavers' union come upon the stage, the result of a controversy over wages at the Farr Alpaca Company. A local union, nourished by national organizers, sprang up, won a 10 per cent wage increase at the Farr mills, and then undertook to enlist the Lyman Mills workpeople. Unsuccessful there, the new union, like the earlier Knights of Labor group of the eighties, gradually melted away. Lacking in business experience, the most capable and far-sighted of union lead-

41. Holyoke *Transcript,* Sept. 24, 1902, May 1, 3, 30, June 8, 9, 12, 13, 15, 16, 17, July 24, 27, Aug. 1, 6, 18, Sept. 18, 1903, June 24, 1904.

ers found it practically impossible to keep their organizations together without the impetus of specific grievances.[42]

There were some exceptions. Several of the textile unions which had a long history in England had branches here in Holyoke that kept their groups together regardless of occasions for collective bargaining. Thus the wool-sorters, the loom-fixers, and the mule-spinners. At the Lyman Mills the mule-spinners, whose national was one of the strongest and best managed of American unions, did indeed act virtually as spokesmen for all the workpeople in the plant after the organization of the Holyoke local in 1891. The agent found it wise to handle problems with the mule-spinners carefully, and in the course of the next few years when wage reductions and short time were frequent, it was the mule-spinners who led the opposition for all the operatives. This group of men, knowing themselves nearly irreplaceable, were in a peculiarly powerful position; ring-spinners, even weavers, could be found or trained without great difficulty, but mule-spinners had to spend at least five or six years in learning the art, and still the international union set such high standards of accomplishment that their numbers were automatically limited. The Holyoke local did not abuse its power, and kept the respect of mill heads and workpeople alike by the discipline its rank and file maintained. In dealing with the officers of the

42. Lyman Mills Papers, Agent's Letter Book, 1899–1900, Lovering to Parsons, June 17, July 27, 1899; Holyoke *Transcript,* Mar. 23, 1885, Apr. 16, 17, 18, 20, 24, 29, 1885, May 26, June 12, 1899. This does not mean that there were not grievances and strikes occasionally in the nineties just as there had been in the seventies without the creation and intervention of unions. For example, the weavers of the Glasgow mill in South Hadley Falls struck in 1890, in hopes of effecting the reinstatement of an overseer unjustly discharged. The next year at the Hadley Thread Mill girls attempted to resist what they considered a "speed up," and the black dyers at the Farr Alpaca Company struck in protest at shortening of hours and so of pay. Holyoke *Transcript,* Nov. 17, 1890, Mar. 14, July 1, 1891. The weavers and spinners at the Germania mills were never formally organized, and yet three times between 1870 and 1900 they struck. They were specially trained workers who could not be quickly replaced. Consequently conflicts there were intra-mural affairs which had no effect upon labor elsewhere in Holyoke. Wm. Mauer (interview).

mule-spinners' union, mill management could know that any agreement reached would be carried out and that any proposal rejected by the union representatives would be repudiated by all. Thus in 1902 the Lyman Mills mule-spinners held out for ten months for a 10 per cent wage increase, corresponding to what had been obtained in Rhode Island. When settlement was reached the new rates amounted to over 16 per cent increase. Such solidarity was an inspiration to weaker labor organizations and sufficed to keep the mule-spinners themselves together through peaceful as well as stormy years.[43]

The other two enduring textile groups, the wool-sorters and the loom-fixers found in Holyoke no occasion to deal with their employers. The wool-sorters were in fact rather a guild than a union, an exceptionally aristocratic group, who regarded themselves as a special caste and their organization as a kind of club. Most of them English by birth, they nourished a tradition of days when the master wool-sorter went to work in a high hat, as much a gentleman in his way as the mill owner in his. Until long after 1903 the difference between a skilled wool-sorter and an ordinary wage earner was never questioned.[44]

Nevertheless it remained true that the factories were not strongholds of unionism. Among the machinery men and the metal-workers a few unions grew up which proved to be permanent, the moulders and core-makers, the machinists and the wire-weavers.[45] The machinists' union grew out of

43. Lyman Mills Papers, Parsons to Lovering, Oct. 11, 1892; Agent's Letter Book, Lovering to Parsons, Aug. 11, Oct. 10, 1893, Apr. 16, Dec. 3, 21, 1894; Holyoke *Transcript*, Nov. 1, 1893; Mass. Bur. Labor Statistics, *Twenty-eighth Annual Report*, 1897, p. 317; *Twenty-fifth Annual Report*, 1894, p. 310; James Burke, Agent Lyman Mills, 1907–1927 (interview); National Spinners' Association of America, *Report of the Twenty-fourth Convention*, 1902; *Report of the Twenty-sixth Convention*, 1903.

44. Not all woolen mills employed wool-sorters. For example, the Germania bought its raw wool already graded and could resort to unskilled help in lieu of wool-sorters.

45. The wire-weavers' was the oldest of these organizations, dating from 1884, but there was no local unit formed in Holyoke separate from Springfield and West Springfield and the members took no active part in the general labor movement in the city. Holyoke *Transcript*, May 23, 1934.

a crying need for a check on hours of work. In a paper-mill city, where the steady running of water wheels or paper machines was considered of utmost importance, the natural tendency was to call upon the repair man at any hour of the day or night, Sunday or weekday alike, if breakdown of a machine threatened. Before the formation of the union, almost any job might be pronounced an emergency demanding skilled machinists' immediate attention at regular pay only. After the organization of the union in 1890 the workmen succeeded in securing pay for overtime and Sundays at the rate of "time and one half," with the magical result that the number of emergency jobs dwindled to a small fraction of what they had been.

The machinists' union was not large compared to the moulders'. This organization, numerically one of the most powerful in the city in the early nineties, played for a time a conspicuous role. Some of its history illustrates the vehement opposition on the part of Holyoke employers of labor to the closed shop and the lengths to which the entrepreneur would go to fight it, just as a later chapter would exemplify the necessity of a union's gaining control of the mechanization of its field if it is to survive indefinitely. In 1891 began a struggle between the owners of the Holyoke Hydrant and Iron Works and their moulders which lasted nearly a year. The foundry owners, determined not to yield on this matter of a closed shop, brought in "scabs," only to find that many either joined the union or soon left town. Union moulders then were haled into court charged with intimidation of non-union men, and after being fined fifty dollars were rebuked by the judge for confounding liberty and anarchy. Rumor labelled the strikers members of the criminal class, so that public opinion would more readily condone the strikebreakers' carrying pistols. Some months later the Central Labor Union, organized the year before, voted to uphold the moulders who thus had behind them the united force of organized labor in the city, even though capitalist Holyoke still viewed them askance. In point of fact there was little or no violence displayed. The union grew in strength, despite its enforced compromise on the

main issue, and the conduct of the labor leaders won for
the city the treasured title of "Banner City of Unionism."[46]

Just as many years later the failure to gain control of
the developments in mechanization of the craft was to un-
dermine the strength of the moulders and eventually to
eliminate them as an industrial factor, conversely the typographical union showed the effect of the successful pursuit
of new processes. The national typographical union, one
of the oldest in America, had been the articulate advocate
of workingmen's rights for decades when the Holyoke
union was formed. In 1894 a strike at the *Transcript* ended
in the victory of the union and the greatly enhanced prestige of the local among workmen. Whether it was due to
exceptionally farsighted leadership, to the numerically
small but highly skilled membership, or to mere good luck,
the union in Holyoke, as elsewhere, consistently kept control for its members of each improvement in printing, so
that when the new presses were installed only union men
could operate them.[47]

The building trades made up the largest section of organized labor. The history of the unions in the building
trades is somewhat obscure, and their importance before
1900 is doubtful. The bricklayers, to be sure, were the very
first to organize in any form in the early eighties, and the
carpenters and painters also early made up unions of a
sort. But there is some evidence that these had no continuous existence, and before the creation in 1887 of the American Federation of Labor the local lodge of the Knights of
Labor apparently exercised such control as there was.
Some strikes were carried on for better pay or shorter
hours and before the slump of 1893 several were successful.
But as soon as that immediate objective had been won or
lost, organization petered out. The treasurers failed to

46. *Ibid.,* Jan. 19, June 9, Aug. 3, 8, 11, 12, Sept. 3, 7, 1891, Mar. 14, 28,
Apr. 1, 1892; John Bleasius, Secretary Central Labor Union (interview);
Mass. Bur. Labor Statistics, *Twenty-fourth Annual Report,* 1893, p. 285.
Years later iron-moulders were again brought into court on charges of
intimidation of non-union men. Holyoke *Transcript,* Sept. 21, 1899.

47. Holyoke *Transcript,* July 13, Sept. 17, 1891, May 8, 11, 21, 24, July
10, 1894; John Bleasius, Urban Fleming (interviews).

keep strict accounts, records were casual at best, and usually what were really new unions had to be set up when a new occasion arose. Building had gone on at such a rapid pace between 1878 and 1893 that it might appear that workmen could dictate their terms without unions. But since the inflow of labor, unskilled and skilled, was quite as incessant as the erection of houses, stores, or mills, the wisdom of regulation of apprenticeship became clear. Thus as early as 1886 the carpenters' union claimed some two hundred members in Holyoke, at least fifty of whom were out of work. In accordance with the accepted arrangements within the national units of the American Federation of Labor, each local union made its own regulations for admission to full membership, three or four years being the usual period for apprenticeship. But until the Central Labor Union was set up in the city and the building-trades unions could witness the potential strength of labor organization, their unions were loose-knit, ill-managed, and weak, their large membership from time to time notwithstanding.[48]

The Central Labor Union of Holyoke has probably been the most important single factor in the strength of organized labor in the city. Formally set up in 1890, it had had already some five years of experience in the guise of an informal association of the labor groups in town. At the beginning of 1891 seven unions were represented, but fifteen months later there were seventeen.[49]

The purpose of the Central Labor Union was to have a clearing house of problems affecting all organized labor in

48. Frank Elting, Agent Holyoke Building Trades Council, 1912–1938 (interview); Holyoke *Transcript,* Feb. 14, 1880, Mar. 23, Oct. 24, Nov. 21, 1885, Mar. 18, 26, 27, 29, Apr. 1, May 3, 4, 5, 1886, Feb. 25, May 5, 1888, Dec. 24, 1891, Oct. 27, 1899.

49. The seventeen unions were: brick makers, tenders, French-speaking carpenters, the English-speaking carpenters, lathers, plumbers, tinsmiths, painters, moulders, coremakers, spinners, paper makers, printers, machinists, day-laborers, cigar makers, and one other unnamed. The paper makers were not recognized as more than a local union until 1893, but they threw in their lot with the working people of the city in the common cause of labor in 1891. Holyoke *Transcript,* Apr. 25, 1885, Oct. 8, 1887, Jan. 19, May 6, July 13, Sept. 7, 1891, Mar. 14, 28, 1892.

the city. Each union might have as many as five delegates
to represent it and at the meetings held every second Sunday of the month any member might bring up for discussion any matter of interest to his fellows. The grievance
committee was perhaps the most important since to it fell
the examination of the rights of each case brought to the
Central Union to enlist the support of united labor in Holyoke. This committee generally functioned with fairness
and efficiency and made the decisions of the Central Labor
Union matters of importance to employers as well as workmen. Indeed during its first few years, the Central Union
gave a vigor and dignity to organized labor which stood
it in good stead in the difficulties of the depression years
following. Between 1893 and 1897 Holyoke workpeople,
whether unionized or not, stood small chance of doing more
than hold on to jobs at slim wages, and they could agree
to the pronouncements of the State Federation of Labor at
the end of 1895 that the stability of the trade union movement was proved by the failure of the panic of 1893 to
destroy it.[50] After suffering a considerable loss of influence
between 1895 and 1899, by the end of the century the Central Labor Union was again showing its strength. Several
new unions had been added and capitalist Holyoke was beginning to realize that labor unions and collective bargaining had come to stay.

The strength of the Central Labor Union inevitably
rose or fell with the power of the unions it included. When
the paper-mill workers won their strike for shorter hours
in 1901, the Central Labor Union boasted forty-six unions
affiliated and a membership of 4,600. After the disastrous
strike in the paper mills in the summer of 1903, the Central Labor Union lost in prestige although it had gained
earlier from the success of the mule-spinners. It seemed to
prove that "an injury to one is the concern of all."[51]

50. Mass. Bur. Labor Statistics, *Twenty-sixth Annual Report,* 1895,
p. 733.
51. *Ibid., Twenty-eighth Annual Report,* 1897, p. 337; *Thirty-second
Annual Report,* 1901, p. 207; Holyoke *Transcript,* Aug. 3, Nov. 28, 1898,
June 12, Oct. 27, 1899.

What were the issues that had brought these labor organizations into existence? Why had not the older methods endured where overseer or superintendent or boss or owner hired his help as individuals, paid them and promoted them or penalized or discharged them according to his own view of their individual merits? The answer is clear. Workpeople had found that improved conditions of labor, higher wages, shorter hours came more readily by means of collective bargaining than by trusting either to the individual initiative of the employer or by obtaining coercive legislation. The struggle of the tour workers in Holyoke doubtless convinced many people of the futility of relying upon enlightened self-interest of the entrepreneur voluntarily to secure the worker shorter hours or better pay, and such labor laws regulating employment of women and children as Massachusetts had enacted may reasonably be said to have been wrung from a reluctant employer group by organization of all the socially-minded forces in the state.

But while careful social planning would probably be carried out more effectively by a complete legislative code, working people found such means slow for securing immediate improvements. Why wait for a state minimum-wage or nine-hour law when by forming a union and forcing concessions by collective bargaining even ditch diggers could help themselves at once?[52] Once sure that unions gave hopes of higher wages and shorter hours of work, workingmen were ready to try local organization.

As soon as a union became firmly established in a trade it was likely to raise the issue of the closed shop, the coercion of all workers in the trade to join the union, the acceptance of the union as the sole agent of labor in that realm. Before 1900, however, only three times did Holyoke unions feel strong enough to raise the closed shop issue.[53]

52. The shovelers' union numbering some 200 members less than a year after its organization won an increase in pay for a nine-hour instead of a ten-hour day. Holyoke *Transcript,* May 25, 1891, Feb. 20, Mar. 14, Apr. 5, 9, 1892.

53. The moulders, the typographical union, and the bricklayers. Mass. Bur. Labor Statistics, *Twenty-fourth Annual Report,* 1893, p. 292.

Generally labor leaders contented themselves with having their unions recognized and winning through them improved wage rates. Naturally the more highly skilled the craft the easier it was to organize and control its workmen. But the problem presented by the continuing influx of labor affected even specialized groups. Short of making a stand for limiting immigration, how could unions cope with this ever-renewing threat to their established position? Yet in Holyoke, though early aware of the implications of the situation, organized labor was unwilling to commit itself to work for the exclusion of newcomers from countries whence many of the union members had themselves recently come. As an alternative, unions strove to enforce regulations anent apprenticeship and limitation of membership, but all through the nineties—as indeed later—the position of labor was greatly weakened by the renewing supply. Another factor in Holyoke's labor market was the large proportion of women employed and their failure to organize. Thus the most significant problem of the workman the unions were unable to handle at all, namely the ensuring of constant employment.[54]

The securing of steady employment seemed an insoluble problem. In 1885, 24.75 per cent of the city's workers were unemployed part of the year, the average being over four and one half months; and ten years later the percentage had risen to 26.42 per cent. This part-time employment was, to be sure, in considerable measure among the unskilled and the builders, the latter as always subject to difficulties of seasonal occupation. But even in manufacturing establishments over 20 per cent of the total number employed at some time were laid off part of the year, and 287 days comprised an average working year.[55] The state reports of unemployment covered in 1884–1885 as well as

54. In 1900 when bricklayers were still being paid forty-five cents an hour, eighty of the hundred union members averaged less than $500 a year income. Holyoke *Transcript*, Mar. 20, 1900.

55. Mass. Bur. Labor Statistics, *Eighteenth Annual Report*, 1887, pp. 268, 277, 183–184; *Census of Mass.*, 1895, *Social Statistics and General Summaries*, VII, 39–40, 96–97, 106; *Manufactures*, V, 266, 330.

in 1895 periods of business depression which gave pictures
not representative of average years. Still to have every ten
years as much as a quarter of the city's employables unemployed during an appreciable part of the year created
a severe problem which served as a check upon the power
of organized labor.[56]

Impatient, perhaps, with the limited achievements of the
unions, some Holyoke workers turned tentatively toward
the end of the century to the Socialist program. As the
Central Labor Union lost in prestige, the Socialists found
themselves for a time increasing in strength. After years
of making little impression upon the labor forces in the
city, the party took on new life in 1898. The old Socialist-
Labor party of the early eighties had survived in spite of
all setbacks, and now comprised an English-speaking as
well as a German-speaking wing. Eugene Debs, addressing
a large gathering in the City Hall in October 1898, proclaimed as not far distant the Socialist revolution which
should eliminate the evils of competition in society. And
as if to strengthen his prophecy a few weeks later, Ward
Three elected for alderman the staunch old Socialist, Max
Ruther, who had run for office on the Socialist ticket every
year since 1884. Probably the enthusiasm of the Socialists
for municipal ownership of the gas and electric-lighting
plants in Holyoke helped carry the vote in 1897 in favor
of purchase of these utilities and prevented the rescinding
of the decision on any later referendum.[57] But otherwise
the practical effectiveness of the party proved insignificant. Ruther failed to be re-elected to the city government
in 1899 and only seventeen delegates materialized at the
Socialist convention held that November. Working people

56. Continuous unemployment reached only 1.13 per cent of the total
numbers considered in the census in 1895. Yet among the thirty-two cities
of Massachusetts, Holyoke ranked twenty-first in 1894–1895 in the matter
of continuous unemployment. This rating was exceeded only by Boston,
New Bedford, Lynn, Taunton, Everett, Chelsea, Worcester, Quincy, Wal-
tham, Marlborough, and Woburn. *Census of Mass.,* 1895, *Social Statistics
and General Summaries,* VII, 107.

57. Holyoke *Transcript,* Dec. 17, 1897, Jan. 4, 26, 31, May 30, June 11,
25, Aug. 3, Sept. 16, Oct. 26, Nov. 14, Dec. 14, 1898.

concluded that Socialism was still too theoretical to be immediately useful to them. In 1901 at a state convention of the American Federation of Labor held in Holyoke the Socialist program was definitely repudiated.[58]

Thus, at the beginning of the new century, despite the growing conviction among Holyoke's working people that to secure a place in the sun for themselves organization was necessary, actual accomplishment was not great. Tenuous beginnings which frequently vanished utterly were the rule. In the building trades, unions were most numerous but at the same time most unstable; the textile industry was virtually still ununionized; and paper makers, who had just begun to feel their union established, were disrupted by the disastrous strike of 1903. The movement had been rather slow to take hold in Holyoke. The preponderance of women in the textile mills, the pitifully low standard of living which many hands brought from their homes overseas or in Canada compared to which wages and living here were almost luxurious, and most important, the continuing opportunity for economic advancement for the thrifty and lucky, all tended to delay the movement toward organization. As long as men could envisage their own emergence into a group economically secure and therefore socially rising they had no desire to put themselves definitely apart from the employer class. In a community which was still growing, where new mills were being started and new personnel added, able conscientious workmen might hope to rise. In papeterie concerns, newly forming in the late eighties and nineties, a man with experience in the paper world might find a chance. And anyone might accumulate enough credit to invest in real estate or a small shop. Not until such hopes began to fade away altogether did unions take vigorous hold.

As the unionized labor movement grew in the city, public opinion shifted somewhat. For a generation articulate Holyoke had prided itself on what it liked to consider the atmosphere of brotherly love existing between employer

58. *Ibid.*, Sept. 28, Nov. 21, 1899, Oct. 9, 1901.

and employe. When Fall River was in the throes of bitter fights between capital and labor, Holyoke pointed to the peace within the mills here. Citizens cited instances when employers voluntarily increased wage rates; and men alluded to the opportunities for promotion from the ranks of labor. But control had been safely in the hands of capital. The increase in power of labor as distinct from or indeed opposed to capital created a new attitude, and the well-to-do became less sure that Christian love and forbearance ruled. But it was more than uneasiness that made for the change of sentiment. In the seventies and early eighties plants were small enough so that employers knew their workpeople as human beings. Sometimes the head of the mill ate his dinner at the company boarding house alongside his employes.[59] The families of her husband's help the owner's wife could know, sometimes in the role of the Lady Bountiful doubtless, but also as a humanly interested neighbor. As the mills expanded and numbers of employes doubled and tripled such relationships gradually ceased. The social gulf widened and with the loss of personal contact loss of understanding followed. To a limited extent for Protestants the Masonic Temple or church still gave common meeting ground to workmen and employers. But working people were chiefly Catholic, mill heads Protestant. True, by the turn of the century paternalism had not set in, and the capitalist group, scarcely as yet labelling itself such, had not as yet any sense of social guilt, a twentieth century social phenomenon. But uncertainty had supplanted confidence.

Organized labor was that "your people" that Hamilton a century before had called "a great beast?" The long strike in the paper mills, although conducted in orderly fashion and concluded without bitterness, gave citizens a jolt. Their faith in the acquiescence of workpeople in the existing social and industrial order had been disturbed. Capital had, to be sure, triumphed, and outwardly a cooperative spirit on the part of labor again prevailed. But

59. *Ibid.,* Feb. 7, 11, 1880; John Hildreth, W. A. Prentiss (interviews).

how must it be fostered? Holyoke had been revealed to be
no stronghold of idyllic Christian brotherhood, but an industrial city where lay a gulf between capital and labor.
To narrow the breach was a problem of the next era.

VIII

MANAGEMENT AND LABOR, 1903–1922

THE industrial history of Holyoke from the first years of the twentieth century to the end of the post-World War depression follows an expected pattern. The city grew in population and wealth, weathering the periodic business slumps before 1914 with encouraging stability. For example, in the depression of 1908 the decrease of output of manufactured goods in Holyoke as compared to the year before was 9.74 per cent, about four million dollars' worth, while the decrease in Lawrence, Lowell, and Worcester amounted to 16.6 per cent, 20.02 per cent, and 21.86 per cent respectively.[1] Despite the increased cost of power in Holyoke, twenty-four new small industries started up between 1909 and 1914.[2] But the next years pinched industrial development badly. The Underwood tariff hit the textile mills and the war in Europe cut off from the paper mills their best source of essential raw materials as well as some markets for finished paper. Then in 1916 came the war boom which set every plant in the city running to capacity, as far as fuel and labor shortage permitted. Brief reaction immediately after the Armistice was again succeeded by eighteen months of nearly unprecedented prosperity. The collapse in 1921 was the inevitable result of excessive expansion during the war.

Although twentieth-century Holyoke was no longer primarily the Paper City, the fortunes of the paper mills still marked the rise and fall in the city's industrial progress. Consistently the independent paper companies seemed to

1. Holyoke *Transcript,* Sept. 13, 1909. Boston and Chicopee, however, lost only 7.77 per cent and 7.31 per cent respectively. The average earning in Holyoke for 1908 the *Transcript* placed at $614 per employe. *Ibid.,* Dec. 23, 1908.

2. *Fourteenth Census of the United States,* 1920, *Manufactures,* IX, 632.

fare better than the trust.[3] To the array of independent
mills was added in 1904 the Crocker-McElwain Company,
organized by the erstwhile manufacturing heads of the
American Writing Paper Company. In the history of the
Crocker-McElwain Company may be traced the course of
one of Holyoke's successful independent paper concerns, a
career which, if not entirely typical, at least suggests the
general pattern.

Probably no other company in the city so well illustrates
under a system of competitive capitalism the necessity of
competent management. Crocker and McElwain withdrew
from the American Writing Paper Company when their
advice was rejected by its executives. The great writing
paper trust, still producing a large percentage of the writing paper output of the country, was shortly to reveal its
incapacity to dominate the market or even to pay the interest on its own bonds. Crocker and McElwain, however,
although not having any great amount of capital to begin
on, proceeded to carry out their ideas as quickly as they
could finance their enterprise. Their underlying principle
was that money could be made in paper manufacture only
by running a mill's machines faster than competitors ran
theirs. Thus the shrewd manufacturer increased volume
without proportionate capital outlay. But in order to speed
up machines to that extent complete overhauling or re-
placement was periodically essential. On the issue of spending $1,825,000 for revamping obsolete and therefore slow-
running machinery, Crocker and McElwain had split with
the American Writing. Now in their own mill they were to
vindicate their policies.[4]

Good luck attended them at the outset, as they were able
to purchase of the Water Power Company on moderate
terms the old Cabot Street mill with ten permanent mill
powers appurtenant. The Water Power Company had sold
its last permanent powers in 1881, and, save by transfer
such as this, permanent power could not be had. With this

3. Holyoke *Transcript,* Jan. 21, 1902, May 13, 1909.
4. Private information.

important initial advantage, the newly equipped mill began manufacture in 1905, operating one Fourdrinier machine. Since the early eighties the amount of capital needed
successfully to launch a paper company had multiplied
considerably. Machinery and plant were far more expensive, for only machines that could run at high rates of speed
could turn out a large enough volume of paper to sell at
competitive prices. All the skill and experience of Clifton
Crocker and Frank McElwain did not suffice to make their
investment profitable until they added in 1907 a second
machine to the mill and so doubled its output. But from
then on, money panic of 1907–1908 notwithstanding, their
mill did well, enabling them to expand again in 1913 by
the purchase of the old Chemical Paper plant of the Newtons. This once prosperous mill had been losing money under half-hearted management and was in need of thorough
modernization of equipment and buildings. But it had sixteen permanent powers and so promised unfailing cheap
water power at a time when non-permanent water power or
coal bade fair to be increasingly expensive. Within a year
of Crocker and McElwain's taking over they had completely reorganized the personnel of the Chemical, and
daily output jumped from thirty-four tons to forty-five
without any additional equipment.[5]

The boom of 1916 brought the Crocker-McElwain mills
such a rush of business that the owners were able to clear
up their indebtedness to the banks and extinguish their
mortgage. They did not then increase their plant but ran
all the installed machinery full blast night and day as long
as the demand held. Not until the depression came after
the war did they replace old machinery and expand their
capacity to be ready for the next upward swing of the
business cycle.[6]

Quite different was the course followed by the American
Writing Paper Company. The problem confronting the

5. Holyoke *Transcript*, Sept. 3, 1914.

6. R. F. McElwain (interview). During the depression of the thirties
output at the Chemical was increased from 90 tons to 120 a day, and by
1936 the company was able to pay off its last indebtedness.

trust was not easy. Fundamentally the difficulties were traceable to the large overcapitalization with which the company had begun. But shrewd independent manufacturers aver that this need not have crippled the company indefinitely. From the beginning the executive heads dedicated company earnings to reducing this loss instead of to modernizing equipment and increasing output and control of the market. The year 1902 was the most prosperous year the paper industry knew, up until the war boom when every paper manufacturer made money, and yet in 1903 company officials, in spite of the comfortable cash balance, stood aghast at the proposal to spend $1,825,000 on new machinery. Million-dollar expenditures were too big for them to contemplate, just as million-dollar sales campaigns and million-dollar profits were unthinkably large.[7] The men in charge had been capable heads of small independent mills; now they could not enlarge their scope to think in terms of millions. By 1906 the company had already lost domination of the writing-paper market, and admittedly faced as keen competition as its individual mills had encountered when the trust was organized. No dividends had been paid, partly because bondholders opposed such a policy. Stockholdings had become so scattered that when early in 1907, after a good year, the directors voted to reduce the capital stock from $25,000,000 to $22,000,000,

7. Holyoke *Transcript*, June 13, 1903. In 1903 when Eagle Lodge first presented its demand for a higher wage schedule, company officials published a long letter in the *Transcript* justifying their refusal. The arguments to the layman might sound convincing: that even before 1898 loft-dried mills were losing business to machine-dried mills, and that book mills outside Holyoke running on wood pulp papers were able to operate more cheaply than Holyoke book mills because these outside mills manufactured their own wood pulp. Thereupon Holyoke book mills were pushed into the field of machine-dried writings and so took more business from the fine mills. To operate at all, the company contended, its labor costs must be no higher than pulp paper mills elsewhere.

The fallacy lay in the fact that seven years out of ten pulp could be bought more cheaply in Holyoke than pulp mills could afford to sell it to their own paper mills. To compete in the cheaper lines meant running the machinery faster and therefore spending money on rebuilding a few of the sixty-six machines every year.

sufficient stockholders could not be found to sanction the measure.[8] Reorganization and recapitalization, prophesied as early as 1905, was not to be seriously considered for another eight years.

The Wall Street panic in the fall of 1907 ushered in a period of reverses. Orders fell off. For months work was staggered through the various divisions of the company in order to divide what work there was among the employes. Water shortage aggravated conditions since steam was far more costly.[9] Instead of pursuing Crocker-McElwain tactics of seizing depression years for remodelling equipment, the American Writing abandoned its building projects.

Then the three years 1910, 1911, and 1912 saw business improve so greatly as to warrant paying small dividends on the cumulative preferred stock. But 1913 brought disaster.[10] General business depression cut sales, prices could not be pushed up in spite of higher costs of raw materials, especially of rags, and a severe drought which closed the canal-head gates for sixteen days caused large coal consumption and hence increased operating expenses. Continued water shortage through much of 1914, soaring prices of imported raw materials after the outbreak of the war in Europe,[11] lack of shipping facilities to carry on export to South America, and, most important of all, drop in demand for paper combined to bring the American Writing by midsummer 1915 to the very brink of bankruptcy. Expenses for 1914 had exceeded income by $100,-000. The 5 per cent bonds of the company were selling at 52, the cumulative preferred stock at $8, and the common stock at 75 cents. Unable to meet the interest on the bonds

8. *Ibid.*, Feb. 18, 1903, Feb. 20, 25, 1905, Feb. 21, 1906, Jan. 16, Feb. 13, 15, 1907.

9. *Ibid.*, Dec. 16, 1907, Jan. 6, Apr. 9, June 27, Oct. 29, Dec. 2, 1908.

10. *Ibid.*, Feb. 16, Aug. 19, 1910, Feb. 8, 1911, Dec. 19, 1912. In 1908, 2 per cent was first paid, 1 per cent in 1909, 2 per cent in 1910, 1911, and 1912, and 1 per cent in April 1913. Payment of 7 per cent was required, but even in its best year, 1902, 5 per cent was the most the company had ever earned. *Ibid.*, June 10, 1915.

11. Notably rags, pulp, china clay, wires, and bleaching powders. *Ibid.*, Aug. 10, 1914.

and still carry on business, the directors, helpless, called for complete reorganization.[12]

Bondholders and stockholders each engaged a competent engineer to make a survey of the condition of the company property and report upon prospects for the future. The report to the bondholders' committee contended that real estate, plant, and equipment were adequate security to cover the amount of the outstanding bonds, provided there was neither forced sale nor complete shutdown. Workable schemes of running the mills profitably must be found. The independent mills in Holyoke were operating successfully. With much the same natural advantages and few inevitable problems not shared by their independent competitors, the American Writing Paper mills, if properly run, also should be able to make money. Many of the water rights and owned permanent mill powers were an enormous asset for a concern producing high grade papers. And another important advantage lay in the character of Holyoke's skilled labor, a group intelligent and still not markedly aggressive.

Responsibility for the sorry state of the company, the report continued, had to be fairly placed upon the old management. Able manufacturers though there had been at the head, they had failed to grasp the need of large-scale, closely coördinated operations and a wide view of business opportunities and demands. The organization had been like a loose association of separate mills using one general superintendent for consulting on manufacture, one chief engineer for construction problems, the general sales office as a jobbing house, and the treasurer for banking. The incentives of individual proprietorship were gone and no rewards to initiative and conspicuous ability had been substituted. Each mill continued to make the principal grades upon which it had run when independent, and consequently the company had several papers of the same grade to be sold for the same purpose with only different water marks or slight mill differences to distinguish them. Thus the costly short runs and resulting

12. *Ibid.*, Aug. 10, 1914, Feb. 4, June 10, 21, July 27, 1915.

waste of stock and time necessary for independent mills had been carried on under the combine. No one knew which lines were profitable and which were not, or, more than in a very general way, what each mill could best make.

Yet obsolescence of machinery was not an outstanding cause of unprofitable operation, for although the company had not bought a new machine for fifteen years, maintenance of the old had been cared for. Closer coöperation, broader vision, properly kept costs, and incentive to hard work by recognition of ability were essential for success in the future, whether the financial problems were met or not.[13]

So much for criticisms of the management. As the moment for reorganization approached, stockholders and bondholders were so at variance about what should be done that action was halted for a time.[14] The interest on the bonds was paid while company officials waited for some concerted move on the part of the owners. And then in 1916 business in paper took a sudden upswing. All talk of shutdown or other drastic measures ceased. As the year wore on the most pessimistic became hopeful for the company's survival.[15]

The only two years in the history of the paper industry when there were enough orders to go around were 1916 and 1920.[16] The 1916 boom came just in time to save the

13. John G. Callan, Report to the Bondholders' Committee of the American Writing Paper Company, Aug. 27, 1915 (in possession of the author).

14. Holyoke *Transcript*, Aug. 4, 1915. The bondholders urged curtailment of salaries and running expenses, while the preferred stockholders wished to scale down the value of the bonds. The stockholders could not be brought together to take any common action.

15. *Ibid.*, Nov. 10, Dec. 17, 1915, July 7, 1916.

16. Ordinarily there is overproduction, chiefly because when the time comes to revamp a mill it is good economy to expand its capacity at the same time. Only the fact that consumption increases almost as rapidly as production prevents complete confusion. Callan lists per capita paper consumption in the United States between 1910 and 1915 as follows:

1910	104 pounds	1913	127 pounds
1911	110.3 "	1914	138 "
1912	119.8 "	1915 (estimated)	151.9 pounds.

Callan, Report to the Bondholders' Committee.

American Writing Paper Company for another eight years. Every paper manufacturer made money, no matter how inefficient he might be, the only trouble being the scarcity and high price of raw material. Some overproduction resulted and had to be absorbed in the course of the next two years, but although prices for paper advanced only 20 per cent as over against 37 per cent for materials, the paper industry throve right up to the signing of the Armistice. Meanwhile in 1917 the American Writing had spent half a million dollars on modernization and a new president had reorganized the personnel and centralized administration.[17]

Labor costs rose rapidly during the war. Most of the paper mills were now running three shifts, and sufficient skilled help to keep all running full time would have been hard to get even had the army not taken men. Eagle Lodge, revived and again powerful, together with other unions concerned secured large wage increases twice in fourteen months. The coal shortage caused the shutdown of several mills, as the federal fuel administrator allowed for a time only water power to be used in paper manufacture. Not until paper was put upon the government essential-industries list in August 1918 could Holyoke mills be sure of power. Then, however, the American Writing mills operated 190 per cent above normal.[18]

The signing of the Armistice brought immediate reaction. Volume of production dropped to half what had been called for three months earlier, and the first six months of 1919 caused the American Writing Paper Company a $500,000 loss. In 1920 again demand rose and net profits for the year were higher than for any year except 1916. But, as in every field of industry, the market was soon glutted and in 1921 came the inevitable depression. The

17. The bonds were reduced considerably and before the end of the war there was hope that they could be extinguished when due in 1919 and leave the company with a surplus from which to make payments on the preferred stock dividends, by then 120 per cent in arrears. Holyoke *Transcript*, Mar. 9, Sept. 27, 1916, July 12, 1918.

18. *Ibid.*, Mar. 28, 1914, Jan. 14, Feb. 7, Mar. 14, 1916, May 23, 28, July 24, 1917, Jan. 15, 17, June 21, July 18, Aug. 5, 1918, Dec. 3, 1919.

combine in Holyoke operating 50 per cent, cut prices, salaries, and wages, and launched an advertising campaign to promote sales. Thus it staggered through the year and held on precariously for another. Its finances were so tangled and its future so dubious that most of Holyoke merely wondered not whether, but when, the company would collapse. In 1923 a petition in bankruptcy was filed.[19]

The death throes of the original company were so protracted that Holyoke was not particularly disturbed. Only the war had postponed the collapse, and the city had definitely steeled itself for the blow as early as 1915. Bankers, merchants, real estate dealers, and city officials could comfort themselves with the knowledge that some of the business the American Writing mills lost went to independent companies in Holyoke. No one denied that the combine had from its inception brought catastrophe in its wake; having long since accepted that fact, citizens turned their attention to more hopeful enterprises. Not only the unaffiliated paper manufacturing concerns, but the converter and papeterie makers had grown greatly in importance to the city since 1903. The value of the product turned out and the amount of wages paid had both multiplied. Furthermore, machine shops producing papermakers' equipment had expanded. Seven new machine shops were opened in Holyoke between 1909 and 1914. Thus while the gradual failure of the American Writing Paper Company was disappointing to Holyoke, the local paper industry still played a large part in the city's prosperity. Holyoke had not continued its one-time domination of the writing-paper industry, but neither had its importance as a paper city altogether faded.[20]

19. *Ibid.,* Dec. 7, 1918, Feb. 28, Mar. 19, May 1, June 20, 1919, Jan. 5, 8, May 9, June 13, Aug. 15, 23, Oct. 18, 1921.

20. *Ibid.,* Jan. 28, 1904, Jan. 15, May 13, July 28, 1901, Mar. 24, 1914, Jan. 5, 22, 1921. See *Holyoke Directory,* 1903 and 1921. For example, in 1914 in the 21 paper and wood pulp establishments 204 more wage-earners than were employed in 1909 netted $276,000 more wages. *Fourteenth Census of U. S.,* 1920, *Manufactures,* IX, 613, 632.

From the point of view of the numbers of persons directly affected, the welfare of the textile mills, as always, was of greater concern than any other of Holyoke's industries. Silk, cotton, woolen, worsted—the only four establishments in the city each to employ over a thousand hands in 1920 were textile companies.[21]

Of the silk and thread concerns there is little to say.[22] In spite of some downs as well as ups, the local silk mills prospered. In 1909 the chief of these, William Skinner and Sons, embarked upon a new method of training help in order to be ready for business expansion at any moment. By older arrangements silk weavers had had to pay $10 down and then work two or three months as apprentices before they were placed upon the mill payroll at all. Now sixty young women were employed at $4 a week to spend a few hours of each day in learning the exacting art of silk weaving. Thus the mill management created a trained reserve corps of help.[23] The American Thread Company mills were increasingly tied to the interests of the great English corporation owning them, the English Sewing Cotton Company. Not only absentee owners but foreign owners directed the fate of the Holyoke operatives. In the general business expansion of 1916, the capacity of the mills was enlarged and 2,000 employes were given a 5 per cent wage increase; when business fell off after the war wages were automatically cut.[24]

The Lyman Mills most of all the Holyoke textile mills

21. *Fourteenth Census of U. S., 1920, Manufactures,* IX, 602.

22. A private family-owned concern in one case, a great foreign-owned corporation in the other, make it impossible to secure more than the most general data.

23. Holyoke *Transcript,* Feb. 28, 1902, Oct. 30, 1909, Feb. 13, 1913, May 18, 1920.

24. *Ibid.,* Jan. 6, June 5, 1908, Mar. 2, June 2, 1914, Aug. 3, 1915, Jan. 21, 1916, June 12, 1919, Nov. 12, 1920. This great trust, largely one with J. & P. Coats and Company, controlled 90 per cent of the domestic thread business in the United States and 60 to 70 per cent of the manufacturers' thread business by 1914, so that the federal courts ordered the trust dissolved. The next year, instead of 18 per cent profits earned on the common stock, the company earned only 10 per cent. Otherwise the court order made no apparent difference locally.

tended to follow the lead in matters of output and wage rates of the four New England cotton centers, Fall River, New Bedford, Lawrence, and Lowell. Partly because of this recognized policy, partly because of the caution bred into the management after the mule-spinners won their ten months' strike in 1902 and 1903, and partly because of a shift in personnel in Holyoke there were no labor troubles whatsoever here until 1916. The week's strike then was so quickly settled by granting the machinists' demands for pay increase that it can scarcely be termed labor trouble at all. In Fall River a bitter twenty-six weeks' strike in 1904 and in Lawrence eight years later another violent conflict between capital and labor had centered Holyoke textile operatives' attention on the wage battles away from home. Other cities had fought out the issues for all New England textile mills and Holyoke, itself not a battleground, merely accepted the verdicts. Thus the Lyman Mills increased wages early in 1907, cut them the next year, and ran at partial operation all the winter following the panic of 1907, and, when the success of the Lawrence strike was clearly predictable, hastily volunteered a small increase for the Holyoke help. Changes in styles, particularly in widths of fine fabrics, necessitated outlay for remodelling machinery in the slack years of 1914 and 1915. Yet a small stock dividend in 1915 proves the continued earning power of the company even in hard times. The Lyman Mills on the whole carried on comparatively even rates of operation and pay.[25]

25. *Ibid.*, Sept. 7, 1904, Jan. 12, 18, 1905, June 1, Dec. 27, 1907, Jan. 6, 24, Mar. 20, 1908, Feb. 17, Mar. 12, 13, 18, 1912, Apr. 6, 12, 1916, May 20, June 30, Nov. 12, Dec. 13, 20, 1920; Lyman Mills Papers, Burke to Mass. Bur. Labor Statistics, Oct. 1907; Burke to Parsons, Feb. 16, Apr. 21, 24, Aug. 12, 22, Sept. 10, 1914, July 24, Oct. 9, 25, Dec. 18, 1915; Parsons to Burke, Sept. 11, Nov. 5, Dec. 8, 1914; Burke to Lovering, Apr. 1916; Directors to Stockholders, Feb. 8, 1915.

The extent of the depression in cotton textiles is evidenced by the agent's report to the treasurer in April 1915. The mill was equipped with 12,368 spindles and 2,700 looms. In 1913, 76 per cent of the spindles were run and 65 per cent of the looms; in 1914, 74 per cent of the spindles and 69 per cent of the looms. *Ibid.*, Burke to Parsons, Apr. 3, 1915.

A new agent appointed in 1907 was a local man, brought up through the mill ranks, and the help had frequent occasion to be grateful for the agent's understanding and sympathetic attitude toward their problems. Here was a link between owners and workers which proved surprisingly effective. At least twice between 1917 and 1922 Agent Burke interceded in the operatives' behalf with the company directors in Boston, once taking upon his own shoulders responsibility for an increase in wage schedule, in 1922 steadfastly refusing to countenance more than a 10 per cent cut. Mutual respect and confidence thus marked the dealings between management and workpeople down to the dissolution of the company in 1927. The mill came through the post-war depression unusually well, having succeeded in preventing cancellation of contracts and having kept inventory low.[26]

As the twentieth century wore on the woolen industry as distinct from worsted manufacture played a less significant

26. James Burke (interview).
The liquidation in 1927, so far from being the result of shaky financial position, was due to the eagerness of a group of stockholders to realize completely upon the substantial assets of the company. The whole story of the circumstances leading up to the vote to liquidate will doubtless never be told. The move was probably initiated by men who had lost money when the Dwight mills of Chicopee were closed up in 1922. When investigation of the financial status of the Lyman Mills revealed that over $200 could be netted on each $100 par value share of stock stockholders were anxious to get their money out. The coarse-goods mill, where southern competition was felt most, was shown to be losing money, but the fine-goods mills were operating profitably still. The story goes that this business was coveted by other New England mills, some of whose stockholders were also Lyman Mill stockholders.
About 1,050 operatives were thrown out of work by the liquidation, but in 1927 jobs were easier to find than after 1929. Some 200 hands had been displaced by machinery between 1920 and 1927. Some of the 1,050 found jobs in other local textile mills, some in textile mills elsewhere, some found new means of livelihood, and some drifted back to Quebec whence they had come. Of the Poles, a number chose the moment to go back to farming, hiring out as hands on the valley onion and tobacco farms until they could scrape together the means of buying a plot of land of their own. For the city taxpayers in the thirties the dispersion of the 1,050 may have been a boon, inasmuch as the city relief rolls swelled to 1,700 families in 1933 without them. Private information.

part in the city's history than before. Two concerns were
blotted out altogether and even the Germania mill gradually ceased to be of vital importance. By running largely
upon high-grade chinchilla and plaid-faced overcoatings
the Germania continued to do well for some years. Apart
from the prosperity brought by the abnormal demands of
the war, the peak of its success was reached about 1912.
Then tariff changes in 1913, additional state laws restricting hours of labor, and cancellation of government contracts after the Armistice contributed to hard times for the
concern. But fundamentally the decline of the company's
business was due to the change in fashion effected by the
introduction of the closed, heated automobile. Heavy wool
overcoatings were doomed.[27]

The city's great worsted concern, the Farr Alpaca
Company, however, enjoyed twenty years of unparalleled
prosperity. By 1903 the company's monopoly was well established. Foreign competition was eliminated by the pro-
hibitive duties of the Dingley Tariff and domestic competition was quickly frozen out. Just as in 1902 the Farr
Alpaca met the threat of American competition by increasing plant and production and thereby decreasing costs per
piece until every rival manufacturer could be undersold, so
the company checked every later attempt to cut in upon
its monopoly by further expansion and speeding up of machinery.[28] Thus through the depression of 1907–1908,
while would-be rivals were obliged to curtail operations,
the Farr Alpaca mills ran at capacity, although as the
treasurer reported, the company had to make lightning
changes in qualities and styles to keep it going. The effect
of the lower duties of the Payne-Aldrich Tariff in 1910
was estimated to be the equivalent of a 5 per cent cut in

27. Holyoke *Transcript,* June 14, 1912, Feb. 3, 1913, June 30, Dec. 13,
1920. The Germania Mills were liquidated in 1931. Part of the plant was
then torn down; part was turned over to a new company, made up of a
few of the stockholders of the old. This greatly reduced plant has operated with success for the last few years.

28. F. A. Co. Records, II, 246, 330. In 1902 the average margin of profit
was 4.37 per cent; in 1909 it was 1.72 per cent.

volume of sales.[29] And still the Holyoke mill made money. In 1913 it had 3,123 looms in operation.

The still lower rates under the Underwood Tariff, put into effect in 1914, necessitated sharp curtailment. The difference in wage rates of the mills of Bradford, England, manufacturing fine quality alpacas, and of the Farr Alpaca plant was a tremendous handicap to offset by more efficient methods and machinery.[30] The United States imports of worsted cloth for 1914 under the new tariff were three-and-one-half times the imports for 1913. At about this time another factor affected the company's business, namely, the experiment adopted by some of the great ready-made clothing houses, who were among the mill's largest customers, of substituting skeleton linings in men's suits for full linings. Shoulders and sleeves were lined and elsewhere seams were merely bound. The resulting shrink-

29. Holyoke *Transcript,* July 21, 1910. In 1908, 147,000 pounds of alpaca were imported into the United States, 165,000 pounds in 1909, and 414,000 pounds in the first six months of 1910.

30. *Ibid.,* July 2, Oct. 19, 1911. The rates paid in 1911 by the chief English firm for a fifty-five-and-a-half-hour week and by the Farr Alpaca Company for a fifty-six-hour week were as follows:

	Joseph Benn & Sons, Bradford, England	Farr Alpaca Company, Holyoke, Mass., U.S.A.
Tenders of Noble combs	$4.80	$10.15
Tenders of heavy drawing frames .	3.00	8.55
Tenders of roving frames . . .	2.64	8.55
Gill box minders	3.00	8.20
Spinning Dept.		
Overseers	7.20	18.00
Spinners (Girls)	2.70	8.10
Doffers (Boys and Girls)	2.16	6.05
Weaving Dept.		
Loomfixers	8.64	17.40
Weavers (average of all)	3.80	13.00
Firemen	6.00	18.30
Mechanics	7.20	18.13
Carpenters	7.64	17.98

To reduce these discrepancies in labor costs the American concern in 1912 replaced a thousand old English looms with new American automatic shuttle-changing looms, thereby greatly cutting weaving costs. New faster spinning frames were also installed. F. A. Co. Records, II, 356–357.

age in volume of linings needed cut into the Farr Alpaca's business appallingly. For a year the Holyoke mills ran only three days a week.

By way of forestalling labor troubles the company directors in 1914 acquiesced in a proposal of the treasurer to share profits with the employes. Wage cuts were expected to follow the new tariff and American woolen manufacturers faced the prospect of "bearing the brunt of the inevitable labor contest." The new bonus scheme provided for paying to each person employed for the full year preceding the same percentage of his year's wages as was paid to the stockholder on his stock. The sums accruing on wages of employes who were not on the payroll a full year were to be put into a pension fund. As if to placate the stockholders, the management at the same time declared a stock dividend increasing the capital stock from $2,400,-000 to $7,200,000 by converting the surplus undistributed profits into capital, so that each stockholder received two new shares of stock for every one he owned before. The sum paid out to the 3,000 employes, it was estimated, when there was full operation would amount to about one quarter the amount paid in dividends. Even in 1915 when for ten months of the year the mill ran only at half time the help received over $79,000 in cash bonuses. The stabilizing effect was exactly what the management hoped for. Workers were grateful to the treasurer for his stand in their behalf, and a committee of employes presented him with an engraved testimonial of their gratitude. Their appreciation of the company's generosity nourished a genuine loyalty to the concern and labor turnover was reduced to a minimum.[31] Here in the largest industrial plant in the

31. F. A. Co. Records, II, 365, 375; III, 2–7, 17, 21; Holyoke *Transcript,* Jan. 28, Feb. 3, Mar. 28, 1914. The inauguration of profit-sharing was not welcomed by some stockholders who were also employers of labor in other Holyoke mills, where the bonus system was deemed too expensive to adopt. The bonus did not eliminate all wage controversy within the Farr organization; twice between 1914 and 1921 the dyers and crabbe-room help protested the rates. Yet even there the matter was quickly settled.

city the breach between capital and labor which at the beginning of the twentieth century had threatened to widen irreparably was effectively spanned for many years.

By 1916 the European war was providing the equivalent of complete tariff protection to all American textile manufacturers, and, skeleton linings notwithstanding, volume of business and profits for the Farr Alpaca Company rose to a new high. Although private customers' orders continued to fall off, government contracts in 1917 and 1918 alone ran 41 per cent of the looms. Raw materials and particularly dyes were hard to secure, but the problem of labor shortage which forced one quarter of the textile machinery in the United States to stand idle in 1918 did not touch the Farr. The bonus was doing its work. The enormous volume this produced netted large profits in spite of the rapid increase in labor costs. The state law of 1919 making forty-eight hours instead of fifty-four the legal working week for women further added to labor charges, since the help expected and received the same pay per week as before. In November 1918 cancellation of government contracts and of civilian orders too brought about a six months' curtailment of output, only to be followed later in 1919 and in 1920 by renewed expansion. English mills after the war were confronted with higher costs, and the rise in English labor rates enabled American mills for a year or two to operate without acute competition from abroad.

More land, more storage space, more power, more looms —the Farr Alpaca Company proceeded as in the past to prepare for keener competition in the future by enlarging its plant. Capitalization was increased for the third time in fourteen years, bringing the total up to $14,700,000. The directors transferred $5,400,000 from undivided profits as a stock dividend and $1,800,000 was raised by marketing new shares. Dividends of 15 per cent were continued through 1919. The general business depression of 1921 affected the concern, although shrewd raw material purchases netted profits even when manufacturing could not.

And after some readjustments the next year again success attended the enlarged enterprise, until the very name of Farr Alpaca seemed to conjure up visions of unending profits, and the management itself, unfortunately, expected wealth to roll in unsought. In part to this complacent optimism, in part to the unwieldy size of the concern must the catastrophes after 1930 be attributed.[32]

For the first twenty years of the twentieth century, Holyoke thus depended for prosperity upon the paper industry and its subsidiaries and upon textiles, although the machinery interests, notably the great pump works, also employed a considerable number of skilled workmen and were important to the city. The International Pump Company, however, encountered financial difficulties which led to reorganization in 1916 and the loss of control of the local plant by the Holyoke men who had developed it. This change made little difference at the time in the running of the works, although years later the Holyoke plant was to be sacrificed to the welfare of company units elsewhere. But the development of electrically transmitted power after 1903 made the city's power advantages less outstanding than formerly. One great machinery establishment built its new factory in 1911 across the river in Willimansett, and other concerns in the course of that decade followed to build where power could be bought as easily from the Holyoke Water Power Company as in Holyoke and where real estate and housing were cheaper.[33] The future of the city was inextricably linked with the power situation. This had various aspects.

When in 1902 the city went into the business of selling gas and electricity in Holyoke, electrical development was in its infancy. The city had paid a good price for the Holyoke Water Power Company plants and it expected the municipal G. and E., as it has been called ever since, to act

32. F. A. Co. Records, III, 24–25, 35–38, 54–55, 71–73, 100–101, 127–129; Holyoke *Transcript,* Jan. 7, 1916, Jan. 30, May 7, 1919, Jan. 9, Dec. 13, 1920.

33. Holyoke *Transcript,* Feb. 10, 1901, Mar. 7, 1904, July 2, 1919, Feb. 15, 1921.

as the sole purveyor of gas and electricity to the community, to private customers and municipality alike. But in 1903 the Holyoke Water Power Company, eager to sell the surplus power it could command whenever the river was high or mills not using all the water their indentures entitled them to, sought and obtained of the legislature the right to generate and sell electricity for power in units of not less than one hundred horsepower. The city's exclusive electrical power rights therefore were lost. At the time there was no opposition to the Water Power Company's re-entering the electrical power field, since users of one hundred horsepower were few and the city could not then have supplied many such customers. In fact in 1903 the G. and E. had only forty-three customers for power altogether.[34]

The next move toward expanding the electrical power possibilities of Holyoke came in 1909, when the Water Power Company, having secured the acquiescence of the city government, obtained an extension of its charter which permitted the company to sell electricity in less than one hundred horsepower units for either power or lighting to manufacturers leasing space in any building owned by the company or upon which the company held a purchase-money mortgage. In seeking the city's consent, the Water Power Company held out prospects of undertaking to erect or to finance new buildings to house infant industrial ventures, and of inducing new industries to come to Holyoke. The citizens, anxious to see the city grow, agreed to the scheme. The result for the city was disappointing. The projected new mill was not put up, few new users of power came to build up new industrial enterprises, and several concerns moved across the river, out of Holyoke altogether. The long story of the bitter feud which flared up between Holyoke Water Power Company and the G. and E. has no place at this point in the industrial history of the city. Cer-

34. *Ibid.,* Dec. 15, 1932, Mar. 19, 1903, Dec. 29, 1904; *Municipal Register,* 1904, p. 324.

tainly the ultimate effect of the conflict was detrimental to
the city as a whole.[35] Probably the Water Power Company's extended charter rights benefited immediately not
the city but the company, and, failing to effect the incom-
ing of new concerns, merely lost to the municipality some
of its power and many of its electric-light customers.[36]

Real estate dealers contended that land not adjacent to
the canals, which years before the Water Power Company
held for sale at moderate prices, the company would now
sell only at exorbitant rates, thereby stifling the growth of
the city. The electric transmission of power made usable
for manufacturing sites property hitherto of comparatively slight value, and the directors of the Water Power
Company, citizens thought, were short-sightedly hoarding
land and power. The company could afford to forego real
estate sales in Holyoke if instead it could sell power in Willimansett. There, in the comparative ease with which power
could be brought to the manufacturer instead of having
to bring the manufacturer to the power, not only in Holyoke, but in all New England, lay the basic clue to Holyoke's failure to grow rapidly. As time went on this power
factor became increasingly significant. With the development of the Turners Falls Power Company, able and anxious to extend its power lines into every town in western
New England, the peculiar advantages for manufacturers
of location in the water-power city by the Holyoke dam
dwindled to the vanishing point. After the war in order
to compete more effectively the Holyoke Water Power
Company built new hydro-electric power plants at the
canal overflows, and by means of offering cheaper rates
succeeded in keeping its customers in the neighborhood
and in bringing to Holyoke a few new ones. But the new
concerns that settled in the city were attracted by offers of
financial backing rather than by outstanding power ad-

35. The rivalry and unfriendliness has continued down to the present,
causing unfortunate delays in needed improvements in the city.
36. Holyoke *Transcript,* Jan. 14, 18, 26, Feb. 10, Mar. 9, 1909, Feb. 7,
1911, Mar. 8, Oct. 15, 1912, Nov. 29, 1920, Dec. 15, 1932.

vantages, and of the new enterprises only one was permanent.[37]

While campaigns launched by the Chamber of Commerce advertising the city's opportunities for manufacture were not able to alter the fundamental fact that the original advantage of power had now been lost, and while real estate prices remained high and decent housing difficult to find, Holyoke still had promising features for her promoters to emphasize.[38] The most outstanding of these for the industrialist was the character of labor to be had. The growth of a radical labor element, dreaded and half expected here in 1902 and 1903, had not materialized. Not only were the working people of the community skilled in their respective trades, they were intelligent and generally conservative.

The years from 1903 to 1916 marked a period of quiescence in the organized labor movement. For women and minors state law in 1907 restricted factory hours to fifty-six a week. Eagle Lodge after the unhappy experience of 1903 virtually ceased to exist for a time in spite of periodic efforts to reorganize it, and thus the Holyoke branch of the Brotherhood of Paper Makers, for all its efforts to dominate labor in Holyoke paper mills, effected little. An attempt to force an eight-hour bill and three-tour system through the state legislature in 1913 proved abortive, since of the 110 Massachusetts paper mills by that date 80 were already reported to be on a three-tour basis.[39] In 1907 the bookbinders' union, urged on by a national organizer, endeavored to force the closed shop upon the National

37. *Ibid.,* Mar. 7, 1907, Feb. 10, 1909, Mar. 8, 1912, Apr. 12, 1915, June 12, 20, July 2, 1919, May 21, 1920, Feb. 5, June 24, Aug. 2, 15, 1921. The Water Power Company, be it said, suffered from greatly increased valuations on their outlying land. They offered the land at the price the city tax assessors put on it.

38. *Ibid.,* Jan. 14, 1909, Oct. 2, 1920, Jan. 10, Mar. 22, 1921.

39. *Ibid.,* June 27, 1904, May 4, 8, 10, 1905, July 30, Nov. 12, Dec. 10, 1906, Feb. 16, June 1, 6, 11, 1907, Apr. 13, 1911, Feb. 10, 1912, Feb. 12, Mar. 3, Oct. 20, 1913, Feb. 5, 1915; Mass. Bur. Labor Statistics, *Thirty-eighth Annual Report,* 1907, pp. 12, 13, 497; *Thirty-ninth Annual Report,* 1908, p. 191; Burns, History of the International Brotherhood of Paper Makers.

Blank Book Company, only to find at the end of an eight months' strike that it was beaten.[40] The building trades in this period made some progress in strengthening their unions, carried on one or two campaigns against the master builders for better wage rates and shorter hours, and, having banded together to form the Building Trades Council with a charter from the American Federation of Labor, and an able, salaried agent in charge, were for the first time in a position to act as an effective and responsible body. A labor newspaper, *The Artisan*, was launched in 1908 to promote the cause of organized labor and for some years was published regularly. But until the boom of 1916, when labor in every field was in such demand as to enable workmen to dictate higher wages, local labor developments were few. The Central Labor Union lost no ground, but neither did it gain any. Employers after the scares of an aggressive labor movement at the beginning of the century were on the whole more conciliatory; and the collapse of the Socialist party in Holyoke, after a wide-open break between the two wings, served to allay apprehensions in the mind of the general public. The appointment of a local man as agent at the Lyman Mills and the adoption of profit-sharing at the Farr Alpaca Company went a long way toward ensuring peaceful relations between labor and capital. Holyoke was no longer a leader in the New England labor movement.[41]

The war years brought gains to the working people in the form of higher wages than ever before, increases only partially offset by the higher cost of living.[42] Founders

40. Holyoke *Transcript,* Feb. 23, June 11, May 31, 1907, May 29, 1908.
41. *Ibid.,* Nov. 9, 1906, Mar. 7, 1907, Apr. 2, Oct. 9, 1908, Mar. 13, Sept. 7, Oct. 11, Nov. 1, 1909, Mar. 16, 1910, Feb. 13, May 10, 16, June 23, 1911, Jan. 26, 29, Nov. 1, 1912, Oct. 3, Nov. 13, 1914, Feb. 19, 1915, Nov. 30, 1920.
42. For example, the wage scale at the Lyman Mills in the spring of 1916 compared to the schedule of 1911 shows the notable increases in pay. The increase averages about 30 per cent. At the end of the year another 10 per cent increase was added. Lyman Mills Papers, Burke to Lovering, Apr. 15, 1916; Burke to Sigourney, Jan. 31, 1916; Sigourney to Burke, Nov. 25, 1916.

and moulders, machinists, paper-mill employes, building tradesmen, and textile workers, all strengthened their positions and, sometimes with strikes, more often without, netted substantial benefits between 1916 and 1919.[43] In 1919 state law made a forty-eight-hour week for women and minors mandatory and some manufacturers felt obliged to continue the fifty-four-hour-week wages for the shorter week. This new schedule made more inevitable wage readjustments downward after the set in of the post-war business depression, and by 1922 workmen's income had been scaled down considerably.[44]

Paper makers at the Crocker-McElwain were confronted with a new issue to fight out when in the spring of 1920 the company undertook to force recognition of a genuine open-shop policy and the signing of individual contracts between workmen and the company. Eagle Lodge protested the move as an attempt to undo all unionization in the local industry, and one of the prompt responses to the scheme was the formation in the city of a new lodge of the Brotherhood of Paper Makers, composed of some 180 unskilled laborers. But the workers were at a disadvantage with the mills operating less and less as 1921 wore on. Unemployment in the paper industry became so general by fall that a committee of manufacturers urged upon the mayor a program of public work relief. While business and steady employment in the paper mills revived by the end of the year, workers and mill owners alike realized the folly

43. Paul F. Brissenden, *Earnings of Factory Workers,* 1899 to 1927 (Census Monograph, X), pp. 194, 210, 212–214. The chief industries of Holyoke were among those that for the United States as a whole showed increases of real wages of from 10 to 24 per cent.

44. Holyoke *Transcript,* Apr. 26, May 8, 15, July 13, 22, Sept. 11, 25, Dec. 4, 7, 8, 20, 22, 1916, Mar. 13, 20, May 12, 1917, Feb. 26, Apr. 12, May 10, 21, July 12, 1918, Feb. 18, 26, Mar. 19, Apr. 2, 17, 21, 23, May 7, 12, Aug. 19, 30, 1919, Mar. 29, Apr. 18, 29, 1921; *General Acts of Massachusetts,* 1919, ch. 113. It was the textile industry that was primarily affected by the forty-eight-hour law of 1919, since over half the operatives in a mill such as the Lyman Mills were women. The Lyman Mills reduced wages accordingly for a time but soon followed the lead of Fall River and New Bedford in paying the old wages for the shorter week. Lyman Mills Papers, Sigourney to Burke, Feb. 3, Dec. 2, 1919.

of a fight to the finish upon the application of union principles. Crocker-McElwain employes signed the individual contracts. Practically in all amity open-shop policies prevailed. It was a far cry from the days twenty years previous when Eagle Lodge had felt strong enough to demand, albeit unavailingly, the closed shop in Holyoke paper mills.[45]

On the whole, Holyoke working people exhibited an unusual degree of moderation over the span of years. Instead of growing more radical as time went on, workers became rather less so. Perhaps in effecting an attitude of non-violence the Catholic church played a part. Certainly to the labor leaders much credit is due. Consistently educating themselves in the public night schools, at political rallies, and at forum discussions, and, after 1920, eagerly embracing the opportunities offered by the Amherst College labor classes launched in Holyoke by Neil Hamilton, the leaders of the Holyoke labor movement proved themselves an able, intelligent group. Their obvious determination to uphold the dignity of labor and to improve its economic condition without crippling capital earned them universal respect. Manufacturers and mill hands by no means always saw eye to eye, but neither group could belittle the intelligence or generally the fair intentions of the other. Bitter industrial labor fights could not obtain as long as such an atmosphere endured.

By 1922 it was clear that Holyoke was not destined to become a great industrial center. Official statistics indicate the progressive slowing up between 1905 and 1920, in spite of the acceleration of manufacturing in the war years. Every industrial community partook of that war prosperity and it can scarcely be regarded as an index of normal growth. The doubling of total wages and more than doubling of listed value of products manufactured here in

45. To the union man open shop had meant the exclusion of union labor. Crocker and McElwain insisted that their individual contracts were to guarantee neither union nor non-union shop. The men eventually all signed. Holyoke *Transcript,* Apr. 9, 17, 22, May 3, 28, Aug. 30, Sept. 29, 1920, Jan. 10, 24, Mar. 11, Apr. 11, Sept. 27, Oct. 4, 14, 18, 19, 1921.

the five years between 1914 and 1919, the years to which census figures refer, must be considered in relation to the purchasing power of the dollar, and that was nearly halved in the same period. The city's total population in 1921 was practically what it had been in 1914. Even in the early years of the century Holyoke was growing much more slowly than other manufacturing cities of Massachusetts.[46] After the war there was no reason to believe in great future expansion here. Holyoke might hold her own as a small manufacturing city, where adequate power, special knowledge of the manufacture of certain products, and a stable, intelligent citizenry gave particular advantages. Otherwise, in economic realms such as cheap transportation[47] and low tax rates, in social opportunities, in schooling, in housing facilities, the city had little to offer. Holyoke had attained her full industrial stature.

46. *Municipal Register,* 1914, p. 422; 1921, p. 86; Mass. Bur. Labor Statistics, *Thirty-eighth Annual Report,* 1907, pp. 396–397; *Thirteenth Census of U. S.,* 1910, *Abstract with Supplement for Massachusetts,* pp. 686–687; *Fourteenth Census of U. S.,* 1920, *Manufactures,* IX, 592, 613, 632; Brissenden, *Earnings of Factory Workers,* 1899 to 1927, p. 194; *Statistics of Mfg.,* 1921, p. 26; *Census of Mass.,* 1905, *Manufactures and Trade,* III, 23, 100. In the decade between 1895 and 1905 fifteen of Massachusetts' thirty-three cities had grown more rapidly than Holyoke. For example, the population of Lawrence increased 34.29 per cent, of New Bedford 34.59 per cent, of Worcester 29.73 per cent, of Springfield 42.74 per cent, of Brockton 44.11 per cent, of Holyoke 23.84 per cent. *Census of Mass.,* 1905, *Population and Social Statistics,* I, p. xxix.

47. Holyoke *Transcript,* Nov. 26, 1920.

IX

CITY GOVERNMENT

WHILE capital investors and industrial workers struggled to evolve a stable economic structure, political life also underwent changes. The immigrant of the fifties and sixties was becoming naturalized by the seventies and by the eighties was demanding a share in city government. The fact that this share had become so large by the nineties as virtually to exclude the Yankee was due in part to the preoccupation of the native American with the great game of money-making. What had government, particularly municipal government, to do with business? For a time the political scene is the obverse of the economic, the foreign-born citizen or his sons dominating the political arena, the native American the industrial.

Whatever ills the community had suffered as a town, confident citizens had hopes of curing in short order once the new city government was inaugurated. With the faith in government machinery characteristic of nineteenth-century America, Holyoke in the fall of 1873 enthusiastically prepared for the new order. The municipal charter created two bodies, a board of seven ward aldermen and a council of twenty-one, three members elected from each ward. Over these stood a mayor, flanked by a clerk and a treasurer. The School Board also was elected.

The personnel of the first city government was able. Judge Pearsons, who had been one of the young lawyers to throw in his fortune with the New City back in 1849, was elected mayor and was supported by a group of representative citizens as aldermen and council members.[1] In spite of some agitation for nominating candidates and carrying on elections without the machinery of national party

---

1. *Municipal Register,* 1874, pp. 19–36; Holyoke *Transcript,* Jan. 17, 1874.

alignment, rival candidates were for years chosen by Republican and Democratic party caucuses. Only once, in 1877, both parties nominated the same candidate and William Whiting was unanimously elected mayor. For some six years the rule of the "Brahmins" endured. Leading citizens were elected to office and tended to their jobs conscientiously. The manufacturing interests of the city were well represented and expenditures were carefully considered with an eye to keeping the tax rate down and the city debt within bounds. In the lean years of the middle seventies such matters were vital considerations to many citizens.[2]

Finances, however, were not easy to administer, for the city was in need of many improvements—sewers, crosswalks, curbings and paving, street lights, and fire hydrants, schoolhouses and furniture; and the elaborate city hall which had been building for two years when the charter was secured was costing the new municipality a small fortune, nearly three times what had been set aside for this purpose in the beginning. Could the city possibly pay as it went? Civic pride coveting a metropolitan appearance wrestled with Yankee canniness. The water works rentals sufficed to meet that department's current expenses and provide a sinking fund for extinguishing the bonds, and the Holyoke and Westfield Railroad, that far-sighted municipal investment, by 1879 was paying dividends into the city treasury.[3] By the opening of 1878 the mayor could counsel more liberal expenditure, announcing his conviction that economy could be overdone and that it was sound policy to make the city attractive as a place of residence, lest capitalists otherwise consider Holyoke as a manufacturing center only. So firmly did Whiting believe in a regime of constructive expenditure that he himself set the example by building a hotel and an opera house in 1878 which immediately gave Holyoke a metropolitan air and

2. Holyoke *Transcript,* Dec. 2, 1874, Nov. 24, 27, Dec. 1, 4, 8, 11, 1875, Nov. 22, 29, Dec. 6, 1876, Dec. 1, 1877, Dec. 13, 1879.

3. *Ibid.,* July 22, 29, 1874, Jan. 4, 1875; *Municipal Register,* 1877, p. 9; 1878, pp. 7–9, 16.

Mayor Whiting doubtless a substantial financial return.[4] But by 1878 the business cycle was on the upturn and a program of spending money for highways and sewers, health inspection, and schools was not only easier to urge but, in view of the increasing rapidity of the city's growth, utterly essential.

But the business boom had another consequence. Substantial citizens who had given time to city administration tended to become too engrossed in their personal affairs to be willing to act as public servants. The city had been economically and honestly governed in the past. Need one fear to relax his personal vigilance a little? The year 1880 marks the beginning of a new order in the city government. There had been evidences before that time of the coming into power of the Irish ward politician, that nearly universal phenomenon in American municipal politics of the day. But here the comparative success of the native American of some education and property in keeping the municipal administration in hand during the seventies led to the lulling of his apprehensions.[5]

The change did not take place overnight. But as 1880 gave way to 1881, and 1881 to 1882, the difference in type of city official began to be evident. In 1882, for example, the Council which a half dozen years before had boasted some of the most outstanding business men of Holyoke now was made up of a preponderance of Irishmen scarcely known outside their own wards, save, perhaps, for the three liquor dealers. With the Board of Aldermen, the more important body, a similar shift in character took place. Even the office of mayor after 1883 was filled by Irishmen, second generation or representative of the better element, but still neither a W. B. C. Pearsons nor a William Whiting.[6]

4. Holyoke *Transcript*, Jan. 8, Dec. 10, 1879.
5. *Ibid.*, Jan. 6, 1877; *Municipal Register*, 1877, p. 9; 1878, pp. 6–17; 1880, pp. 5–17.
6. See lists of officeholders from 1874–1887 in *Municipal Register*, 1887, pp. 294–307. The thirty-one council members for 1877 included eleven mill men, two lawyers, two doctors, one farmer, eight merchants, one con-

To some extent this situation was not only inevitable but desirable. The number of naturalized citizens was increasing every year, not, to be sure, in proportion to the increase in the total number of voters, but naturalized voters coupled with native voters born of immigrant parents made up an overwhelming proportion of the total voting list. Second-generation Irish by the eighties were by mere force of numbers entitled to considerable parts in the political arena.[7] Thanks to interested cultivation of these opportunities these new Americans soon dominated the political scene, and while Yankee indifference had largely created this state of affairs, once the Irish regime was established in the city hall it was not to be dislodged without a fight. The number of legal voters in comparison to the total population was small, partly because of the excess of females over males in the city, and partly because of the large percentage of aliens. Even in 1900 there were less than 2,000 men of voting age in the whole city who were of native American parentage, whereas foreign-born or American-born of foreign parentage numbered 9,808.

In view of this distribution what reason was there for regarding the Irish control of city politics as detrimental? Was it not reasonable and ultimately cheap compensation to the pride of the underprivileged to feel themselves in authority in some realm? Certainly their economic opportunities were not great. How did the municipal government function in the eighties as compared to its performance in the seventies under the "Brahmin" regime? Were

tractor, one teaming contractor, and one clerk. Holyoke *Transcript,* Dec. 6, 1876. Sixteen of the twenty-eight aldermen and councilmen owned real estate.

7. In 1879 the *Transcript* published a letter complaining of the Irish rule of the city. The answer was just in every respect: ". . . You say we rule or ruin, and own no mills. . . . You could not run your mills, except we did the work from which you realize your profits. You say we own nothing, yet rule the city. This is another lie, and for evidence I refer you to the books of the City Clerk Delaney and Collector Andrews for evidence of the truth of this statement and you will see we pay more than you have any idea. . . . In conclusion let me say we have not ruled Holyoke, but in the future we shall endeavor to do so." Holyoke *Transcript,* Feb. 15, 1879.

taxes higher, disorder greater, or public health less efficiently cared for? Was the patronage abused or outright
graft in evidence? How did the nineties differ from the
eighties and how did the full-fledged machine run by and
in the interest of the "Kaffir King," that adroit politician,
"Mikeleen" Connors, come into existence?

To answer these questions fairly it is necessary to examine the status of city administration in the three decades with care. It is true that the tax rate in the seventies
averaged considerably higher than in the eighties, and the
amount raised by taxation in 1875 was almost three quarters of the total raised ten years later, although the property valuation was only three fifths in 1875 of what it was
set at in 1885. By 1897 assessed valuation had again increased notably, and the amount taxed upon it had risen
but little.[8] Superficially, therefore, it might appear that
the city was run with greater regard for the taxpayers'
pocket in the eighties or nineties than it had been earlier.
But to offset this was the jump in the city debt, the device
for sliding the burden on to the future, a scheme discovered by Council and Board of Aldermen in the middle
eighties by approving expenditures long after all funds
for meeting them had been exhausted. Statutory limitation of municipal borrowings promulgated in 1885 checked
this system somewhat. Furthermore the municipality in
the seventies had needs some of which could not arise again
for a generation or more—trunk sewers, macadamized
main roads, fire engine houses, and the like.[9] That the city
fathers of the seventies undertook to pay for important
permanent improvements from current taxation is testi-

8. *Ibid.*, Mar. 13, 1886, Apr. 16, 1897; *Municipal Register,* 1898, p. 587.

Date	Tax Rate	Amount of Taxes	Valuation
1875	$20.80	$208,534	$ 9,681,127
1885	17.20	290,433	16,135,515
1895	16.80	486,293	27,704,625
1898	14.40	546,811	36,415,800

9. Holyoke *Transcript,* Oct. 4, 1876, Jan. 7, Mar. 31, 1885, July 21,
1894; *Municipal Register,* 1875, pp. 49, 92–104, 110–125; 1879, pp. 88–116;
1887, pp. 7–22.

mony not to their extravagance, but to their courage.
Such thrift also made possible the lower tax rates of the
next aldermanic generation. Still between 1892 and 1899
the city debt was nearly doubled.[10]

Supervision of public health was undeniably better carried out at the end of the century than in the seventies.
Medical knowledge had widened enormously and the fa-
miliarity of the medical profession with the germ theory
of disease enabled city Boards of Health everywhere to
act with an intelligence impossible a generation earlier.
Yet definite ideas of how to proceed often did not elicit
the means of carrying out wise measures, and meanwhile
the continued growth of the city was multiplying health
problems.

In the seventies there was in fact no formal Board of
Health. The selectmen had usually acted as such in the
days of town government, and after the city charter was
granted, a city physician appointed by the Board of Aldermen supervised public health. Providentially, despite
the poverty that made undernourishment and thence disease all too common in the poorer sections of the city,
public health in the seventies was unusually good. Typhoid
took heavy toll particularly among the French Canadians
where sanitary conditions were at their worst, but no epidemic resulted.[11]

In 1880 a Board of Health of three was created which,
together with the health officer, took over the widening
duties of health supervision. Then for the first time the
city instituted a regular service for collecting garbage,
and the improvement in the cleanliness of alleys and streets
was noticeable. Collecting ashes and rubbish as well as

10. Holyoke *Transcript,* May 3, 1899. City debt was as follows:

Year	Amount	Year	Amount
1892	$ 850,000	1896	$1,474,000
1893	1,029,000	1897	1,553,000
1894	1,190,000	1898	1,603,000
1895	1,334,000		

11. *Ibid.,* Apr. 1, 15, May 10, 1876, Dec. 26, 1877, Jan. 11, Apr. 5, 1879;
Municipal Register, 1874, pp. 182–189; 1879, pp. 123–126.

house offal was added to the matters in the province of the Board of Health in 1882. An adequate sewerage system and proper connections with private houses and tenements were its concern only incidentally until the nineties. Milk inspection was inaugurated early in the eighties but consisted chiefly of a perfunctory fat-content test which revealed little about the purity of the milk.[12] During the eighties also a health officer pursued the unvaccinated new arrivals in Holyoke in hopes of checking smallpox, and children were vaccinated before being admitted to the public schools. The truant officers kept track of quarantines of school children for measles, scarlet fever, and diphtheria, and in the winter of 1887 over one thousand school children were quarantined for measles alone.[13]

Indeed there is indication that lack of funds was largely responsible for the inadequacies of the health administration.[14] In 1893 a much needed plumbing inspector was appointed to whose good work was due the enforced improvement of several tenement houses where owners had omitted any proper provision for drainage. But the whole sewerage system, laid out for a city of 10,000 inhabitants, was inadequate for a city of 30,000 to 40,000. The building by private funds of a hospital where many of the city poor received free care took some financial burden from the city. But despite the genuine concern of the personnel of the Board of Health and of many private citizens in this matter of public health, the City Council refused to take the demands of the health officers very seriously.[15] The new charter with the "reformed" administration was necessary

12. *Municipal Register,* 1881, pp. 161–166; 1882–1883, pp. 150–152; 1885, pp. 101, 149–150, 174; Holyoke *Transcript,* May 1, 1880, Aug. 8, 1885.

13. Holyoke *Transcript,* Aug. 7, Sept. 19, Oct. 3, 1885, Mar. 1, 1886, Mar. 5, 1887.

14. Holyoke health officers in the early nineties were lax, however, about reporting to the State Board of Health. For several years Holyoke was the only city in the state failing so to report. Mass. State Board of Health, *Annual Reports,* 1890–1895.

15. *Municipal Register,* 1895, pp. 67–84; Holyoke *Transcript,* Aug. 28, 1897.

before money enough was forthcoming to make the public health administration even moderately efficient.

Holyoke's death rate was not excessively high as compared to cities the country over, but in comparison to cities in the neighborhood where conditions of climate and soil were similar, Holyoke's death rate was not creditable. In 1878 for Holyoke it was 21.67 per thousand of the population, whereas Springfield had 15.30 per thousand. In 1891 the rates stood Holyoke 20.45, Springfield 20.09, Northampton 16.90. The mean death rate based upon the five census years 1870 to 1890 inclusive placed Holyoke third highest in the state, only Boston with a mortality rate of 24.1 and Fall River with 23.4 exceeding the 23.1 of Holyoke.[16]

But it was infant mortality that was shockingly high for a city healthfully located, 312.56 per thousand of the population under one year of age in 1890; in 1900 31 per cent of the total deaths were babies under one year of age. Still on this score Holyoke in the nineties was in less sorry case than other manufacturing cities of the state.[17] A gen-

16. Holyoke *Transcript*, Oct. 29, 1881, Jan. 1, 1892; Mass. State Board of Health, *Tenth Annual Report*, 1879, p. 284; *Twenty-fifth Annual Report*, 1893, p. xlii; *Twenty-sixth Annual Report*, 1894, p. xciv.

17. *Municipal Register*, 1900, pp. 181–200, 311; *Eleventh Census of U. S.*, 1890, *Vital and Social Statistics*, VI, Pt. I, 566–567. Tables of infant mortality in Massachusetts cities between 1881 and 1890 ranked Holyoke ninth. Per one thousand births the mortality of infants under one year of age for the ten year periods was as follows:

City	1881–1890	1891–1897
Fall River	239.7	255.3
Lowell	222.5	227.5
Lawrence	213.9	200.5
Boston	188.6	164.9
Salem	180.6	168.2
New Bedford	177.7	200.0
Chicopee	176.1	214.2
Cambridge	172.3	152.2
Holyoke	168.1	156.5

Mass. State Board of Health, *Twenty-eighth Annual Report*, 1896, p. 753. During the years 1891–1897 the rate the state over for the urban group was brought down from 174.9 to 164.2 per thousand births. Mass. State Board of Health, *Thirtieth Annual Report*, 1898, p. 802.

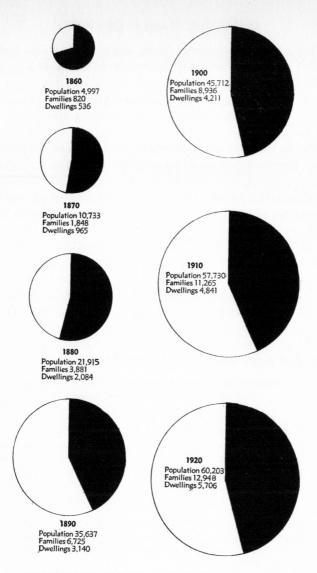

1860
Population 4,997
Families 820
Dwellings 536

1900
Population 45,712
Families 8,936
Dwellings 4,211

1870
Population 10,733
Families 1,848
Dwellings 965

1910
Population 57,730
Families 11,265
Dwellings 4,841

1880
Population 21,915
Families 3,881
Dwellings 2,084

1920
Population 60,203
Families 12,948
Dwellings 5,706

1890
Population 35,637
Families 6,725
Dwellings 3,140

HOUSING IN HOLYOKE, 1860–1920

*Census of Massachusetts, 1860, p. 146. Tenth Census of the
United States, 1880, Population, I, 670. Eleventh Census of the
United States, 1890, Population, I, Pt. I, cxci. Twelfth Census of
the United States, 1900, Population, II, 606. Thirteenth Census
of the United States, 1910, Population, I, 1290. Fourteenth Census of the United States, 1920, Population, II, 1269.*

eral house-to-house sanitary inspection was urged by the
Board of Health and the need of closer inspection of babies' milk was recognized, but the reform city government
had not been sufficiently impressed with the public need to
act by the turn of the century.[18]

Inadequate housing which accentuated all the health
problems was not regarded in these days as a public concern. In 1880 only two cities in the United States had a
housing problem as acute as Holyoke's. New York with
16.37 persons per dwelling and Hoboken with 11.50 were
more crowded than Holyoke with 10.52 persons to each
dwelling. Five years later, despite the rate at which building had gone on, there were still two wards of the city
that averaged fourteen persons per dwelling while a third
less crowded ward boasted one tenement where sixty-seven
persons used one front door.[19] But the street railway en-
franchised in 1884 opened up new sections of the city for
residence so that some of the worst overcrowding was relieved. Unsightly and unsanitary tenements were abandoned as workpeople began to build small homes along the
higher terraces of the river to the south and west of the
business section, in South Hadley Falls, and, particularly
after the building of the bridge in 1890, in Willimansett,
that part of Chicopee across the river from the third-level
canal mills.[20] Yet even then the tenements near the mills
were packed so that Holyoke in 1896 housed more persons
per room than any city in Massachusetts except Boston.

18. *Municipal Register,* 1900, pp. 180–185; Holyoke *Transcript,* Dec.
28, 1892.

19. *Tenth Census of U. S.,* 1880, *Population,* I, 670–671; *Census of
Mass.,* 1885, *Population and Social Statistics,* I, Pt. I, 118, 165; Holyoke
Transcript, Apr. 13, 1883, June 27, 1885.

20. Holyoke *Transcript,* Mar. 19, 1884, Jan. 1, 1885, July 28, 1888, May
2, Aug. 17, 1890, Dec. 3, 1891, Feb. 6, 1894, Apr. 22, 1898; *Census of
Mass.,* 1895, *Population and Social Statistics,* I, 597–598. See above, p. 173.
Neither South Hadley Falls nor Willimansett were part of Holyoke. Occasionally citizens voiced interest in adding to the city the regions across
the river with which economic ties were close, but South Hadley belonged to Hampshire County not Hampden, and Willimansett was too
largely peopled by the impecunious to be worth a fight to annex.

In 1900 Holyoke still averaged 10.9 persons to every dwelling.[21]

Maintaining cleanliness in streets and alleys, another factor in public health, fell to the street department. The task was overwhelming. An observant citizen in the seventies wrote:

Not a stone's throw from "the finest building in western Massachusetts," looking southward from our magnificent city hall, what is the prospect? A heap of waste timber rotting in the stones; a dilapidated shed, roofed over a pile of truck; in the background a stable and hoggery. . . . Loose litter is scattered all about. . . . Nor is this in the purlieus of the city, (where things are a hundred times worse) but close by the business center, and near some of the most pleasant residences.[22]

Goats and cows browsed in vacant lots. Brick blocks and wooden tenements lined many streets, with untidy rear premises, sometimes filthy. Pursuing an idea of creating an urban appearance the street department cut the trees along city streets and demolished the pine grove on "Depot Hill." Later as the city spread out and the well-to-do built elaborate houses set in wide lawns, pains were taken to conceal the obvious crudities of the city. But the alleys remained foul.[23]

In the administration of the police department the question of efficiency also is problematical. Upon the police de-

21. Holyoke *Transcript,* Dec. 10, 1896; *Twelfth Census of U. S.,* 1900, *Population,* II, Pt. II, clxi. In 1900 the housing situation in the cities over 25,000 population was as follows:

	Persons per dwelling
Manhattan and the Bronx	20.4
Chicago	8.8
Boston	8.4
St. Louis	7.0
Hoboken	14.2
Fall River	11.0
Holyoke	10.9

22. Holyoke *Transcript,* Apr. 21, 1877.

23. *Ibid.,* June 30, Aug. 18, Sept. 12, 1877, June 13, 1884, May 21, 1890.

partment hung all enforcement not only of law but of
liquor license regulations as well. Consequently the personnel of the police force was always of vital concern to
the liquor interests. Favoritism and laxity of police officers
could disturb the honest liquor dealer as much as an officer's incorruptible sense of duty could frighten the dis-
honest. Massachusetts by the end of the seventies had tried
most variations of liquor traffic regulation but had come
apparently to only one conclusion, that enforcement must
rest with the local authorities. The seventies saw Holyoke,
for all the arrests for drunkenness, an orderly young city,
patrolled by eleven officers and a marshal, responsible men
proud of their posts. Other than the tasks of enforcing the
Sunday closing law, of occasionally raiding the dens of the
unlicensed vendor, and the daily arresting of the drunken
disturber of the peace, the police force had little to do. As
the depression years of the seventies wore on there were an
increasing number of tramps to be lodged and kept track
of, some of them perennial vagrants, more of them men
migrating in their search for work. But the regime of
Chief of Police Ham, till his resignation in 1881, was one
of order.[24]

The eighties saw a change. In 1879 and 1880 the city
took a sudden forward bound in growth. Hundreds of poverty-stricken French Canadians and Irish, and tens of
British and Germans came pouring into the town, ready
to work in the mills, as day-laborers or skilled artisans, but
numerous enough, ignorant enough, and sometimes stub-
born enough to make the task of maintaining order a far
more difficult one than it had been. The police force was
enlarged, but the very enlargement of the force inevitably
complicated the administration of the department. Houses
of ill fame grew up in a city which recently had boasted,
albeit ostrich-fashion, that none were to be seen within the
city limits. Brawls, murders, and violence of other descrip-

24. *Ibid.*, May 27, 1874, Apr. 14, 1875, Nov. 30, 1881; *Municipal Register,* 1875, pp. 13–14; 1876, p. 12; 1880, pp. 113–117. In 1875 when the
population of the city was listed as 16,208, the police fed or lodged 1,161
tramps.

tion became sufficiently frequent to give Holyoke a reputation for urban badness probably as exaggerated as her pristine self-assumed name for virtue. But certainly the number of places licensed to sell liquor had so increased by 1885 as to make proper supervision difficult for a far bigger police force than Holyoke maintained. In 1883, 140 shops and saloons paid fees into the city treasury for the right to sell spirits and informed citizens tacitly conceded that others unlicensed existed.[25] The power of patronage vested in the hands of aldermen who allotted the licenses was enormous and the temptation to lax enforcement for the police was more than negligible.

In 1887 and 1888 the police were put under the civil service and tenure of office during good behavior was secured, an arrangement which freed the department from immediate dependence upon the favor of the mayor.[26] But with every passing year the power of the liquor dealers in town was growing stronger and the task confronting the police to enforce the law became more difficult. On the other hand one section of public opinion was in turn becoming aroused by the extent of control of public affairs in the hands of the liquor interests. Every city election since the early eighties had entrenched the "rum power" more securely until 1888 brought a minority of temperance aldermen to the board. The granting of licenses that year nearly split the city government into impotent fragments, for the "drys" determined to restrict licenses to those who had never violated the law. All other city business was thrust to one side while the fight went on, and although the result was satisfactory to no one, the number of licensees was cut from 163 to about 100.[27] The temperance men then strove to have the police strictly enforce the

25. Holyoke *Transcript*, Feb. 28, Mar. 3, Apr. 21, May 1, 1880, July 24, Nov. 27, Dec. 4, 1883, Mar. 5, 14, July 14, Dec. 3, 1884, Apr. 21, 29, 1885, Oct. 20, 1888.

26. *Ibid.*, June 9, 18, 1888; *Municipal Register*, 1887, p. 31; John Hildreth, Chairman License Committee of the Board of Aldermen, 1887 (interview).

27. The mayor's official figures of licenses granted was 163, but Hildreth set it at about 240 in 1887.

law against the unlicensed and against licensed dealers
who resorted to illegal practices. But it was disillusioning
for the drys and disheartening for the conscientious police
officer to have the arrested saloon-keepers all discharged
without even a fine.[28] When at length the temperance forces
succeeded in having the licenses of violaters of the law re-
voked, it was still impossible to shut up their saloons. Since
saloon-keepers were still licensed to sell cigars, the saloon
doors remained open, and the police were thus powerless to
prevent much illegal liquor selling.

And then in 1889 a new complication was added by a
state law forbidding any municipality to grant more than
one license to each thousand of the population. A city that
had been estimated as having one saloon to each hundred
inhabitants was to be reduced to having one tenth that
number. The scramble to be one of the privileged thirty-
five was naturally tremendous. Placing the fee at $1,000
for a first-class license had no great effect upon eliminating applicants, and the first year eighty-nine dealers applied. The result was twofold: the power vested in the
Board of Aldermen in granting these coveted licenses made
the liquor question overshadow utterly every other in city
elections and led to the candidacy of men for posts of aldermen who from the standpoint of public spirit were ill
suited to the place; and second, many of the disappointed
applicants or impecunious simply sold without license. The
reign of the "blind pig" made the police nearly helpless.[29]

Thus the nineties found the city government operating
primarily in the interests of liquor men. Who were these
"liquor men"? Among them were God-fearing, honest citizens convinced of the legitimacy of their business; and
then there were the unscrupulous with no compunctions
about defying the law provided they could do so profitably. To secure a license and protection from interference
in the conduct of their business most men were willing to

28. John Hildreth (interview); Holyoke *Transcript,* Apr. 28, June 2,
Sept. 15, Oct. 13, Nov. 17, 1888; *Municipal Register,* 1887, pp. 28–29.
29. Holyoke *Transcript,* Apr. 27, May 4, 11, 1889, July 28, 1890, Jan.
13, 1891; *Municipal Register,* 1891, p. 31; Thomas Carmody (interview).

pay, preferably to legally constituted authorities, but if need be to extra-legal powers too. It was by way of the cigar business that Holyoke's Tammany was built up. A shrewd young Irishman, Michael Connors, who came to Holyoke in 1888, launched a small cigar business selling Kaffir cigars to the local saloon-keepers. His ready tongue quickly created for him a following which sent him from Ward Three to the Board of Aldermen for four successive years from 1891 on. The struggle for licenses was at its height. Connors lined up with himself three other aldermen and was thus in control of the board of seven, and the combination for several years worked with the utmost smoothness. Saloon-keepers who wanted licenses—so the story ran—were expected to buy at least 100,000 Kaffir cigars at $60.00 a thousand, so that Connors' private business grossed $6,000 from each license. Connors and his cohorts could well afford substantial inducements to wavering members of the Board of Aldermen to allot the licenses as directed.[30] The better elements in the city were slow to bestir themselves, but succeeded in 1894 in defeating some of the ring. The mayor, a bitter opponent of the "combine," in that year secured from the state legislature the right to vest the granting of licenses in the hands of a commission appointed by himself. Since as long as a License Commission functioned instead of the Board of Aldermen there was "nothing in it" to be an alderman, apparently the era of ward bossism was ended.[31]

But here the matter of the police and of law enforcement entered in. If an incorruptible License Commission of three, each appointed for three years, was to allot the licenses for a sum of $1000 apiece, it was simpler for the unscrupulous to sell without a license, provided the police could be fixed. That system also enabled the unlicensed vendor to sell on Sunday regardless of the closing law. Some of the police force were won over, so that citizens were suddenly frightened at the Scylla looming up in the

30. Holyoke *Transcript,* Jan. 5, 22, 1894, Mar. 22, Apr. 18, 1895.
31. *Ibid.,* Dec. 3, 1894; *Municipal Register,* 1895, pp. 23–24.

form of a corrupted police force and the "blind pig" after the city had newly escaped the Charybdis of a government controlled by the liquor ring. How extensive corruption or at least laxity was among the police can only be surmised. Private opinion and official reports did not agree.[32] Take the control of the police force out of the hands of the local machine, was urged by one group of agitated voters. And so again Holyoke affairs were brought before the legislature in Boston and a bill passed the House placing the control of the Holyoke police under a commission to be appointed by the governor. But the governor vetoed the bill, pronouncing it unwise to take home rule from the city, since a sufficient body of public opinion could surely be maintained to ensure law and order. Thus challenged, uneasy citizens turned back to the local scene, uncertain how to proceed. At least, some said, Holyoke by implication was no worse than other municipalities in the Commonwealth, her tax rate as low and arrests for drunkenness no more numerous.[33]

The License Commission continued its arduous task, but taxpayers now watched the city hall with an attention that had been lacking for years. A good deal of unpleasant publicity had attached to Holyoke's name during the discussions in the legislature and citizens began to hunt about for means of redeeming the city's reputation. One measure agreed upon by all was the securing of a new city charter. The new charter was carefully thought out. The old cumbersome bicameral system was abolished, and one body, a group of twenty-one aldermen, fourteen elected at large together with one from each ward of the city, took over the duties which before had been divided between Board of Aldermen and Council.[34] Henceforward responsibility could not be shunted back and forth. But revamping the machinery of government could not by itself remake the administration. Two more years were to pass before that

32. *Municipal Register,* 1895, pp. 24–25, 338–342.
33. Holyoke *Transcript,* Apr. 12, 18, May 19, 1895.
34. *Ibid.,* July 22, 1896; *Municipal Register,* 1897, pp. 5–6.

reform was accomplished. In December 1896 an upright citizen was elected mayor and hopes ran high that now at last law, efficiency, and economy were to rule. But as had been found to be the case before, personal honesty and good intentions on the part of the mayor did not suffice to produce an effective or even an honest administration. The year 1897 saw the city in constant political turmoil, with two of the three license commissioners at length resigning in weary disgust and at the end of the year the leader of the liquor ring himself, "Mikaleen" Connors, reappearing on the front of the stage, elected mayor.[35]

The reign of the "Kaffir King," however, began less disastrously than many persons feared. Police were instructed to carry out the law rigorously against illegal liquor sellers without showing any favoritism. But the leopard after all was not to change his spots. Arrests for illegal liquor selling were so blatantly not followed up that Connors' first moves were labelled bluff to conceal the ensuing laxity. And then in midsummer the mayor himself departed on a spree which wound up by his sailing for Ireland. Even his henchmen resented that.[36] Still his machine might have regained its equilibrium and continued to function had it not been for a scandal which came to light during his absence, although one unconnected with either liquor grafts or machine activities. The tax collector, elected yearly by the Board of Aldermen, was charged with embezzlement of taxpayers' monies. The case did not come into court until after Connors' return, and as the collector had been serving for a third year in 1898, there was no way of laying the disgraceful business at the door of the Kaffir ring. The tax collector, an aimiable, bluff Irishman, universally known as "Honest Jim," was popular in the city, and many citizens for months continued to believe that Honest

35. Holyoke *Transcript*, Jan. 20, 21, Feb. 2, Aug. 21, Oct. 19, Nov. 24, Dec. 10, 15, 1897. Connors, no unprejudiced witness, to be sure, in his inaugural address accused the regime of the preceding year of a corruption which made possible the open sale of liquor on Sunday and unwarranted political pressure upon the purchasers of licenses. *Ibid.*, Jan. 3, 1898.

36. *Ibid.*, Jan. 13, May 2, July 2, 1898. Private information.

Jim would soon produce the missing funds and confound his accusers. It took much legal evidence plus the forcing of his bondsmen to make good to the city some $65,000 of vanished city taxes to convince many of Honest Jim's malfeasance.[37] But meanwhile city finances were in an appalling muddle. City employes had to wait for their wages as there were no funds with which to pay them, and suddenly anger at a regime which had allowed such loose administration sprang up and the Kaffir ring found itself unpopular because of what it was after all only partly responsible for. "Turn the rascals out" became a general cry. This Irish rule was after all too costly.

At this juncture there came into evidence the workings of a new political machine headed by W. F. Whiting, son of Holyoke's trusted and wealthy paper manufacturer, William Whiting. "W. F.," as the younger man was always called, without his father's nation- or state-wide political ambitions, clearly found pleasure in acting as the boss of the local scene. No motive, financial or moral, prompted him other than the feeling of power. Never willing himself to hold city office, W. F. for some fifteen years was to control city administration through his henchmen. His followers were bound to him by direct personal ties, a large financial backing here, a staunch support for office there, or the virtual guarantee of contracts for city supplies. In 1898 the Whiting machine was just beginning to manifest its possibilities. Seizing the magnificent opportunity afforded by the unpopularity of Connors' regime, Whiting decided to

37. Holyoke's tax collector always had been required to give a personal bond on taking office, and his bondsmen were personally responsible to the city for any financial discrepancies in his returns. Only blind belief in the collector's honesty could have led his bondsmen to commit themselves as they did. There was a shortage of $109,903 dating back to 1895 and a total of about $225,000 for the three years up to Keough's resignation in August of 1898. The tax collector's books he considered his own property and had never allowed others to examine. Legally his bondsmen were responsible for the whole $225,000, when "Honest Jim's" personal bankruptcy was proved. The settlement for $65,000 was effected by political pressure upon the new and ambitious young mayor. Holyoke *Transcript*, Aug. 16, Sept. 6, 9, 12, Oct. 8, Nov. 1, 26, 1898, Jan. 21, Oct. 20, Nov. 9, Dec. 1, 1899. Private information.

run his young brother-in-law, Arthur Chapin, for mayor. Not only Chapin, but five public-spirited, able men as aldermen were elected in December 1898, and the reform of city government was inaugurated.[38]

There was much to reform. Rigid economy was necessary to recover from the loss of the $160,000 of taxes which Keough's bondsmen were not forced to make good. The police had to be encouraged to more active enforcement of the law and the performance of the License Commission was to be checked. Two lawsuits had to be pressed on toward settlement, the Lyman Mills tax-abatement suit and the Municipal Lighting case between the city and the Holyoke Water Power Company. New schoolhouses had to be built, and the pauper department, recipient of nearly one tenth of the annual taxes, had to be more carefully watched.[39] Public interest in civic affairs was kept alive by a series of spectacular developments, first and most dramatic perhaps the charges brought by mayor and city solicitor against the head of the License Commission. The unsavory dealings of the License Commission—the extent of the graft amounting in some instances to virtual blackmail and extortion—were varied, although timorous witnesses, fearing the overthrow of this "reform administration" in a year or two and the subsequent revenge of the accused, failed to testify in court as conclusively as the reformers hoped. A more scrupulous commissioner was appointed when the offending incumbent was at length ousted, and thenceforward the liquor situation was honestly dealt with.[40] The winning of the tax case against the Lyman Mills next brought credit to the new administration and

38. Holyoke *Transcript,* Jan. 3, Apr. 18, 1898, Jan. 1, 23, Apr. 18, 1900.
39. *Ibid.,* Nov. 26, 1898.
40. Private information; Holyoke *Transcript,* Mar. 7, 15, 29, 30, Apr. 8, 11, 1899, Jan. 1, Apr. 18, 26, Dec. 15, 1900. More meticulous standards of public morality might have charged graft upon the succeeding commissioners, Whiting men all, who undertook as a matter of course contracts for the city or received commissions on real estate purchases for the city. But since in each case the business had to fall to some one the machine giving the city good government might reasonably defend its system of awards.

then the successful campaign for reduction of city expenses. Chapin's cohorts even netted some glory from the profitable and capable management of the Board of Water Commissioners and of the Holyoke and Westfield Railroad, although in each case lucrative returns had been the accepted order for some years.[41]

Other realms of city administration were not immediately affected by the change. The fire department had long been well run, largely, it is presumed, because insurance rates were so cut for cities whose fire departments and equipment were considered efficient that influential citizens had for years made a point of seeing that that department was properly administered. In order to take it out of politics in 1891 the department was put under a commission. Holyoke's bountiful water supply also contributed to the light record on fire losses. But about one ninth of the city's income was devoted to fire protection, more than was allotted for many years to any other one city department except the School Board.[42] Other factors than political reorganization chiefly influenced the management of the pauper department. Municipal lighting was a question apart. And the School Board, elected by the voters, ran its independent course.

The pauper department was not exceptionally well administered either in the eighties, the nineties, or the early years of the twentieth century, but the problems attending poor relief varied so with the numbers to be helped, and the numbers, in turn, so directly with the business cycle of depression or prosperity, that comparisons become difficult. In the seventies when the country-wide depression

41. Holyoke *Transcript,* Nov. 2, 1899, Dec. 1, 1900; *Municipal Register,* 1900, pp. 5–6. The Board of Water Commissioners had extended the water system by the laying out of new reservoirs from time to time. The work was always well and economically done.

42. *Municipal Register,* 1885, pp. 212–219; 1891, pp. 20, 82–94; 1895, pp. 280–308; 1898, pp. 401–402; 1899, pp. 201–203; 1900, pp. 209–210. Once, in 1891, the police department received a larger appropriation than the fire department, and in 1900 the Board of Public Works received a larger amount than either fire or school departments, but that was for the special expense of building three new schoolhouses, an expenditure which could logically be called part of the school appropriation.

was at its worst the city was hard pressed to care for the destitute, a situation aggravated by the revision twice within five years of the state laws of settlement. The result each time was an enormous addition to the burdens of the city. The number of families seeking public aid grew each year.[43] By 1879, discovering how much the settlement laws had been eased, old people applied for city aid who before had been unwilling to become state cases lest they be sent to the state almshouse in Tewksbury. Where nine old people had been city charges in 1878 there were sixty-seven in 1879. The number of vagrants to be fed and lodged for a brief time also ate into the appropriation for city poor relief. Nevertheless on the whole the municipality viewed the work of the overseer of the poor as done humanely and economically. Only three Massachusetts cities had so small a per capita expenditure for poor relief in 1876, namely forty-four cents per capita per year, and only seven equalled Holyoke's record in 1881. On the other hand, as many a good Catholic pointed out periodically, the city's reliance upon the House of Providence hospital and orphanage shifted a large burden annually from the city. Holyoke pauper bills must have been much larger had there been no such institution here.[44]

The House of Providence was not, however, the only private charity which supplemented the city efforts. The St. Vincent de Paul Society and the Union Relief rendered valuable assistance in the seventies, as other organizations were to do in later years. Most unusual help came after 1878 from a legacy of Whiting Street, the strange-seem-

43. Once a family or individual was recognized as having legal settlement within a town of Massachusetts, that town must be responsible for aid—if need be, for total support—of that family. Before 1874 ten years of residence and five years of paying taxes by the men of the family was required before settlement was won in the town. The revised statute cut the time requirement in half as concerned residence and from five years to three for paying taxes. In 1879 a new law granted women settlement after five years of residence in a town. Holyoke *Transcript*, Oct. 21, 1874, Jan. 23, Dec. 25, 1875, Feb. 5, May 31, 1876; *Municipal Register,* 1875, pp. 51–66; 1876, pp. 61–74.

44. Holyoke *Transcript,* Jan. 6, 1877, Jan. 12, May 1, 1878, Jan. 8, Sept. 10, 1879, Jan. 15, Feb. 19, 1881, Jan. 21, 1882, Dec. 26, 1883.

ing old Yankee who, having grown wealthy from the growth
of river towns of the Connecticut, turned back to their use
part of his fortune. His will created a fund the income of
which was to be used for the aid of the "worthy poor" of
some six or seven of these Massachusetts cities or towns,
Holyoke and Northampton netting the lion's share.
"Worthy poor" was to be interpreted as persons not paupers. The trustees were limited thus in their assignments
of the income, but it proved a helpful source of relief for
over fifty years.[45]

As prosperity returned with the eighties the numerous
demands upon the pauper department diminished. Costs,
however, did not at once decrease and the city almoner was
accused of negligence and inefficiency. Yet over 1,100 persons were given aid in 1880 at a cost to the city of $9,905.
At that time while the city still owned neither poor farm nor
almshouse, relief was given in the form of orders on the
city merchants for supplies of the necessaries of life,
namely, "bread, crackers, flour, meal, meat, potatoes, fish,
salt, molasses, soap, oil, wood, coal, and clothing"; and
paupers entirely dependent on city support were boarded
out. But apparently no amount of supervision sufficed to
prevent the abuse of this system, the transmuting of bread
into confectionery, tobacco, or liquor.

At length in 1888 in hopes of eradicating the greatest
evils of such methods, the city bought and stocked a farm
of some seventy-three and a half acres. But neither was
this arrangement ideal. The almoner of twenty-two years'
standing was dismissed in 1894 as being too old to super-
vise the farm work properly, since the crops raised had
netted very little. With a new almoner in charge a new
scheme was adopted. Able-bodied men applying to the city
for assistance were given work on the city farm and paid
accordingly. The system worked well, particularly as numbers of applicants increased. The depression of the nineties had by then taken effect and costs for poor relief again

45. See above, p. 91; Holyoke *Transcript,* Aug. 3, 1878, Jan. 28, Apr. 5,
1882, Aug. 9, 1884.

rose sharply. The almshouse had to be extended until 120 persons were accommodated there in 1897. Nearly 800 families were given aid in that year at a total cost to the city of $51,526. Again in 1898 the almshouse was added to by the building of two well-equipped hospital wards. Although mutterings of discontent were heard in the city from time to time over the bad management of almshouse and farm, investigation generally proved complaints unwarranted. Mayor Chapin's administration in fact found the pauper department sufficiently well run to keep in office the overseer and city almoner appointed several years before, and the return of prosperity cut the expenses of the department so noticeably as to remove its doings from public attention.[46]

In the field of street lighting the city government had had little to do.[47] The Holyoke Water Power Company supplied the gas for much of the street lighting of the seventies and eighties at reasonable rates. A number of naphtha lamps had been used in the seventies, because the light was considered better in proportion to the cost, but by 1884 the proportion of naphtha to gas lights was one to two. At that juncture the lighting problem in the city was altered by the building of an electric plant. Operated first by a company as a subsidiary of the Holyoke Water Power Company, the control was taken over by the Water Power Company some three years later. As early as 1885 electric lights were installed on the principal streets, and in 1890 the city entered into a five-year contract with the Water Power Company to furnish electricity for street lights.[48]

The percentage of electric street lights continued to

46. Holyoke *Transcript,* Jan. 3, 1881, Oct. 20, 1888, Sept. 14, 1889, Jan. 6, 9, 1894, Mar. 8, 1896, Jan. 28, 1897, Sept. 14, 1899; *Municipal Register,* 1895, pp. 389–392; 1898, pp. 571–572; 1899, pp. 571–580; 1900, pp. 315–331.

47. Under the first city charter a committee of aldermen and council members had charge of supplying fuel and street lights. After 1897 under the new charter the Board of Public Works had control of all that pertained to the streets, lights, paving, sewers, cross walks, etc.

48. Holyoke *Transcript,* Jan. 1, Feb. 7, 1885, June 22, 1890; *Municipal Register,* 1877, p. 157; 1885, p. 285; 1891, p. 321. By 1891 of the 333 street lights in Holyoke, 183 were electric, 49 gas, and only 39 still naphtha.

mount, and at the expiration of the first contract a new one was signed. But meanwhile city officials and many private citizens, dissatisfied with the terms and high-handed methods of the power company, began to investigate the question of having the city supply its own electricity. In 1891 the legislature had passed a law permitting any municipality upon vote of the electorate to go into the lighting business, on condition, however, that if a private concern owned a plant, gas or electric, which it offered to sell to that city, the city must accept it. If the terms of sale were disputed, a commission appointed by the Supreme Court of Massachusetts should fix the price. After nearly two years of discussion the question of municipal ownership came up for referendum at the polls in Holyoke and was carried.[49] As a consequence of this vote, when soon thereafter the Holyoke Water Power Company offered both its gas and electric lighting plants to the city, the city was bound to accept them. The Water Power Company's price of $1,000,000 was, however, rejected as the city considered $400,000 a fair value. Thereupon the Supreme Court was called upon to name a commission and for nearly five years the hearings went on before the price of $708,790 was settled upon. Not until December 1902 did the city take over the plants and, organizing the municipal Gas and Electric Department begin to furnish city and citizens with gas and electricity.[50] Thereafter, by the

49. The only ward in the city in which the vote opposed the proposal of municipal lighting was Ward Seven where a considerable proportion of the people of means lived. The conviction that government, whether municipal or state, should leave business to private enterprise was most strongly entrenched where property was most extensive. Holyoke *Transcript*, Dec. 1, 9, 13, 14, 22, 1897.

50. The Municipal Lighting Case, as it was generally called, was deemed sufficiently important to lead to the state's ordering the stenographic reports of the hearings to be published. Twenty volumes of material cover the case. The material I have employed is taken from *Holyoke Water Power Company Petitioner v. City of Holyoke*, XVI, 399–459, and XX, 119–128. Feeling in the city ran high about the case and the issues involved. Various attempts to sidetrack negotiations were made, and Mayor Chapin urged a new vote reconsidering the question. The example of the fine service of the municipal water board was frequently

successful operation of this enterprise plus the economical running of the city water works and the profitable management of the Holyoke and Westfield Railroad, Holyoke became a stronghold of municipal ownership of utilities.

The G. and E. for some years was headed by the men who had been in charge of the plants under the Water Power Company. But a number of employes were needed, and as years went on the political patronage which this circumstance gave to the permanent head of the department created in the city administration a kind of *imperium in imperio*. Irritated citizens sometimes alluded to the department as "the retired alderman's home." No one, however, was able to justify accusations of inefficient management, and the G. and E. grew in importance to the city as the city itself grew.

The city's reform administration continued in control for twelve years. Periodic attempts were made to overthrow the regime, by charges of favoritism, extravagance, and outright graft. Of these only the first could be substantiated, for the mayor presented conclusive figures which proved the economy and honesty with which the city was run. Favoritism in granting of jobs and contracts was tacitly admitted, but a large majority of citizens considered that not only an inevitable but a small price to pay for efficient service.

City finances were in sound condition, the city debt reduced $150,000 in ten years, the tax rate in 1910 set at $17 per thousand dollar valuation and yet many new services and permanent municipal improvements added to the city budget.[51] In 1910 alone $197,000 was spent on per-

cited in the newspapers. On the other hand opponents bemoaned the probable graft of a city-owned utility. A new vote was in fact taken on the question of revising a contract with the Holyoke Water Power Company and abandoning municipal ownership for a period of years. But again the electorate favored city control and refused the proposed contract. Holyoke *Transcript*, Jan. 3, 13, Feb. 24, Mar. 5, 1898, May 15, Nov. 9, 1899, Jan. 1, Mar. 12, 13, July 11, 19, 1900, Dec. 15, 1932.

51. Holyoke *Transcript*, Oct. 21, Nov. 9, 1903, Dec. 13, 1905, Dec. 4, 1908, July 7, 1909, Jan. 2, Mar. 9, Apr. 26, July 26, 1910; *Municipal Register*, 1904, pp. 11–19; 1908, p. 3; 1910, p. 346.

manent improvements, schoolhouses, highways, playgrounds, parks, and the purchase from Northampton of Smiths Ferry, the elongated sausage-shaped territory between the river and the Mt. Tom range stretching northward to Mt. Tom Junction. And even that year a payment of $365,590 was made upon the city debt. Well might the city pride itself upon its efficient administration. Its three great municipal enterprises were financially profitable: the Holyoke and Westfield Railroad, free of debt, paid 14 per cent or about $31,000 a year to the city treasury; the water works offering the cheapest household rates in the United States, so officials boasted, paid $10,000 yearly into the city; and the Gas and Electric Department, by law untaxed and obliged to supply the municipality at cost, saved the city nearly 38 per cent in six years on its street lighting and cut household rates 40 per cent below the old rates of the Holyoke Water Power Company.[52] The municipality performed many services not generally included for citizens, free servicing of gas appliances in homes, removal of ashes, garbage, and rubbish from inside the houses, paying one half the cost of laying sidewalks and installing good sewers, providing for street sprinkling in summer.[53]

But in spite of care in budgeting, fixed charges for city maintenance rose steadily. Between 1905 and 1910 the city auditor estimated that while population increased 11 per cent and property valuations 19 per cent, the city debt rose 43 per cent, amount of city taxes 15 per cent, state taxes 37 per cent, county tax 9 per cent, payments on the city debt 300 per cent. Every city department demanded and spent increasing sums, so that 1910 as compared to 1905 saw the school department increase expenditure by 28 per cent; police department, 27 per cent; fire department, 22 per cent; relief department, 14 per cent; Park Commission, 33 per cent; the Board of Public Works for

52. *Municipal Register,* 1901, pp. 6, 46–47; 1904, p. 324; 1907, pp. 8, 68; Holyoke *Transcript,* May 28, 1909, Apr. 26, 1911, Dec. 15, 1932.
53. *Municipal Register,* 1908, p. 263; 1910, pp. 372–381.

alleys, street cleaning, and bath houses, 34 per cent, 112 per cent, and 40 per cent respectively; the Board of Health, 62 per cent; and these additions took no account of the new expenses incurred by the creation of city playgrounds in 1910. As the auditor pointed out, each administration expected to economize but a month after it was elected the public demanded the best of everything, regardless of cost. And public conceptions of the best were becoming yearly more comprehensive. Elsewhere the same tendencies were noticeable. An excerpt from a United States Census report dealing with per capita costs of administration in the 158 largest American cities listed the comparison between 1902 and 1907. The average increase in cost of health administration was about 583 per cent, of education 22 per cent, of charity and corrective work 23 per cent, of fire protection 21 per cent.[54] Running a city had become a difficult and exacting business.

Partly because of the growing demands on the time of the conscientious officeholder, in the fall of 1910 capable Mayor Avery refused to run for another term. His successor was generally considered competent to carry on the honest administration as a member of the Whiting machine. But either because public vigilance had been lulled into too great a sense of security to examine John White's qualifications, or because the power of office affected White's convictions, the new order soon proved disastrous. By 1912 Holyoke had slipped back into the hands of self-seekers to whom the public interest was of secondary importance. The $197,000 devoted to permanent city improvements in 1910 was reduced to $25,000 in 1912 and the sum dedicated to debt payment was cut by one third; only the mayor's contingency fund was increased. After two years in office, White was replaced by more able men, but for many years the city was not again to be run with the honest efficiency of the Chapin-Avery regime.

Expenditure rose steadily, much of which was indeed inevitable under any administration in view of the new

54. Holyoke *Transcript*, Mar. 9, 1910, Apr. 26, 1911.

public services demanded by public opinion and by state law, until the tax rate in 1921 was 41 per cent above the 1910 rate. More schools, more streets and sewers, extensions to the water supply and to the gas and electric plants —all were necessary as the city grew. With the population in 1921 standing at 61,680, the amount raised per capita by taxation had jumped from $15.18 in 1910 to $36.80. Assessors' valuations also were pushed up to keep pace with the higher costs of everything after the war. And still the city debt increased. Population in the second decade of the century had increased 6 per cent, the ordinary costs of running the city 200 per cent.[55]

Confronted with such figures, the electorate was roused to making charges of extravagance and graft against city officials. Incumbents in the city hall were not alarmed. From the adoption of the Eighteenth Amendment and the Volstead Act on, illegal liquor selling in Holyoke proceeded undeterred, and reason suggests that some of the city fathers and police force alike found it a profitable arrangement. They were entrenched with the support of the liquor interests, and a more public-spirited administration was not to be elected for some years. Federal enforcement agents concentrated upon raids in Holyoke during 1920 and 1921, but the speakeasies learned to cover their tracks more skillfully, and city government in the twenties remained largely in the hands of the liquor forces.[56]

Of all the city departments, that of poor relief expanded less in the years from 1900 to 1920 than was to be ex-

55. *Ibid.,* Oct. 23, Nov. 12, 25, 1912, Jan. 5, 1913, Nov. 13, 14, 1919, Nov. 16, 1921; *Municipal Register,* 1914, pp. 8–9; 1921, p. 8; Lyman Mills Papers, Burke to Lovering, Aug. 18, 29, 1919.

56. Holyoke before prohibition days had always faced trouble in controlling the liquor interests. Although the police force was included in the civil service and a conscientious staff rendered good service on the whole, the temperance groups in the city were critical of the efficacy of the law enforcement. Holyoke *Transcript,* Oct. 12, 21, Nov. 12, 13, 1901, Jan. 9, 1902, Apr. 27, 1905, Nov. 12, 1906, Apr. 9, 25, Dec. 2, 1908, Jan. 1, 1910, Dec. 18, 1911, May 12, 1913, Apr. 3, May 18, 1915, Apr. 4, 28, Sept. 11, 26, Nov. 3, 29, Dec. 4, 1919, Mar. 29, Aug. 24, Sept. 3, 1920, May 11, 27, June 7, 28, Nov. 15, 1921; *Municipal Register,* 1908, p. 8; 1914, pp. 13–14; 1921, p. 61.

pected. As always the demands for aid rose or fell with the fluctuations in local industry. Just as 1908 with shutdowns in the mills proved the most difficult in the city's history up to that time, so 1909 with the return of prosperity brought an immediate marked let-up in the calls for help. The city expended $62,210 in the depression year in giving aid to 676 families, whereas in 1897, the hardest year before 1908, $10,000 less had sufficed to tide over nearly 800 families. The larger cost per person in 1908 was attributed to the more general unemployment which made it impossible for friends and relatives to give assistance. Organized charity under the Holyoke Relief Association rendered valuable help in 1908, but so completely had conditions changed by the end of that year that the volunteer group disbanded.

In the fall of 1913 pessimists were prophesying that the effect of a newly enacted state child labor law would be the doubling of the relief charges in the city, a grievous commentary upon the then extent of child labor in Holyoke. Actually the heavy burdens put upon the relief department in 1914 and 1915 were caused by the widespread unemployment brought about by the industrial slump of those years. The city, by state law, in the fall of 1913 had another expense added in the form of aid to dependent mothers, a charge which thenceforward added regularly some thousands of dollars to the budget. Aldermanic investigation of the conduct of the city poor farm revealed that inefficient management there, if not outright dishonesty, was costing the city considerable. And meanwhile the numbers of applicants for work at the city hall increased. Then in 1916 the situation again reversed and there was work enough for all. Not until the winter of 1920–1921 was the relief department again flooded with requests for assistance. With many heads of families working only two or three days a week through much of 1921 the situation was hard. Seven hundred twenty-six families were given help in the course of the year. Yet, according to a state Chamber of Commerce survey, unemployment did not reach the proportions of 1914 and 1915 in Holyoke. In the fall of 1921 the Board of Aldermen, urged on by a committee of manufacturers and employers in other fields, voted to borrow $50,000 to expend on street building within the city as a way of providing work relief. And by the end of the year a new era of general steady work in the mills was calculated to avert excessive charges for the immediate future in the relief department.

Otherwise there was no fundamental change in methods of giving poor relief in these years. The city farm under the direction of a resident superintendent housed the permanent city charges, an arrangement made humane by the hospital wards for the infirm. All able-bodied inmates of the farm were expected to work on the place. On the farm between 120 and 240 persons were cared for in 1920 and 1921 of whom about half were hospital cases.[57]

The most notable increase in city expenses came with enlarging the functions of the Board of Health. As medical knowledge widened, the essential character of proper health protection in thickly populated areas became manifest to city dwellers, and a series of new state laws and local ordinances added new duties for health officers and necessitated in time multiplication of staff. Six posts in 1901 had grown to eleven by 1910 and to eighteen by 1921. Quarantining of contagious disease, making of bacteriological examinations, particularly in cases of suspected diphtheria, and inspection of tenements and plumbing, barns and livery stables, undertaking establishments, bakeries, fruit and vegetable stands, slaughter houses and meat markets, and of milk, vinegar, and petroleum—these varied tasks fell to the Board of Health in 1901.[58] Con-

57. *Municipal Register,* 1904, p. 347; 1906, p. 87; 1908, p. 97; 1910, pp. 316–317; 1914, pp. 8, 453–454, 514–515; 1921, pp. 8, 357–378, 372–373; Holyoke *Transcript,* Jan. 4, 1904, Apr. 10, May 23, 27, Oct. 22, Dec. 1, 1908, Jan. 1, 1909, Sept. 2, Nov. 13, 1913, Jan. 22, May 6, 1914, Apr. 3, 1915, Jan. 1, 1917, Dec. 4, 1919, Nov. 27, 1920, Sept. 27, Oct. 19, Nov. 2, 1921.

58. *Municipal Register,* 1901, pp. 167–194; 1910, pp. 6, 430–453; 1921, pp. 438–474. The increase in numbers of salaried officials was unfortunately a means of paying political debts rather than a necessity. Providence, Rhode Island, a city four times the size of Holyoke, performed

scientious though the officers might be, to cope adequately
with many of the health problems of the city, professionally trained personnel with wider powers supported by enlightened public opinion was needed.[59] The unsanitary
crowded tenements in the city bred disease rapidly and the
poverty and ignorance of the foreigners living in them
multiplied difficulties. Demolition of the worst of the tenements, rigid enforcement of proper building ordinances,
medical inspection in the schools with a system of following cases into the homes, a public milk station for infant
care, a campaign of education to prevent tuberculosis, and
means of locating and treating active cases of tuberculosis,
such were the most vital needs for public health in Holyoke. To arouse public opinion was a task that occupied
nearly a decade, and even after some general realization
of the urgency of action it took another decade to carry
part of the program into effect.

By 1910 new building ordinances in the city provided
against further construction of dark, unventilated tenements, but added to the expense of building inspection.
Medical inspection in the schools was inaugurated in that
year also. Increase in the work of the city bacteriologist,
the building and maintenance of a tuberculosis sanitorium,
the opening of a public dispensary for diagnosing tuberculosis, the erection of a contagious disease hospital, and
the institution of a Municipal Milk Station partly supported by city funds in the next five years further multiplied costs. But the public could see the results in the
gradual decline of the death rate to 12.68 per thousand in
1914 and to 12.20 in 1921. Only the influenza epidemic of
1918 brought an increase for that year to 18.58.[60] A separate municipal department of Child Welfare was created
in 1919 to enlarge the scope of the work for infants and
pre-school children and to provide maternity care. So in-

notable health service with a far smaller staff. Murray P. Horwood,
Health Survey of Holyoke with Relation to Tuberculosis, pp. 203–204.
59. Holyoke *Transcript,* May 9, 1914.
60. *Ibid.,* Sept. 21, 1906, Jan. 31, 1919; *Municipal Register,* 1910, pp.
113, 432, 452, 565–566, 568–569; 1914, pp. 358–386; 1921, pp. 441, 568–573.

fant mortality, the death rate of children under one year
of age per thousand born, was reduced from 150 in 1910
to 85 by 1921.[61] Between 1918 and 1921 alone, infant
mortality was cut by a third.

These new services, let me repeat, were recommended by
the Board of Health before state law or public opinion demanded them or taxpayers were ready to pay for them.
That numbers of shockingly unsanitary, overcrowded
tenements existed in the city had long been a familiar fact
to the health officers. Yearly their published reports gave
information from which citizens might have drawn a picture of conditions. People read of the removal of a few of
the worst old buildings and failed to envisage the state of
the many that still stood. Meantime ambitious contractors
were adding new tenement buildings, no better built,
scarcely less ill ventilated, lighted, or piped than the oldest.[62] The first public awakening came in 1908 when a survey made of Holyoke housing by a competent visiting doctor gave comparisons of conditions in Holyoke with those in
other American cities. Only eleven of the thirty odd cities
of over 100,000 inhabitants had proportionately more
tenement houses than Holyoke, with about 55,000 inhabitants. In these tenements occupied by the foreign-born,
health conditions were appalling, and the mortality of infants under a year was so high as to bring the total for the
entire city up to one third of the whole mortality.[63]

The crowding in the poorer sections of the city had been
disgraceful in 1900; in 1910 it was worse, 11.9 persons per
dwelling, only Hoboken, New Jersey, and New York City

61. Holyoke Child Welfare Commission, *Annual Report,* 1936, p. 1.
The creation of this department, separate from the Board of Health, was
due to a legal complication which made it impossible for the city merely
to contribute funds to the private organization, the Infant Hygiene Association. See below, pp. 386–387.

62. See *Municipal Registers,* 1901 to 1910; Holyoke *Transcript,* Dec. 4,
1905, Feb. 4, 1908, Feb. 7, Mar. 12, 21, 1913.

63. Holyoke *Transcript,* Nov. 2, 1908. By 1910 there were fifty cities in
the United States of over 100,000 population, but in 1900 only thirty-six.
Thirteenth Census of U. S., 1910, *Population,* I, 1289.

showing more per dwelling. In 1915 Holyoke's Ward Two still averaged 22.3 persons to a dwelling.[64] (See chart, p. 259.) But not only were these tenements crowded, they were built with dark rooms, narrow courts and air shafts, with insufficient plumbing, and no proper fire protection. These facts were not comprehended quickly. Reports of various civic organizations formed between 1906 and 1912 piled up the evidence year after year. In 1912, 50 per cent of the cases of tuberculosis were laid at the door of improper housing, and a large part of the high infant mortality.[65] In 1910, 86 per cent of the city's infant mortality occurred in Wards One, Two, and Four, where housing conditions were most deplorable. Groups of citizens urged more careful sanitary inspection, more stringent enforcement of existing sanitary laws and building ordinances, and additional means of public control. Gradually this campaign of education made some headway. The worst tenements were abandoned as newer dwellings were built. But still public opinion was not strong enough to force upon the city government an ordinance compelling the improvement or destruction of unsanitary tenements.[66]

But in spite of the good intentions of the Board of Health, its personnel was not technically trained, particularly in the case of the tuberculosis visitor and physician in charge of the dispensary. Political favor, not professional

64. *Fourteenth Census of U. S.*, 1920, *Population*, II, 1268–1270; *Census of Mass.*, 1915, p. 110. Holyoke *Transcript*, Jan. 23, 1911.

65. Holyoke *Transcript*, Mar. 7, 1907, Sept. 2, 1908, Jan. 28, 1911, Jan. 13, Dec. 7, 1912. Racial susceptibility to tuberculosis has in recent years been found to be a more important factor in the spread of the disease than overcrowding. The French Canadians are not highly susceptible, whereas the Irish, Russo-Poles, and Irish born in Canada are extremely so. Therefore despite the overcrowded living quarters in Wards One and Two where most of the French Canadians live, tuberculosis is less prevalent there than would be the case were unsanitary living conditions the chief cause. Horwood, Health Survey of Holyoke with Relation to Tuberculosis, p. 11.

66. Frank Elting, Agent Holyoke Building Trades Council, 1907–1938 (interview); Holyoke *Transcript*, Mar. 13, Apr. 30, Oct. 4, 1913, Jan. 29, 1914, Feb. 5, 1915, Mar. 11, 1916, July 6, 1919, Apr. 6, 1920; Lyman Mills Papers, Burke to Parsons, June 3, 1914; Parsons to Burke, June 8, 1914.

competence, was the basis of selection, and the lack of any municipal program of public health education resulted.[67]

The increasing costs of running the city did not prevent the adoption of a municipal playground program in 1910. Specifically voted by the electorate at the city elections of 1909, the opening of playgrounds marked the beginning of a new era of civic consciousness. Authority to acquire and organize the supervision of these playgrounds was vested in a commission appointed by the mayor. Like the members of the other municipal commissions, the Playground Commissioners served without pay and by their devoted attention contrived to keep the playground administration unusually free of politics. It was public service such as the city had seen too little of. Three women had place on the commission.[68]

The ratification of the Woman Suffrage Amendment and the flinging of several thousand women into participation in city government might have been expected to accelerate the movement to extend municipal social services. But woman suffrage was too new before 1922 to affect local government. In fact while still unenfranchised, women, as members of various volunteer organizations, had been as effective in promoting civic improvements as they were as voters.

City politics continued to be a great sport for the part of the population whose economic opportunities were smallest. As the yearly municipal elections drew near and candidates for office began their speaking campaigns, working people swarmed to the political rallies to cheer their friends or hiss their foes. Pre-election days were Roman holidays, although the gatherings where the ward gladiators carried on their word combats were goodnatured.

Thus Holyoke, begun as a company town, emerging confidently from village government to city, encountered the usual ups and downs of American municipal adminis-

67. See above note 58.
68. *Municipal Register,* 1910, pp. 213–241; 1921, pp. 138–158.

tration of the late nineteenth and early twentieth centuries. Civic pride conflicting with individual interests, benevolence toward the underprivileged competing with absorption in the game of money-making, made the participation of the business leaders in city affairs spasmodic. When political control slid into hands too blatantly and expensively self-seeking, public opinion aroused and the taxpayers returned to office more zealous guardians of the public weal. Some departments were always efficiently and economically run. But city government was administered of necessity without long-time policy, one regime supplanting another sometimes once a year. Only taxes, poverty, squalor, and misery were certain. Social maladjustments went deeper than city politics, however clean and probing, could reach. Social irresponsibility had been to blame for much, ignorance and stupidity for much, cupidity and lack of idealism for the rest. Some persons still hoped to see the evils remedied by education of the oncoming generation. The endeavor to eliminate indifference and ignorance by enlightenment was to be made through the schools, while materialism was only to be countered by religion through the churches. Yet the quickening of civic conscience, first marked in the nineteen-twenties, was to be brought about neither by schooling nor by the churches alone but by social forces distinct from both.

X

SCHOOLS, 1873–1922

THE mental habit of considering any social problem as solvable by the oncoming generation if it were given proper education was widespread in nineteenth-century America. Let this generation struggle to give the next a chance and the future would be secure, for greed, lust, stupidity, callousness, all the fundamental human weaknesses must yield before the onslaught of enlightenment which education of the younger generation could bring. Discouragement over conditions in the present could not endure where such hope prevailed. Therefore men vaguely troubled in their hearts by the misery about them in this land of promise turned their eyes upon the schools. Money was voted to the school department and men gave generously of their time to serve on the School Committee, since there lay the easing of their social conscience.

The Holyoke School Board was elected, one member from each ward of the city and two members at large, to hold office for three years, three of the nine to be re-elected or replaced each year. After 1893 women also, upon payment of the poll tax or a state or county tax, might vote for school committeemen, an arrangement which may have helped thereafter to diminish the influence of politics in the running of the schools.[1] Appropriations were made by the Board of Aldermen, but the disbursement of monies lay with the School Committee. Until 1897 the mayor was *ex-officio* chairman of the School Board, and presided at meetings with some regularity for years. No salary was attached to the post of school committeeman, only minor prestige and some patronage. Yet until after 1903, through good city administrations and corrupt, Holyoke produced

1. Holyoke *Transcript,* Dec. 9, 1897.

fairly able School Committees, generally representing the city's best interests even if not always her most distinguished intellects.[2] The program of education was laid out by the superintendent of schools, but the committee was supervisory. In the appointment of teachers lay the chief possible source of patronage for committeemen. Teaching posts were after all jobs. For purposes of administration the board divided the schools into three districts, over each of which a committee of three board members kept special watch. Thus the appointing power came by custom to lie in the hands of the district committee as the persons best informed about the needs of their own bailiwicks. Still the superintendent of schools exercised some authority, and his recommendations carried weight. Probably Holyoke's corps of teachers were as capable as that of most Massachusetts cities of the seventies and eighties.[3]

Although the city spent more money for schools than for any other single purpose save interest payments, there was perpetual need of a larger teaching staff and much of the time of more school rooms. Until 1878 two factors served to offset the limited accommodation and small number of teachers, first, the circumstance that attendance was highly irregular until a truant officer began to function in 1876, and then that the business depression led families to leave the city. The school population in 1876 was nearly four hundred less than in 1875, a loss of about 12 per cent.[4] The increase in capacity of the parochial schools also relieved the stress in the public schools. Nevertheless, from 1878 on, even by the standards of the eighties, the inadequacy of the primary schools in particular to meet the demands of the growing city was chronic. As truancy was checked somewhat, as amplification of state laws

2. *Report of the School Committee,* 1897, pp. 98, 149. In the letting of contracts for school supplies and new buildings there were opportunities for showing favoritism inevitably, but the School Board seemed to keep its hands fairly clean. E. N. White, School Committeeman, 1897–1900 (interview).

3. *Report of the School Committee,* 1879, p. 8; 1883–1884, pp. 8–9; 1894–1895, p. 14.

4. Holyoke *Transcript,* Aug. 16, May 6, 1876.

brought larger attendance at school for working children, and as reviving prosperity enabled more parents to keep children in school instead of breadwinning, school needs confronted the city sharply.[5] The situation by 1880 is clearly described by the superintendent of schools in his report:

Hundreds of these pupils [of foreign nationalities], knowing not a word of English, enter our schools at the lowest grade. Some can read their mother tongue and know something of numbers, while others know nothing. While some have passed their thirteenth birthday, others . . . require . . . evidence . . . that they have passed their fifth. Differing widely in age, in degree of maturity, in home influences, in ante-school attainments, and of course in quality of character . . . agreeing in but one thing,—ignorance of the language— placed forty or fifty in a room at the beginning of a term, to be increased to sixty, seventy, or eighty within a few weeks, under one teacher, perhaps the last appointed and least experienced—this picture I hold up to your contemplation. . . . And this condition will continue . . . what means will you adopt to secure . . . the speediest judicious advancement of the individual pupil from grade to grade? Will you divide these schools and increase the number of teachers by three? or will you place in each of the three buildings where these disadvantages are greatest, a principal's assistant to be used chiefly in these schools?[6] or will you choose for such schools teachers qualified by nature, culture, and experience for the peculiar and great amount of work demanded?

The above conditions do not affect the lowest grades alone but are felt . . . in every schoolroom in the city.[7]

What did the city do about it? What that was effective could it afford to do? If education was the panacea of social ills, what could it afford not to do? In the 1930's when progressive educators advocate one teacher for every seven

5. *Report of the School Committee*, 1879, pp. 7, 21–27, 58–60.
6. The term *school* is used in the sense of group.
7. *Report of the School Committee*, 1879, pp. 41–42.

primary pupils, it might seem a miracle that the public schools of the eighties could successfully teach anything. And after 1884 state law required cities to supply school children with free textbooks.[8]

The School Board therefore first of all undertook to convince the taxpayers and the city fathers of the necessity of a large increase in appropriations. They succeeded. The cost of the school system in 1880, $34,175, ran up to $54,530 in 1884. Seventy-six teachers instead of forty-nine were employed in the grammar and primary schools, although pupils enrolled increased from 2,433 to 4,153. By 1890 expenditures totalled nearly $80,000 for about 4,700 pupils and ten years later $171,355 for some 6,500. In the second place, irrespective of action by the School Board and in spite of the resentment of some of the Protestant element of the population, the parochial schools were expanded until about three eighths of the city's school children were no longer a city charge.[9] And in the third place, the board launched a teacher's training school in 1891, where students had opportunity to do practice teaching in the elementary grades.[10] The Park Street School, near the third-level canal, was rearranged for the purpose so as to have four primary grades available for training-school teachers, and under competent instructors for several years the training school proved useful. In 1895, 25 per cent of the teachers in the city had attended the school.[11] Still it was at best a partial and unsatisfactory solution of

8. *Ibid.*, 1883–1884, pp. 37–38.

9. *Ibid.*, 1880, pp. 7, 61; 1883–1884, pp. 32–33; 1889–1890, pp. 42–43; 1900, pp. 18–19, 28; Holyoke *Transcript*, Apr. 20, 1890.

10. Fifteen years earlier a similar scheme had been tried, and two or three high school graduates were accepted as pupil teachers for each of the lowest grades at the Park Street School. These pupil teachers supervised the children on the playground too. But although the plan was reported to work well at first, it lapsed for lack of applicants for training. *Report of the School Committee,* 1876, p. 34; Holyoke *Transcript,* June 7, Dec. 16, 1876, June 30, 1877.

11. *Report of the School Committee,* 1890–1891, pp. 85–91; 1894–1895, pp. 52, 128–140. Before 1897 the need of professional training for teachers was not recognized here. Although a state normal school was barely ten miles away in Westfield, only 39 out of 141 teachers in the Holyoke

the many difficulties. As more effective for securing properly trained teachers, the board ruled in 1896 that thereafter at least normal-school training should be a requisite
qualification for teaching posts and that the training school
consequently should be discontinued.[12] New buildings in
some sections of the city and repairs and improvements to
existing structures from time to time relieved the worst
overcrowding.[13] But there remained that more fundamental problem of how to find teachers who under adverse circumstances could make the most of their small pupils' intelligence in the four or five school years at their disposal.

For always Holyoke's school problem and opportunity
lay in the primary grades. Every effort to improve the
record notwithstanding, superintendents had to report at
intervals that a large proportion of the total school population of the city dropped out of school every year after
completing the fourth grade. The same general situation
existed in nearly every growing American industrial community before 1900, a reproach and a challenge.[14] In Holyoke in 1874 the number so dropping out was over 75 per
cent of those completing the fourth grade. Five years later
thirteen first grades converged to four fifth grades, not
counting the ungraded schools for part-time working children and the mixed schools in the suburbs. The four fifth
grades fed two ninth grades. As late as 1898 thirteen fifth

public schools had attended any normal school in 1895. Therefore the 27
graduates of the Park Street training school tended to leaven the mass.
Twenty years before, however, only one teacher in thirty had had as
much training as a normal school course.

12. *Report of the School Committee,* 1897, pp. 69–92, 99. The school
could offer practical experience in teaching only for the primary grades.
From the standpoint of general training the state normal schools were
better qualified to meet Holyoke's needs.

13. *Ibid.,* 1893–1894, pp. 14–17; 1900, pp. 30–31.

14. The figures of the State Board of Education as cited in 1899 by the
superintendent of schools show Massachusetts children averaging seven
years of schooling as compared to four for the United States as a whole.
Holyoke as a city subject to Massachusetts laws had thus a record better
than many manufacturing communities. See above, p. 133. *Ibid.,* 1899,
p. 31.

grades sufficed for twenty-six first grades, although there were seven ninth grades.[15]

The explanation is not far to seek: first of all the poverty of a large part of the population of a mill city put pressure upon parents to put children to work as soon as possible, and secondly there was the ignorance of many immigrant parents of the potential uses of education beyond the legal minimum. Probably also a third factor entered in, namely the reluctance of the child itself to go further with a schooling that offered little play to the imagination, opened up few new horizons, and promised merely continuation of a dreary routine.[16] Social regeneration by education could not be carried far unless children could be kept in school beyond the fourth grade. Only the extension of the school laws as time went on bettered school attendance.

What were the legal requirements for schooling? Free, compulsory, nonsectarian education had been a Massachusetts ideal for generations and had become law in 1858 for children between the ages of seven and fourteen. At least the equivalent of the free public schooling must be given to every child whether in church or other private school. After the Civil War the difficulty of enforcing attendance in a state where child labor in the mills was legal for children over ten had resulted in the stipulation first of three months, and then twenty weeks of school attendance out of every school year for children under fifteen years of age. And in the seventies these laws were strengthened by obliging towns and cities to provide truant officers among whose duties were to be the check-up on certificates of age and schooling required of every child under sixteen employed in mill or shop. Furthermore, no child less than fourteen years old who could not read and write might be employed while the public schools were in session. If children were

15. *Ibid.*, 1874, pp. 22–23; 1879, p. 66.
16. The recognition of this feature of the problem is indicated by Search, superintendent from 1896 to 1899, in his declared aim to bring individualization into mass education in the public schools. *Ibid.*, 1895–1896, pp. 21–35.

sent to private schools the course of study must be as thorough as in the public schools and teaching must be in English. In 1887 the literacy requirement became a stipulation of literacy in English for all under sixteen, with an arrangement whereby night schooling might be substituted for regular day schooling by children between the ages of fourteen and sixteen. Later, thirty weeks instead of twenty of day schooling for children under fourteen was required. Eleven years later the law forbade entirely the employment of children under fourteen and explicitly required the attendance at school of all minors between the ages of seven and fourteen during the entire time the public schools were in session. Thus little by little the laws of the state reached out to force upon the wariest immigrant's child such education as he could acquire in school before he was fourteen years old.[17]

Holyoke in the early seventies was admittedly remiss in executing the school laws. Four years late in issuing a truancy ordinance, the city had a percentage of absentees from school of about one third the total school population in 1875, well over one thousand daily according to the official estimate.[18] When in 1876 the School Board appointed a truant officer and instituted the systematic investigation of the whereabouts of all children of school age in the city, the picture changed rapidly. Boys who made a game of evasion gave up the sport when it was found to end in the dark room of the basement at the city hall, and although at first some parents resented the interference of the school authority and announced that they would do with their children as they, the parents, pleased, gradually they gave way. Attendance jumped in the fall of 1876 to 95 per cent. Habitual truants were sent to a county truant school

17. *Ibid.,* 1879, pp. 58–60; 1897, pp. 92–93; 1899, pp. 61–62; Mass. Bur. Labor Statistics, *Seventh Annual Report,* 1876, pp. 270, 271, 276, 280, 302, 346–347; *Twenty-eighth Annual Report,* 1897, p. 363; Mass. State Board of Education, *Fifty-second Annual Report,* 1887–1888, pp. 88–117.
18. Holyoke *Transcript,* May 16, 1874; *Report of the School Committee,* 1875, p. 17.

but their numbers were few.[19] As the truant officers, aided
by mill overseers, enforced the law requiring work cards
for minors, there were continued attempts at stating false
ages for children. Parents, particularly among the newly
arrived French Canadians, insisted that their children's
wages were needed to keep the wolf from the door, and the
literacy requirement of 1880 was there felt to inflict great
hardship. When in 1883 the age limit for employment of
minors was set at twelve instead of ten in Massachusetts,
this situation was merely somewhat aggravated.[20]

The fight for better school attendance had to be waged
unceasingly. In the seventies the percentage of withdraw-
als from the schools before the end of the term averaged 26
per cent of the enrollment, children who had completed
their twenty weeks of schooling taking up jobs relinquished by those who had not. These children generally
were assigned to special ungraded schools where their irregular attendance need be a lesser handicap. The laws of
the eighties made possible some improvement here. Illness
and quarantines against contagious disease many years
cut in largely upon attendance. But it was truancy which
was the constant problem. The effective but drastic methods of earlier years, detaining truants in temporary con-
finement without warrant from court, had to be abandoned, since "champions of personal liberty" protested.[21]
Corporal punishment also had to be discontinued, and altogether the school authorities were baffled. The law of
1898 which penalized the parent with a fine for failure to
coerce the child into regular attendance had not produced

19. Holyoke *Transcript*, May 6, 10, 13, 17, 20, June 7, Sept. 2, 6, 20,
Oct. 4, 1876; *Report of the School Committee*, 1877, p. 20; 1879, pp. 25–
26. Truancy was ruled to be absence from school for three successive
days without the parent's knowledge.
20. See above, p. 134. Holyoke *Transcript*, Sept. 16, 1876, Feb. 19,
1879, May 8, 1880, Nov. 16, 1889; *Report of the School Committee*, 1881,
p. 27; 1883–1884, p. 27.
21. *Report of the School Committee*, 1880, pp. 29–30; 1883–1884, pp.
17–30; 1891–1892, pp. 23–38; 1893–1894, pp. 43–44; 1894–1895, pp. 75–77;
1900, pp. 34–35; Holyoke *Transcript*, Dec. 28, 1878.

the desired result by the turn of the century. The number of arrests and commitments to the county truancy schools was still discouragingly large.[22]

Truancy and indifference to the opportunities of schooling were often traceable directly to the homes. While many of the poorest parents were ambitious for their children, in view of the high percentage of illiteracy among the foreigners coming into the city every year, it is perhaps not strange that some of these immigrant parents regarded schooling for their children as superfluous. (See table.) Yet illiteracy did gradually decline. In 1885 Holyoke with 15.99 per cent had a higher percentage of illiteracy in proportion to the population ten years old and over than any other city in Massachusetts except Fall River, where the figure ran up to 20.65 per cent. New Bedford with 12.70 per cent stood third in this sorry race. And this in the land of the little red schoolhouse! By 1895 illiteracy in Holyoke had dropped one third compared to 1885, one in every nine being unlettered instead of one in every six. About two fifths of these illiterates by the later date were in domestic service, approximately one third employed in mills. Still in 1900 there were nearly 2,700 persons in the city who could not speak English.[23]

To meet this situation obviously the regular day schools could not suffice. Free public night schools were the only answer. Evening schools for persons, whether adult or mi-

22. *Report of the School Committee,* 1898, pp. 147–148; 1899, p. 61; 1900, pp. 58–60. The question of discipline within the schools was troublesome for many years. Corporal punishment was employed so regularly in the seventies that the suggestion was made that no more than one case a month for each school room in the city should be allowed. In the eighties as an innovation the ruling was made that corporal punishment might be by striking upon the hands only; neither gags nor dark rooms were to be permitted thereafter. The result was announced as better discipline. Holyoke *Transcript,* Feb. 12, Sept. 20, 1876, Dec. 28, 1878, Feb. 8, 1879, June 3, 1884, May 6, 1885.

23. Holyoke *Transcript,* Nov. 22, 1876, Jan. 25, 1882; *Census of Mass.,* 1885, *Population and Social Statistics,* I, Pt. II, lxxv; *ibid.,* 1895, *Social Statistics and General Summaries,* VII, 210, 211, 224; *Twelfth Census of U. S.,* 1900, *Population,* II, Pt. II, 500; *Report of the School Committee,* 1900, p. 52.

ILLITERACY 1870–1920

	1870	1880	1890	1900	1910	1920
Total population	10,733	21,915	35,637	45,712	57,730	60,203
Population over ten years of age . .		17,068	27,662	35,045	45,963	48,166
Foreign-born over ten		10,082	15,976	18,247	22,411	19,973
Illiterates over ten	2,201*	2,976	3,516	4,001	3,108	2,487
Foreign-born illiterates over ten . . .		2,858	3,285	3,733	2,912	2,372
Percentage of illiterates over ten of total population over ten		17.44	12.71	11.4	6.8	5.20
Percentage of foreign-born illiterates over ten of total foreign-born population over ten . . .		28.34	20.56	20.5	13.00	11.9
Population over ten unable to speak English . .			3,175	2,693	4,843	2,083
Percentage of population over ten unable to speak English of total population over ten . . .			11.48	7.68	10.5	4.3

Holyoke *Transcript*, Sept. 17, 1870. * Children under twelve excluded. *Census of Mass.*, from the *Tenth U. S. Census*, 1880, p. 476. *Eleventh Census of U. S.*, 1890, *Population*, II, lvii, lxv, 222, 224, 228. *Twelfth Census of U. S.*, 1900, *Population*, II, Pt. II, cxx, 440, 446, 458–459, 500. *Thirteenth Census of U. S.*, 1910, *Population*, I, 1252, 1282; II, 881. *Fourteenth Census of U. S.*, 1920, *Population*, II, 1218, 1259.

nor, whose employment made impossible daytime schooling had been opened by the town in 1870 and then dropped.
But in 1874 after the passage of the ten-hour day these
were again tried, this time with marked success. From then
on evening schools were an accepted part of the city school
system, and soon in fact were called for by state law. Attendance could not be legally required in these schools even
for the illiterate, but enough interest in learning English
or in getting other elementary schooling existed to make
the classes a boon to numbers of young men and women.
The average age in the evening schools at first was between
eighteen and nineteen. Some children over the school age
attended irregularly, but during the early eighties attendance lagged and often fell below 50 per cent of the enrollment. Other mill cities, however, had scarcely better records.[24] Then in 1887 the evening schools took on new
importance owing to the enactment of a state law forbidding the employment of any minor who could not read and
write English unless he were regularly attending either day
school or an evening school.[25] Thus in order to get employment many foreign children had to secure school certificates by attending the evening schools until they could
read and write English or until they became sixteen.[26]

24. Holyoke *Transcript,* Oct. 24, Dec. 5, 16, 1874, Feb. 20, Mar. 6, Apr.
17, Dec. 5, 9, 12, 1875, Mar. 8, Nov. 15, Dec. 2, 20, 27, 30, 1876, Dec. 29,
1877, Jan. 2, 1878, Jan. 29, Feb. 15, 1879, Jan. 14, Oct. 20, 1880, Oct. 15,
1881, Oct. 2, 1883. In 1883 attendance averaged only 185 to some 600 en-
rollments. As this was attributed partly to race quarrels, separate schools
for French, German, and English-speaking pupils were provided, and attendance improved perceptibly the next year. *Report of the School Committee,* 1875, p. 20; 1878, p. 9; 1883–1884, pp. 49–50.

25. Holyoke *Transcript,* Oct. 8, 1887. "Regular" attendance was defined as presence at 70 per cent of the sessions, "which attendance at
evening school is accepted for time 'not exceeding the length of the public school year minus twenty weeks, in place of attendance at day school
as now required by law.' " *Report of the School Committee,* 1897, pp.
92–93.

26. Holyoke *Transcript,* Sept. 29, Oct. 13, Dec. 27, 1888; *Report of the
School Committee,* 1893–1894, pp. 21–22; 1894–1895, pp. 17–20. Holyoke
did not open her evening school to children under fourteen and required
for them the thirty weeks' attendance at the regular day schools. The
statute of 1887, obscurely worded, was clarified by the law of 1898.

After 1898 evening school was obligatory for all children employed between the ages of fourteen and sixteen.

The presence of illiterates and children who, not yet sixteen years old, had already spent long hours at work in mill or shop retarded progress in many evening schools. Classes in drafting or mechanical drawing were for years part of the evening school program and attendance here averaged better than in the other classes.[27] But otherwise the evening schools were mostly used by young people not interested in going beyond primary grade work. Yet when a new superintendent in 1896 induced the School Board to organize an evening grammar school with additional sessions beyond the forty evenings theretofore thought sufficient, response was immediate. Forty students were graduated from this grammar school in the spring of 1898 and these promptly petitioned for an evening high school. Only financial stringency led to the postponement of this extension. But the School Board increased the elementary school sessions from forty evenings to sixty in hopes of making the work accomplished of more permanent value to the pupils, and the superintendent gave greater attention than ever before to selecting the teaching force. The evening schools were at last becoming true schools for hardworking young men and women of the city, not merely makeshifts to satisfy legal requirements.[28]

With the practical necessities of teaching reading and writing in English and some arithmetic to the swarms of Holyoke children, English-speaking, French Canadian, German, and at the end of the century Polish, it was possible to have few variations of curriculum in the primary grades. A little music and drawing and a smattering of geography were the only additional subjects. The wisdom of making the utmost use of time available for schooling for children soon to be at work in mills led to conscientious

27. Holyoke *Transcript,* Apr. 3, July 14, 1875, Nov. 16, 1889; *Report of the School Committee,* 1883–1884, p. 48; 1891, pp. 16–18; 1895–1896, p. 17; 1897, pp. 158–159.

28. *Report of the School Committee,* 1895–1896, pp. 12–15; 1897, pp. 94–97, 159; 1898, pp. 44–45; 1900, pp. 31–32.

efforts to find the best methods of teaching, but content differed little in the nineties over what it had been in the seventies.[29] Uniformity of material used or methods employed was not demanded of Holyoke teachers and some interesting and successful experiments resulted in the nineties. A little handwork was introduced in some of the primary grades in 1893, and four years later kindergartens were opened. The discovery that many first graders were taking a year and a half or two years to do that first year's elementary work was a strong argument in favor of kindergartens. But besides this preliminary training for the children, more better-trained, better-paid, primary-grade teachers and better books and working materials were badly needed to bring the quality of primary work up to the standard of accomplishment maintained in the higher grades.[30]

The higher the grade the more adequate became the schooling. Less time was wasted and better work accomplished. This was partly because the teachers' salary scale rose in the upper grades, because superintendent and supervisors gave more assistance here, because numbers of pupils per teacher dropped, and, what is perhaps the fundamental explanation of the other facts, because taxpayers' children were predominating in the upper grades and taxpayers were better able to demand their money's worth. In 1879 a ninth grade was added to the grammar school course to make time for review and make surer of sufficient preparation for high school work. Two years of United States history at the end of the grammar school had been

29. Holyoke *Transcript,* Feb. 7, 1874, Dec. 30, 1876; *Report of the School Committee,* 1879, pp. 35–36; 1883–1884, pp. 46–47; 1893–1894, p. 173. In the seventies there was some discussion of adding the teaching of French or German in the public grade schools in order to enroll foreign children whose parents wished them to know their parents' native tongue. Many of these were sent to special French or German schools, lay and parochial. But sectarian jealousy, not true interest in education, apparently prompted the series of letters to the *Transcript* on the subject. Holyoke *Transcript,* June 3, 10, 14, 17, 28, July 8, 15, 18, 19, 1876.

30. *Report of the School Committee,* 1893–1894, pp. 12, 81–83, 98–99, 127; 1894–1895, pp. 108–144; 1897, pp. 175–177.

part of the general schedule since the seventies, but there
were little but the tool subjects taught below the eighth
grade until the nineties brought interest in scientific
studies. At the same time the teaching of United States
history was pushed into the lower grades, since several
principals felt the importance of giving to children who
would never reach the eighth grade a background of their
country's past, especially where it was their adopted country.[31] Unhappily this came to result in much repetition of
work, until pupils were known to have studied history in
the grade school for five years and never have gone beyond
the American Revolution.

Still the general problem of enrichment of the curriculum below the high school was recognized in the city and
attempt was made, beginning in 1894, to make available
to grammar school children some knowledge of science. A
little elementary physics and chemistry was presented in
some schools through simple experiments which the children themselves performed, but equipment was necessarily
so limited as to make the educational results negligible.
Here also geometry, algebra, and Latin were added in the
top grades. Some manual training was tried out although
without either special manual-training teacher or shop the
results were an indication of what could be done rather
than evidence of accomplishment.[32]

A new era in the schools bade fair to be inaugurated
with the coming in 1896 of Preston Search as superintendent. His boundless energy and careful educational program in 1897 and 1898 were felt all through the schools,
and affected the quality of the work from the primary
grades up. Outlines of literary study, insistence on the
purchase of more adequate text and reference books, elimination of duplication of instruction, laboratory methods
rather than recitations, all aroused interest verging on excitement at the potential development of the public schools.

31. *Ibid.*, 1879, pp. 34, 50; 1890–1891, pp. 66–73; 1894–1895, pp. 92, 107,
113.

32. *Ibid.*, 1894–1895, pp. 107–108; 1895–1896, pp. 84, 90, 95–97, 102–105.

With his resignation after two and a half years of service inevitable reaction set in, the exhilaration subsided, and only part of the tonic effects of his administration survived. Citizens began to voice doubts as to whether children were being schooled to a point to unfit them for their future places in the community and the resulting drag upon the school program lasted long after 1900.[33]

The costliness of building up a good school system was at the bottom of much of Holyoke's educational troubles. Alarm at the expense of Search's program created opposition to his plans. Unwillingness to spend money for buildings and teachers ended in the overcrowding and unsuccessful teaching in the schools of the eighties and early nineties. Why should the taxpayer be heavily burdened in order to give a free education to the mill hand's child? The possible recompenses in the form of a more friendly, more intelligent working population, of an informed, judicious electorate in the next generation of this republic, and of satisfaction of any individual altruistic desire for sharing had to be weighed against the expense. Solve the social problems of the future through education by all means, but keep the cost within bounds. In view of the cost per child of schooling even of a perfunctory sort it may seem surprising that there was any opposition to the founding of the Catholic parish schools. Yet some there was.[34]

The Convent School for girls and the Institute for boys in St. Jerome's parish were accepted by the town at the end of the sixties with more surprise than disapproval. The relief these afforded the public schools at first offset the religious or civic distress of conscience which anon assailed some of the New England citizenry. Sectarianism was not to be downed by consideration of cost. But there were other aspects of the question of parochial schools. Unprejudiced persons viewed with some uneasiness the dividing of the community by schools which set apart one

33. *Ibid.*, 1897, pp. 7–12, 73–114, 157–214; 1898, pp. 42–70, 99–135; 1899, pp. 31–32; 1900, pp. 7–9; Holyoke *Transcript*, Oct. 26, 27, 1898.
34. Holyoke *Transcript*, Apr. 14, 1880, Jan. 14, 1882, June 22, 23, 1883.

group of children from their fellows. When the first parochial schools were opened in Holyoke, division on religious
lines already existed, but through the public schools many
thoughtful citizens still hoped to minimize such differences.
Yet it was determination to strengthen the religious wall
which caused Father Harkins to open the parish school of
St. Jerome, so that Catholic children might receive adequate instruction in their religion.

When the French school was started in 1876 objection
could be made on another score, namely that here was a
group taught in French for whom no direct means of
Americanizing existed. By law the School Committee had
the duty of keeping private schools up to public school
standards and of seeing that teaching was in English. Actually the School Committee could do little or nothing in
that respect. In 1878 the French school was accepted as
part of the school system since English was taught in one
session. Grey Nuns from Canada toook charge and by
1880 some five hundred French Canadian children attended. Here, however, unlike the other parochial schools
in the city, no children were accepted who would attend
only for the legally required twenty weeks. Such part-time
pupils had to go to the public schools. Gradually opposition to French parochial schools subsided, affected by the
realization on the part of employers that only by encouraging the French Canadian to bring with him his church
and its appendant, the church school, where French Canadian church history and doctrine could be taught, could
the movement countering repatriation and its consequent
emigration be developed. Since French Canadian labor
had become an important industrial factor in New England, persons interested in stabilizing it must logically
withdraw opposition to French parochial schools.[35]

The eighties saw the multiplication of the Catholic

35. Mass. Bur. Labor Statistics, *Thirteenth Annual Report,* 1882, pp.
88–92; Holyoke *Transcript,* Sept. 9, 1876, Sept. 11, 1878, Oct. 29, Nov. 9,
Dec. 14, 1881, July 12, 1882, Mar. 30, 1889; Minutes of Meetings of the
School Committee, 1877.

schools in the city. With the completion of the diocesan orphanage at Mt. St. Vincent just south of the city proper, the Sisters of Providence organized a school for the children there. In compliance with the instruction of the Plenary Council held in Baltimore in 1884, the priest of the English-speaking parish of the Sacred Heart also opened a school, whither Sisters of St. Joseph were brought to teach, while in 1890 a second French parochial school, for the Perpetual Help parish, opened its doors. By 1890 five different orders of nuns were teaching in these church schools.[36] The enrollment mounted regularly, by 1895 totalling some 2,485, about one third of all the school children in the city. Two thirds of these parochial school children were born of foreign parents. The protests at the establishment of a German Lutheran Church school in 1890 indicates that the opposition to these parochial institutions was by no means born exclusively of Protestant bigotry.[37] In this large growth well might the person opposed to parochial schools on principle find cause for alarm.

Apart from the disapproval of church schools on the grounds of unwise segregation along religious lines, a policy labelled by its opponents as un-American, were there sound reasons for objection to the parochial schools? In Holyoke at the end of the century they were saving the taxpayers, estimating from official data, $51,199 a year.[38] If the education given by the parochial schools was as far-

36. These were the Sisters of Notre Dame conducting their Convent School for girls, the Sisters of Providence carrying on the St. Jerome's Institute for boys and the schools at the orphanage, the Sisters of St. Joseph in the Sacred Heart parish, and the two French orders, the Sisters of Ste. Anne who in 1887 replaced the Grey Nuns in the Precious Blood school, and the Sisters of the Presentation of Mary teaching at the Perpetual Help school. In 1900 the Holy Family school at Brightside was listed separately. *Report of the School Committee*, 1900, p. 53; McCoy, "Diocese of Springfield," *Catholic Church in N. E.*, II, 675–680, 600–605.

37. Holyoke *Transcript*, Apr. 22, July 31, 1890; *Census of Mass.*, 1895, *Social Statistics and General Summaries*, VII, 129.

38. This figure is computed from the reported cost per public school child of $15.94. It excludes the children in the schools of the diocesan orphanage. *Report of the School Committee*, 1900, pp. 18, 53.

reaching and as thorough as that of the public schools then the case against the former was much weakened. The curriculum in the parochial schools of the English-speaking parishes in secular subjects corresponded to that of the public schools. Sister Mary of Providence, head of St. Jerome's school for boys, herself laid out the course and chose to use the same texts as the public schools in all save history.[39] In the French schools the study of French, of French history and church history took much time, and as the Sisters who taught were all educated in Canada and unfamiliar with United States history there was no instruction in American history. French Canadian children were sent back to Quebec for further education if their parents could afford it. Thus in the case of the French parish schools the charge of un-Americanism might be sustained. The teaching in English and science or mathematics also was admittedly below that of the public schools.

But undoubtedly the impression existed quite generally in the city that the preparation in all the parish schools was less satisfactory than in the public. To the annoyance of Father Harkins many Catholic parents consistently dubbed the parochial school inadequate and by preference sent their children to the public.[40] Of the five orders of nuns conducting the Catholic schools, only two, the Sisters of

39. After the separation from the mother house in Canada in 1892, Sister Mary became Mother Mary. A person of continuing influence in the church school and in the community for another forty years, she was of the utmost value to the Institute School. McCoy, "Diocese of Springfield," *Catholic Church in N. E.*, II, 611; Mother Mary of Providence to the author, May, 1934.

40. The high school records at the end of the century reveal little. In the entering class in 1898 there were forty children from the parochial schools, twenty from St. Jerome's, seventeen from the Sacred Heart, and three from the Precious Blood. Of these at the end of the term sixteen, five, and one respectively showed deficiencies. On the other hand of the public schools only four had better records than the last two named parochial schools. But obviously one term's data are insufficient for generalization, and no other such table is available for comparison. In 1897 there were some 1,200 children attending the Precious Blood school. Yet only three entered the public high school upon graduation. Holyoke *Transcript*, Nov. 4, 1895, Jan. 19, June 25, 1897; *Report of the School Committee*, 1898, p. 90.

St. Joseph, and the Sisters of Ste. Anne, were primarily
teaching orders, and thus the teaching was presumably less
good than that of the trained public-school teachers. Moreover the poverty of the Catholic parishes made it difficult
for their schools to have much equipment, a disadvantage
keenly felt by the hierarchy, and in fact a source of continuing irritation at the refusal of the state school authorities to divided appropriations with the parochial schools.
Nevertheless in Holyoke by the turn of the century the
relations between parochial schools and public were har-
monious. Search spoke in the warmest terms of the coöperation he received from the Catholic schools. One high school
which served for all, parochial and public grammar school
graduate alike, was a uniting influence.[41]

In the high school, the schools of Holyoke reached their
peak. Pride in the high school had always run high from
its beginning in 1852 to days a generation later when its
renown was less well earned. Experiments in a course of
study adapted to a mill town had resulted first in a general
course, then in 1874 in an additional classical course designed for college preparation, and still later in the seventies in a scientific course to prepare students for entrance
into the higher scientific schools. Although opinion varied
in the city about the wisdom of offering three separate
courses in a school of about one hundred pupils (in 1879)
with a staff of four teachers, general satisfaction over the
records of the graduates of each department allayed criticism. The general course was the most popular through
the eighties, the work in Greek and Latin was demanded
by a smaller but insistent group of young persons, while
the laboratory work in the scientific courses, though claiming comparatively few pupils, had special appeal in a paper
city where research in chemistry might be of much importance. As pressure of numbers increased in the high school
it became necessary to combine the classical with the gen-

41. McCoy, "Diocese of Springfield," *Catholic Church in N. E.*, II, 605;
Holyoke *Transcript,* Apr. 14, 1880, Jan. 19, Sept. 14, 1897; *Report of the
School Committee,* 1898, pp. 55, 90.

eral course for a time so that students wishing to enter college generally had to take five years to prepare.[42]

Enrollment in the high school mounted steadily but, hampered by cramped quarters, the calibre of the work shrank. The instruction in scope and character failed to keep pace with the numerical growth. Dissatisfaction with the conduct of the school began to be general by 1895, until the public would no longer accept as excuse the limitations imposed by lack of physical space. Plans for a large new modern building were completed that year and construction begun. Then the following year the calling of Preston W. Search to take the superintendency of all the schools quickly effected the desired vitalizing of the high school work.

Search had accepted the post on express condition that he be in fact as well as name head of the schools, and the School Board had therefore been obliged to revise its rules and vest the power of appointing teachers in the superintendent, with the board merely confirming his nominations. Search, consistently refusing to allow political considerations to affect his course, brought to Holyoke a number of new teachers who were not local citizens.[43] Most outstanding was the new high school principal, Charles Keyes, who took charge in the fall of 1897. In place of the old curricula under which there had come a stratification of the school "into the aristocracy who go on to college, and the plebeians who cannot," seven courses of study with almost unlimited opportunity for variation were presented. These comprised a course in the classics, in modern languages and literature, a Latin-scientific and English-scientific course, a business course, an art course, and one in manual training. And more significant still, each pupil was assigned to a section officer to direct him, conferences between pupil and teachers and teachers and parents were

42. *Report of the School Committee,* 1879, pp. 43–51; 1884, pp. 47, 54; 1891, pp. 63–64; Holyoke *Transcript,* Sept. 19, 1881.

43. *Report of the School Committee,* 1893–1894, pp. 73–75; 1894–1895, pp. 9–15, 63–70, 83–87; 1895–1896, pp. 20–44, 48–49, 79–80; Holyoke *Transcript,* June 2, 1896.

put into operation, and individual work in place of class work arranged. Visitors flocked to see the workings of this new model scheme.[44]

The new building delayed of completion was not occupied until the fall of 1898 so that the most important educational reconstruction was undertaken in the old hampering quarters. Upon the move to the spacious new building equipped with fine laboratory facilities and with accommodation for eight hundred pupils the work of the new regime proceeded with even greater vigor. Five hundred and eighty-three students enrolled and a staff of twenty-one teachers carried on the program.[45] The elective system and the flexibility of the program inspired the pupils with ambition. "The idea of getting something for nothing is gone," wrote the principal at the end of 1898. "A good education costs good hard work and the large majority of our boys and girls show by their application that they believe in and enjoy good hard work."[46]

Having now for the first time a gymnasium, high school students confined before to calisthenics in small classrooms pursued gymnastics also with enthusiasm. Athletic teams— football, basketball, baseball, and track—were organized and won envied interscholastic championships. The *High School Herald*, published monthly, soon proved a well-managed sheet, while the forming of dramatic clubs, of a

44. *Report of the School Committee*, 1897, pp. 75, 79–81, 98–101, 157–168, 178, 199–214; Holyoke *Transcript*, Oct. 27, 1898. Each student kept a notebook for each subject which enabled his teachers to keep readier track of his progress or difficulties, and to lend aid. English work improved noticeably. These notebooks were an innovation. *Report of the School Committee*, 1897, p. 216. The attention of the educational world was for two years fixed upon Holyoke. The large attendance at the Teachers Institute held here in 1897, the wide interest in the speeches given at the dedication of the new high school building, the congratulatory letters sent in by persons qualified to judge of the value of work done, all prove the interest in these experiments outside the city itself. The elective system was still an experiment in Massachusetts high schools. See Mass. State Board of Education, *Sixty-fourth Annual Report*, 1899–1900, p. 13.

45. *Report of the School Committee*, 1898, pp. 41, 88, 94–95; 1899, p. 40.

46. *Ibid.*, 1898, pp. 93–94.

literary society, and the Banjo Club gave further evidence of the quickened interest in all that touched the high school.

In addition to the opportunities thus opened up to school children, the high school was made as never before into a means of education for the community as a whole, "the People's College." Constructive effort went into a program of evening lectures and entertainment open to the public. The lectures, held in the great high school auditorium, were so largely attended as to suggest a wide public longing for intellectual nourishment. The years following the resignations of Search and Keyes saw a continuation of these lectures, albeit upon a less comprehensive scale.[47]

Under the successors of these pioneering educators the high school curriculum was again revised. Without the expert guidance of its originators and a highly trained staff the seven-course scheme with the wide elective variations proved impracticable. Though teachers were supposed to plan their work so that half of each period could be allotted to supervision of pupils' study and preparation, as worked out, the long eighty-minute periods became prolonged recitations. Pupils unaided in individual work lost their bearings. The only answer seemed to be to revert to a system of requirements for all students with comparatively few opportunities for choice of courses. Mass education was resumed in less stereotyped form than before the late changes, but at the cost of the sacrifice of many individual interests.[48]

There followed several years during which taxpayers' zeal was concentrated first upon reducing expenditure for the schools, not upon getting the best possible education for the city's children. The policy of retrenchment handicapped the schools particularly because of the difficulty of securing able teachers at the salaries Holyoke would pay. Holyoke in 1901 had the highest cost for schooling per

47. *Ibid.*, 1898, pp. 67–70, 75–76, 87; 1900, pp. 36, 48; Holyoke *Transcript*, Jan. 21, 1888.

48. *Report of the School Committee*, 1899, pp. 45–48; 1900, pp. 47–48; Holyoke *Transcript*, Oct. 26, 1898, June 9, 1900.

child of any city in the state, and in 1902, after two years' attempts at economy, only Springfield and Newton had higher costs per child.[49]

But the trouble went deeper than costs. Opposition to Search's program had been stirred up on the grounds of expense, but his policy of appointing the best teachers he could find regardless of their habitat also aroused consternation in the bosom of the old guard. The fact that his appointees were teachers of wide experience and unusual capabilities did not lessen local resentment. Upon his resignation, however, the School Board ruling anent the appointing power was not at once changed. The centralization of responsibility had clearly been of benefit to the whole school system.[50] A first modification of the superintendent's authority was effected in 1900 which permitted the School Committee to retain any teacher who had given satisfactory service for three years. Still such a "tenure of office" act only partly reopened the schools to political influence. But by 1905 the School Board had accepted the working principle that Holyoke applicants should be given the teaching posts. The regime of economy made easier a return to the old system of considering local candidates only. The appointment of teachers was evolved into a kind of patronage scheme for members of the School Board whereby each member of the board in turn had the privilege of nominating a candidate for a vacant position in the public schools. The superintendent then made the appointment. Where storekeepers and other persons anxious for public favor were members of the board—as was generally the case—the staff of the schools tended inevitably to be

49. *Municipal Register*, 1901, pp. 100, 114; 1902, pp. 7–8; 1904, p. 82. The cost per child for Massachusetts cities in 1901 was listed in part as follows:

Holyoke $32.60	New Bedford $25.84
Lowell 28.68	Chicopee 22.63
Northampton . . . 26.40	Fall River 22.47

50. *Report of the School Committee*, 1899, pp. 7–8, 17–35; Holyoke *Transcript*, May 2, 3, Sept. 7, Nov. 12, 14, Dec. 8, 1898.

composed of persons having "pull" rather than exceptional qualifications as teachers.

The political manoeuvrings of the School Board indeed became little short of a public scandal between 1903 and 1909. Able candidates for school committeemen, anxious to eradicate politics from the running of the schools, were defeated or so in a minority on the board as to be nearly helpless. The superintendent of seven years' standing was supplanted in 1906 by a young lawyer in the city, a member of the "Gorman" machine. The new superintendent was a persuasive politician, but in no other respect qualified for the job. During his years in office an inner cabal prepared in advance topics for presentation at School Board meetings, and the votes were cast accordingly. The system was overturned finally by revelations of petty graft in connection with purchases of supplies for the schools. The superintendent, proclaiming his innocence of all connivance, was at length replaced by a more capable, experienced man.

The change was beneficial. The appointment of teachers was thenceforward again vested in the superintendent of schools and the patronage of the school committeemen limited. The board raised the scale of teachers' salaries until Holyoke salaries ranked third in the state for cities under 100,000 population, and superintendents selected teachers with at least normal-school training and a year of teaching experience.[51]

Meanwhile the parochial schools had been growing rapidly. In 1904 with the opening of a Polish parish school every Catholic church in the city had its own school. At the turn of the century, Father Harkins of St. Jerome's had put the blame for the prevalence of lax sexual morality upon the public schools, and had declared that training in

51. Fred Webber, School Committeeman, 1908–1911 (interview); Holyoke *Transcript,* Feb. 17, Mar. 17, 1905, Sept. 20, Dec. 7, 10, 13, 22, 1906, Nov. 5, 25, Dec. 3, 1907, Jan. 3, 14, Feb. 21, Mar. 3, Apr. 6, 7, 1908, Feb. 2, Apr. 6, 7, 1909, Jan. 5, May 2, 1911, Feb. 3, 1914, Dec. 18, 1918; *Municipal Register,* 1906, p. 270; 1910, pp. 150–151; 1914, pp. 135–136.

the parochial schools would put an end to it. Every Catholic parish had endeavored then to expand its schools, and at the end of his life in 1910 Father Harkins could see seven parochial grade schools and two Catholic high schools in Holyoke as well as the diocesan orphanage school at Brightside. Forty-eight per cent of the city's school children attended these private schools.[52] Until 1912 the teaching in the Catholic schools was divided among six different orders, but after that date in the English-speaking parishes the order of St. Joseph alone took charge.[53]

How the teaching and fields covered in these parish schools compared with those of the public schools became less easy to determine after the opening of parochial high schools, for where the Holyoke High School had served as a common measuring stick for all grammar school graduates who went on in school, ever increasing numbers of parochial grade school pupils now entered their own parochial high schools. For example, ten comprised a graduating class at the Rosary High School in 1910; in 1921 seventy.[54]

The lightening of the tax burden for the city through the extension of the parochial school system was evident;[55] yet many Protestant taxpayers continued to deplore the division of the city school children into two groups, and many assumed parochial school education to be woefully inferior to the public school. As in earlier years the parochial schools were financially too limited to be able to af-

52. There was also the German Lutheran parish school and a small co-operative private school which together had about eighty pupils enrolled. *Municipal Register,* 1904, p. 77; 1908, p. 178; 1910, p. 194; Holyoke *Transcript,* Apr. 25, 1901, Feb. 19, 1904.

53. Vladislous Rabinski, Sister Anne of Order of Ste. Anne (interviews); *Holyoke Directory,* 1908; Lucey, *History of St. Jerome's Parish,* p. 57. The Sisters of Notre Dame continued their convent school, and the Sisters of Providence conducted the schools at Brightside.

54. Holyoke *Transcript,* June 19, 1918, June 19, 1919, June 15, 22, 1921. In 1910, 25 per cent of the pupils entering the high school came from other schools than the public grammar schools; in 1914, 18 per cent; in 1918, 10.5 per cent; and in 1921, 16 per cent. *Municipal Register,* 1910, p. 157; 1914, p. 154; 1918, p. 143; 1921, p. 296.

55. The superintendent in 1908 estimated that the parochial schools saved the city nearly $160,000 a year. *Municipal Register,* 1908, p. 188.

ford expensive books or scientific laboratory apparatus. For some phases of high school work this lack was highly disadvantageous, and necessitated a mere text-book course in the sciences. On the other hand, the classical courses were generally thorough, and, an outgrowth of careful preparation in Latin, the English grammar courses. Much of the teaching in the parochial grade schools, notably in spelling and penmanship, was excellent, and most fair-minded observers were also ready to admit that in discipline of attitude the parochial school child was as well or better prepared than the public school child. Before 1922 the diocesan direction of education was too superficial to limit greatly the authority of each pastor over the schools of his own parish, and thus upon the conservatism or liberalism, educating zeal or indifference of the individual priest depended the character of his parochial schools. Manual training, home economics courses, and physical education the parochial schools had to forego for lack of funds; in the high schools the business training courses, the scientific courses, and modern languages other than French had to be slighted. Yet the church hierarchy, conscious of the antagonisms to its school system that persisted, set itself to raise its standards and as years went on achieved great improvement.[56]

For both public and private schools the need of careful supervision, patience, and painstaking teaching was evident, as surveys and census reports revealed the extent of illiteracy in the city. Nineteen per cent of the children in the public schools in 1913 were retarded.[57] Percentage of illiteracy of persons over ten years of age in the city had, to be sure, gradually declined from 11.4 per cent in 1900

56. Private information; *A Century of Catholicism in Western Massachusetts; Municipal Register,* 1921, pp. 257–260. To-day some of the parochial high schools offer business courses. But the decentralization of the church schools in Holyoke has been particularly disadvantageous to the high schools. In Springfield where the Cathedral High School serves all the city's parochial grade schools the calibre of the parochial high school work is pronounced unusually good.
57. Holyoke *Transcript,* Feb. 3, 1914.

to 6.8 per cent in 1910, to 5.18 per cent in 1920. Still the number of persons over ten years of age unable to speak English in 1910 was nearly 5,000, or 10.5 per cent, and in 1920 was about 2,000 or 4.32 per cent. (See table.) Such a situation indicated the handicap under which many children labored whether in school or not, and, as in earlier years, among the poorest families the need of putting children to work led to cutting down the period of their schooling to the legal minimum. The schools therefore had to concentrate upon essentials in the primary and early grammar grades if many future citizens were to have any education worthy of the name.

The vital importance of the primary grades and the wisdom of stressing English were recognized by the superintendent of schools in 1910 when he carried out an examination of the methods of teaching reading employed in the first grades of the city schools, conducted a discussion of these methods among primary grade teachers, and then adopted a revised list of books for primary reading. Later, revised reading lists for the grades above the first and new arithmetic texts were added. Four years later the School Board issued a complete revised list of texts supplied for every grade and for the Holyoke High School. School executives in the interests of better teaching made great efforts to reorganize staff so as to reduce the number of pupils per grade school teacher and in this respect Holyoke by 1910 rated fourth of the twenty-four principal New England cities. But improvement in elementary teaching and stressing English was lost to many of the immigrant children for whom it was primarily designed because numbers of them attended the French Canadian and Polish church schools where they might study the language and history of their parents' native lands. Although English was also taught in these parochial schools, inevitably the emphasis was shifted somewhat from mastery of English to a perpetuation of the parents' language. In 1908, 46 per cent of the foreign children in the city were estimated to be in parochial schools, a proportion which probably did not drop greatly in later years.[58]

Most Holyoke children in the first decade of the century got no high school work at all. In 1910, 89 per cent of the public school children were in the grades below the high school, so that any extension of curriculum which affected only the high school touched a very small part of the school population. To give some manual training to grammar school children in 1910, cooking and sewing for girls and shop work for boys in the three upper grades was added. In 1919 state legislation obliged local authorities to create a system of continuation schools for working children between the ages of fourteen and sixteen. Four day-time hours a week must be devoted to school, where courses, some of them specified by the state, were to be taught. Anyone who reached the age of sixteen without having completed fourth-grade work must attend evening classes. The industrial depression in 1913–1914 and again in 1920–1921 made jobs for minors in the mills fewer and served to keep in school children who would otherwise have gone to work. Thus the length of time available for preparing future citizens for their places in the community was slightly extended.[59]

In the high school the resulting increase in numbers of pupils of limited cultural background and little intellectual ambition had the unfortunate effect of lowering somewhat the scholastic standard which could be maintained and led to the conviction upon the part of wealthier citizens that their children must be sent away to private schools to prepare for college. The inevitable outcome was a sharper class demarcation than had existed before. Only

58. *Ibid.*, Nov. 2, 1908; *Municipal Register,* 1910, pp. 102–107, 155, 165; 1914, pp. 154, 185–197; 1918, p. 143; 1921, p. 297. Public kindergartens were increased in number from seven to ten, but the number of children attending remained fairly constant over the span of years.

59. *Municipal Register,* 1910, pp. 97, 102–105; 1914, pp. 165, 173; 1921, p. 227; *Acts and Resolves of Massachusetts,* 1913, ch. 779; *General Acts of Massachusetts,* 1919, ch. 311; Holyoke *Transcript,* Feb. 9, 1921.

the severe economic pressure upon the capitalist class after 1929 was to offset partially this movement and to bring back to the public high school children of the more well-to-do.

School attendance, however, improved slowly as years went on, for such children as were not regularly employed. Sporadic truancy diminished and confirmed truancy became rarer. By 1908 Holyoke had a larger percentage of pupils graduating from the high school of those who entered than the average city in Massachusetts, and Holyoke's proportion, just under 13 per cent, was thought creditable. But the number who yearly dropped out of schools to find employment in mills and shops as soon as the law allowed at fourteen continued to be depressingly high. During the war this number reached a peak of 1,328 children under sixteen years of age. In the depression of 1921 the numbers of such minor employes dropped to one half that figure.[60]

To keep children in school beyond the legal requirement meant in some cases educating parents in the importance of the extension of schooling for their children, in more instances interesting the children themselves in further school work. To interest parents, superintendent and principals hoped that the formation of Parent-Teacher Associations might prove helpful. Between 1911 and 1920 a number of separate Parent-Teacher Associations were formed. But, meetings becoming merely social occasions or sessions of destructive criticism of the school, the futility of the associations as means of parental education became patent and they were allowed to die. Interesting the children in further education might conceivably have been accomplished by making school work more varied in content or perhaps by more inspired teaching. The director of the Continuation School opened in 1920 declared that most of the children obliged to attend it had dropped out of regu-

60. *Municipal Register,* 1904, p. 126; 1906, pp. 272, 254; 1908, pp. 200, 207, 237–238; 1910, pp. 140, 198–199; 1914, pp. 142, 170; 1918, pp. 100, 131, 156; 1921, pp. 285, 308; *Thirteenth Census of U. S.,* 1910, *Population,* I, 1,171; *Fourteenth Census of U. S.,* 1920, *Population,* II, 1,101.

lar school to go to work not from economic necessity but from choice. Work was more attractive.[61] More convincing testimony to the ineffectiveness of public school education could hardly be found.

The failure to adjust the school curriculum to a changing world—the slighting of social studies and of work in science, and an over-emphasis upon the tool subjects—cost the schools the interest of many pupils and of some parents. The situation, arising in part from the limited range of subjects taught, was aggravated by the calibre of much of the teaching. The inadequacy of professional training of large numbers of the teaching staff, particularly in the grade schools where long years of experience were considered by an unthinking public a sufficient substitute for training, tended to become more marked as years went on. Teachers' salaries were not increased at a rate comparable to the rise in cost of living. The difficulty of bringing into Holyoke schools gifted teachers at Holyoke salary rates was heightened by the continuing pressure upon the superintendent of schools to engage local teachers only. But the full extent of the lacks in the school system was not to be widely apprehended until the 1930's.[62]

In view of the high percentage of young people who were to earn their livings in industry in Holyoke, many persons early became interested in the possibilities of vocational education. For nearly ten years before the Holyoke Vocational School was established in 1913, advocates of industrial training had pointed to the scarcity of skilled labor in the city and urged the opening of a trade school here. The first response was the launching of industrial classes in the city evening schools. A course in steam engineering first offered in 1908 was enthusiastically attended, and other courses followed—wood-turning, pattern-making, and electrical engineering; for girls, cooking and sew-

61. Superintendent of schools (interview); Holyoke *Transcript,* Nov. 10, 1907, Oct. 4, 1913, Feb. 3, 4, Mar. 27, 1914, Apr. 5, 1915; *Municipal Register,* 1921, p. 267.

62. *Report of the Survey of the Schools of Holyoke, Massachusetts,* 1930, pp. 360–400.

ing. Then the day high school offered classes in carpentry
and machine-shop work; and manual training was offered
for seventh, eighth, and ninth grade day pupils. A course
in bookkeeping, opened first in 1906 in the day high school,
was offered four years later also in the evening high school.
But with the passage of state laws providing state aid for
properly constituted vocational schools, Holyoke was not
content with so restricted a program.[63] In 1913 an independent vocational school, under the direction of a Board
of Trustees appointed by the School Board and confirmed
by the Board of Aldermen, was opened to carry on both
day-time and evening courses.

The vocational school was housed in the new high school
gymnasium building, althought the Board of Trustees
promised to have the city erect a special mill-type building
for the school, a promise not fulfilled until 1932. For the
evening vocational classes where six to seven hundred persons were enrolled, the high school building itself had to
accommodate the overflow.

With the assistance of the State Board of Education,
the trustees mapped out a course of studies for the day
school. Of four trade departments opened—carpentry and
building, machine-shop practice, pattern-making, and
printing—the first three were chosen because foremen and
manufacturers in the city agreed that there lay Holyoke's
greatest industrial needs, and there also greatest opportunities for training boys. Students might complete the
course as quickly as their capabilities permitted, normally,
according to the first plan, in four years, later, according
to a revised, more efficient plan, in three years. To receive
a diploma a boy must spend the last five months of his final
year in full-time employment in the trade for which he had
trained. Such an arrangement necessitated close coöperation between the school officials and employers and labor
organizations. To facilitate this an advisory committee

63. *Municipal Register,* 1906, p. 270; 1908, pp. 180; 1910, pp. 97, 99,
125–132, 137–139; *Acts and Resolves of Massachusetts,* 1911, ch. 471;
1912, ch. 106.

was created, composed of three representatives of every trade or occupation taught in the school, a committee whose duties were voluntary but whose interest in the problems and knowledge of the local situation made their advice valuable. In addition to the shopwork and studies in related fields the curriculum included some cultural subjects, English, civics, industrial history or science, hygiene.[64]

While attendance fell off somewhat during the war years, the school was an asset to the community from the beginning. It is noteworthy that labor organizations were more coöperative in its successful operation than were manufacturers in the city, although a group of young men trained in special trades would seem to have been of greater advantage to capital than to labor.[65] In the depression of 1921 the school encountered the problem of scarcity of places for the advanced students to practice their trades, and a corresponding lack of accommodation for boys wishing to enter the school. The difficulty was enhanced by the agreement of the school to take charge of classes for vocational rehabilitation of disabled soldiers. Federal money supplied shop equipment for rehabilitation classes and by 1922 these were housed in a separate building. Meantime federal aid, as provided by the Smith-Hughes Act of 1916, brought in some money to the vocational school for its own use. Trade school students generally found jobs for themselves, and as business revived after 1921 openings for them multiplied.[66]

Part of the usefulness of the vocational school came from its evening classes. From the beginning provision was made for short, intensive instruction in special problems of several trades for men employed during the day and for courses in practical arts for women. The courses which ran

64. *Municipal Register,* 1914, pp. 210–286.

65. Labor leaders recognized the value of training, for experience had proved that it is the untrained workman who only half knows his trade who is at the mercy of an employer.

66. *Municipal Register,* 1918, pp. 185–190, 199–202; 1921, pp. 329–339; Holyoke *Transcript,* Mar. 7, 1917, Aug. 1, 1919, Dec. 22, 1921; Matthew Herbert, Director Holyoke Vocational School, 1918–1938 (interview).

about twenty-five weeks offered at first work in the trades
taught in the day school, and in brick-laying, cabinet-mak-
ing, steam-engineering, electricity, chemistry of paper-
making, and drawing for carpenters and for machinists;
for women dressmaking, cooking, millinery, embroidery,
and home nursing. As interest or opportunity shifted each
year courses were dropped and new ones added—paper-
making and brick-laying classes abandoned, textile classes
organized, and during the war, work in automobile repairing or radio signalling. In 1918 special classes in Morse
telegraphy were offered women to fill posts vacated by enlisted men. Year after year several hundred men and women
availed themselves of these opportunities. State university
extension courses opened in 1920 drew upon another group
of persons and apparently affected the vocational evening
school attendance very little.[67]

The most important agent in combatting illiteracy in
the city was the system of regular evening schools. In
1910 five elementary schools and one high school averaged
somewhat over seven hundred pupils in regular attendance
four evenings a week, for the elementary schools, thirteen
weeks a year, for the high school, twenty-four weeks. About
two hundred of these pupils attended the high school. Enrollment and attendance had increased notably since 1905
in the evening high school, but had remained fairly static
in the grades. The amending of state law in 1913 requiring
all illiterates between sixteen and twenty-one years of age
to attend evening school enlarged the elementary classes.
The superintendent of schools after 1910 insisted upon

67. The course in papermaking was disappointing. Eagle Lodge had
been interested in the project and some of the heads of the American
Writing Paper Company. But to have a course which would be valuable
meant finding a thoroughly trained paper chemist to conduct it and a
plant big enough to work in. One was too costly; the other could be had
only by agreeing to impossible conditions laid down by the American
Writing Paper Company in return for the use of one of its mills. Consequently the course had to be dropped as a part of the public vocational
school program. Private information; Holyoke *Transcript,* Jan. 14, 1916,
Mar. 7, Sept. 16, Oct. 10, 1917, Aug. 31, Sept. 27, 1921; *Municipal Register,* 1914, pp. 233–247; 1918, pp. 191–205; 1921, pp. 346–349.

proper provision for the evening schools in teaching staff and curricula, and not long after invested in special text books adapted to evening school use. Three groups had to be kept quite distinct in the management of the evening schools. First, there were regular pupils, ungraded beginners, intermediate, or advanced; second, there were those who could speak no English, some of them educated in their own language, some of them not; and third, there were persons seeking special work, instruction in cooking or sewing or the like. As soon as the foreigners had learned enough English to be classed with the first group they were shifted. Thus the numbers of persons in the city unable to speak English was halved between 1910 and 1920, although the drop in immigration after the outbreak of the World War also contributed to this decline. (See table.) Regular evening school enrollment and attendance fell off during the years of the United States' participation in the war just as it did in the day high school, but both revived after the war.[68]

Special Americanization classes were launched in 1919 in an effort to wipe out adult illiteracy which the draft had revealed during the war to be extensive in Massachusetts as elsewhere. Evening school classes, mothers' classes, neighborhood classes, and industrial classes held in manufacturing plants in the city—in 1921 there were thirty-six different groups taught by twenty-seven part-time teachers all under the direction of the school department with state supervision. The number of aliens of voting age had decreased both absolutely and in relation to the number of foreign-born in the city by 1921, and the Americanization classes were to contribute further to the making of citizens as well as a literate population.[69]

68. *Municipal Register,* 1910, pp. 110–111, 163–164, 138; 1914, p. 155; 1918, p. 149; 1921, pp. 264–265; Holyoke *Transcript,* Mar. 22, 1910, Nov. 7, 1911, July 30, 1912, Feb. 3, 1914, Feb. 18, Nov. 3, 1916, Oct. 9, 1917; *Acts and Resolves of Massachusetts,* 1913, ch. 467.

69. Only with the restriction of immigration did these classes cease to be important. Citizenship classes in the evening high school for persons seeking naturalization had been opened in 1916. *Municipal Register,* 1921,

Such were the schools which for nearly fifty years were hopefully looked to for the saving social enlightenment of the community. No one could think that their purpose had been fully accomplished. Some might doubt that it had been approached. Improvement had unquestionably been achieved in the course of the two generations. Yet the steady influx of penniless and uneducated foreigners down to the time of the war constantly presented new problems of schooling to the city while it was still struggling with the old. Clearly public school education alone could not quickly remake the social order.

pp. 249–250; Holyoke *Transcript,* Nov. 13, 1905, Nov. 3, 1916, Feb. 23, Oct. 13, 1917.

XI

RELIGION, 1850–1922

WHAT men could not accomplish by city ordinances and schooling might be done by the regeneration of humanity through Christianity. Must not the evils arising in a community dominated by materialism vanish where Christian idealism prevailed? Altruism early found a natural outlet through the churches and many an earnest Christian viewed the solution of questions of social ills as purely one of bringing religion to each individual. The churches in Holyoke's first generation endeavored to effect social well-being by the salvation of souls of the individuals. In the next generations additional means were sought.

Holyoke of the first generation was peopled by New Englanders and immigrants. As the church had been the *raison d'être* of the early New England village, the necessitating reason for group living, so the conception of the inevitability of a church in any coherent community had persisted, a deep-rooted conviction in the mind of the average New Englander. Hence at the very beginning, the builders of the "New City" here organized their churches, the Congregational in 1848, and a year later the Baptist. But it was more than habit and perfunctory adherence to a familiar social code that inspired these. There existed in the hearts of many persons a vital spiritual craving which a church and Christian fellowship could best appease.[1] Here were no philosophizing transcendentalists who could secure in individual mystical communings a satisfying inner life, but simple, hardworking people to whom the

1. *Fiftieth Anniversary Second Congregational Church, Holyoke, Massachusetts,* pp. 76–79. A large part of the data for this chapter has been derived from interviews with living persons, too numerous to name. Where no other authority is cited it is of this oral kind.

church spelled religion and to whom religion was necessary. There were probably always persons in the town who found the accepted religious attitudes of the existing churches not wholly adequate. And there were some heathen, some rebels against an oversevere application of Christian discipline. But for all its newness, the "New City" partook sufficiently of its New England background to find religion expressed in the church less an instrument of ordering the course of society than an essential of individual existence.[2]

The theology of this mill village was not profoundly subtle. Among the Roman Catholics, in 1860 already about one half the total population, complete authoritarianism held sway. They were accustomed to accept without question the pronouncements of the priest, who, set aside by the Sacrament of Ordination, was an essential intermediary between God and the layman. The Sacraments of the church, one for each great event of human life from birth to death, as administered by the priest, were a necessary part of Christian living for every true Catholic.

Of Protestant ideology the predominating concepts were those of the two original denominations, the Congregational and the Baptist. These were the first churches of the "New City"; and these two from the first presented two diverging religious points of view. Fundamentally the two creeds were not dissimilar: belief in an omnipotent and loving God, the workings of whose providence might be obscure but whose wisdom was infinite. In theory man was saved by God's free gift of salvation, the receiving of which was not to be determined by human actions, but, in the phrase of the old Calvinists, by election of God. So prayer, kind deeds, unselfish living were merely "evidential" of God's grace indwelling in the individual. God's voice speaking to man through the human conscience and Holy Writ, the inspired Word of God, were the ultimate authorities on earth. Man's duty, therefore, could be summed up in obedi-

2. Holyoke *Mirror,* Feb. 7, 1857.

ence to the will of God as thus revealed to man.[3] It was a faith which by its stress upon the acceptance of God's will and upon God's satisfaction with a successful stewardship of one's earthly talents lent itself peculiarly well to the material interests of a growing industrial community. It was straight Calvinism. But the superstructure built upon this foundation by the Congregationalists varied from that of the Baptists in use, if not greatly in form.

The Second Congregational Church was possessed of a flexibility which was denied the Baptist. Strict observation of the Sabbath including attendance at church twice in the day, and a conscientious endeavor to spread the Kingdom of Christ by example as well as precept—so much was expected of church members; also acceptance of the words of the Covenant and of the Confession of Faith. But the Congregationalist was still free to arrive at his own conception of the meaning of these words, free to evolve his own ideas of revealed truth: man's depravity through Adam's fall and eternal fire for all but the chosen, or man's free agency, and ultimate salvation for all truly repentant sinners.[4] Darwin's *Origin of Species* with its disturbing ideas was not published in 1859 and was not apparently heard of in Holyoke until the late sixties. Higher criticism in America was still unknown. So no doubts of the authority of the Bible existed until the Second Congregational Church was nearly a generation old. Then, as always, although examination of a person wishing to join the church included an oral probing of his religious faith, greater latitude of personal interpretation was possible for the member of the Second Congregational Church than for any other until the Unitarian Church was launched in 1874. For twenty-five years the Second Congregationalists were the leaders of liberal religious thought in Holyoke.

Not so the Baptists. Their chief doctrinal differentiation lay in their insistence upon adult baptism by total immer-

3. Records of the Second Baptist Church in West Springfield, I.
4. Holyoke *Transcript*, Oct. 8, Dec. 3, 1864.

sion, an essential commitment of the convert to the Christian life. For this the Baptists cited Scriptural command, and the Bible was literally word-for-word inspired. Hence there was no choice. No person who had not obeyed the clear command of the Bible about washing clean his soul might join the baptized elect in communion at the Lord's Table.[5] From this firm belief in the closed circle of the godly arose many of the characteristic attitudes of the Baptists. Here was a flavor of the seventeenth-century Massachusetts theocracy. The hedge must be guarded to keep the fold of the faithful safe from the ravening wolves without. Therefore strict watch must be kept lest a wolf in sheep's clothing slip in, and what amounted to a system of espionage developed. The Covenant pledged the faithful to a life of righteousness, to spreading the Gospel and to keeping watch over each other:

To have no fellowship in any way with those sins evidently condemned by the Gospel of Christ, such as using intoxicating drinks except as a medicine, holding our fellowmen in bondage, desecration of the Sabbath, licentiousness, lying, profanity and fraud: also to guard against foolish talking and jesting which are not convenient; . . . disregarding promises, tattling and backbiting.[6]

The backslider, he who had seen the light but had returned to ways of darkness, was the most reprobated of humans. Hell yawned for him. At times the devout seemed to dwell upon the torments awaiting the unregenerate with a morbid pleasure. Nevertheless there was a certain splendid dignity to the austere Baptist. His care for his fellow cove-

5. *Centennial of the First Baptist Church of Holyoke,* p. 24. Even in the seventies so strong was the feeling of the special sanctity of the Baptist communion that a kindly deacon at the Baptist church was nearly excommunicated for having passed the bread and wine to visiting Methodists.

6. Records of the Second Baptist Church of Holyoke, I. The proof of the sinfulness of drinking strong liquors was a citation from I Timothy 5: 23, "Drink no longer water, but use a little wine for thy stomach's sake, and thine often infirmities."

nanters like his ardor for converts was born of his intense
conviction that in his way alone lay salvation.

Less severe in doctrine but equally straight-laced in their
conceptions of conduct were the Methodists. The Methodist Episcopal Church had been founded in 1853 under the
aegis of the New England Conference in response to the
desires of the Methodists who for a dozen years had had to
cross the river to worship with the Wesleyans in South
Hadley Falls. Theirs was the usual Wesleyan faith, with
emphasis upon the "New Birth" of the spirit after conversion. As part of the highly organized Methodist Episcopal
Church of America the local group had no independent
creed or discipline. The Conference pronounced it sinful
to drink, dance, or play cards, and the Holyoke church
acquiesced.[7] But the harsher aspects of Calvinistic theology
the Methodists rejected.

Similarly the teachings of the other two Protestant
churches established in the sixties. The Episcopal Church,
organized as St. Paul's in 1863, was obliged in self-defense
to stress its anti-Roman character, its reliance on Bible as
well as Prayer Book. A generation later the Episcopalians
could feel closer to the Roman Catholic Church than to the
Protestant, but in the sixties and seventies the religious
climate of Holyoke was too uncongenial to anything that
smacked however faintly of "Popery" to make such development possible. Certainly a larger spirit of toleration
existed among the Episcopalians than among the Baptists.
The German religious society, which flourished in South
Holyoke from 1866 on, was primarily a national church
for the German Protestants who had poured into Holyoke
after 1865. Services were conducted in German and the society was significant not for any variation of the dominant
Protestant ideology but for its segregating of the Germans
from the rest of the community.[8]

7. Osgood, *Story of the Holyoke Churches*, p. 41; *Fiftieth Anniversary
Second Congregational Church*, Appendix, p. 172.

8. Osgood, *Story of the Holyoke Churches*, pp. 85–87; H. L. Foote,
Historical Sketch . . . of St. Paul's Church.

In 1874 about fifty well-to-do persons startled the orthodox by organizing the Liberal Christian Congregational Society based upon Unitarian doctrine:

We believe in freedom of Reason and Conscience as the method in religion, in the Fellowship of the Spirit as the bond of religion and in the progressive establishment in the life of the individual and society of the Divine Commonwealth of Truth, Justice and Love.

In the love of truth we unite for the worship of God and the service of man; and as His followers, we accept the religion of Jesus, holding accordance with His teaching that practical religion is summed up in love to God and love to man.

We covenant with God our Father and with each other to insure perpetually to this community a reverent worship of God, free and untrammeled preaching of the truth, the religious training of our youth, the upbuilding of character and the promotion of benevolence and good-will among men.[9]

Each signer of the Covenant was utterly free to interpret the Bible for himself. The denial of the Trinity and a belief in the unity of the God-power completed a creed which shocked Holyoke of the seventies. Right thinking in Holyoke was felt to be as important as right living, and one's own salvation, a concern between the individual and God, more vital than service of one's fellowmen.

Despite the fundamentally religious character of the town, the churches whether of liberal view or narrow all had an uphill struggle for existence until after the Civil War. The perpetual changing of population—disappointed or ambitious people moving away, newcomers moving in, and after a time, in turn departing—this constant shifting in membership had presented a problem to the churches in the fifties. The panic of 1857 had been followed by what the Baptist records term "a precious season of revival," but that wave of religious enthusiasm had been

9. Records of the Liberal Christian Congregational Society of Holyoke, I, 21; "History of Holyoke's Churches," *Thirtieth Anniversary Holyoke Daily Transcript.*

country-wide and in Holyoke it had not sufficed to offset
the effects of the community disasters. Only the two parent
churches in Baptist Village had not been greatly affected
by the business slump, since they served the agricultural
district of the town. Their crippling loss of members in
1849 when many were dismissed to form the churches in
the "New City" had been partly compensated for in the
ensuing decade,[10] and thereafter while neither First Congregational nor First Baptist Church was to grow largely
until the city crept out to them in the nineties, for a generation both were spared most urban problems. But in the
town the troubles of the manufacturing community were
reflected in the church life. Indeed the business revival in
1863 and 1864 had no counterpart in the town's religious
history, zealous efforts of evangelists notwithstanding.
"There was a state of things in the church neither pleasant
nor hopeful," reported the Baptists.[11] Growth and effective
influence had to await the years of Holyoke's rapid industrial expansion after 1865. From then on till after the turn
of the century the churches were probably the most important single conscious factor in the social evolution of the
city.

Of happiest influence was the young pastor who came in
1867 to take charge of the Second Congregational Church,
a man of rare charm and spiritual force. In his fifteen
years of service here John Trask saw his church emerge
from insecurity to occupy a dominant place in the life of
the town.[12] A better picture of the quality of the religion

10. Holyoke *Mirror,* Apr. 3, June 12, 19, Oct. 30, 1858; *Fiftieth Anni-
versary of the Second Congregational Church,* p. 138; Records of the
Second Baptist Church, I; Records of the First Orthodox Congregational
Church in Holyoke, I; Records of the Second Baptist Church in West
Springfield, I, 113–114; Records of the First Baptist Church of Holyoke,
I. Thirty-six persons were admitted to the First Baptist Church in 1858.

11. Records of the Second Baptist Church, I; *Fiftieth Anniversary
Second Congregational Church,* p. 138; Holyoke *Transcript,* Jan. 30, Feb.
6, 27, Mar. 27, 1864; A. J. Rand, History of the First Seventy-five Years
of Second Baptist Church, 1849–1924 (in possession of the clerk of the
church).

12. Allyn, "Sketch of Holyoke," *Thirtieth Anniversary Holyoke Daily
Transcript.*

of that church at this period can hardly be found than in Trask's own description of one of his deacons:

He went to the house of God to worship, and reverential attention is worship. If at any time his pastor trembled as he denounced wrong or summoned the indifferent to a duty that had been neglected, the first man to quiet his apprehensive fears and to stiffen his questioning courage was Deacon Allyn. He loved the gentle things of Christian faith and hope. "The bruised reed and the smoking flax" were emblems of his own distrustful and timorous heart. But he loved just as much the thunderous voices of the law and the loud tones which announced man's awful responsibility. His great, true nature responded with equal clearness to mercy and to penalty. Because he was a "burning and a shining light" he was a power, not only in the congregation but in the meetings of prayer. How often have I seen this modest but intense Christian rescue a prayer meeting from the valley of the shadow of death. A dull silence had settled over all. The hymns were powerless to awaken religious feeling. The prayers seemed to reach no realm beyond the walls of the room. This man rises in his place and begins to speak. He makes no allusion to the stagnant atmosphere. He is never critical. Perhaps he has been so much absorbed in silent prayer that he has not noted the situation. Some text of Scripture may have engaged his mind and he has been thus engrossed. It is evident as he begins to talk that whoever else is dead, he is inwardly and outwardly alive. God has been filling his soul. "As the hart pants for the water brooks" is the picture that rises before him. The description of it is clear, intense and thrills with emotion. He grasps the seat in front to steady himself as he vibrates with the inspired passion. Every one listens. Every one is moved. The power of his speech has cleared the air. The bench shakes under the movement of his hand. He speaks not more than three minutes. The hour is saved. Down into the cold, arid, sterile depths falls the quickening influence of his fervid, glowing, fruitful thought.[13]

13. *Fiftieth Anniversary Second Congregational Church*, pp. 136–137.

Here was religion personal, intimate. While the whole congregation could not perhaps maintain such depth of feeling for long, still such emotion was a living reality to most of them.

Two years after Dr. Trask's coming to Holyoke, Reverend R. J. Adams was called to the Second Baptist Church, there to embark upon a pastorate of nearly twenty years. Almost at once that church also began to grow. The year 1870 brought the longed-for revival and that year when ninety-one were received into the Congregational Church,[14] "Brother Adams" immersed ninety-five converts for the Baptists. As the annual letter to the Westfield Baptist Association narrates:

One evening it seemed as if all unconverted ones in the room had come, the windows of heaven were opened, and we had but to ask Sinners to come for the influences of the holy spirit were truly in our midst. . . . We saw those whom we had watched with interest as they had for years come up to the house of God and gone away with no hopes, coming now, and saying, pray for us. . . . Again we saw husbands whose wives had prayed for them many years, kneeling and desiring forgiveness of sin. Now the family Altar is reared in those homes and the praying wife has some one to lead in the family devotions. . . . One Sabbath our pastor baptised forty-four in twenty-two minutes, thus establishing the fact of his being equal to his proportion of the 3,000 in one day. . . . Our social position as a church has greatly improved during the year, and if we follow Christ, as we ought, we see no reason why we may not command our share of respect.[15]

In 1870, as twenty years before and twenty years later, there was, however, little social intercourse between the different churches. Each church was to an extraordinary degree a self-sufficient social unit. Perhaps, in fact, as the sixties turned into the seventies and the town grew into a city this centripetal tendency became more pronounced. It

14. *Ibid.,* p. 33.
15. Records of the Second Baptist Church, II.

was no longer possible to know everyone in town and therefore the church groups tended to become even more than before the centers of social existence. Women met in their church sewing societies and carried on their own church auxiliaries for Foreign Missions. With leisure still a restricted quantity, where the well-to-do families were still few and great wealth was not yet known, there was scarcely time to pursue a wider circle of social contacts. Only less true was this of the men of the community. Sundays were devoted to churchgoing and generally two evenings of the working week to prayer meeting and midweek services. In Holyoke's first generation each man's church meant to him not only spiritual refreshment, but sociability as well.[16]

But it was each church to itself. There was even little coöperation between the denominations in matters of general community concern. In the early years save for a brief collaboration in the revival of 1858 and in a union Sunday School picnic or two, Baptists and Congregationalists, Methodists and Episcopalians, had little traffic with each other. The chief common enterprise of the Civil War period had been the Ladies' Soldiers Aid Society which, sponsored by the women of the churches, forwarded boxes of clothing and supplies to the regiments in the field, direct to hospitals and to the Christian Commission in Boston and the Sanitary Commission in New York. But with the conclusion of the war this kind of coöperating philanthropy was abandoned.[17]

In the fall of 1866, it is true, a few young men in town banded together for union prayer meetings and later rented rooms as a Holyoke Young Men's Christian Association, to serve as a social center rival to the saloons. In inspiration the enterprise was definitely religious rather than social. "It is earnestly desired that all who feel an interest in the conversion of the souls of our town and of the

16. *Fiftieth Anniversary Second Congregational Church*, pp. 81, 84, 91–94.

17. Holyoke *Mirror*, Apr. 3, 1858; Holyoke *Transcript*, Sept. 12, 1863, Dec. 17, 1864.

world will be present at all the meetings," ran one notice.
But for all its successful inauguration, the organization
survived only a short time and when twenty years later a
new Y.M.C.A. was founded, memory of the first society
had vanished.[18]

A Valley Sabbath School Union, which after 1864 met
for some years in quarterly sessions to discuss methods of
giving religious instruction, furnished the other chief example of collaboration. A joint Sunday School mission in
South Holyoke was undertaken in 1866 by men of all four
Protestant churches, but it soon was taken over by the
Germans in that neighborhood and ceased to be an inter-
denominational project. Most charity work was simply
neighborliness, spontaneous in inspiration, direct and personal, if occasionally injudicious, in execution. Such organized charity as existed had only the churches for outlet. In an endeavor to prevent duplication of labors for the
help of the town's needy, the women of the Second Congregational Church Sewing Circle attempted in the seventies
to organize a kind of united charities, the Union Relief,
but there is scant evidence of widespread interchurch co-
operation. On the contrary, each society expected to care
for its own poor, and did.[19] Organized, nonsectarian or
secular philanthropy was to be a contribution of a new
generation.

Perhaps the temperance societies might be cited as exceptions to this rule, the Women's Christian Temperance
Union, the Temple of Honor, and several others. Active
temperance drives encouraged these. The great Murphy
temperance movement as launched in the city at the end
of 1877 was the most notable achievement of this kind. Inaugurated by the Baptists, the campaign was carried on
by a committee made up of representatives from every

18. Holyoke *Transcript,* Nov. 17, 1866, May 11, June 15, 1867, Jan. 4,
1868, May 15, 1869, May 14, Dec. 31, 1870.

19. *Ibid.,* Jan. 16, 1864, Oct. 21, 1865, Jan. 19, 1867, Mar. 11, 1869; MS.
in possession of F. S. Webber; Osgood, *Story of the Holyoke Churches,*
p. 85; *Fiftieth Anniversary of the Second Congregational Church,* pp.
77, 92.

Protestant church and from every temperance society in town. An eleven-day drive got 2,300 persons to sign the pledge, and wound up with arranging for a series of Sunday evening union temperance meetings in the city hall which were calculated to keep the new converts steady in their course. In this battle even the Roman Catholic society, the St. Jerome's Temperance Society, was called on and gave help.[20]

Meanwhile the Roman Catholic Church was growing steadily. Established as a parish in 1854 with its church building dedicated four years later, St. Jerome's by 1865 was firmly entrenched. The dignity and selfless virtues of Father O'Callaghan, the first priest, were kindly remembered after his death in 1861 by Protestant and Catholic alike, while his successor, Father James Sullivan, by a sweetness and gentleness of manner, abetted by a cultivation all too rare in the little mill town, succeeded in ingratiating himself in the community at large. His wisdom in counselling his parishioners against taking part in anti-draft riots in 1863, and his tact in dealing with his Protestant fellow-townsmen built up a mutual good-will that augured well for the future. A kindness of tone creeps into the local press accounts of Catholic activities which must have been most refreshing to these alien communicants. But the very rapidity of growth in prestige and in numbers of the Holyoke Catholic Church served to disturb the Protestants and threatened thus to create a permanent rift.[21]

In 1866 gentle Father Sullivan was replaced by a man of very different ilk, Father Patrick J. Harkins, energetic, quick-tempered, but perhaps better able than his predecessors to cope with the uncouth turbulent "Paddies" pouring

20. Records of the Holyoke Women's Christian Temperance Union (in possession of Mrs. Edward Whiting of Holyoke); Holyoke *Transcript*, Dec. 29, 1877, Jan. 2, 5, 12, Feb. 27, Apr. 17, May 4, July 13, 1878, July 25, 1884.

21. Holyoke *Mirror*, Mar. 2, 23, May 11, 1861; Holyoke *Transcript*, July 25, Aug. 1, 1863, July 17, 1865; Lucey, *History of St. Jerome's Parish*, p. 39.

into Holyoke with every passing year. As the number of
French Canadians from Province Quebec increased, they
were set off by the bishop in 1869 into a separate French-
speaking parish with their own French Canadian pastor
and their own church, *Le Sang Precieux.* Yet so quickly
did St. Jerome's recover from this loss of parishioners that
in 1876 it was necessary to subdivide the English-speaking
church by the creation of a parish in the more southern
part of the town, the parish of the Sacred Heart. Thus less
than twenty-five years after the founding of St. Jerome's
there were in existence here two English-speaking Catholic
churches and one French Catholic church, each possessed
of a church edifice, of a considerable debt, and of a devoted
but materially poor congregation.[22]

Needless to say there were practically no converts to
Protestantism. To disappointment over this failure to
wean the erring from "Popery" probably much of the antagonism of many a zealous Protestant may be attributed.
The seventies saw the Catholic community expanding more
rapidly than the Protestant. To quote from that fruitful
source the annual letter of the Second Baptist Church to
the regional association:

We have to constantly regret that we are surrounded (as
perhaps no other church in the association is) with an im-
mense population that are bound by ignorance and supersti-
tion to a church of forms and ceremonies. A church that neither incites nor demands Holiness or purity and hardly morality in its members. Upon such a people the Gospel has but
little effect or impression even when they can be reached
which is but seldom, owing to the strictness with which their
spiritual advisers admonish them of the sin of hearing any
protestant preaching. Some progress, however, has been
made among this class during the year by the labors of a
French Calporteur (Brother Edward Raleoux) in our city

22. McCoy, "Diocese of Springfield," *Catholic Church in N. E.,* II,
675–677. The substitution of Father Harkins for Father Sullivan was deplored by the Protestant part of the community and from the standpoint of toleration was unfortunate. Holyoke *Transcript,* Apr. 23, 1870.

during most of the year. A number have been brought into
our Sabbath School and three persons (formerly Catholics)
have become hopefully converted and united with our church.
Mr. Raleoux was chiefly supported by our Sunday School.[23]

Whether or not this attitude was typical of the Protestant
community at large, many Catholics so felt it to be. They
in turn were beginning to resent their lack of social recognition although it was obvious that differences of economic
status often produced that result, and although the fact
was well known that each Protestant society was a group
only to itself. Oppose to this resentment on the one hand
the uneasiness on the other hand caused by the failure of
the Catholic Church to care for the bodily ills of its need-
iest,[24] and append possibly also the dislike of self-contained
New Englanders for the aggressive Irish Catholicism of
some of the newer arrivals, and one is confronted with the
materials for an untiring feud.[25] In fact, considering the
New England background, the marvel is not that some
mutual intolerance existed but that it was so little developed at the end of the first generation of the town.

But no amount of Protestant disapproving could check
the spread of Catholicism in Holyoke. The seventies turned
into the eighties, and the eighties into the nineties, and
still the phenomenal growth continued. To the unobservant
or apprehensive Protestant the Roman Church may have
presented a solid front of strength. Yet from the end of
the sixties on there were differences within the Catholic
Church, and two strands of Catholicism, the English-
speaking Irish church and the French-speaking Canadian,
developed along quite separate lines.

The Irish by virtue of priority, numbers, and determination always led the way. The growth of the Irish Catholic
church is in no small measure to be traced to the extraordinary vigor, spiritual and physical, of Father Harkins, who
from his coming to St. Jerome's in 1866 guided the desti-

23. Records of the Second Baptist Church, II, Sept. 17, 1871.
24. See above, p. 125; Holyoke *Transcript*, Mar. 13, 1869.
25. Lucey, *History of St. Jerome's Parish, passim.*

nies of a large part of Holyoke down to the day of his death in December 1910. Because of his unusual capacity to realize his aims concretely this enterprising, rough, irascible, but honest, able, and loveable man of Donegal was known for years as "Harkins, the Builder." Founder of one of the first parochial schools in western Massachusetts, he also built a convent to house the nuns teaching his charges. He brought Sisters of Charity to Holyoke to care for the sick and helpless and contrived with the aid of these Sisters to purchase and equip a small hospital and an orphanage. With vision sustained surely by mighty faith he bought tens of thousands of dollars' worth of real estate for his own congregation and for others still to be formed; and as building after building arose upon these lots, the pride of his parishioners in these outer and visible signs of their faith seemed to eradicate largely any memory of the financial sacrifices demanded of them. Among people not of the faith now and again criticisms were voiced of the weight of the debts put upon the parishes, both St. Jerome's and the newer ones. But certainly the more articulate of the Catholic laity suppressed any disapproving questionings, if they had any. Although by 1880 there were a number of Irish families in town who had risen in the economic scale to positions of comparative ease, still such were very much the exception. The total annual income of the Sacred Heart Church in that year was listed as $2,700. Yet the Roman Catholic building program went on.[26]

Urged on by the untiring zeal of Father Harkins and later priests of other churches, for the next thirty years the Irish people of the city piled up the material evidences of their devotion to their faith. Two more parishes were set off from St. Jerome's, the Holy Rosary in 1886 down in the Flats near the river, and Holy Cross in 1905 in the "Highlands." Despite the fact that the Flats was the poorest section of the city, the Church of the Rosary was acclaimed as being one of the most beautiful in the diocese.

26. *Ibid.*, pp. 40–56; McCoy, "Diocese of Springfield," *Catholic Church in N. E.*, II, 675–677.

In the older parish of the Sacred Heart an imposing array of parochial buildings filling a whole city block was completed by 1896 where twenty years before had been a sand bank. By the end of the century, Holyoke had the distinction of being the only city in the Springfield Diocese to have two permanent rectorships, an honor accorded a parish only when its self-support is assured and it is complete as to church buildings, schools, and equipment. The parish of the Sacred Heart was in turn divided in 1913 to make still a fifth English-speaking parish.

Father Harkins was, however, far more than a builder in brick and stone. He was a power in the public life of the city. His tongue-lashings and his roaring injunctions to the "toughs" from "Tiger Town," one of the least God-fearing spots within miles, kept the troublemakers in check; while his essential straightforwardness, his common-sense, and his love of justice made him both feared and respected. His creation was the St. Jerome's Temperance Society, a Catholic weapon against the saloon. Personal friend of Protestant clergymen in town, he refused to confine the expression of his humanity to his own coreligionists. Within his church his influence was paramount. The Holy Name Society to promote the use of reverent language only, the Ladies' Sodalities, religious societies for the encouragement of more devout living, the numbers of girls dedicating their lives to service as nuns, the St. Jerome boys taking Holy Orders, all these indicate a spiritual force in this Catholic community that could not be gainsaid.[27] Thus the English-speaking church.

The development of the French Catholic Church, however, did not duplicate that of the Irish. Ever since the formation of the first French parish, the Precious Blood, in 1869, the attachment of the French Catholics to their own church has been unwavering. Their increase in numbers also was only less than that of the Irish; in 1890 it was

27. *A Century of Catholicism in Western Massachusetts,* published by the *Catholic Mirror* (Springfield, 1931); Lucey, *History of St. Jerome's Parish,* pp. 75, 100–102.

necessary to create a second French Catholic parish, Our
Lady of Perpetual Help, and in 1903 still a third, The
Immaculate Conception.

In spite of this devotion and in spite of their numerical
expansion, the French Canadian Catholics failed to give
the impression of determined aggressiveness of the Irish.
To begin with, the generality of "Canuks," as they were
called, temperamentally more stolid, more completely of
peasant background than the Irish, had no expectations
and no great desire to play a leading role in the life of the
city. Irish Catholics represented the church militant, and
were not content with easygoing, patient ways. Tolerant
French Canadians of a later generation attributed the aggressive attitude of the Gael to the memory of ancestral
persecutions of Cromwell's day, or to the need, more recently, of developing defenses against New England bigotry. Whatever the reason, the Irish Catholics displayed a
kind of energy in building up their church forces which
was unknown to their French Canadian coreligionists. The
Irish drive was aimed not only at supplying spiritual nourishment for the sheep of the fold but also at securing recognition of the power of their great organization from a
Protestant public generally depicted as yielding them only
grudging admiration. The French Catholics, on the other
hand, were comparatively unconcerned with the rest of the
world, Catholic or Protestant, and were therefore more
tolerant, more ready to live and let live. To immigrants of
the first generation, the church meant *home*, the village in
Province Quebec, French Canadian patois, French Canadian customs, relatives, friends; the church gave vent to
all that complex of feelings tied up intimately with home.
Thus the French church commanded a tenderness which
the church of the Irishman, filled with defiant memories of
the "old country," could never attain.

Services in the French churches were always distinctive.
Save for the Latin of the Mass, French was the only language employed. An emphasis on music, the use of Grego-
rian chants, and an appeal to the congregation's aesthetic

sense, such as it was, betokened a subtle but vital difference in approach to religion. Unsophisticated though the artistic sense of the first generation of French Canadians was, distressing though some of its cruder manifestations were, the whole of aesthetics as the Canadian immigrant saw it was expressed in his church. In the heyday of American gingerbread architecture when native American artistic taste was dormant, the church of the Precious Blood surpassed from an architectural standpoint what might reasonably have been hoped for. With its stone ornamentings it was regarded as exquisite in the seventies.[28]

Just as the French Canadians treated their religion as the deepest expression of their culture, so the better educated of them by the end of the century were ready to adopt a critical attitude toward it. The pronouncement of the priest was by no means accepted unquestioningly on all matters, and a willingness to look at all sides of a question, even where it might involve a study of Protestant views, denoted an attitude of mind which the Irish Catholic was prone to label reprehensibly lax. Conversely French Canadians felt that the Irish were often shallow in the exercise of their faith, too ready to accept unthinkingly what the priests had not carefully enough explained. Yet rarely would the French Canadian critic point this out. Some of this easygoing tolerance perhaps developed later with the increase of intercourse with American non-Catholics, and as a result of the alignment in local politics of the French Canadian with the Protestant in opposition to the dominating Irish. But certainly the twentieth century saw a certain amount of antagonism between French and Irish Catholics.[29]

28. Holyoke *Transcript,* May 1, 29, 1878.
29. Only across the river in Willimansett, by 1894 virtually an extension of Holyoke, was a working arrangement evolved whereby one church sufficed for both English-speaking and French Canadian Catholics. For several years before the appointment of a resident pastor in 1897, the Irish and German Catholics were shepherded by one priest, the French by another. Three masses were held every Sunday in one hall, two for the French and one for the English-speaking, and the rental cost of the hall was divided. With the coming of a priest who spoke both French and

Save for the Poles, Catholics of all other nationalities
in Holyoke had to content themselves with attendance at
one of the English-speaking churches. The numbers of
German Catholics or of Italian or Lithuanian did not warrant separate national churches and apparently these
peoples did not ardently long for such. The Poles, on the
contrary, were perhaps only less nationalistic than the
French Catholics in regard to the church. The Polish
Catholic Church was the product of the influx of Poles in
1893 and 1894. In 1896 the bishop appointed a resident
Polish priest who in spite of all difficulties soon gathered
into his fold 320 parishioners from a shifting population
of about 500.[30] The Poles though painfully poor in those
early years rallied to their priest's support and by 1900
had embarked upon the erection of a church building. The
Polish Church, Mater Dolorosa, claimed a devoted and devout parish over which it exercised a most civilizing influence. A passion to have their sons be altar boys in the
church led many Polish parents to send their boys on in
school to a study of the classics. And the eastern love of
ceremony found expression in the use of ten to fifteen altar
boys at a time in the service and in a more extended ritual
than the Irish or even the French Catholic churches employed.

Eight Catholic churches by 1905 in a city of approximately 50,000 inhabitants numbered nearly 35,000 fol-

English, and the building of a church in Willimansett and a chapel on its
outskirts, some unity in the parish was achieved. McCoy, "Diocese of
Springfield," *Catholic Church in N. E.,* II, 667.

30. *Ibid.,* II, 681–682. A stormy episode marked the year before the
establishment of the first resident Polish priest. In 1895 an unscrupulous
man, a priest who had been unfrocked in Poland, tried to establish here
an "Independent Polish Church." He was driven from the city shortly
by the police for "drunkenness and worse," but his project had caused
such dissension in the Polish colony that many Poles had ceased to go to
church at all. This state of affairs, unusual with a people who ordinarily
looked to the church as their guide and protector in a strange land, made
it imperative in the eyes of the bishop to detach the Holyoke Poles from
the Chicopee Falls parish and to settle a Polish pastor here. When
Father Sikorski came in September 1896, he found nine Poles faithful to
the church.

lowers and owned property valued at $697,740. A decade later with a ninth parish added, parishioners were about 5,000 more. Thirteen Protestant organizations at the earlier date could muster only about 9,000 adherents, and at the later date about 2,000 more.[31]

For all their national differences, the Roman Catholics of whatever parish did not allow mutual antagonisms to interfere with the establishment and promotion of Catholic charities. Even in the seventies when the Protestants were still sharply divided into denominations for all organized philanthropy the Holyoke Catholics were valiantly working together for the creation and maintenance of a hospital and orphanage. Before 1870 Roman Catholic relief work could not be carried on effectively. The congregations of St. Jerome and the Precious Blood both were made up almost wholly of families of mill operatives or other manual laborers who could barely contribute to the building and support of their churches. The priests were primarily concerned for the spiritual well-being of their parishioners, and bodily ills had to be cared for by kindly neighbors or from the funds of the Holyoke Catholic Mutual Benevolent Society. This mutual benefit society organized in the fifties could not begin adequately to meet the situation, even had every Catholic in town belonged to it. In cases of serious accidents in the mills, subscriptions were frequently taken up from among the victims' fellow operatives. The Overseers of the Poor could use public monies only for persons with a settlement in the town, and then only sparingly, and possible accommodations for the disabled or orphans were meagre. As the town grew, such methods could not suffice. Recognition of the need of a hos-

31. United States Bureau of the Census, *Religious Bodies,* 1906, I, 381, 446–447; 1916, I, 337, 412. The numbers cited for 1906 are 29,379 Roman Catholics, but that is listed with deductions made for children under nine years of age. Some 5,586 children are listed as attending Catholic Sunday Schools. Protestant church members are given as 4,697; and 4,398 children attended Protestant Sunday Schools. In 1916 Catholic communicants numbered 34,503, Protestant 6,627.

pital and orphanage was general, but it was Father Harkins who took the initiative.

When visiting Sisters of Charity from a house in Kingston, Canada, came on a fund-raising tour in 1873 Father Harkins enlisted their interest in a scheme for securing a body of nuns from their community to come to Holyoke to take charge of a working girls' hospital home which he hoped to build. One of his parishioners, a physician, warmly seconded the proposal as a practicable answer to the town's most pressing medical need. Arrangements completed, four Sisters of Charity came in November to assume the care of the ailing and helpless.[32]

The hospital home for working girls did not after all materialize because more urgent demands were immediately made upon the time and strength of the eager Sisters— care of many aged infirm and of some fifty orphans. Fortunately four more Sisters came in the winter of 1874–1875 and soon after that some of the Sisters and the orphans were moved across the river to South Hadley Falls where the old rectory was made over into quarters for girls and a wooden dormitory put up for the boys. Meanwhile the task of providing hospital facilities and nursing was carried on by the Sisters in Holyoke and the Falls as well as could be. In 1877 at last they were able to open their hospital supplied with fifty beds and for that day well equipped for medical care. The next year the Holyoke mission was incorporated under the name of The House of Providence and thus the Sisters were able to maintain the hospital without taxation. At the same time the orphans were brought back to Holyoke because the property in South Hadley Falls was needed by the priest of the newly separated parish there.[33] The orphans were crowded into the

32. Holyoke *Mirror,* Mar. 20, 1858, Mar. 23, 1861; McCoy, "Diocese of Springfield," *Catholic Church in N. E.,* II, 608–611. The account of the work of the Sisters of Providence as given in the following paragraphs is derived chiefly from the story as told me in June 1934, by Mother Mary of Providence, one of the original sisters of the Holyoke mission.

33. Thenceforward although the needy of South Hadley Falls relied

third floor of the Institute built for a parochial school for boys of St. Jerome and there were housed for some two years.

The multiplicity of demands upon the Sisters was great. But the public was appreciative. Protestants as well as Catholics contributed generously to the support of the hospital and the work for the orphans, and the Sisters of Providence speak gratefully of the broad spirit of charity in the city at large which made possible much of the work of the order. Indeed the ailing were tended as far as means sufficed without reference to their faith. The problem of an orphanage was solved in 1880 when, after Herculean labors on the part of the Sisters, a tract of land to the south of the city was bought and a building put up for the orphans not only of Holyoke but of the whole Springfield diocese. Here at Mt. St. Vincent under the eyes of the tireless Sisters boys and girls were watched over, educated, and bred in the faith. Having paid off the debt on the House of Providence hospital, the Sisters were now confronted with the task of financing operation of the new institution. As a diocesan project Mt. St. Vincent was of course not dependent on support from Holyoke alone, but Holyoke gave generously through direct donations, through fairs and benefit entertainments, and through the purchase of the nuns' needlework. As time went on this diocesan charity was greatly expanded. Therefore in 1892 these Sisters became the Sisters of Providence with their mother house here.[34]

for help upon the charity of the Sisters in Holyoke, the Parish of St. Patrick's was distinct and no longer under the pastoral care of Father Harkins. After 1875 some of the Sisters added to other duties the teaching of the boys of the Catholic Institute, a responsibility which the nuns of this order carried on until 1912.

34. The Sisters were frugal administrators and used the farm land at Mt. St. Vincent for a herd of milch cows. In 1887 the original building was added to and five years later the adjacent property was bought and a separate orphanage for the boys founded at Brightside. Here also was erected the Bethlehem Infant Asylum and a home for aged men, all diocesan charities. So effective in their work were these Sisters that the Bishop of Springfield in 1892 had them detached from the order in Kingston and made the charity order of the Springfield diocese.

All during these years the Sisters were carrying on their hospital in Holyoke. It was desperately needed. The number of people seeking care in its wards was far in excess of what could be provided for, and the burden upon the nuns was heavy. Although the opening in 1893 of a secular institution, the Holyoke City Hospital, lightened the demands upon the Catholic foundation, a larger, more modern hospital for the Sisters' work became a necessity. In 1894 therefore a new House of Providence hospital was completed and four years later the Harkins Home was opened where chronic patients were accommodated. The bishop's gift of surgical instruments enabled Catholic doctors to perform operations at the hospital, and thus the House of Providence was fitted to meet the needs of its community.

Despite the magnificent organization of the Roman Catholic church in Holyoke, its charities could scarcely have been carried on so ably without the aid of lay societies, notably the local branch of the Society of St. Vincent de Paul. Members of this nation-wide association, organized for the sole purpose of giving secret help to the needy, were all laymen, but conducted their work of relief under the direction and inspiration of the church. Less altruistic but little less useful in relieving want were the mutual benefit societies which through the decades grew in numbers and activity. More social than religious in character these organizations still were useful as means of extending help where it was needed, although it was self-help rather than charity as such.[35] These societies supplied not only social groupings and valuable aids to charity but also con-

---

35. Alexandre Belisle, *Histoire de la Presse Franco-Américaine*, p. 20; Lucey, *History of St. Jerome's Parish*, p. 126. The declared purpose of the Massachusetts Catholic Order of Foresters is typical, "the promotion of fraternity, unity and true Christian charity among its members, and for the purpose of raising and maintaining a fund, so as to enable us to give substantial assistance in time of sickness and distress; to make suitable provision for the widow and orphans; and to do all in our power to further the interests of our fellow members." *A Century of Catholicism in Western Mass.*, pp. 270, 260, 265.

venient nuclei through which to work for the extension of the sphere of the Church Triumphant.

As the Roman Catholic Church expanded it might be assumed that there would be among the Protestants an acceleration of the anti-Roman feeling, just as there had been earlier. But this apparently was not the case. As the first generation of Holyoke gave way to the second, such hostility as existed seems rather to have sprung from the Catholic side, where the second generation of Irish was beginning to hope for greater social recognition. Among the Protestants, however, a certain indifference had come to prevail. Perhaps the business leaders of the community, still almost exclusively Protestant, were too much engrossed in the excitements of building up great industries and possible fortunes to be concerned with nonessentials in religion. The city was growing rapidly in the late seventies and the eighties and it might well have seemed logical to Protestants that the immigrants' church must grow too. Thus as long as the members of an alien church did not too far outnumber the Protestants, the latter were on the whole ready to accept the inevitable. The futility of trying to effect Catholic conversions was recognized by most of the Protestant churches, and the contributions of non-Catholics to Catholic charities made for mutual good feeling.[36] All later innuendo to the contrary and an occasional contemporary expression of mutual distaste notwithstanding, the second generation of the booming young city saw a decade of friendly relations between the people of the two faiths.

The increase of parochial schools, later a source of friction, caused in the eighties no deep feeling of concern. The public grammar schools still enrolled many Catholic children every year, and to the city high school went virtually all the boys and girls of whatever creed who could afford

36. McCoy, "Diocese of Springfield," *Catholic Church in N. E.*, II, 610. It is possible that these gifts to Catholic charities are evidences of a kind of paternalism, whereby sops to the religion of the mill operatives were considered a good investment. But I do not so interpret the evidence.

additional schooling, save always of course the few who were sent back to Canada. The school children mingled with each other regardless of religion and school friendships grew up naturally. But difference in economic status, and its consequence, differences in the part of the city in which children lived, affected these friendships as geography will. Between the families of children who had bridged the geographical or economic gap, however, there was no social intercourse. Here the distinction unquestionably had its chief origin in the difference in world's goods, making a gulf that no amount of good will could span easily for long. No one expected it to be otherwise. Indeed the priests were not anxious to have their charges mix with the heretics, and sometimes dictated the breaking up of what they considered dangerous friendships.[37] Perhaps the Protestants, as a class possessed of far greater means and infinitely greater social prestige, were sometimes guilty of a tactless disregard of their Catholic fellow citizens, but if so it was generally unconscious. Later the acute problem of the mixed marriage arose occasionally, in which the Protestant with considerable bitterness felt that all the concessions were demanded of him and none given in return. But before 1900 by reason of the lack of general social mingling, that situation was rare; not until the erstwhile indigent Catholics had risen to a position of comparative wealth did it present itself. Religious antagonism as such in the second generation was limited until after 1890.

Unfortunately for the cause of toleration, religious is-

37. An extreme example of the Catholic fear of social intercourse with Protestants was quoted in the *Transcript* from an article in the *Catholic Journal.* Urging the necessity of Catholics' living apart from Protestants the article concluded: "No other means of ridding one's self of their consequences is given us but avoiding the associations that lead to these and kindred evils. It is nearly impossible for us to avoid the associations of any one or a number of persons if we are continually in their presence or constantly meeting them at their and our homes: hence the great desirability of Catholics living among themselves as much as possible." Holyoke *Transcript,* Aug. 4, 1880. Later in the eighties a day nursery for children of working women had to be given up because Catholic women would not place their children in the care of Protestants. *Ibid.,* Jan. 3, 24, May 5, 1885, Jan. 2, Feb. 12, May 28, 1887.

sues came to be associated with local politics. The United States census report of 1890 revealed the overwhelming preponderance of Catholics in the community, 18,828 Catholics to 3,128 church members of all other churches.[38] Thus with priest, patriot, and politician urging the transformation of aliens into citizens, political control became relatively simple. All that was connected however remotely with the unsavory regime of the local Tammany was viewed with distaste by a suspicious public. Unjust though it patently was, in the minds of Protestants the associating of the Catholic church with the reign of graft followed. With the inauguration of a "reform" city government, the misdirected animosity subsided only in part. Perhaps the propaganda of the dying American Protective Association after all made some impression. Be that as it may, from about 1895 on Protestant Holyoke had ceased to be indifferent to the Catholic church.

The end of the century saw a rivalry between the two faiths which though rooted in secular soil bore fruits of mutual intolerance. The gradual supplanting of Protestant teachers in the public schools by Catholics was declared by irritated non-Catholics to be the result of religious prejudice. The large majority over a Protestant rival which a staunch Catholic might expect to secure in any municipal election if he skillfully played upon the intolerance of his coreligionists offered a temptation to the not too nice that was hard to resist.[39] Yet fundamentally these antagonisms were not truly religious in origin. The value in any industrial community of a great conserving and conservative force like the Roman Catholic Church

38. *Eleventh Census of U. S.*, 1890, *Statistics of Churches*, XXVII, VII, 91.

39. For years the resulting bitterness endured and first in 1908 did the local press indicate a changing tone. "The City has about arrived at a point when a man's religious belief when running for office, takes a secondary place to his standing in the community, both morally and from a business standpoint, and it will not be many years when the religious warfare on both sides of the fence will be a thing of the past." Scrap Books of Grace Church (in possession of clerk of Grace Church, Holyoke).

was not fully appreciated even by industrial leaders, and the petty annoyances of everyday living temporarily blinded them to its worth.

The Protestant churches of the city in comparison to the overpowering growth of the Roman Catholic Church grew slowly. Between 1885 and 1892, however, four new church groups were organized, a second Methodist Episcopal church, a Presbyterian, a French Congregational[40] and in 1892 a second German Lutheran society. The new German church resulted from the organization in 1888 of the original South Holyoke society as a Lutheran Church of the Missouri Synod, the most rigid in its theology and reactionary in its practice of any Lutheran association in the United States. The irreconcilables therefore formed their own group as a German Reformed Church. Both German churches established parochial schools and thereby intensified their isolation from the other Protestant churches. In the case of the older church, complete dissociation from other denominations was deliberate policy, and as its membership was not very large, most of Holyoke knew little about it.[41]

But centripetal tendencies were still characteristic of all the Protestant churches, and social contacts outside the church one attended were few. It was not a question of denominational exclusiveness, for there was little intercourse between the two Congregational churches or the two Baptist groups, in spite of the fact that the street railway in the nineties brought the older churches into easy communication with their offshoots. Although the Methodists, the Episcopalians, the Presbyterians, and even more markedly the Unitarians, had their typical organizations and their individual church lives, it is through the two most powerful churches, the Second Congregational and the Second

40. The small flock of French Protestants always had to receive some financial support for their church from the Massachusetts Congregational Conference and it was therefore years later abandoned.

41. United States Bureau of the Census, *Religious Bodies,* 1906, I, 381; Reverend Martin Steup to the author, Mar. 1933.

Baptist, that the dominant characteristics of the religion of that whole generation can best be surveyed.

The liberal religious element of Holyoke continued to be most widely represented by the Second Congregational Church. For all the intellectual breadth of the Unitarian Church, and the assured social position of many of its members, it was of secondary importance. Modification of religious ideology, as of practice, was gradual among the Congregationalists. Here a succession of unusual pastors facilitated readjustments. From the intensely personal religion of the first generation which Dr. Trask described to the more social pragmatic point of view which began to make itself felt at the end of the century the path was rendered smooth by the wisdom and intellectual adaptability of Trask himself and the men who followed him. Notably Dr. Edward Reed, in whose hands the church serenely rested from 1886 to 1914, was the spiritual heir of John Trask, and the gentle graciousness of this minister and his wife permeated the whole congregation. A lovely kindliness of spirit directed his course and gave effect to his utterances. Himself not in the van of religious thought, he was still willing to accept change with the march of time. But his sermons never varied from Scriptural themes and the interpretation of the duty of the individual Christian. Typical is his language in 1899:

Brethren and friends, today is the anniversary of Pentecost, when the Holy Spirit came with power to abide in the church. Let us remember that the only truly successful Church is a consecrated Church; that the only abiding, saving power is "power from on high." Let us stand in the old paths; let us not be ashamed of the Gospel of Christ in which our fathers believed; let us "contend earnestly for the faith which was once for all delivered unto the saints"; let us believe in the Holy Ghost; "let us love one another, for love is of God," "and he that dwelleth in love dwelleth in God, and God in him"—and so transmit to those who shall come after us the priceless heritage we have received from the past.[42]

42. *Fiftieth Anniversary Second Congregational Church*, p. 44.

Yet the first year of his pastorate saw the founding of a parish library which included books covering a considerable range of subjects, varying from dissertations on theology to works on urban sociology. From the titles of some of these books one can judge of the intellectual fare made accessible to the parish: J. S. Van Dyke, *Theism and Evolution;* James McCosh, *Religious Aspect of Evolution;* A. H. Sayce, *Higher Criticism and the Monuments;* George Hodges, *Faith and Social Service;* Henry Drummond, *Natural Law in the Spiritual World;* Jane Addams, *Democracy and Social Ethics;* H. C. King, *Theology and the Social Consciousness.*[43] No narrowly confining creed presented painful problems to the rising generation of choosing between science and theology. The transition to a newer order of religion in its intellectual aspects, the members of this church apparently made without great travail of spirit.

The exceptionally high order of the music of the church, the fine organ, and the choral singing gave to the services even as early as 1885 an aesthetic appeal still unusual in a New England Congregational Church. The cruder of the old revival hymns were relegated to oblivion and the congregation could join heartily in singing the finer ones. The gifted musician who served as organist after 1885 collected rare church music suitable for use by the choir and trained a large chorus, until the most hardened sinner looked forward to going at least occasionally to the Second Congregational Church to hear the lovely old anthems and carols. The music probably also was important in familiarizing a Puritan community with the great contributions of the Roman Catholic Church to the realm of sheer beauty. Far more than was realized at the time, the developing interest in the music of the service simplified the acceptance of the usage of a new day.

Here was a kindly congregation made up in the days of Dr. Trask of young people of fairly similar means—of

43. Catalogue of the Parish Library (vault of the Second Congregational Church). This library was almost completely destroyed when the church burned in 1918.

professional people, mill executives, clerks, storekeepers, and some mill hands, a church which had been for years scarcely confronted at all with the problem of urban churches, of rich people versus poor. As the mills expanded and disparity of wealth increased, the women of the church made a point of contriving to give help to the poor of the parish in such unostentatious fashion that no one's pride need suffer. In fact as time went on, some poor people were secretly suspected of joining the church for the sake of the security they attained that they would be well taken care of in this world, regardless of what might happen to them in the next. By the dawn of the new century this church included most of the persons of large wealth in the city as well as a number of poor people. With the possible exception of St. Paul's Episcopal Church, in this congregation were to be found as nowhere else in Holyoke the two extremes of wealth and poverty. Yet just as change in religious ideology during these years was gradual, the difference in social approach to religion was itself almost imperceptible. The juxtaposition of capital and labor had not yet been keenly felt within this church.

Instrumental in easing the shift from the religion of the first generation to the more social religion to which the church was to be accustomed in the twentieth century was the Young People's Society of Christian Endeavor. Following in the wake of the first Christian Endeavor Society founded in Portland, Maine, in 1881, the young people of the Second Congregational Church of Holyoke organized about 1884 a society which soon boasted forty-three active members and forty-five associate members.[44] To the younger generation the old Thursday night prayer meetings which were a source of such profound spiritual refreshment to their fathers were simply a bore. These young people of the eighties seized upon the Christian Endeavor

44. *Directory of Second Congregational Church,* 1886. A definite pledge to take active part in the society's weekly prayer meetings deterred the less ardent or the more timid from joining on the basis of full membership.

meetings as a means of escape from the older order, but supported their own prayer meetings with enthusiasm.

The project which was to overshadow the work of the Christian Endeavor entirely had an earlier inception. In 1879 Dr. Trask's New Year's sermon on the theme of "Doing Something Definite for the Master" had so stirred the boys in one of the church Sunday School classes that they pledged themselves to open a Sunday School in the lower part of the city where they might hope to reach children who would otherwise receive no religious instruction. A canvass of a poor section of the city revealed the possible usefulness of such an undertaking and classes were accordingly started. From a modest beginning with eight pupils and only the boys of the Second Congregational Sunday School class for teachers came the interesting experiment, Holyoke's "Institutional Church," Grace Church. For years the Sunday School was conducted by this same group of boys, grown to be men. In answer to criticisms from other churches, particularly from the Roman Catholic, the founders of Grace Chapel were at pains to see that it was ministering only to children who would not otherwise have church connections. Children of many nationalities flocked to the afternoon sessions, interested to have a good time if they could. Often, doubtless, religion was not the chief goal of the pupils, in spite of the teachers' valiant efforts.

Gradually the parents of the children were sought out for evening services and so began an adult permanent association. Older people in the Second Congregational Church had helped with financing from the first, and in 1892 again they stood by when it was decided to secure a resident pastor to carry on the work now offering opportunities of service beyond the power of a group of volunteer workers, however earnest, to handle. Thus the rise of Grace Church. In 1894 a church edifice was built. But the boys who started Grace Chapel continued to conduct classes in person and to be vitally interested in the now greatly enlarged enterprise. Indeed of all the significant features of the Grace Church work, the most important of all was not the variety of social service which it came to perform in this downtown field, not the opening of reading rooms and classes for adults and children, not the equipping of a gymnasium and the supplying of hot water for baths, not the stereopticon lectures and the bringing in of college speakers on a wide range of economic, social, and scientific topics—not any of these important aspects of the undertaking, but the socially significant fact that the boys who began the job carried it on.[45] Several of them had come to be men of importance in the city and two or three of them had become heads of great mills. But this personal touch with the downtown church answered criticisms of an excessive self-sufficiency on the part of the Second Congregational Church, and suggested that the relation between rich and poor in this Congregational community was not one of patronizing paternalism but more nearly one of Christian brotherhood.

An enterprise in its beginning somewhat similar to Grace Chapel was undertaken in 1886 by the Baptists. Endeavor Chapel was the special charge of the Young People's Society of Christian Endeavor of the Second Baptist Church. But it failed of the breadth of scope of the Congregational Chapel. The aim had been to reach the Protestant families left stranded when the church moved uptown and to serve families without definite church affiliation. A Baptist chapel across the river in Willimansett was also fostered by this parent church, and for a time Beulah Chapel shared with Endeavor Chapel the services of its pastor. But though Beulah Chapel came to be a small independent Baptist Church, Endeavor Chapel shrank with the gradual moving away of Protestant families until in 1916 it was abandoned altogether.[46]

The Second Baptist Church of the second generation from many standpoints offered a greater contrast to its Congregational neighbor than had been the case earlier.

45. Scrap Books of Grace Church; *Fiftieth Anniversary Second Congregational Church,* pp. 147–160.

46. Osgood, *Story of the Holyoke Churches,* pp. 97–98.

While the Congregationalists had moved slowly the Baptists did not move at all. Before 1901 the Second Baptist Church stood on dogma and discipline just where it always had. Probably this imperviousness to change was partly due to the fact that its membership continued to be recruited from the middle classes, from neither the very rich nor the very poor. A "one class church" it was called. Such of the congregation as had accumulated money were to be viewed as good and faithful servants of the Lord who had wisely husbanded their talents. The Baptists could therefore more easily blind themselves to the new religious problems of the growing industrial city and as of yore could direct their eyes inward upon the weal of their own souls. The uncompromising old deacons staunchly believed in the regenerating force of the Holy Spirit and were ready repeatedly to testify to their experiences of personal conversion. Theirs was a Calvinism of an order unmodified by the findings of higher criticism and little affected by the discoveries of scientific research. The Church published in 1889 its Declaration of Faith which settled the questions raised by science thus:

God has written in the natural world the evidences of his wisdom and omnipotence and omnipresence. He had laid down in the Bible an infallible standard of religious doctrine and duty to guide men to heaven. Any differences between these two revelations, any contradictions are apparent only and not real. Consult the Bible to learn your duty to God and man, consult the divine book of nature for light on questions of natural science.[47]

The belief in the realities of heavenly bliss and the torments of everlasting hell were fully accepted. To secure to oneself a share in the former as strict an observation of the Sabbath was demanded in 1900 as had been considered necessary twenty years before, and the mutual watchfulness over the conduct of one's fellow members was still

47. *Declaration of Faith of the Second Baptist Church of Holyoke,* pp. 5–6.

reminiscent of the days of Increase Mather. Strict Sab-
batarianism was, to be sure, not confined to the Baptists,
but was the rule in all the evangelical churches. A walk in
the cemetery after dinner was the extent of the entertainment to be expected between church services.

The continued stress laid upon both discipline and
dogma in the Second Baptist Church is exemplified by the
sermon given by the pastor on the occasion of the laying
of the cornerstone of the new church building in 1884:

A nation of Atheists is simply *impossible*, because some divine
sanction is essential to the influence of law, and obedience to
law is the condition of national life. The Bible with its Free
Gospel, the church and Sabbath-schools moulding the rising
generation and reproducing the old personal and social good-
ness, the strong, deep-rooted faith of the founders of this Republic—this is the adamant on which our nationality must
rest or it will fall to pieces.

It may be that the present generation will decide the fate of
this great nation, by deciding whether the Sabbath and the
public worship of Almighty God, shall be preserved or blotted
out. No people and no government can have any assured
prosperity unless there is a reverent recognition of the claims
of Jehovah. . . . No true church can be reared which does
not embrace and hold the true doctrines respecting Christ,
especially those which pertain to His incarnation, his divine
nature, his teachings, his example, his atonement, his resur-
rection and intercession. Everything essential to a gospel
church depends on correct views of the Son of God.[48]

Correct thinking and impeccable conduct were both expected.

In their Covenant the Baptists engaged

That we will maintain private and family devotions; reli-
giously educate the children committed to our care; abstain
from the sale and use of intoxicating drinks as a beverage;
and endeavor, in purity of heart and newness of life, and

48. Records of the Second Baptist Church of Holyoke, II.

goodwill toward all men, to exemplify and commend our holy
faith, win souls to the Saviour, and hold fast our profession
till He shall come and receive us to Himself in the heavenly
mansions.[49]

Thus the Church made prohibition part and parcel of its
pledge. In the Sunday School a flourishing Loyal Temperance Legion was nourished which chanted with gusto:

> We're coming, we're coming, a brave little band
> On the right side of Temperance we now take our stand.
> We don't like tobacco, do you know what we think?
> That those who do use it are quite sure to drink.

Even cider was looked upon with disfavor by the zealous.

The Junior Christian Endeavor Society was fostered by
the ardent Sunday School teachers.[50] On the other hand,
from the Junior Endeavor boys and girls quite regularly
went on into the Young People's Society of Christian Endeavor. There the hymn singing, as in the similar societies
in the other churches, played a great part. Revivalist
hymns were the order of the day:

> Brightly gleams our Father's Mercy
> From his lighthouse evermore
> But to us he gives the keeping
> Of the lights along the shore.
> Let your lower lights be burning
> Send a gleam across the wave
> Some poor fainting struggling seaman
> You may rescue, you may save.

---

49. *Declaration of Faith,* p. 41; Covenant.

50. One ingenious teacher evolved a point system whereby Christian
virtue was to be developed. She awarded five points to any child who
would arise to offer up a prayer, five points to any who would offer a
testimonial, two points for the recitation of a bit of Scripture, and one
point for remembering to bring the Bible to Sunday School each week,
and at the end of the year the winner of the most points was presented
with a prize—one time a gold bracelet, again, if a boy, with a five dollar
gold piece. The incongruities of this system of bribery apparently impressed no one as humorous.

But of less cheerful variety were the hymns sung in the church service itself:

Sin Revived: I Died.

Lord, how secure my conscience was,
And felt no inward dread!
I was alive without the law,
And thought my sins were dead.

My guilt appeared but small before,
Till terribly I saw
How perfect, holy, just, and pure,
Was thine eternal law.

My God, I cry with every breath
For some kind power to save,
To break the yoke of sin and death,
And thus redeem the slave.[51]

Rescue the Perishing

Rescue the perishing, care for the dying,
Snatch them in pity from sin and the grave.
Weep o'er the erring ones, lift up the fallen
Tell them of Jesus the mighty to save.

Chorus

Rescue the perishing, care for the dying
Jesus is merciful, Jesus will save.

Down in the human heart, crushed by the tempter,
Feelings lie buried that grace can restore.
Touched by a loving heart, wakened by kindness
Chords that were broken will vibrate once more.

Rescue the perishing, duty demands it,
Strength for thy labor the Lord will provide.
Back to the narrow way patiently win them
Tell the poor wanderer a Saviour has died.

51. *The Calvary Selection of Spiritual Songs with Music for the Church and Choir,* selected and arranged by Charles S. Robinson and Robert S. MacArthur, no. 387.

Into this close community, which contained many of the representative men of the city, came in 1901 an unexpected force with the installation of Dr. J. S. Lyon as pastor. Here was no hard-shelled old-time Baptist, but a man whose views of Christian duty were increasingly moving away from the old conception of salvation through personal piety in the direction of practical service to one's fellowmen. Greatly troubled by the misery and squalor to be found in this mill city, Dr. Lyon set himself to direct the attention of his congregation away from their own experiences of conversion toward the crying needs, physical and spiritual, of their fellowmen. While he was obliged to work slowly with deacons who gasped at a minister who did not confine himself to preaching the Gospel, his tact and his ardor gradually combined to win many of his congregation to his own point of view.

A men's Bible Study Class under his aegis became the Men's League, a discussion group of modern social problems viewed in the light of religion and philosophy. By relating the discussions to local industrial issues the pastor soon made the league an eagerly interested and growing organization. Law enforcement, child labor, legislation to regulate unemployment, labor's rights—the topics discussed were immediately pertinent. For the first time in years the men of the church began to take the lead in church affairs, instead of leaving matters to women as before. The Men's League became a power also in the community. It was a far cry from the attitude of the earlier generation of Baptists when the Men's League in a concerted effort to clean up local politics endorsed the candidacy for district attorney of an Irish Roman Catholic!

Such revolutionary approaches to religion naturally aroused some protests. But while these came from a few of the older church members who professed to have experienced divine revelation direct to themselves, the main body of the congregation followed Dr. Lyon's lead enthusiastically. The impact of his vigorous personality was widely felt, and the Second Baptist Church throughout his fif-

teen-year pastorate was again a vital force in the city. Dr.
Lyon's successor was a kindly, conservative preacher of
the Gospel, unable or unwilling to walk in his predecessor's
footsteps, and so after 1916 the Baptists gradually slid
back into greater conservatism. But the church was never
again wholly oblivious to the city around it.

In 1914 the Second Congregational Church also was
brought under the influence of a new pastor, a stirring
preacher who was convinced that the church to be a regenerating social factor must work through groups rather
than with individuals. Nineteen years earlier Dr. Reed had
encouraged the formation at the church of a Men's Christian Industrial League, intended to be an undenomina-
tional, mutual benefit society, "to promote patriotism,
sobriety and . . . furnish the necessary aid in case of
sickness or disability." At the Chapter meetings social
questions might be discussed. "We believe it is proper and
high time that the Church was broadening her lines of effort and bringing men to Christ and the Church that ought
to be their home."[52] But the organization never became
any force in the city at large, and by the time of Dr. Wicks'
advent the church was ready for other means of expression. General adult discussions were inaugurated. Great
attention was paid to making the Sunday School inspiring
to the younger generation, and the Young People's Society, an offshoot of the earlier Christian Endeavor, became an active, intelligently interested group. By such
means the influence of the church was kept at an unusually
high pitch into the twenties. Attendance at midweek service dwindled to the vanishing point, as was the case in all
the Protestant churches, but Sunday was still generally
set aside for church-going by young people as well as older.

A Gothic chapel, the Skinner Memorial Chapel, built in
1912, was a source of great pride to the Congregationalists, and when the main church burned in 1918 the congregation turned to the rebuilding with the determination to
make the church compare architecturally with the chapel,

52. Folder (vault of the Second Congregational Church).

regardless of cost. The old amphitheatre with its yellow oak pews, characteristic of New England Congregational church architecture of the preceding era, was replaced by a pseudo-Gothic hall with stone pillars and vaulting and a chancel that, to the astonishment of the foreign-born and of Episcopalians, created the general appearance of a Catholic church. Efforts to meet the large debt thus in-curred kept the congregation busy.

Coöperation among the Protestant churches made headway after the nineties. First the Y. M. C. A. and the other philanthropic projects led to new collaboration. In 1907 the whole of the Protestant community devoted over a week to a great revival campaign. The coming of the evangelists, Wilbur Chapman and his eight assistants, was advertised by posters and articles in the newspapers days in advance and the city hall auditorium was chartered for the meetings. While less sensational than Billy Sunday, Chapman and his cohorts resorted to typical revivalist tactics, and it is indicative of the continued unsophistication of Holyoke's religious life that the appeals made deep impression. The mayor himself, having given much time to the campaign, naïvely proclaimed the investment a profitable one for the city in dollars and cents.[53]

While the city in general was divided into two major religious camps, the Catholic and the Protestant, there were other religious groupings. Most important of these were the Jews. Russian and Polish Jews were to be found here as early as 1883 and 1884, but no Jewish congregations were established until 1891, since by Hebrew law there must be at least ten heads of families in order to form a congregation. The East-European Jews had been preceded by three or four families of German Jews, but these professed to have nothing in common with the poor immigrants arriving later. Before 1882 Jews could not get Kosher meat from Springfield and with the enforced abandonment of the dietary laws, these early comers, doubtless

53. Holyoke *Transcript,* Nov. 10, 14, 1907; Scrap Books of Grace Church.

never devout, gradually drifted away from Judaism altogether.

The first congregation of Russian Jews to be formed was called Agudas Achim, Society of Brothers. In 1902 it changed its name to B'nai Zion, Congregation of the Sons of Zion, and by then much enlarged moved into a synagogue of its own, bought—thus picturesquely do things happen in this polyglot country—from the Société de St. Jean Baptiste. This congregation was Conservative Orthodox; that is, willing to have English-speaking, seminary-trained rabbis to conduct the festivals at Yom Kippur and ready to make concessions to a kind of American Judaism. Jewish families were coming to Holyoke at the rate of about twenty-five a year, so that where there had been four orthodox families in 1890 there were by 1906 one hundred forty in spite of a restlessness which carried many a family out of town again. In 1904, Jews who longed for a Strict Orthodox congregation were strong enough in numbers to build a synagogue in South Holyoke. The Raidphi-Sholum (Seeking Peace) and the Sons of Zion divided fairly evenly between them the Jewish families of the city. The Jews kept careful watch over their newly arriving brothers, and except for the German Jews let none slip away from Judaism. It was supervision unostentatious but effective.

There were other groups. Christian Brethren of the Apostolic Line or the Plymouth Brethren, Scotchmen and Englishmen mostly, numbered forty or fifty. The characterizing belief of this sect was their recognition of "the gift of preaching" and the repudiation of any ordained ministry. In the nineties also arose a coterie of advocates of New Thought, largely women who adopted the faith-healing "success cult" and organized a local society. The coming in 1900 of the editor and publisher of a New Thought magazine, *The Nautilus*, failed to stimulate the local society although later the wide circulation of the money-making magazine outside Holyoke connected the city with that movement in the minds of readers. A somewhat similar society was the Holyoke Lodge of the Theosophical Society chartered in 1899 with thirty members. The Theosophists maintained their connection with their churches and devoted their weekly meetings to delving into the esoteric and to the study of Madame Blavatsky's pantheism. But while the preachment was beguiling, that the spiritual thought power of Theosophy might make everything ours by divine right, a belief particularly pleasing to persons possessing little worldly goods, the Theosophical Society remained a minor episode in the religious life of the city. In 1912 Christian Scientists formed a church here which strengthened gradually, but Holyoke was too overwhelmingly a Roman Catholic community to lend ready ear to Mary Baker Eddy's teachings. An Eastern Orthodox Church with membership composed of the four or five hundred Greeks in the city was built in 1917. And in this same year the Unitarians sold their church property and temporarily disbanded.

Outside the churches some religious work was carried on by the Young Men's Christian Association and the Salvation Army. The former, organized in 1886, soon emphasized its social and civic character more than its religious, although Bible study classes were given for years and in the early part of the twentieth century Sunday afternoon religious meetings were held which had such large attendance that church pastors began jealously to regard the "Y" as a kind of union church for young men. But the decline of interest in these meetings and the eventual abandonment of that feature of the program ended any nascent hostility. The Salvation Army post had been founded here in 1890 and attempted some social work, but without local funds it could accomplish little and not until after the World War did it have enthusiastic support in the city. Its purely religious endeavors, however, were not without result. The Army preached a Christianity based on a belief in the divine inspiration of the Bible and a literal acceptance of all its teachings from Genesis to Revelation. With fervent evangelizing methods, with deeds as well as hymns, the Soldiers endeavored to teach the importance of the New Birth of the Soul. The Army had a checkered career of ups and downs. By the very nature of the Army organization the quality of the work accomplished at any local post must depend upon the personnel of the local force. A particularly successful adjutant had worked up a fairly numerous soldiery at the opening of the century, only to have it dwindle not long after. Opposed by the Roman Catholic Church as the preacher of an apostolic religion, and mildly derided by the Protestants when it was not actually resented as drawing people from the churches by an unstable emotional appeal, the Army could claim few members in 1916.[54] The church was still felt to be the proper channel for religious work.

In 1916 the Catholic women of the city undertook the organization of a charitable enterprise, civic rather than religious. Through St. Agnes Guild made up of a number of separate circles these women launched a day nursery for the care of children of working women. Sisters of the House of Providence took charge. But in one important particular this enterprise differed from earlier Catholic charities: its supporters aligned themselves with the city as a whole and in the twenties after the founding of the Community Welfare League and the Community Chest the day nursery served as a strong link between the Catholic and the Protestant philanthropists.[55] And as always Catholics supported their diocesan charities.

By 1922 the Catholic Church, externally powerful, was still a growing rather than a diminishing force in the life of the city, and the Protestant churches viewed its strength as a challenge. Sunday morning church attendance among Protestants was a matter of course until after the war, although first the midweek services and then the Sunday evening services ceased to be largely attended. After 1900 more young people than a generation before spent their Sundays canoeing up the river, and as the automobile came

54. United States Bureau of the Census, *Religious Bodies,* 1916, I, 412; *Thirtieth Anniversary Holyoke Daily Transcript;* Records of the Holyoke Y. M. C. A., 1887–1911; *Salvation Army Handbook of Doctrine.*
55. Holyoke *Transcript,* Apr. 1, 1916.

into general use more and more took Sundays in mild
weather for all-day outings. But there had always been
some hedonists who leavened the church-going mass with
their frivolous philosophy of life, and many of these contributed financially to local good works, pleasantly allay-
ing thereby apparently any occasional sense of uneasiness
about the hereafter. Still even in 1920 these young people
were no considerable proportion of the whole community.
More there were probably to whom religion consisted in a
superficial lip service without vital personal significance,
merely a way of "playing safe" in case priest or pastor
should be right.

Gauged by the increase in membership in the Masonic
lodges, a greater number of men than heretofore found
some religious life through Masonry. To be sure, the
charge was brought from time to time that Masonry was
undermining the church through allowing the ceremonies
in the Masonic Temple to take the place of church services.
Undoubtedly in the lodge some Masons did find satisfaction for their ritualistic cravings to which Protestant tradition gave no other outlet, and felt in the fellowship and
elaborate ceremonial in the lodge inspiration to right living such as the church itself stood for. But most Masons
were rather brought into closer touch with their church
than turned from it.

There was of course some deliberate repudiating of the
church. Even a generation before there had been individuals whose religious feeling sought expression only in the
pietist's exclusive emphasis on personal virtue, who found
such virtue easier without the church. For them the mystic
element in the universe could perhaps not be confronted by
the group so well as by the individual. Furthermore, on intellectual grounds there was some rejection of the church
as an institution. Bob Ingersoll had had his local admir-
ers.[56] And there had been also a few German Marxian So-

56. When Ingersoll spoke at the Empire Theatre in 1896 the house was
packed. Many of the audience went doubtless out of curiosity and for
sheer delight in the oratory of the famous agnostic.

cialists who were convinced enemies of the church and of all organized religion as the preacher to the proletarian of acquiescence in his lot. Themselves courageous, decent, hard-working men, most of them, in the early years of the new century they made with their teaching no impression upon the city at large and after the country-wide Bolshevik scare of 1920 these few were lost sight of. But of any pronounced, widespread, intellectual conflicts within the churches or without, of any repercussions of the "Warfare of Science and Theology," there was no sign.

Thus Holyoke continued to be a community imbued with a sense of the importance of religion, seeking spiritual life through its churches. For some citizens religion was inevitably an unthinking or perfunctory kind of continuation of the past. For some, whether Protestant or Catholic, a species of compartmenting of ideas must have existed: on Sundays church-going and Christian worship of the God that gave to each his appointed place, and on weekdays vigorous pursuit of that worldly destiny, the hoped-for place in the sun. God was in His Heaven and by and by all would be well with the world. Yet for all the acceptance of the existing order with its misery and squalor, its disease and corruption, the city's prevailing atmosphere, religious and mundane, was kindly. Rivalry, even some hostility, between Catholics and Protestants still existed, not fully terminated by the growing realization of the necessity of community coöperation if the city was to be made a wholesome place in which to live. But as yet there was surprisingly little of that impatience at the futility of the Protestant church that had long been voiced in the big cities. Holyoke's intellectual and social points of view lagged in general more than a decade behind that of urban centers. The pragmatic Christianity which had been written and talked of in New York and Chicago since the late nineties was just beginning to command hearing here.

For nearly two generations the purpose of religion and the church had been regarded as the salvation of the soul of the individual. Too much engrossed in the business of

becoming herself urbanized, and too far removed from the
sources of a rich intellectual life, Holyoke had been largely
unconscious of the changes in attitude toward the church
and religion which had taken place elsewhere. With the return of the men who had seen service with the army in
France and in training camps in this country a new point
of view was to make itself felt. Holyoke was to find her
erstwhile church members indulging in that kind of ro-
mantic religious individualism which rejected the church as
a vital force, recognized no form of worship, and regarded
"a Christianity of the 'Spirit' and of disposition, a religion of humanitarian activity and an entirely individual
interpretation of the intellectual aspect of religion"[57] as the
only kind worth having. But in the early twenties in Holyoke religion and the church were still sufficiently one to
lead men to hope through the church to fill the heart of
each human being with Christian idealism, and thus to
bring to an end the evils of a materialistic civilization.

57. Ernst Troeltsch, *The Social Teachings of the Christian Churches*
(translated from the German by Olive Wyon), II, 798.

XII

SOCIAL LIFE

THE cultural life of Holyoke in its early years had been similar to that of any small New England mill town. Because of its sudden, artificial growth with even the native American element transplanted from other towns, there probably had been less social mingling here than elsewhere. And from the beginning foreigners had been a large part of the population, foreigners who lived in separate colonies, simple people devoted to their own churches, too poor and too occupied with the struggle for subsistence to have leisure for other things.

As the city emerged from the town and wealth increased, this situation was somewhat modified. Population rose from 16,260 to 21,915 between 1875 and 1880, and by 1900 stood at 45,712. By 1917 it had reached its peak, 62,210, and by 1920 had shrunk slightly to 60,203.[1] But the nationality make-up of the community continued to be a dominant factor in its cultural development.

Irish and French Canadian were the chief constituents of the population down to 1900. Through the eighties the Germans kept up their earlier proportion of the whole, but British immigrants were fewer. After 1884 Russian Jews began to drift in and in the nineties began the Polish immigration. The Jews and the handful of Italians who came set up small shops as a rule; the others went into the mills. The color question never entered into population problems here. From the town's beginning there were a few Negroes, and in the seventies several Chinese boys came as students. But neither Africans nor Orientals were important factors here.[2]

1. See chart.
2. *Census of Mass.*, 1885, *Population and Social Statistics*, I, Pt. I, 519; *Eleventh Census of U. S.*, 1890, *Population*, I, Pt. I, 670–673, 713; *Census*

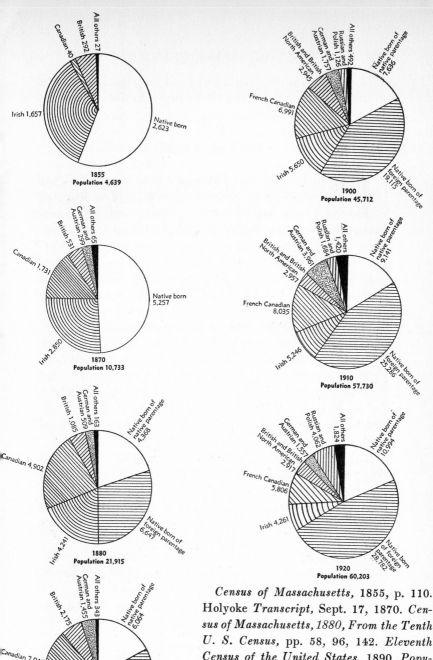

All others 27
British 292
Canadian 40
Irish 1,657
Native born 2,623
1855
Population 4,639

All others 65
German and Austrian 299
British 531
Canadian 1,731
Irish 2,850
Native born 5,257
1870
Population 10,733

All others 163
German and Austrian 509
British 1,085
Canadian 4,902
Native born of native parentage 4,568
Native born of foreign parentage 6,647
Irish 4,241
1880
Population 21,915

All others 343
German and Austrian 1,455
British 2,175
Canadian 7,046
Native born of native parentage 6,064
Native born of foreign parentage 12,561
Irish 5,993
1890
Population 35,637

All others 492
Russian and Polish 1,126
German and Austrian 1,751
British and British North American 2,945
French Canadian 6,991
Irish 5,650
Native born of native parentage 7,636
Native born of foreign parentage 19,115
1900
Population 45,712

All others 1,420
Russian and Polish 1,684
German and Austrian 3,961
British and British North American 2,957
French Canadian 8,035
Irish 5,246
Native born of native parentage 9,141
Native born of foreign parentage 25,286
1910
Population 57,730

All others 1,824
Russian and Polish 4,062
German and Austrian 1,571
British and British North American 2,917
French Canadian 5,806
Irish 4,261
Native born of native parentage 10,924
Native born of foreign parentage 28,182
1920
Population 60,203

Census of Massachusetts, 1855, p. 110. Holyoke Transcript, Sept. 17, 1870. Census of Massachusetts, 1880, From the Tenth U. S. Census, pp. 58, 96, 142. Eleventh Census of the United States, 1890, Population, I, Pt. I, clxiii, 670–673. Twelfth Census of the United States, 1900, Population, I, Pt. I, 714, 796–799. Thirteenth Census of the United States, 1910, Population, II, 880–881. Fourteenth Census of the United States, 1920, Population, II, 65, 762–763.

NATIONALITIES IN HOLYOKE, 1855–1920

The native Americans born of native parents remained a minority until the twentieth century. Approximately 52 per cent of the population in 1875 was foreign-born, proportionately the largest foreign population of any city in Massachusetts.[3] By 1890 the percentage of foreign-born had shrunk slightly, but still Fall River, Massachusetts, with 50.15 per cent, and Duluth, Minnesota, with 48.17 per cent, alone of American cities exceeded Holyoke's percentage of 47.67. In 1890 Americans born of native parentage were only 17.02 per cent of Holyoke's whole population. Only Milwaukee had a smaller percentage, 13.64.[4] Another decade again lowered Holyoke's percentage count of native-born of American parentage, but the percentage of foreign-born was less outstanding. At the end of the century there were seven other American cities which had larger foreign-born elements, all but two of the seven being New England manufacturing cities.[5]

By 1920 Holyoke had ceased to be the city of foreigners that it had once been. Only a third of the population was foreign-born and of this third about 49 per cent was naturalized or had first papers. Some Poles and a few Italians and Greeks had been added to the permanent population between 1905 and 1920, although many Polish immigrants

of Mass., 1895, Population and Social Statistics, II, 623; III, 105; Twelfth Census of U. S., 1900, Population, I, Pt. I, 796–799, p. cxx; Holyoke Transcript, Aug. 2, Sept. 20, 1873, June 21, 1876, July 17, 1878, July 23, 1881.

3. Five years later in 1880 while Holyoke had a foreign population of about 49 per cent of the whole, Fall River had 48 per cent foreign-born, Lawrence, 44 per cent, and Lowell, 38 per cent. Mass. Bur. of Labor, Thirteenth Annual Report, 1882, p. 199; A Compendium of the Census of Mass., 1875, p. 47.

4. Eleventh Census of U. S., 1890, Population, I, Pt. I, p. clxiii. New York had 19.54 per cent American population born of native parents at this same census.

5.

	Per cent Foreign-born		Per cent Foreign-born
Fall River	47.7	Honolulu	44.4
Passaic, N. J.	46.4	Lowell	43.1
Lawrence	45.7	Manchester, N. H.	42.6
Woonsocket, R. I.	44.4	Holyoke	41.4

Twelfth Census of U. S., 1900, Population, I, Pt. I, pp. cix, cx.

stayed in the city only long enough to accumulate from their mill wages means to purchase farms in the valley. In 1914 there were, it is true, fourteen different nationalities represented in one evening school in the city.[6] Nevertheless seventy years after its founding Holyoke was mostly inhabited by the children and grandchildren of foreign-born, not newly arrived immigrants. Irish and French Canadian still outnumbered all other national stocks, with New England, British, and German coming next.

The diverse nationality constituents of this community, like other American cities, had to live side by side. The invisible line between the Irish and the French Canadian quarters was the most generally recognized in the seventies and early eighties. But the Germans also, dividing their distaste equally between Irish and "Canuk," tended to keep apart as far as possible, forming a separate group in South Holyoke. There within the fold of the Lutheran church the German colony held closely together till nearly the end of the century. The Poles, late-comers, built up their colony in the neighborhood of the Lyman Mills, their first work headquarters. Jews, Italians, and Greeks were too few to form distinct colonies, but they too, each group to itself, maintained close ties. No new group was ever welcomed into the city except of course by the employer of labor, but outspoken hostility was rare.

Only the Irish–French-Canadian feud was of any duration, save perhaps a spasmodic boys' war between Americans and Irish. Friction between Irish and French Canadian dated back into the sixties. Then at the end of the seventies the extent of the immigration from Quebec alarmed the Irish. These "Canuks," who lived "packed like mackerel in a barrel" were competitors for jobs which had been scarce; their low standard of living, that of the "Chinese of the Eastern States," as the State Commissioner of Labor called them in 1881, filled their Irish rivals with indignation rather than pity. With the return to Canada of some of this labor and the formation of naturalization

6. Holyoke *Transcript,* Feb. 21, 1914, July 21, 1921.

clubs among much of what remained, some of the most
acute hostility to the French Canadians died down. But
Irish disapproval of the French Canadian custom of sending their children to work in the mills at the earliest possible age, with all its implications of indifference to their
children's welfare, ran high and mutual dislike of Irish and
French lingered. It was nursed by the rivalry of their
churches. The elaborate service in the French churches and
the beauty of the music excited no admiration in the Gael.
In the political world Canadian voters could be counted
upon to support any opponent of the dominating Irish.[7]

The Irish were always the most convivial people. Wed-
dings were festive occasions and wakes scarcely less so.
With the warm-heartedness common to their race they
cared for each other in trouble or made merry at each
others' homes. Unless there was no other possible bread-
winner the mother of an Irish family did not work in the
mills, as was frequently true of other nationalities. Hers
was the rôle of home-maker, and husband and children alike
bent every effort to maintain her in it. In consequence the
Irish family had a unity and a dignity which neither poverty nor prosperity could destroy. St. Patrick's Day was
the great day of their year with Christmas and Easter
next in importance on the calendar. But for all their good-
humored enjoyment of life's small pleasures their cultural
background was limited, and even the sun of wider opportunities produced little fruit. They greeted a full-blooded
joke with more gusto than lovely music or subtly presented
ideas.

Among the foreigners it was the Germans who cultivated
interest in music, and on several occasions German societies
gave concerts and conducted festivals which aroused general enthusiasm. To these music-lovers, abetted by New
Englanders, was due the inauguration in 1911 of a public
concert course and thus, with the support of the Mt. Holyoke College department of music, orchestras and soloists

7. *Ibid.,* Mar. 1, 29, Apr. 5, 1879, Aug. 9, 12, Nov. 11, 1882, Jan. 1,
1885, Sept. 31, 1887, Apr. 7, 15, 16, 1888. Private information.

of note yearly brought fine music to the city. The other unique contribution of the German population to Holyoke was their passion for physical culture. The Turnverein originated in the seventies and systematic gymnastic training was as much a part of the life of the German colony as church-going. In the gymnasiums and appendant beer halls of the two Turnhalls centered much of the German social life.[8]

The French Canadians were less sociable than either Irish or Germans. The sombre habitant heritage of stolid acquiescence in the hard conditions of a working world was not lightly cast aside. Work, go to Mass, save money, and return to Province Quebec—that was long the order. As time wore on the dream of final return to Canada lost much of its charm and the French Canadian accepted Holyoke as his home. Yet although many of these people became naturalized citizens, they were not soon or easily Americanized. Their children attended French schools; they spoke French Canadian at home; they read the locally published French newspaper; they celebrated their own special holidays, New Year's and St. John the Baptist's Day. Outside their church few knew much pleasure. The organization of the Société de St. Jean Baptiste in 1872 gave another outlet to their social instincts, but even this society began as a mutual insurance group and only later became a nucleus of sociability.[9] While some of the French Canadians by the end of the century had risen to positions of comparative wealth and were a recognized part of the American population, they were the exception. Here was no font of a rich culture.

The Poles during their first decade in Holyoke, 1893–1903, played no notable part. The completion of a Polish Catholic church at the end of that period marked the beginning of their importance as a unit in the city. The Pol-

8. Holyoke *Transcript,* June 19, 1898, Mar. 9, 1909, Apr. 9, 1910.

9. *Ibid.,* Oct. 7, 17, Nov. 14, 1874, Apr. 21, 28, 1875, Aug. 19, 1876, May 4, 1885; *Hampden County History,* III, 113; Edouard Cadieux (interview); A. Belisle, *Histoire de la Presse Franco-Américaine,* pp. 128–134.

ish church school was directed by the pastor whose scholarly cultivation made deep impress upon the younger generation. Constantly he urged parents to keep their children in school, out of the mills. By 1913 a considerable number of Polish children were entering the public high school with a firm grasp of English and an unusually good foundation in Latin. The building in 1915 of Kosciusko Hall equipped with bowling alleys and other means of diversion supplemented the church as a social center.[10] Yet not until the twenties had enough Poles attained any economic security to give them the leisure necessary for fuller cultural life.

The contribution of other foreign nationalities is less susceptible of analysis. The English and Scots were imperceptibly assimilated into the native American population, although the Union Club of the English and the Caledonian Club and Clan MacLaren of the Order of Scottish Clans served as foci of separate group activities. The Jews after 1913 launched a Y.M.H.A. and Y.W.H.A., and through other societies devoted some attention to promoting Zionism. Italians and Greeks were too few in number to be of significance. The Greek Orthodox church opened in 1917 made a center for the latter, while the Italians made social contacts through their national society, the Italian Progressive Club.

National societies, early formed by almost every foreign group, helped to perpetuate national differences. The Ancient Order of Hibernians, the German Benevolent Society, the Sons of Hermann, the Société de St. Jean Baptiste, the Sons of the Order of St. Michael—these are but a few of many. Some of them were mutual benefit societies; others were purely social. All maintained large memberships. Toward the end of the nineteenth century fraternal organizations with no particular national basis began to appear, bringing together the separate groups. The Odd Fellows, the Masons, the Knights of Columbus, and the Elks all functioned as unifying social factors, and after

10. John Zielinski, Laura Rabinski, Adele Allen (interviews).

the building of an Elks Home and the Knights of Columbus Hall were still more useful in this respect.[11]

New Englanders of Holyoke's first generation were as
self-contained as any of the foreign groups. Most social
gatherings were centered in the separate Protestant
churches, save for the singing societies' occasional concerts
or the Lyceum debates. Gradually, however, some social
life developed that transcended church bonds. In 1873 the
newly launched magazine club—pretentiously named the
Book Club—included most of the leading spirits in the
community, not only Congregationalists but Episcopalians
and one Baptist as well. But while election to the Book
Club constituted for years the peak of social success, its
meetings were too rare to influence literary taste in the
city. For that purpose rather the increase in number and
variety of books in the public library served. As the city
grew in wealth it was first and foremost the native Americans who achieved the leisure to widen their cultural horizons. They formed dinner and discussion clubs, a chess
club, and a whist club. A few began to travel and later to
buy *objets d'art* and pictures. When a new public library
was built in 1902 a small art gallery and museum was included where a few good paintings were hung.

Taste in music was encouraged by the oratorio and
choral societies and after 1886 by the organ recitals given
at intervals by the gifted organist at the Second Congregational Church. The rare church music collected by William Churchill Hammond and played by him for a public
quick to sense its quality went far in the next thirty-five
years toward creating in the whole city an appreciation of
fine music.[12]

In the seventies the nearest approach to metropolitan

11. Holyoke *Transcript*, June 13, 1877, Mar. 4, 1882, July 14, 1888, Feb.
9, 1889, Feb. 24, 1901, Aug. 26, 1905, Jan. 1, 1908, Mar. 9, 20, July 13, 17,
1909, Nov. 27, 1911, Aug. 27, 1915, Jan. 1, 1916; *Thirtieth Anniversary
Holyoke Daily Transcript;* Daniel Kenney, Harry Burman, Edouard
Cadieux, George Chioles, Demetrius Nicolaides (interviews); *A Century
of Catholicism in Western Massachusetts,* pp. 260–271.

12. Minutes of the Book Club, 1873–1909; Holyoke *Transcript,* Jan. 28,
1880, Apr. 27, 30, 1881, Feb. 18, 1882, May 24, 1898.

sophistication came by way of the Opera House. Built in 1878 by William Whiting partly as an investment, partly as a public-spirited gesture, for twenty years it was a means of education and pleasure-giving to a large public. Some of America's best plays and finest actors came here, and Holyoke theatre-goers received them enthusiastically. The opening of the Opera House was a gala occasion. Proudly the *Transcript* reported: "That portion of the public who use tobacco kindly respected the wishes of the owner of the Opera House, and to their credit be it said that the floor was stained but by one or two persons."[13] But at the end of the century the theatre fell upon hard days. Country-wide theatre chains preëmpted the best plays and Holyoke was no longer able to secure plays or actors worth seeing. Theatre-goers were obliged to go to Springfield and at the Holyoke Opera House only third-rate burlesques were shown. Movie houses after 1906 supplied the entertainment which earlier the Opera House had furnished.[14]

Throughout the years leisure meant to most of the population opportunity for simple diversion. Croquet had some vogue in the seventies, and in the eighties boating and canoeing on the river were organized by a group of young Americans who formed the Canoe Club. Membership in the Canoe Club, however, was generally not opened to Catholics, and later when land was bought on the river bank at Smiths Ferry and tennis courts and a ball field laid out only the Protestant minority could enjoy them. Similarly the Mt. Tom Golf Club, opened in the nineties, was restricted. But for the most part interest in sports cut through social barriers. Anyone who could afford a pair of skates could enjoy the ice in winter, who owned a gun might join the Rifle Club, and who could buy a two-wheeler in the nineties could bicycle. Devotees of horse racing could watch if not participate in that pastime at the Trotting Park in South Holyoke, just as boxing enthusiasts might

13. Holyoke *Transcript,* Mar. 27, 30, Apr. 30, 1878. A month later the report read: "The manners of good society are observed by everyone."
14. *Ibid.,* Nov. 16, 1906.

follow their favorite's career at "sluggers' soirees" in the eighties. Baseball fans for years supported the Holyoke Shamrocks and then the Sharps in the ranks of professional leagues until the cost of high-salaried players put them out of Holyoke's reach. But meanwhile the Holyoke High School began to have athletic teams whose careers excited much general interest in the city. And after the opening of public playgrounds in 1910 various baseball teams carried on games there.[15]

In summer by the nineties the well-to-do began to take brief holidays at the seashore or in the mountains, while the mill population took trolley rides in the evenings or sat on the benches in the city parks. The opening of an amusement park in the outskirts of the city at the foot of Mt. Tom, a venture of the Street Railway Company, proved a source of entertainment to the public in the nineties and of revenue every summer to the trolley company. The merry-go-round, the shooting booths, and the dance hall were popular and after 1898 a funicular railway up the mountain added to the charms of Mountain Park. And year in and year out, winter as well as summer, the saloons offered sociability. Much of the year only the high school lectures, the reading rooms of the Y.M.C.A., or, more accessible to all persons regardless of age, sex, or religion, the public library, offered more serious pastime.[16]

Holyoke's third generation found social life more unified than it had been, but there was still some cleavage between Protestant and Catholic. While economic rise in the world had brought Irish, Germans, and some French Canadians into the professions and into positions of comparative social prominence, there was no widespread mingling between the adherents of the two faiths. Catholics, looked at

15. *Ibid.,* May 8, June 16, Aug. 28, Nov. 13, Dec. 22, 1875, Oct. 7, 21, June 3, 1876, Aug. 15, 1877, May 21, Sept. 25, Oct. 2, 9, 12, Nov. 6, 1878, Apr. 10, July 28, Dec. 23, 1883, Feb. 14, 1885, June 28, 1886, July 14, 21, 1888, May 23, 1903, June 20, 1911.

16. *Ibid.,* May 26, 1880, Aug. 2, 1883, Oct. 11, 1884, Jan. 1, 1885, June 12, 1903, May 23, 1904; *Municipal Register,* 1885, pp. 226–230; 1901, pp. 200–201.

askance as members of the Mt. Tom Golf Club, formed their own Country Club. Excluded fairly consistently from membership in the Canoe Club, Irish and French Canadians and Polish organized outing clubs with headquarters at Hampden Ponds beyond the western reaches of the township.[17] Although the social units gradually ceased to be church groups, no city-wide social life developed. Instead there grew up a multiplicity of clubs in which membership seemed to be determined by chance of neighborhood or business association. "Holyoke Club life" still furnished most of what there was in the nature of sociability.

There was one notable exception among the men of the city. For them bridge-playing became a common and unifying interest. Women were inclined to club together in small groups of neighbors to play. But the men of the community sought the game wherever able players were to be found, and the Park Lyceum, before 1910 a stronghold of whist enthusiasts, became after that time the meeting ground of auction bridge players of every station of life. City employes, mill executives, trolley conductors, clerks, doctors, lawyers—there was here no distinction save ability to play the game indifferently or well.

While differences in national heritage, in religion, and in economic status kept the city divided into a number of separate social and cultural groups, the awakening interest in general civic betterment was gradually to cut through these lines. Determination to make Holyoke a cleaner, freer place to live, with wider opportunities for rich life for all, was not confined to any one group. Citizens in the twenties were to set themselves to the task.

17. *Ibid.*, May 25, 1908, Aug. 11, 1919.

XIII

THE GROWTH OF SOCIAL CONSCIENCE

FOR a generation Holyoke depended upon her churches to undertake all philanthropic work while the city pauper department assisted the destitute. At the end of the seventies the legacy of Whiting Street created a fund which made it possible to give aid to persons not paupers,[1] but otherwise until the late eighties there was no source of help for the needy other than the churches. Catholic charities far outdid anything the Protestant churches attempted and eventually stirred the more well-to-do Protestant groups to emulating collaboration. So in the second generation the city saw the growth of a series of non-sectarian philanthropies.

The first community enterprise of this kind was the Young Men's Christian Association. The crying need of decent living quarters for the many young men whom business opportunities brought to the city in the boom years of the eighties and their want of place for some social life apart from the saloons aroused members of the Protestant churches in 1885 to found a Y.M.C.A.

The members of this Association [so the Constitution read], shall seek out young men, residents, or strangers in Holyoke, and endeavor to bring them under moral and religious influences by introducing them to members and privileges of the Association, by aiding them in the selection of suitable boarding places and employment, and by securing their attendance at some place of worship, and by every means in their power surrounding them with Christian influences.[2]

The evangelical character of the Association's origin was thus plainly stamped upon it. All the Protestant

1. See above, pp. 271–272.
2. Records of the Holyoke Y.M.C.A., 1886–1911.

churches worked for its success and raised funds for the
building, completed in 1894. There with reading and pool
rooms and a large gymnasium Holyoke for the first time
had a gathering place for young men regardless of creed
or economic status.

So consistently was the social and civic value of the "Y"
stressed that a number of Catholic boys made use of it for
some years. The program of the Education Committee
early proved useful. An elementary course of schooling was
mapped out and volunteer teachers carried it out in evening classes. Before adequate public night schools had been
opened in the city, the schooling hereby offered the immigrant boy who had to work during the day was appreciated. Curiously enough among the most enthusiastic supporters of these sessions of the Christian Association were
young Jews whose ambitions to learn were thus satisfied
with no sacrifice of their Judaism. In time the "Y's" spon-
soring of various intra-city athletic leagues for series of
games—basketball, volley ball, bowling, baseball, and later
tennis—kept interest alive among men whose religious zeal
was slight, and in 1916 in the Boys' Department the first
permanent Boy Scout troop in the city made a focus of
activity for the twelve- to sixteen-year-olds.[3] Thus steadily
the Y.M.C.A. evolved from a religious foundation to a social.

Like the Y.M.C.A., the next humanitarian undertakings
in the city also were organized by coöperating committees
of the Protestant churches. But the inspiration came not
from the churches but from individuals who as members
of the local churches naturally turned to these bodies as
offering the easiest means of organizing philanthropies.
To give working girls of the city facilities for recreation
and instruction similar to what the Y.M.C.A. offered men,
women of the Protestant churches started in 1888 the
Young Women's Association. In spite of cramped accom-

    3. *Ibid.;* Benjamin Wolman (interview); Records of Holyoke Boy
Scout Council; Holyoke *Transcript,* Apr. 21, 1903, Jan. 13, 1919, Dec. 27,
1921.

modations and a limited program the Y.W.A. gave to many young women opportunities for diversion and self-improvement. For nearly fifteen years the religious element in the Association was purely incidental. Then in a reversal of the incipient trend of the community, the association affiliated with the national Y.W.C.A. and membership was confined to women professing an evangelical faith. The new alignment was justified on the grounds of its giving the local association needed backing by a powerful country-wide movement. In the following twenty years the Y.W. C.A. did expand the scope of its activities, bought and furnished a building which supplied inexpensive decent living quarters for women, a gymnasium, and other recreation rooms, offered classes in domestic science and dramatics, opened a summer camp, and from time to time conducted investigations of conditions in the city which gave rise to new organizations. The religious restriction proved in time to be little limiting to the civic usefulness of the Association.[4]

Again in 1890, through the efforts of coöperating women of the Protestant churches, the Holyoke Auxiliary of the Children's Aid Society was formed. The purpose of this society was to give help to neglected or abused children of the community, sometimes by supplying clothing and financial aid to the family, sometimes by giving necessary instruction to ignorant parents, and occasionally by finding temporary or permanent homes for the children whose own homes were unfit. The county agent reported seven months after the forming of the local auxiliary that forty-two Holyoke children had been cared for by the association that year. The conditions in which some of these young ones had been found were described as "revolting in the extreme." Whether such cases were due to poverty, ig-

---

4. The originators of the first associations were chiefly Unitarians who as persons denying the divinity of Jesus were excluded from membership in a Christian association. The affiliation with the Y.W.C.A. was thus a matter of considerable controversy. Holyoke *Transcript,* Sept. 30, Oct. 5, 1905, July 13, 1907, Apr. 27, 1908, Sept. 24, 1919, Jan. 31, Feb. 4, 12, 1921; *Thirtieth Anniversary Holyoke Daily Transcript.*

norance, or viciousness, or to a combination of those factors, whether such circumstances were due to chance, to
exceptional social maladjustments, or to some inherent rot-
tenness in the whole social and economic system, the women
of the auxiliary did not stop to ask. Appalled at the existence of such conditions in this erstwhile village, they bent
themselves to relieve the immediate need, not to remake the
social order. Funds were raised by individual soliciting but
also by having Sunday collections in the churches donated
to the work. The function of the auxiliary, however, was
more than that of finding money for the expenses incurred
by the county agent for the society. The local board of
managers also undertook directly to abet the work by investigating cases. In 1905 the state census counted 241
neglected children in the city but two years later the Holyoke Auxiliary had 118 under its view. By later standards
of social work the volunteer service of the Holyoke Auxiliary members was doubtless not highly efficient. But it
marked a departure from the casual kind of church charity
work theretofore thought sufficient.[5]

The day of secular philanthropies was dawning. Early
in the nineties another important philanthropy was begun,
namely the Holyoke Boys' Club. The club was patterned
on a New Haven experiment and met with immediate success here. Although in 1892 open country and the river
were still fairly accessible to the boys of the Ward One
tenement blocks as to the dwellers in the shanties of the
Patch or to the Hill boys, recreation rooms and organized
leisure activities were a greatly needed supplement. Under
the auspices of a committee of six men, representing at
least four different churches in town, the Boys' Club was
financed and planned. An able superintendent took charge
in the old Methodist Church building on Main Street, from
which the Methodists had moved uptown some time before.

5. Records of the Holyoke Branch Hampden County Children's Aid
Society (in possession of president of the Holyoke branch); Holyoke
Transcript, Jan. 17, 1917; Census of Mass., 1905, Occupations and Defec-
tive Conditions, II, 247.

Here classes in carving, bookbinding, and printing were carried on. A gymnasium was equipped and reading rooms were furnished and both were much used. The club early became an ordered undertaking professionally supervised and supported by men devotedly interested in the boys who used it. And the number of these boys of all creeds or none was legion. Perhaps no other philanthropy in the city received such general endorsement, although it was without church backing or religious purpose. People of all kinds patronized the club benefits, or gave outright sums to abet the work. In 1917 a new club house with a large gymnasium and an able instructor in charge inaugurated an era of expanding usefulness. The boys themselves, most of them from the tenement districts below the canals, refused to allow the club to be labelled a charity and dues were collected from every member. In this way one of the earliest of Holyoke's humanitarian projects grew into a great civic enterprise.[6]

Of somewhat different character was the inception and evolution of the Holyoke City Hospital. Probably because here obviously was an undertaking the need of which was felt by all classes, the project launched by business leaders in 1891 and forwarded by committees from each Protestant church at once emerged into the realm of a secular philanthropy. Public-spirited men devoted themselves to organizing a city-wide campaign for funds and the incorporated group succeeded so well that by June 1893 a forty-bed hospital was opened free of debt. It was completely furnished by the Hospital Aid Association, the women's branch of the enterprise, which also undertook to provide a fund to meet the expenses of patients unable to pay for themselves. A nurses' training school was established which supplied a competent corps of nurses both for the hospital and for home service.

6. Secretary Boys' Club (interview); *Thirtieth Anniversary Holyoke Daily Transcript;* Holyoke *Transcript,* Feb. 22, Oct. 12, 1908, Jan. 1, 1910, Oct. 8, 1921; Lyman Mills Papers, Burke to Sigourney, Nov. 17, 1916.

But the hospital failed to become an institution for which the general public took any great responsibility. A large part of the Catholic population could reasonably contend that the House of Providence was their responsibility and that while the need of additional hospital facilities was manifest their duty lay in the support of the earlier foundation. In fact the work of the House of Providence expanded yearly. The Protestant minority together with the French and Polish Catholics might have evolved a systematic method of financing an adequate permanent endowment for the City Hospital, but it seemed unnecessary. For thirty years any deficit was quietly met by a few persons of wealth who made the hospital their special charity. The settling of financial problems in this easy way induced no extravagance but on the other hand led citizens to take the hospital for granted in a fashion that was to be disastrous when later the original benefactors were unwilling or unable to carry it on.

The Hospital Aid Society continued its work and cared for many patients. Some money, it is true, was raised for a fund from time to time, but immediate demands tended to eat it up. The directors and staff had only the satisfaction of knowing that the institution was performing important services for the public, and doing them well. In 1919 the American College of Surgeons gave the Holyoke Hospital a first rating.[7]

The history of the hospital was repeated in part in other Holyoke philanthropies. To meet many public needs, not the general public but a few individuals sponsored the wanted agency. The early years of the twentieth century produced several such undertakings which became somewhat like a series of proprietary charities, secular, to be sure, but not truly community projects.

What came in the course of years to be a downtown social center was started in 1902 as a family philanthropy dedicated to the memory of William Skinner, the founder

7. *Thirtieth Anniversary Holyoke Daily Transcript;* Holyoke *Transcript,* Dec. 31, 1909, Jan. 10, Nov. 24, 1919, Jan. 14, 1921.

of the great Skinner Silk Mills. The Skinner Coffee House originally was a place where mill girls, primarily those employed in the Skinner mills, could get hot drinks and soups at a nominal cost at lunch time. The undertaking was early expanded and in 1916 was established in a new building in the heart of the tenement district inhabited by French Canadians, Greeks, and Poles. Here the uses of the Coffee House became still more varied—mothers' classes in cooking American foods, dressmaking, folk dancing, and dramatics. A resident director took charge, and the Skinner Coffee House became a permanent neighborhood settlement.[8]

The Aged Peoples' Home and the District Nurse Association, while not supported by any one family, both fell into the category of charities carried on by a few. The former was projected by a social club of women, the Rain or Shine Club, which, unsatisfied with outings to collect wild flowers in the neighborhood, in 1902 embarked upon raising money to found a home for old people. It took some six years to bring in the necessary funds, and not until the gift of a site for the home in 1908 was the building begun. The home from the beginning was partly self-supporting in that residents who had savings contributed. A matron managed the house competently and the home, almost at once become an Old Ladies' Home, gave peaceful shelter to a number of old ladies, not all Holyoke citizens. Somewhat similarly the District Nurse, later called the Visiting Nurse, Association was launched. There was clearly need of a staff of nurses to go into homes where was illness and where poverty and ignorance often made decent care impossible, and again it was a public-spirited few who shouldered the responsibility of the undertaking for the whole community. Persons who could pay something for this nursing service did so, but the nurses gave care and instructions for self-help to many families who could pay nothing. The revelations of appalling health conditions in

8. Holyoke *Transcript*, Nov. 15, 1902, Sept. 30, 1910, Nov. 15, 1916, Mar. 7, 1917, June 28, 1921.

many parts of the city which the visiting nurses brought to
the sponsors of the association and so to a wider public
served in time to awaken the whole city to some awareness
of the necessity of community action.[9]

But the growth of social conscience was slow. In so far
as citizens thought at all about civic needs, they tended to
salve their consciences with thoughts of generosities to
some particular philanthropy. It was the business of the
city government, of the churches, of the schools, of the
state, perhaps of the medical profession, to attend to the
city's wants. Let everyone lay by something for a rainy
day and use his talents like a good and faithful steward of
the Lord and then there would be no occasion for anyone
to rescue his neighbor. The old Calvinistic philosophy lingered on and indeed the Catholic attitude reinforced it with
the preaching of the relative insignificance of material welfare compared to the importance of spiritual.

Alarm at the discovery of the prevalence of tuberculosis
in the city brought into existence the first agency which
deliberately set itself not only the task of alleviating the
worst of conditions immediately but of educating the public to the urgency of full coöperation. The Holyoke Tuberculosis Association began its work in 1908 by opening
a small day camp for consumptive patients during the summer months and instituting a clinic and class for instruction of patients. Upon the erection of a city sanitorium in
1912 the Association camp was closed, and the District
Nurses carried on the home nursing for a time. To the
Holyoke Tuberculosis Association's campaign of education
was partly due the opening of the public sanatorium which
supplied care to Holyoke tuberculosis patients free and to
non-residents who were partly subsidized by the state. The
Association again was instrumental three years later in
getting the city Board of Health to start a dispensary
where diagnoses were made and free advice was given. The
dispensary, however, received little publicity and its potential usefulness was further minimized by the circum-

9. *Ibid.,* Mar. 25, 1902, Nov. 16, Dec. 15, 1905, Apr. 29, 1908.

stance that the dispensary physician and tuberculosis visitor were not trained in tuberculosis diagnosis, a technique particularly difficult in the earlier stages of the disease.

It fell to the Holyoke Tuberculosis Association as a group of private citizens to educate the public in methods of prevention. The Association distributed to school children instructions for avoiding infection, furnished rubber stamps for marking textbooks with ten rules of health, financed movies, lectures, and dissemination of literature to mill workers. Unhappily the high percentage of illiteracy among the foreign industrial population frequently rendered printed information useless. For two years the Association endeavored to organize an Industrial Tuberculosis League in the city to which mill hands and mill owners alike should contribute, but in 1912 it had to be abandoned because of failure to interest working people. In 1916 a summer day "Kinderkamp" for children likely to contract the disease was launched and for years thereafter carried on its good work. The Association not only thus sponsored the preventive work, it cared for tuberculous persons through the visits of the Association Secretary-Nurse and the supplying of milk, eggs, and warm clothing in impoverished households where the disease existed. The fact that long after 1921 Holyoke had a death rate from tuberculosis about 20 to 25 per cent higher than the rate for the state as a whole or materially higher than that which prevailed in the United States Registration Area merely emphasized the magnitude of the tuberculosis problem in the community, if not the futility of attempting to cope with a community problem through one private agency.[10]

More effectively was civic conscience aroused by publicity given to Holyoke's excessive rate of infant mortality. Early in 1911 an enterprising young altruist presented at a meeting of the Mothers' Club of the Y.W.C.A. carefully

10. Horwood, Health Survey of Holyoke with Relation to Tuberculosis, pp. 16, 97, 202–210; Records of the Holyoke Tuberculosis Association, 1907–1918 (office of the Association); Holyoke *Transcript,* Dec. 15, 1905, Sept. 2, 1909, Dec. 30, 1911, Jan. 13, Dec. 23, 1912, Mar. 12, June 22, 1914, Feb. 5, 9, Aug. 3, 1915, Jan. 24, June 14, 1916, Sept. 4, 1917.

compiled data showing the extent of mortality among Holyoke infants under one year of age. The report was well calculated to stir a group of women, and when the figures —long available in the City Hall and in the annual health board reports in the local press—were flung out as a challenge to mothers of the city, the response was prompt. Doctors and laymen joined in petitions to the city government to vote funds for a Milk Station, so-called, where mothers might be given instructions in the care of their babies and where proper infant feeding could be supervised. Milk should be supplied at moderate cost or free for the poor. The city gave $900 toward expenses and the Milk Station was opened in the summer of 1911 with a nurse and doctor in charge. Three years later the Infant Hygiene Association was formed under the general auspices of the City Board of Health with a competent child specialist as director, a graduate nurse and three trained assistants, and two station physicians in charge. The city supplied $3,000, and the rest of the costs were met by mothers using the station or by private donors, members of the Association. Where 49 babies were cared for in 1912, there were 350 by 1919. Nurses' visits to the homes were soon included as part of the program, but lack of funds obliged the Association to limit the prenatal care it undertook.[11]

Still in 1918 Holyoke's infant death rate compared to other American cities was high, 124 deaths per thousand births. Only thirteen cities had worse. The fact that the death rate for babies in the care of the Association stood at 45 per thousand births inspired efforts to extend the work. With the creation of the Child Welfare Commission, as a separate department of the city government, the next

11. The deaths occurring at the Catholic diocesan orphanage at Brightside, most of them not Holyoke babies, made the figures of Holyoke infant mortality always appear higher than the city itself rated, and the local Association was at pains to compile its statistics for Holyoke-born children only. Hence state or United States census data are of little use, save for very general comparison with figures for other cities. Holyoke *Transcript,* Jan. 28, Apr. 26, 1911, Mar. 20, May 9, 1912, Jan. 20, 1914, Nov. 10, 1915, Aug. 6, 1916, Apr. 4, June 15, July 3, Nov. 14, 1918; *Municipal Register,* 1914, p. 362.

year the Infant Hygiene Association went out of existence. The municipal administration carried on the work with no break, and, thanks to an increased appropriation, was able to widen its field by adding to the staff a nurse for prenatal care and a pre-school-age and nutrition clinic. For such community enterprise the community as a whole was beginning to see the need.[12]

Two other features of a growing sense of community responsibility were the citizens' concerted efforts to keep the city clean, undertaken under the leadership of the Civic Improvement and the Women's Municipal Leagues, and the adoption of a city playground program. To stop the dumping of rubbish and the general custom of throwing paper into alleys and streets called for a series of publicity campaigns, which over a period of years after 1908 gradually effected great improvement. The epidemic of infantile paralysis in 1916 gave some impetus to the drive for general city cleanliness.[13] The public playground movement was also begun about 1908 and by vote of the city three municipal playgrounds were opened in 1910. The city parks had been for years a recognized boon, and their extent had been enlarged by purchases between 1901 and 1908. But except for the wading pool, tennis courts, cricket grounds, and baseball fields in Riverside Park in South Holyoke there had been no place in the city for any kind of supervised play. In the most crowded sections of the city there were five schools without any yards whatsoever for play. With an estimated population of 25,000 per square mile in the city in 1910 the need of sunny playgrounds was evident.

The playground program was ambitious in spite of financial limitations. Four playgrounds—the one in Riverside Park already fairly well equipped—were opened in

12. Holyoke *Transcript,* Mar. 7, Apr. 5, May 6, 24, Oct. 1, 18, 1919, Jan. 12, 16, June 16, 1920, Jan. 20, 1921; *Municipal Register,* 1921, pp. 569–577. See above, pp. 281–282.

13. Holyoke *Transcript,* May 29, July 9, 1908, July 31, Aug. 7, 1909, Jan. 21, 1910, Apr. 30, 1914, June 26, 1915, Apr. 30, May 4, July 14, Sept. 22, 25, Nov. 24, 1916.

1910 with supervisors and instructors in charge during
July and August. That first season 60,000 children were
cared for here, taught group games, folk dancing, chair-
caning, or raffia work. Some 1,500 children frequented
these playgrounds most afternoons. The cost to the city
was about ten cents a week per child. The benefits to children and city alike were patent, and playground undertakings grew year by year. New projects were added and
the earlier expanded: classes in sewing and darning, simple athletics for girls, reed basketry, story hours, baseball
games, and other boys' athletic contests. At one school
shower baths were installed and nearly 7,800 children were
bathed there in one season. The demand for bath houses
and pools where children could swim became every year
more urgent and the numbers using the only one remaining in the city in 1921 lent force to the plea. That summer
35,446 boys and girls had used the Ward Four bathhouse.
But though the city appropriation for playground work
by 1921 was double what it had been in 1910, there was not
money enough to meet all the hoped-for extensions of the
work. The supervisor and commissioner in 1914 tried opening two of the playgrounds for evening sessions, and the
floods of people who made use of this opportunity led to
evening sessions on three other playgrounds in succeeding
years. In 1921 the supervisor estimated an average nightly
attendance of 1,789 on the five playgrounds open.[14]

Regular baseball teams were early organized, two, later
three, for each playground, and the parents and friends
followed the games with enthusiasm. Some of the games
played on Sunday—in defiance of the state law—evoked
comment from the Massachusetts Civic League in 1913:

Picture the condition there: a crowd of twenty-five hundred
people, ten to fifteen nationalities, men and women from the
shops and mills, each a partisan of one of the nines, doubtful

14. *Ibid.*, Feb. 16, 1905, May 29, 1908, Jan. 19, Mar. 18, July 2, Aug. 27,
1910, Feb. 15, 1911, May 6, 1915, July 11, 1918, Aug. 27, 1919, June 3,
1920; *Municipal Register*, 1901, pp. 200–201, 354; 1910, pp. 213–241; 1914,
pp. 339–352; 1921, pp. 138–158.

decisions by the umpire, favorites being battled all over the
field, a victory, a defeat, no police, no disturbance, eight such
situations each Sunday demanded by law-abiding, self-con-
trolled crowds and by nine citizens out of ten, and especially
by the mothers of boys over fourteen. The query forces itself
as to which is more sacred—such a period of wholesome life,
or a period of twenty-four hours' duration called "Sunday."[15]

Private organizations, a City Baseball League, and a
group of industrial teams, the "Dusty League," also made
use of the playground and park diamonds.

Supervised skating on the playgrounds and sliding on
streets blocked off at certain hours of the day in winter
gave the playground commissioners after 1914 a nearly
year-round task.[16] The usefulness of this community project was more generally recognized than almost any other.

Coördination of efforts for community welfare received
some impetus by war organization. As early as 1912 a
United Charities had organized in the city with a paid secretary and carefully kept records to prevent overlapping
of philanthropic endeavor. With the coming of the Red
Cross Civilian Relief and Liberty Loan drives the city had
further examples of the efficiency of organization. War
Chests proved to many American communities the economy
of one concentrated campaign for funds and in Holyoke
later the Community Chest and Community Welfare
League were to emerge.[17]

As the city entered upon the postwar years its recent
experiences in effecting collaboration between separate
groups and agencies left their mark. Zeal for war work was

15. *Municipal Register,* 1914, p. 344. When in 1919 the state authorities
called a halt to this persisting evasion of the law against Sunday baseball, Holyoke advocates carried the issue to the legislature and won. Holyoke *Transcript,* Mar. 25, May 28, July 1, 14, 20, Aug. 6, 1919, Apr. 3,
1920; *General Acts of Massachusetts,* 1920, ch. 240.

16. *Municipal Register,* 1914, p. 347; 1921, pp. 146, 148.

17. Holyoke *Transcript,* Jan. 30, 1912, May 6, 1913, Feb. 3, Nov. 10,
1914, Sept. 14, Nov. 19, 1915, Apr. 1, 6, Aug. 6, 1916, Apr. 4, June 15,
1918, Oct. 19, 1919, May 22, 1920, Jan. 10, 22, Feb. 14, Mar. 22, 1921.

succeeded by passion for community service. Spurred on by
societies such as the United Charities and the Municipal
Improvement League, by the Chamber of Commerce—the
old Holyoke Business Men's Association in new guise—
and by the Rotary and Kiwanis clubs, societies and clubs
of many kinds adopted some form of civic purpose. Community service, that twentieth-century slogan, became the
watchword of most of the organizations in the city. Some
of this ardor later burned itself out, but through 1921 interest in community welfare ran high. It served to complete
the shift from belief in only church-centered charities
through an intermediate stage of faith in non-sectarian
philanthropy to conviction of the necessity for community
action upon community problems. Citizens were at last conscious of Holyoke as a community.

In seventy-five years the community had seen many
changes. The company village had given way to the booming, self-confident town and that in turn to the industrial
city. The substitution of great impersonal trusts for the
multiplicity of independent mills had emphasized the distance between entrepreneur and wage earner and threatened for a time to create an unbridgeable separation of interests in the community. The city had grown up on the
principle of every one for himself and the devil take the
hindmost. Luck and courage and hard work in the earlier
years had contrived to raise some men above their fellows,
and many of the shrewd or unscrupulous had prospered to
become leaders in the business world and in the rather form-
less social life. But by the twentieth century, class differences had marked out leaner opportunities than of yore.
Labor had organized as a group to withstand capital. Few
Holyoke capitalists were callous or unaware of the poverty
and misery about them. But who was to take command of
the situation and what could be done? Experience had
showed that all could not escape by individual effort into
the capitalist class. Sporadic altruism had not sufficed to
raise notably the whole level of the lower social stratum.
Paternalism and philanthropy had been ineffectual. Such

education as the public schools afforded proved too meagre
and too superficial to equip men with adequate means of
self-help. Labor unions themselves tended to be opportu-
nistic and inevitably lacked social vision.

Social irresponsibility had gone no further here than in
most American cities. The leaders of industry, more residents than absentees, the men looked up to in this materialistic society, were simply not organized to confront the
problems of the general community welfare. Am I my
brother's keeper? The social idealism of Christianity offered no workable answer. The rift between Protestant and
Catholic continued to approximate to the gap between rich
and poor, much as it had in the first generation between
New Englander and immigrant. And the Catholic Church
itself with its elaborate hierarchy could not view even Christian socialism as any solution to the problem of the social
order. Men still shrank from the contemplation of socialism. Communistic groups set up in the United States by
tens in the nineteenth century had petered out. Where
those simpler agrarian communities had failed, how could
such experiments succeed in a more complex industrial society?

Laissez faire, the keynote of the entrepreneur's philosophy for over a century, implied a faith in opportunism, belief that by delaying, by muddling along without outside
interference something might eventually turn up to save
any given situation. It was a hand-to-mouth policy of never
anticipating any social problem. Therefore, careful social
planning in the interest of the community as a whole was
a conception unconsidered by business leaders after mer-
cantilism was discredited. A planned scheme of community
living which reached down to the fundamental order of society had not been possible in nineteenth-century Holyoke.
Individualistic capitalism stood in the way.

But as the water-power city ceased to expand and social
problems continued to grow, the community was stirred to
take thought for the future. The fifteen years after 1922
were to bring many blows to the industrial city. One great

textile mill was to liquidate, another, part of a great trust, was to shut down in Holyoke to remove its business to company mills outside Massachusetts, a third was to shrink its capacity to a small fraction of its one-time productivity, and a fourth was to prepare to abandon two thirds of its plant in an endeavor to operate the rest successfully. The pump works for five years were to be shut down in the interest of the New Jersey units of the company, only to be reopened in part in 1937. The one-time great paper trust by the late thirties was to operate only seven of its sixteen Holyoke mills. The big industrial units were to prove too cumbersome. Holyoke, the water-power city by the great dam, Holyoke the paper city, Holyoke the city of "pleasing Catholicity"—all these characterizations citizens might consider still apt. Whatever the future of hydro-electric power, of variations of paper converting, of Catholic relations with Protestant, of adjustments of labor with capital, Holyoke dwellers were beginning to see that the city must develop not as a series of disparate interests but as a community. Individualistic capitalism was still the accepted economic order. Citizens knew little better than they had a generation before just how to solve the community problems. But the day of social irresponsibility was coming to an end. Intelligent social conscience was dawning.

BIBLIOGRAPHY

I. *UNPUBLISHED SOURCES*

THE materials for a study so nearly contemporary have included necessarily much data not written at all. Where personal reminiscence has been used as a primary source I have been at pains to check the reliability of the informant. Much valuable information has been given me on express condition that I suppress the name of my informant. In such instances I have cited my authority as "Private information." While some of this confidential material might be considered controversial, I have reason to believe it fairly representative of one prevalent point of view.

Industrial Records

The papers of many of the mills in the city have been courteously put at my disposal, and have been invaluable. The most important single source of this type is the Lyman Mills Papers, 1851–1927, a large collection, officially housed in the Baker Library of the Harvard Business School, but still unsorted and uncatalogued. I have used chiefly payroll books and correspondence between the treasurer in Boston and the agent in Holyoke, a source replete with information about the town in its early days as well as with business data. Until recently the records of the Hadley Falls Company were included in the Lyman Mills Papers, but have now been turned over to the Holyoke Water Power Company and are therefore no longer accessible. The Hadley Falls Company records, 1847–1859, especially the Directors' Records, are an important source for the period of the founding of the town.

The papers of the Carew Manufacturing Company of South Hadley Falls are valuable, partly because they are complete back to 1847 and partly because together with the records of the Hampshire Paper Company, the affiliated concern, which date back to 1866, they constitute the only extensive paper-mill records of the vicinity which antedate 1877. The Directors' Records of the Parsons Paper Company, 1854–1887, are extant but too brief to be highly useful. Otherwise the records of all Holyoke's early paper mills have been destroyed. Even of later date there are few paper-mill records available. The sketchy minutes of meetings of the Newton Paper Company, 1876–1905, and six-monthly statements of the mills of the American Writing Paper Company, 1899–1904, exist. But many of the papers of the American Writing Paper Company have been destroyed in the course of the two reorganizations of the company, and for the years 1905–1922 I have relied upon the company's semi-annual statements as published in the Holyoke *Transcript*. Much carefully compiled data about the American Writing Paper Company is contained in the report of the engineer engaged by the company's Bondholders' Committee in 1915. The bound typescript, John G. Callan, Report to the Bondholders' Committee of the American Writing Paper Company, is in the possession of its author.

William Skinner and Sons Cash Book and Farr Alpaca Company Papers represent records of textile mills other than the Lyman Mills. The four volumes of the Farr Alpaca Company Records, 1874–1922, are particularly valuable as they include analyses of the market and general conditions of the worsted company year by year.

Original manuscript sources for the labor movement have consisted only of the unpublished History of the International Brotherhood of Paper Makers, compiled from the union records in Albany by Matthew Burns, once secretary, now president of the International Union. Early local union records have not been found. Published records of the International Mule Spinners' Union were kindly lent me by Urban Fleming, one time head of the Holyoke local, now president of the Holyoke Central Labor Union.

Banking records consist of Hadley Falls Bank Directors' Records, 1851–1875, property of the Hadley Falls Trust Company.

Records of Churches and Social Agencies

Records of many of the Protestant churches are extant in the hands of the clerks of their respective churches, although the Second Congregational Church lost by fire in 1918 its earliest books. Books of the First Baptist Church and the First Congregational Church are among the very few original sources for the period before 1845. Most illuminating, however, are the Records of the Second Baptist Church, 1849–1901, which contain in lengthy annual letters to the Westfield Baptist Association detailed accounts of the progress of religion in the community. The only other significant unpublished church records available are those of the

Liberal Christian Congregational Society, 1874–1918. The Catholic parish records, filed family by family, are private.

Social agencies' records are generally unrewarding. The signal exception is the study made for the Holyoke Tuberculosis Association in 1929 by Dr. Murray P. Horwood of the Boston Institute of Technology, a careful survey of conditions in the city, ethnological, geographical, and political, which account for the high percentage of tuberculosis in Holyoke: Murray P. Horwood, Health Survey of Holyoke with Relation to Tuberculosis.

The papers of such organizations used in this study are as follows:

In possession of the clerk of the First Baptist Church of Holyoke: Second Baptist Church in West Springfield, Records, 1803–1850; First Baptist Church of Holyoke, Records, 2 vols.

In possession of the clerk of the Second Baptist Church of Holyoke: Second Baptist Church of Holyoke, Records, 3 vols., 1849–1924; A. Judson Rand, History of the First Seventy-five Years of Second Baptist Church, 1849–1924 (typescript).

In possession of the clerk of the First Congregational Church of Holyoke: Third Congregational Church, Ireland Parish, West Springfield, Records, 1794–1825; First Orthodox Congregational Church in Holyoke, Records, 2 vols., 1842–1913; First Orthodox Congregational Society in Holyoke, Records, 1855–1918.

In vault of the Second Congregational Church: Second Congregational Church, Records, 1882–1892; Catalogue of Second Congregational Church Parish Library, 1886–1919.

In possession of the clerk of the Liberal Christian Congregational Society of Holyoke: Liberal Christian Congregational Society, Records, 2 vols., 1874–1933.

In possession of the secretary of the Holyoke Y.M.C.A.: Y.M.C.A. of Holyoke, Records, 2 vols., 1886–1911.

In possession of the president of the Holyoke Branch of the Hampden County Children's Aid Society: Holyoke Branch of Hampden County Children's Aid Society, Records.

In possession of the president of the Women's Christian Temperance Union of Holyoke: Holyoke Women's Christian Temperance Union, Records.

In the office of the Holyoke Tuberculosis Association: Holyoke Tuberculosis Association, Records; Murray P. Horwood, Health Survey of Holyoke with Relation to Tuberculosis, 1929 (typescript).

In the office of the Holyoke Boy Scout Council: Holyoke Boy Scout Council, Records, 1923–1938.

Town and County Records

Unpublished official records that bear on Holyoke history are found in several places. These materials supply data for the period when this locality was part of other townships. I have cited the volumes located in the office of the city clerk of Springfield as Springfield Town Records. There is also a published version of the records to 1736, Henry M. Burt, *First Century of the History of Springfield, Massachusetts,* 1636–1736, 2 vols. (Springfield, 1898). The Springfield records give the only specific information about this locality before 1745, save for a few entries in the earliest volumes of the Hampshire County Court Records now located in the Registry of Probate, Hampshire County, in Northampton. The Registry of Probate of Hampden County, 1812–1938, in Springfield I used only for examination of the inventories of estates of outstanding manufacturers of Holyoke of the late nineteenth century. West Springfield Town Records, in possession of the town clerk of West Springfield, include one volume pertinent to this study. Here also is the volume, Records of the Second Parish of Springfield, which deals with local affairs on the west side of the river, 1694–1774.

In addition to these official records there are a few sheets of manuscript in a folder marked "Chicopee," housed in the library of the Connecticut Valley Historical Association in Springfield. Among these are lists of polls of the fifth parish.

Private Papers, Diaries, and Letters

Sources of this type are few in number and meagre in historical content. The most useful of these have been: Papers of the late Ralph Snell of Agawam, Massachusetts, now in possession of Mrs. Ralph Snell. This collection of material in the form of notes, newspaper clippings, pamphlets, and periodicals bearing upon the history of the paper industry in the United States was copious although unordered. I have cited it as Snell Manuscript. Deeds and Papers of Mrs. E. T. Hastings of Holyoke; Account Book of Caleb Humeston, 1787–1813, in possession of Thomas Humeston of Holyoke; Pliny Jones Day Book, 1823, in possession of Mrs.

W. G. Dwight of Holyoke; the papers of Mrs. W. F. Whiting of Holyoke which include the diary of Anna Fairfield, 1856–1859, and the scrap book of Mrs. William Whiting, 1859–1890; the papers of Mrs. Edwin Chase of Holyoke, consisting of the diary of Oscar Ely, 1859–1863, and the diary of Chloe Ely, 1857–1861; autobiography of Joel Webber, 1866, in possession of Fred Webber of Holyoke; Minutes of the Book Club, 1873–1908, in possession of Miss Adele Allen of Holyoke; Scrap books of Grace Church, in possession of the pastor of the church; History of the Holyoke Water Power Company, and Ralph Smith, Development of the Holyoke Water Power Company, typescripts in possession of the Holyoke Water Power Company; J. Roy Lewis, History of the New England Telephone Company in Holyoke, in possession of its author.

Reference has also been made to an unpublished master's thesis, Gertrude Dunn, History of the Schools of Ireland Parish, West Springfield, Massachusetts, 1730–1850, in the Smith College Library.

II. *PUBLISHED SOURCES*

Newspapers and Periodicals

FAR exceeding all other published sources in usefulness for this history has been the Holyoke *Transcript,* issued under different titles but continuously since 1849 save for a gap of months in 1861 and 1862–1863. Appearing first weekly as *Hampden Freeman,* then Holyoke *Freeman,* Holyoke *Weekly Mirror,* and then Holyoke *Transcript,* it gives the most intimate picture of the town to be had. After 1872 the paper was published twice a week and in 1882 daily. A weekly edition summarizing the most important local events of the week continued to be put out for some years, but the files were not kept after 1891. After 1923 the daily is published under the title Holyoke *Daily Transcript-Telegram.* All these files are in the office of the Holyoke *Transcript.*

I have referred occasionally also to *Hampshire Gazette,* the files of which are in the Forbes Library, Northampton, and to Springfield *Daily Gazette* and Springfield *Daily Republican* in the Springfield Public Library, Springfield, Massachusetts.

One trade paper of particular local importance is *Paper World,* 1880–1898. Complete files are in the Springfield Public Library.

Its peculiar value for this study lies in the fact that it was published in Holyoke in the heyday of Holyoke papermaking—and after 1887 for some years in Springfield—by a man well informed about the local paper industry.

The issues of the Holyoke *Directory,* published in 1869, in 1871, in 1874–1875, and thereafter annually, are chiefly valuable for the specific information contained in the appendices—lists of the manufacturing enterprises of each type, the invested capital, number of employes, estimated monthly payroll, and the like. After 1897 the *Directory* curtails the space given to this section, with results unsatisfactory to the historian. The issues complete from 1871 on are in the office of the Transcript Publishing Company of Holyoke. The first issue, 1869, which includes in a foreward a brief history of the town, is in the Holyoke Public Library.

Official Publications

Holyoke *Town Records,* 1850–1873, bound in one volume are to be found in the Holyoke Public Library. City records are cited as *Municipal Register. The Report of the School Committee* for each year after 1873 is so listed except where, bound with the *Municipal Register,* it is paged in with the other reports. From 1900 to 1922 school reports are cited from the *Municipal Register.* In the office of the school department is located also the valuable *Survey of the Schools of Holyoke,* 1930, compiled by the Institute of Educational Research, Division of Field Studies, Teachers' College, Columbia University.

Publications of the Commonwealth of Massachusetts are numerous and informing. In 1837, in 1845, 1855, and 1865 there were official surveys of industry issued by the Secretary of the Commonwealth, and after 1855 decennial census reports. Beginning with 1870 the annual reports of the Massachusetts Bureau of Statistics of Labor appear, a mine of detailed information about conditions in the industrial towns and cities of the state. After 1886 there are also *Statistics of Manufacture* published annually. Add to these the annual reports of the State Board of Health, which begin in 1870, the annual reports of the Secretary and Board of Education, dating from 1837, and the *Acts and Resolves of the General Court,* year by year, and the materials for close knowledge of any city in Massachusetts are at hand. After 1900, however, the data are not generally presented in detail city by city. For Holyoke the twenty volumes of transcriptions of the court hearings, *Holyoke Water Power Company, Petitioner versus City of Holyoke* (Boston, 1899–1903) are useful.

United States Government publications relied upon consist principally of the decennial census reports from 1850 through 1920 and special reports such as *Religious Bodies,* published in 1906, 1916, and 1926, and Census Monograph, X, Paul F. Brissenden, *Earnings of Factory Workers, 1899 to 1927* (Washington, 1929). In addition to these main sources I have used: *Report of the Secretary of the Treasury,* 1832, *Documents Relative to the Manufactures in the United States,* 2 vols. (Washington, 1833), *House Executive Documents,* Twenty-second Congress, First Session; and *Pulp and Paper Investigation Hearings,* 3 vols. (Washington, 1909), *House Documents,* Sixtieth Congress, Second Session, 1908–1909.

Other contemporary published materials are: *Calendar Record and Log Book of the No. One Mill of the Agawam Paper Company . . . January 1885 to May 1911,* copied and published by Ralph Snell, pamphlet in possession of John Gardiner of Valley Paper Company, Holyoke; Timothy Dwight, *Travels in New England and New York,* 4 vols. (New Haven, 1821); *Early Maps of the Connecticut Valley in Massachusetts,* reproduced by Wright and DeForest (Springfield, 1911); *Fiftieth Anniversary Second Congregational Church of Holyoke, Massachusetts* (Holyoke, 1900); A. Forbes and J. W. Greene, *The Rich Men of Massachusetts* (Boston, 1851), *Our First Men, A Calendar of Wealth, Fashion and Gentility* (Boston, 1846), both to be found in the collection of College Pamphlets of Yale University Library; Joseph G. Martin, *Twenty-one Years in the Boston Stock Market* (Boston, 1856); Joel Munsell, *Chronology of Paper and Paper Making* (4th edition, Albany, 1870); *Plan of the New City of Holyoke,* circular in possession of Carew Manufacturing Company, South Hadley Falls; *Thirtieth Anniversary Holyoke Daily Transcript* (Holyoke, 1912); *Report of the History and Present Condition of the Hadley Falls Company* (Boston, 1853), pamphlet Holyoke Public Library; *Report of the Committee appointed by the Stockholders of the Hadley Falls Corporation submitted March 1, 1854* (Boston, 1854), pamphlet in possession of Frank Metcalf estate of Holyoke; *Time Table of the Holyoke Mills,* 1853, broadside formerly in possession of the Farr Alpaca Company of Holyoke; Harry A. Wright, ed., *Indian Deeds of Hampden County* (Springfield, 1911).

III. *SECONDARY WORKS*

SEVERAL works which deal with United States industrial history have been referred to, notably Victor Clark, *History of Manufactures in the United States,* 3 vols. (New York, 1929); Arthur H. Cole, *The American Wool Manufacture,* 2 vols. (Cambridge, 1926); Davis R. Dewey, *Financial History of the United States* (8th edition, New York, 1922); Charles E. Persons, "The Early History of Factory Legislation in Massachusetts" in *Labor Laws and Their Enforcement with Special Reference to Massachusetts,* II, edited by Susan M. Kingsbury, 2 vols. (New York, 1911); Caroline Ware, *The Early New England Cotton Manufacture* (Boston and New York, 1931). Into this classification may also be put Vera Shlakman, *Economic History of a Factory Town (Smith College Studies in History,* vol. xx, Northampton, 1936), a study of Chicopee, Massachusetts, where some of Holyoke's early promoters had been interested.

There are a number of books or pamphlets covering some aspects of the history of the region. For the earliest period most useful are: Sylvester Judd, *History of Hadley* (Northampton, 1863); William B. Sprague, "Historical Discourse . . . 1824" in *Sermons,* II, 2 vols. (Hartford, 1825), College Pamphlets of Yale University Library; and Josiah G. Holland, *History of Western Massachusetts,* 2 vols. (Springfield, 1854). Other material on the Springfield era are contained in George Bliss, *An Address Delivered at the Opening of the Town Hall in Springfield, March 24, 1824* (Springfield, 1828); Henry Morris, *Early History of Springfield, an Address delivered October 16, 1875, on the 200th Anniversary of the Burning of the Town by the Indians,* Appendix K (Springfield, 1876); Oliver B. Morris, *An Historical Address Delivered on the 200th Anniversary of the Settlement of Springfield, May 25, 1836* (Springfield, 1881).

Of later works I found most helpful R. O. Dwight, "Historical Address" in *History of the Sesqui-Centennial Celebration of the Town of South Hadley, Mass.* (1906). There are also: *History of the Connecticut Valley in Massachusetts,* 2 vols. (Philadelphia, 1879), and Alfred M. Copeland ed., *History of Hampden County,* 3 vols. (Springfield, 1902), both semi-commercial rather than scholarly works. On local paper making there is material in the pamphlets published by the Paper Makers Chemical Corporation, Ralph Snell, ed., *Superior Facts,* 1926–1933.

For religious history outstanding is J. J. McCoy, "Diocese of Springfield," *History of the Catholic Church in the New England States,* II, 2 vols. (Boston, 1899). On Catholic charities in the diocese additional information is to be found in *A Century of Catholicism in Western Massachusetts,* published by the *Catholic Mirror* (Springfield, 1931).

For Holyoke specifically secondary works are few: H. L. Foote, *History of the First Twenty-five Years of St. Paul's Church, Holyoke, Massachusetts* (Holyoke, 1889) ; G. C. Osgood, *Story of the Holyoke Churches* (Holyoke, 1890) ; Patrick J. Lucey, *History of St. Jerome's Parish, Holyoke, Massachusetts, Diocese of Springfield* (Holyoke, 1931).

INDEX

ABATTOIR, 173
Absenteeism, 29, 78, 92, 175–
176, 181, 236, 391
Academy, founding of, 8; made
into district high school, 33;
closed, 128 n
Accidents, industrial, 103, 340
Act of 1773, effect of, 5
Adams, R. J., pastor of Second
Baptist Church, 329
Agawam River. *See* Westfield
River
Agawams. *See* Indians
Aged Peoples' Home, 383
Agnosticism, 363–364
Agriculture, early development of,
2; in nineteenth century, 10
Agudas Achim, Congregation of,
360
Albion Paper Co., organized, 88;
ownership of, 92 n; disasters of,
185; reorganized, 186; sells out
to American Writing Paper Co.,
193 n
Aldermen, Board of, 273 n; elec-
tion of, 251; composition, 251,
253–254; policies, 255; appoints
city physician, 256; controls liq-
uor licenses, 263–265; under new
charter, 266; vote work relief,
280
Aliens, numbers of, 254, 319
Alleys. *See* Streets
Allyn, Deacon, 328
Almoner, city, 272, 273
Alpaca manufacture. *See* Farr Alpaca Company
Alvord, Broughton, 91
American Association of Paper
Manufacturers, 146; reject tour
workers' plea, 208–209
American boys' feud with Irish,
369
American Federation of Labor,
grants charter to paper makers,

212; state convention repudiates
socialism, 224; grants charter to
Building Trades Council, 247
American Protective Association,
propaganda, 346
American Thread Co., formed, 181,
182; activity of, 194; later course
of, 236
American Writing Paper Co., organized, 188–193; policies, 193,
228, 230; strikes against, 193,
213; effects of, 195; decline of,
231; dividends, 231; reorganization discussed, 232–233; report
to bondholders' committee, 232–
233; war-time operation, 234;
collapse of, 235; interested in
course in paper making, 318 n;
in the thirties, 392
Americanization, in schools, 299;
lack of, in French schools, 301,
303; classes in, 319; of French
Canadians, 371; at Skinner Coffee House, 383
Americans, native, in politics, 254;
of native parentage, 254, 368
Ames, David, Junior, founds paper
mill in Canal Village, 14
Ames, John, 14
Ames paper mill, 85
Amusement. *See* Leisure; Recrea-
tion
Ancient Order of Hibernians, 372
Appleton, family, 92 n
Appleton, head of Riverside Paper
Co., 189
Apprenticeship, 198, 219
Arbitration, State Board of, cre-
ated, 200 n; condemns work
hours, 209
Art gallery, 373
Artisan, The, 247
Assessors' valuations, 183, 246 n,
278
Athletics, 306; in high school, 375;

350; social prestige of members, 373

Esleeck, A. W., builds paper mill, 193; reduces workers' hours, 208

Evening schools, first opened, 134, 135; required by law, 296; attendance in, 296–297, 318–319; curricula for, 297, 319; grammar school, 297; vocational work in, 315–316; high school, 318; supplemented by Y.M.C.A., 378 *See also* Vocational school

Everett, unemployment in, 223 n

Ewing, George C., promotes Hadley Falls development, 19–22

Exports, colonial, from Springfield, 2; of paper, 146, 193–194

FALL RIVER, hours of labor in, 48; mill directorates, 76; living conditions in, 117; migration of labor to, 139; strikes in, 148, 225, 237; growth of, 148; death rate, 258; housing, 261 n; illiteracy in, 294; school costs, 308 n; foreign population, 368

"Falls Fields," 11

Farming. *See* Agriculture

Farr, Herbert, 140, 141, 170

Farr Alpaca Co., founded, 140–142; employes of, 141; leases Glasgow mill, 166 n; expansion, 168, 170, 242; capitalization, 168, 241, 242; payroll, 168; wage rates, 168 n, 179, 240–242; dividends, 169, 179–180, 194–195, 242; number of stockholders, 175; in depression of 1893, 178–180; tries employes' insurance, 197 n; weavers' union organizes, 214; strike at, 215, 241 n; profits, 239–240, 242–243; profit-sharing, 241–242

Felton Paper Co., 92 n

Fenians, raid on Canada, 114–115 *See also* Fraternal organizations

Ferry, first established, 4; swing, 15; swing, purchased, 64

Ferry Mill, 88 n

"Fields," Ireland Parish, 15

Fifth Parish of Springfield, 5–6

Finances, city, 252, 255–256, 275–277; condition of, 268–269 *See also* Taxation

Fire department, 270; increased cost of, 276

Fire protection, 122; assumed by Hadley Falls Co., 31; volunteer companies for, 34; in mills, 44, 103; inadequacy of, 283

First Baptist Church, a country church, 327

First Congregational Church, 327

First Congregational Society formed, 7

Fisheries, spring salmon and shad, 4, 10–11; shad-fishing on Sunday, 8; rights above dam safeguarded, 24

Flats, 43; living conditions in, 112; sewers for, 121

Flour mill. *See* Gristmill

Foreign-born, 32, 48–49, 367–368, 385; poverty of, 124–125; numbers of, 254, 368; living conditions of, 282–283

Foresters, Massachusetts Catholic Order of, 343 n

Foundries, 164, 165 *See also* Machinery manufacture

Fourdrinier machines, power needed for, 74; in paper mills, 88, 90

Franklin Paper Co., organized, 87; control of, 90, 92 n; reduces hours, 208

Fraternal organizations, 372–373; Odd Fellows, 29, 51; Masons, 51, 110, 363; St. Jerome's Temperance Benevolent and Literary Society, 109–110; Fenians, 109, 114–115; German Benevolent Society, 109, 111, 372; Turnverein, 111, 371; Elks, 372–373; Knights of Columbus, 372–373

Free will, belief in, 323

Freight costs, for South Hadley canal, 13; railroad, 96–97

French Canadian Church. *See* Catholic Church; Precious Blood Church; Immaculate Conception